HIGHLANDS

ARCADIA
DE SOTO

VENUS

OKEECHOBEE
BRIGHTON

Battle of Okeechobee
FORT VAN SWEARINGEN

STUART
MARTIN

SEMINOLE INDIAN RESERVATION

CHANCY BAY

Lake Okeechobee

ST. LUCIE CANAL

FORT MACRAE
INDIAN TOWN

FORT JUPITER
JUPITER

[MARS]
Jupiter Inlet

CHARLOTTE

GLADES

FORT CENTER
LAKEPORT
PALMDALE

FORT MAYACA

Loxahatchee

KELSEY CITY
Lake Worth Inlet

Fisheating Cr.

LA BELLE
ORTONA LOCKS
DENAUD
OLGA ALVA
FORT THOMPSON

MOORE HAVEN

[Lake Flirt]

[L. Hicpochee]

Caloosahatchee R.

CLEWISTON

RITTA I.

CANAL POINT

W. PALM BEACH

PALM BEACH

BAYSHORE
CALOOSA
FT. MYERS
LEE

HENDRY

LAKE HARBOR
S. BAY
BELLES

BELLE GLADE

OKEELANTA
SHAWANO

PALM BEACH

GREENACRES CITY
HYPOLUXO
L. WORTH
LANTANA
BOYNTON

FORT DULANEY
PUNTA RASSA
ESTERO
Estero R.

DEVIL'S GARDEN

BOAT LANDING

DELRAY BEACH
YAMATO
BOCA RATON
DEERFIELD

Sanibel I.
Big Carlos Pass

FT. SIMON DRUM
IMMOKALEE

SAM JONES OLD TOWN

FT. SHACKLEFORD

THE EVERGLADES

POMPANO

BONITA SPGS.

Okaloacoochee Slough

SEMINOLE INDIAN RESR.

BROWARD

COLOHATCHEE
FORT LAUDERDALE

NAPLES

SUNNILAND

BIG CYPRESS SWAMP

COLLIER

Fakahatchee Slough

INDIAN RESERVATION
DANIA
HOLLYWOOD
LITTLE RIVER
OJUS
LEMON CITY

MARCO
Marco I.
CAXAMBAS

OCHOPEE

HIALEAH

Cape Romano
Panther Key

EVERGLADES
Turner R.
CHOKOLOSKEE BAY

MONROE

MIAMI

MIAMI BEACH
[FORT DALLAS]

Ten Thousand Islands

CORAL GABLES

Key Biscayne
Cape Florida

TAMIAMI TRAIL

S. MIAMI
COCO-
NUT GROVE

DADE

PERRINE

Lostman's R.
Rodger's R.
Broad R.
Harney R.
Ponce de Leon Bay

CHITRI'S ISLAND

GOULDS
MARANA

FORT WESTCOTT

Biscayne Bay

HOMESTEAD
FLORIDA CITY

ROYAL PALM STATE PK.

NORTHWEST CAPE
MIDDLE CAPE
EAST CAPE

Cape Sable
FLAMINGO
FORT POINSETT

Mangroves

Key Largo

ROCK HARBOR

Florida Bay

Upper Matecumbe Key

Names in brackets indicate places no longer in existence

INDIAN KEY
MATECUMBE
Lower Matecumbe Key
CRAIG

Long Key

Pine Islands

BIG PINE
BAHIA HONDA
PIGEON KEY

KEY VACAS

FLORIDA KEYS
(MONROE CO.)

Marquesas Keys

Boca Grande Key

KEY WEST

Gulf Stream

Lower Florida

— GEORGE ANNAND —

To Diane —

Enjoy the history of Florida!

Love,
Michele

The Everglades:
RIVER OF GRASS

BY

Marjory Stoneman Douglas

ILLUSTRATED BY

Robert Fink

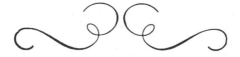

60TH ANNIVERSARY EDITION
Pineapple Press, Inc.
Sarasota, Florida

Inquiries should be addressed to:

Pineapple Press, Inc.
P.O. Box 3889
Sarasota, Florida 34230

www.pineapplepress.com

Original edition copyright 1947
        by Marjory Stoneman Douglas
Rinehart editions: 1st printing, 1947,
        seventh printing 1962
Hurricane House edition: 1965
Banyan Books revised edition: 1978
Mockingbird edition: 1st printing 1974
Pineapple Press revised edition: 1988
Pineapple Press 50th Anniversary Edition: 1997
Pineapple Press 60th Anniversary Edition: 2007

Library of Congress Cataloging-in-Publication Data

Douglas, Marjory Stoneman.
  The Everglades : river of grass / Marjory Stoneman Douglas ; illustrated by Robert Fink ; [update by Michael Grunwald]. -- 60th anniversary ed.
      p. cm.
  Original ed.: New York : Rinehart, 1947.
  Includes bibliographical references and index.
  ISBN 978-1-56164-394-3 (hbk. : alk. paper)
  1. Everglades (Fla.)--Description and travel. 2. Everglades (Fla.)--History.
3. Everglades (Fla.)--Environmental conditions. 4. Natural history--Florida--
Everglades. 5. Florida--History. I. Grunwald, Michael, 1970- II. Title.
  F317.E9D6 2007
  975.9'39--dc22
                                                            2007028384

Design by Stephan Salter
Illustrations by Robert Fink

10 9 8 7 6 5 4 3 2

Contents

1

The Nature of the Everglades

I. THE NAME

THERE are no other Everglades in the world.

They are, they have always been, one of the unique regions of the earth, remote, never wholly known. Nothing anywhere else is like them: their vast glittering openness, wider than the enormous visible round of the horizon, the racing free saltness and sweetness of their massive winds, under the dazzling blue heights of space. They are unique also in the simplicity, the diversity, the related harmony of the forms of life they enclose. The miracle of the light pours over the green and brown expanse of saw grass and of water, shining and slow-moving below, the grass and water that is the meaning and the central fact of the Everglades of Florida. It is a river of grass.

The great pointed paw of the state of Florida, familiar as the map of North America itself, of which it is the most notice-able appendage, thrusts south, farther south than any other part of the mainland of the United States. Between the shin-ing aquamarine waters of the Gulf of Mexico and the roaring deep-blue waters of the north-surging Gulf Stream, the shaped land points toward Cuba and the Caribbean. It points toward and touches within one degree of the tropics.

More than halfway down that thrusting sea-bound peninsula nearly everyone knows the lake that is like a great hole in that pawing shape, Lake Okeechobee, the second largest body of fresh water, it is always said, "within the confines of the United States." Below that lie the Everglades.

They have been called "the mysterious Everglades" so long that the phrase is a meaningless platitude. For four hundred years after the discovery they seemed more like a fantasy than a simple geographic and historic fact. Even the men who in the later years saw them more clearly could hardly make up their minds what the Everglades were or how they could be described, or what use could be made of them. They were mysterious then. They are mysterious still to everyone by whom their fundamental nature is not understood.

Off and on for those four hundred years the region now called "The Everglades" was described as a series of vast, mias-mic swamps, poisonous lagoons, huge dismal marshes without outlet, a rotting, shallow, inland sea, or labyrinths of dark trees hung and looped about with snakes and dripping mosses, malignant with tropical fevers and malarias, evil to the white man.

Even the name, "The Everglades," was given them and printed on a map of Florida within the past hundred years. It is variously interpreted. There were one or two other names we know, which were given them before that, but what sounds the first men had for them, seeing first, centuries and centuries before the discovering white men, those sun-blazing solitudes, we shall never know.

The shores that surround the Everglades were the first on this continent known to white men. The interior was almost the last. They have not yet been entirely mapped.

Spanish mapmakers, who never saw them, printed over the unknown blank space where they lay on those early maps the words "El Laguno del Espiritu Santo." To the early Spanish they were truly mysterious, fabulous with a wealth they were never able to prove.

The English from the Bahamas, charting the Florida coasts in the early seventeen hundreds, had no very clear idea of them. Gerard de Brahm, the surveyor, may have gone up some of the east-coast rivers and stared out on that endless, watery bright expanse, for on his map he called them "River Glades." But on the later English maps "River" becomes "Ever," so it is hard to tell what he intended.

The present name came into general use only after the acquisition of Florida from Spain in 1819 by the United States. The Turner map of 1823 was the first to use the word "Everglades." The fine Ives map of 1856 prints the words separately, "Ever Glades." In the text of the memorial that accompanied the map they were used without capitals, as "ever glades."

The word "glade" is of the oldest English origin. It comes from the Anglo-Saxon "glaed," with the "ae" diphthong, shortened to "glad." It meant "shining" or "bright," perhaps as of water. The same word was used in the Scandinavian languages for "a clear place in the sky, a bright streak or patch of light," as Webster's International Dictionary gives it. It might even first have referred to the great openness of the sky over it, and not to the land at all.

In English for over a thousand years the word "glaed" or

"glyde" or "glade" has meant an open green grassy place in the forest. And in America of the English colonies the use was continued to mean stretches of natural pasture, naturally grassy.

But most dictionaries nowadays end a definition of them with the qualifying phrase, "as of the Florida Everglades." So that they have thus become unique in being their own, and only, best definition.

Yet the Indians, who have known the Glades longer and better than any dictionary-making white men, gave them their perfect, and poetic name, which is also true. They called them "Pa-hay-okee," which is the Indian word for "Grassy Water." Today Everglades is one word and yet plural. They are the only Everglades in the world.

Men crossed and recrossed them leaving no trace, so that no one knew men had been there. The few books or pamphlets written about them by Spaniards or surveyors or sportsmen or botanists have not been generally read. Actually, the first accurate studies of Everglades geology, soil, archaeology, even history, are only just now being completed.

The question was at once, where do you begin? Because, when you think of it, history, the recorded time of the earth and of man, is in itself something like a river. To try to present it whole is to find oneself lost in the sense of continuing change. The source can be only the beginning in time and space, and the end is the future and the unknown. What we can know lies somewhere between. The course along which for a little way one proceeds, the changing life, the varying light, must somehow be fixed in a moment clearly, from which one may look before and after and try to comprehend wholeness.

So it is with the Everglades, which have that quality of long existence in their own nature. They were changeless. They are changed.

They were complete before man came to them, and for centuries afterward, when he was only one of those forms which shared, in a finely balanced harmony, the forces and the ancient nature of the place.

Then, when the Everglades were most truly themselves, is the time to begin with them.

II. THE GRASS

THE Everglades begin at Lake Okeechobee.

That is the name later Indians gave the lake, a name almost as recent as the word "Everglades." It means "Big Water." Everybody knows it.

Yet few have any idea of those pale, seemingly illimitable waters. Over the shallows, often less than a foot deep but seven hundred fifty or so square miles in actual area, the winds in one gray swift moment can shatter the reflections of sky and cloud whiteness standing still in that shining, polished, shimmering expanse. A boat can push for hours in a day of white sun through the short, crisp lake waves and there will be nothing to be seen anywhere but the brightness where the color of the water and the color of the sky become one. Men out of sight of land can stand in it up to their armpits and slowly "walk in" their long nets to the waiting boats. An everglade kite and his mate, questing in great solitary circles, rising and dipping and rising again on the wind currents, can look down all day long at the water faintly green with floating water lettuce or marked by thin standing lines of reeds, utter their sharp goat cries, and be seen and heard by no one at all.

There are great shallow islands, all brown reeds or shrubby trees thick in the water. There are masses of water weeds and hyacinths and flags rooted so long they seem solid earth, yet there is nothing but lake bottom to stand on. There the egret

9

and the white ibis and the glossy ibis and the little blue herons in their thousands nested and circled and fed.

A long northeast wind, a "norther," can lash all that still surface to dirty vicious gray and white, over which the rain mists shut down like stained rolls of wool, so that from the eastern sand rim under dripping cypresses or the west ridge with its live oaks, no one would guess that all that waste of empty water stretched there but for the long monotonous wash of waves on unseen marshy shores.

Saw grass reaches up both sides of that lake in great enclosing arms, so that it is correct to say that the Everglades are there also. But south, southeast and southwest, where the lake water slopped and seeped and ran over and under the rock and soil, the greatest mass of the saw grass begins. It stretches as it always has stretched, in one thick enormous curving river of grass, to the very end. This is the Everglades.

It reaches one hundred miles from Lake Okeechobee to the Gulf of Mexico, fifty, sixty, even seventy miles wide. No one has ever fought his way along its full length. Few have ever crossed the northern wilderness of nothing but grass. Down that almost invisible slope the water moves. The grass stands. Where the grass and the water are there is the heart, the current, the meaning of the Everglades.

The grass and the water together make the river as simple as it is unique. There is no other river like it. Yet within that simplicity, enclosed within the river and bordering and intruding on it from each side, there is subtlety and diversity, a crowd of changing forms, of thrusting teeming life. And all that becomes the region of the Everglades.

The truth of the river is the grass. They call it saw grass. Yet in the botanical sense it is not grass at all so much as a fierce, ancient, cutting sedge. It is one of the oldest of the green growing forms in this world.

There are many places in the South where this saw grass,

with its sharp central fold and edges set with fine saw teeth like points of glass, this sedge called *Cladium jamaicensis*, exists. But this is the greatest concentration of saw grass in the world. It grows fiercely in the fresh water creeping down below it. When the original saw grass thrust up its spears into the sun, the fierce sun, lord and power and first cause over the Everglades as of all the green world, then the Everglades began. They lie wherever the saw grass extends: 3,500 square miles, hundreds and thousands and millions, of acres, water and saw grass.

The first saw grass, exactly as it grows today, sprang up and lived in the sweet water and the pouring sunlight, and died in it, and from its own dried and decaying tissues and tough fibers bright with silica sprang up more fiercely again. Year after year it grew and was fed by its own brown rotting, taller and denser in the dark soil of its own death. Year after year after year, hundreds after hundreds of years, not so long as any geologic age but long in botanic time, far longer than anyone can be sure of, the saw grass grew. Four thousand years, they say, it must at least have grown like that, six feet, ten feet, twelve feet, even fifteen in places of deepest water. The edged and folded swords bristled around the delicate straight tube of pith that burst into brown flowering. The brown seed, tight enclosed after the manner of sedges, ripened in dense brownness. The seed was dropped and worked down in the water and its own ropelike mat of roots. All that decay of leaves and seed covers and roots was packed deeper year after year by the elbowing upthrust of its own life. Year after year it laid down new layers of virgin muck under the living water.

There are places now where the depth of the muck is equal to the height of the saw grass. When it is uncovered and brought into the sunlight, its stringy and grainy dullness glitters with the myriad unrotted silica points, like glass dust.

At the edges of the Glades, and toward those southern- and

11

southwesternmost reaches where the great estuary or delta of the Glades river takes another form entirely, the saw grass is shorter and more sparse, and the springy, porous muck deposit under it is shallower and thinner. But where the saw grass grows tallest in the deepest muck, there goes the channel of the Glades.

The water winks and flashes here and there among the saw-grass roots, as the clouds are blown across the sun. To try to make one's way among these impenetrable tufts is to be cut off from all air, to be beaten down by the sun and ripped by the grassy saw-toothed edges as one sinks in mud and water over the roots. The dried yellow stuff holds no weight. There is no earthly way to get through the mud or the standing, keen-edged blades that crowd these interminable miles.

Or in the times of high water in the old days, the flood would rise until the highest tops of that sharp grass were like a thin lawn standing out of water as blue as the sky, rippling and wrinkling, linking the pools and spreading and flowing on its true course southward.

A man standing in the center of it, if he could get there, would be as lost in saw grass, as out of sight of anything but saw grass as a man drowning in the middle of Okeechobee—or the Atlantic Ocean, for that matter—would be out of sight of land.

The water moves. The saw grass, pale green to deep-brown ripeness, stands rigid. It is moved only in sluggish rollings by the vast push of the winds across it. Over its endless acres here and there the shadows of the dazzling clouds quicken and slide, purple-brown, plum-brown, mauve-brown, rust-brown, bronze. The bristling, blossoming tops do not bend easily like standing grain. They do not even in their own growth curve all one way but stand in edged clumps, curving against each other, all the massed curving blades making millions of fine

12

arching lines that at a little distance merge to a huge expanse of brown wires or bristles or, farther beyond, to deep-piled plush. At the horizon they become velvet. The line they make is an edge of velvet against the infinite blue, the blue-and-white, the clear fine primrose yellow, the burning brass and crimson, the molten silver, the deepening hyacinth sky.

The clear burning light of the sun pours daylong into the saw grass and is lost there, soaked up, never given back. Only the water flashes and glints. The grass yields nothing.

Nothing less than the smashing power of some hurricane can beat it down. Then one can see, from high up in a plane, where the towering weight and velocity of the hurricane was the strongest and where along the edges of its whorl it turned less and less savagely and left the saw grass standing. Even so, the grass is not flattened in a continuous swath but only here and here and over there, as if the storm bounced or lifted and smashed down again in great hammering strokes or enormous cat-licks.

Only one force can conquer it completely and that is fire. Deep in the layers of muck there are layers of ashes, marks of old fires set by lightning or the early Indians. But in the early days the water always came back and there were long slow years in which the saw grass grew and died, laying down again its tough resilient decay.

This is the saw grass, then, which seems to move as the water moved, in a great thick arc south and southwestward from Okeechobee to the Gulf. There at the last imperceptible incline of the land the saw grass goes along the headwaters of many of those wide, slow, mangrove-bordered fresh-water rivers, like a delta or an estuary into which the salt tides flow and draw back and flow again.

The mangrove becomes a solid barrier there, which by its strong, arched and labyrinthine roots collects the sweepage of

13

the fresh water and the salt and holds back the parent sea. The supple branches, the oily green leaves, set up a barrier against the winds, although the hurricanes prevail easily against them. There the fresh water meets the incoming salt, and is lost.

It may be that the mystery of the Everglades is the saw grass, so simple, so enduring, so hostile. It was the saw grass and the water which divided east coast from west coast and made the central solitudes that held in them the secrets of time, which has moved here so long unmarked.

III. THE WATER

In the Everglades one is most aware of the superb monotony of saw grass under the world of air. But below that and before it, enclosing and causing it, is the water.

It is poured into Lake Okeechobee from the north and west, from that fine chain of lakes which scatter up and down the center of Florida, like bright beads from a string. They overflow southward. The water is gathered from the northwest through a wide area of open savannas and prairies. It swells the greatest contributing streams, the Kissimmee River, and the Taylor River and Fisheating Creek, and dozens of other smaller named and unnamed creeks or rivulets, and through them moves down into the great lake's tideless blue-misted expanse.

The water comes from the rains. The northern lakes and streams, Okeechobee itself, are only channels and reservoirs and conduits for a surface flow of rain water, fresh from the clouds. A few springs may feed them, but no melting snow water, no mountain freshets, no upgushing from caverns in ancient rock. Here the rain is everything.

Here the rain falls more powerfully and logically than anywhere else upon the temperate mainland of the United States.

14

There are not four sharply marked seasons, as in the North. Here winter and spring and summer and fall blend into each other subtly, with nothing like such extremes of heat and cold. Here, actually, there are only two seasons, the wet and the dry, as there are in the tropics. The rains thunder over all this long land in their appointed season from the low clouds blowing in from the sea, or pour from clouds gathered all morning from the condensation of the wet below. Then for months it will not rain at all, or very little, and the high sun glares over the drying saw grass and the river seems to stand still.

This land, by the maps, is in the temperate zone. But the laws of the rain and of the seasons here are tropic laws.

The men who make maps draw lines across seas and deserts and mountains and equatorial rain forests to show where the Temperate Zone is cut off sharply from the middle equatorial belt. But the sea and the land and the winds do not always recognize that rigidity. Nor do southern Florida and the Everglades.

To the west the map shows the Gulf of Mexico, that warm land-sheltered, almost inland ocean; and from it, moved by the power of the turning world itself, the Gulf Stream pours its warm deep indigo and white-flecked waters north of Cuba and ever northeastward. "The Stream" is a huge swift-running river of warm salt water forced between the Florida coast, which it has shaped, and the Bahama banks, until high up on the blue globe of ocean it swings far across into the gray latitudes, toward frozen seas.

With all that surrounding warm sea water and not forgetting Okeechobee's over seven hundred shallow watery square miles, east forty miles from the sea, and from the Gulf eighty, the whole southern part of Florida might as well be an island. All summer long the trade winds, or winds blowing so steadily nightlong and daylong from the southeast that it makes no

15

difference if weather men quarrel about their being called the true trades, pour across the land their cool stiff tides of ten miles an hour.

Summer and winter its climate is more equable than that of the mainland regions to the north. And because of its average sixty-five inches a year of rainfall on the east coast and sixty-three in the interior of the Everglades, this region actually resembles certain warm and rainy but not too hot tropic lands more than it does those other dry and mountainous countries which lie exactly on the equator. It is a question of the ratio between the temperature and the rainfall and the evaporation. There is an arc at the very tip of Florida, up the lower west coast to Gordon Pass and up the east coast to the Miami and New rivers, which is the only place on the mainland of the United States where tropical and West Indian plants will grow native, because of that warmth and rainfall.

The northern Glades, and Lake Okeechobee, would seem to be in the South Temperate Zone, but the rainfall is subtropic here too.

The rains begin in the spring, in April or even late in May. There may be a few days of stuffy wet heat and brassy sunlight and a great piling up and movement of clouds by the heavy fretful southeast winds. There may be a continuous bumping of thunder far off. The winds that change their compass positions, east to south to west to north to east again, never on the east and south coasts, in any other way but clockwise, are thrashing and uncertain. Then in a sudden chill the rain may shut down in one long slashing burst in which even hailstones may bounce like popcorn against all that darkening land. Then the rain has moved away and the sun flashes again.

Somewhere thereafter it rains over the Glades or the lake for an hour or two every day in switching long bright lines through which the hot sun glistens. Then the marching wet will start again the next day or so, hissing and leaping down in narrow sharply defined paths as the clouds are pushed about here and there in the bright sky. Sometimes the rains may last only a few weeks in May. After that the summer is a long blazing drying time of brilliant sun and trade winds all night under the steady wheeling of the stars. The great piles of vapor from the Gulf Stream, amazing cumulus clouds that soar higher than tropic mountains from their even bases four thousand feet above the horizon, stand in ranked and glistening splendor in those summer nights; twenty thousand feet or more they tower tremendous, cool-pearl, frosty heights, blue-shadowed in the blue-blazing days.

On summer mornings over the Glades the sky is only faintly hazed. The moisture is being drawn up from the sheen among the saw grass. By noon, the first ranks of the clouds will lie at the same height across the world, cottony and growing. The moisture lifts the whipped and glistening heights. The bases darken, grow purple, grow brown. The sun is almost gone. The highest clouds loose their moisture, which is condensed into cloud again before it can reach the earth. Then they grow more heavy. The winds slash before them and the rains roar down, making all the saw grass somber.

Sometimes the rainy season goes on all summer, casually raining here and there so that the green things never quite dry out while salt-water mosquitoes from the brackish pools about the coasts blow on the west wind in thin screaming hordes. When high water in the Glades flows south, the mosquitoes do not breed in it.

But in late August, or perhaps in September, the rainy season sets in in earnest. White-heaped Gulf clouds, colored by afterglows in some tremendous summer sunsets stand like Alps of pure rose and violet and ice-gray against the ultimate blue until they are harried by the more irregular winds. White

17

streamers are blown from their tops, veils from their sides, and they themselves are pushed and scuffled and beaten down into long moving snowy sheets or rolls of gray, yellowish-gray, lavender-gray, greenish-gray—until they smash down in long marching, continuous, reverberating downfalls.

You can see it raining darkly and fiercely far off over there at the horizon across the scorched saw grass. The sky will be a boiling panorama of high and low cloud shapes, cumulus, strato-cumulus, alto-cumulus, dazzling and blue and dun. Sometimes far up, far away, between all that panoply, there will be a glimpse of outer space as green as ice.

Then the lion-colored light shuts down as the rain does, or the clouds fill with their steely haze every outline of the visible world and water falls solid, in sheets, in cascades. When the clouds lift, the long straight rainy lines blow and curve from the sagging underbelly of the sky in steely wires or long trailing veils of wet that glitter in some sudden shaft of light from the forgotten sun.

There will be the smack of cool, almost chilling hard air and the rising sound of long drumming as if the grassy places were hard and dry, or the earth hollow. You hear the tearing swish of the rain on the stiff saw grass as it comes over and beats and goes by slashing its steely whips. There may be short bursts of thunder and veins of lightning cracking the whole sky. They are dwarfed by the power of the rain and the wind.

Below all that the glistening water will be rising, shining like beaten pewter, and the light will lift as if itself relieved of all that weight of the rain. It will change from pewter to silver to pure brightness everywhere. The brownness that has been dullness will be bright tawniness and the reaches and changing forms of the sky will lift higher and higher, lifting the heart. Suddenly all those thousands and thousands of acres of saw grass that have been so lightless and somber will burst into a million million flashes from as many gleaming and trembling drops of wet, flashing back their red and emerald and diamond lights to the revealed glory of the sun in splendor.

Inches of water will have fallen in an hour and still far off the rain will trample below the horizon, undiminished.

In the course of a single day so much rain will fall, as much sometimes as ten or twelve inches, that the glitter of rising water will be everywhere. The blue of the sky is caught down there among the grass stems, in pools stretching and spreading. In a few days of rain, acre after acre of new water will flash in sheets under the sun. Then, as the rain clouds go over every day, the currents will be gathering their small visible courses, streaming and swirling past every grass blade, moving south and again south and by west. Places of open currents have been measured to show a steady running four miles an hour, in the old days, in watercourses and wandering streams among the straight bristle of the saw grass. Sometimes more than half the year's average will have fallen in less than two months.

Meanwhile the rain has been falling far to the northward. Over Okeechobee it has been moved here and there as the steady drive of the trades is changed to fitful inland airs. Thunderstorms roll and reverberate over the surface and lightning marbles the clouds as storms seem to come together from every direction while the greenish and grayish world blinks with acid radiance. The lake may be blotted out by white falling water that sings with a rising note as the surface brims and is beaten. The curtains of rain, the rain fogs, move off or hang and sway in a dirty gray half-light as the descending water smacks on the pitted and broken waves. The world is all water, is drowned in water, chill and pale and clean.

North, still farther up that chain of lakes, the rains fall and brim the fine green-ringed cups. The waters begin again their southward flow. The Kissimmee River is swollen and strongly swirling between its wet marshy banks, but still the water does not move off fast enough. The banks are overflowing and the spongy ground between it and Fisheating Creek is all one swamp. The rains fling their solid shafts of water down the streaming green land, and Okeechobee swells and stirs and creeps south down the unseen tilt of the Glades.

The grass, like all the other growing things after the long terrible dry seasons, begins in the flooding wet its strong sunward push again, from its ropy roots. The spears prick upward, tender green, glass green, bright green, darker green, to spread the blossoms and the fine seeds like brown lace. The grass stays. The fresh river flows.

But even from earliest times, when in the creeping spread of water the grass turned up its swords and made the Everglades, there was too much water in the great lake to carry itself off through the Glades southward. There was nothing but the east and west sandy ridges to hold back the water. To the east from Okeechobee it seeped and was not carried off and stood along an old wandering watercourse soon filled not only with saw grass but reeds and sedges and purple arrowy lilies and floating masses of grass and small trees. That is still called the Loxahatchee Slough. "Hatchee" means "river" in that same Indian tongue which named the lake. "Slough," in south Florida, means any open swampy place which may once have been a tongue of the sea or a river of fresh water, green, watery, flowery country, a place of herons and small fish and dragonflies and blue sky flashing from among the lily pads.

Loxahatchee is pitted with innumerable pools held in by the coastal rock. South of that, from the overflow of the Glades basin itself, the rivers of the east coast run, St. Lucie and the Hillsborough, the New River and Little River and the Miami River, spilling over the rock rim to the tides.

In the same way, west of Lake Okeechobee, at least twice

20

as far from the Gulf, the water spilled and crept out over soggy level lands, half lakes, half swamps, and so into the Caloosahatchee, the left shoulder of the Glades region.

The Caloosahatchee never rose directly in Okeechobee, but in a wide rain-filled funnel of shallow, grassy lakes between Hicpochee and Lake Flirt. Often they dried up and were not there.

West of Lake Flirt, the Caloosahatchee began in earnest, a river so remote, so lovely that even in the days when it was best known it must have been like a dream. It was a river wandering among half-moon banks hung with green dripping trees and enshrouding grapevines, green misted, silent, always meandering. It has that quality of dreaming still, neglected and changed as it is, to this very day.

But in the days of full flood, Caloosahatchee rose and overflowed the flat country for miles, north and south. The water crept and flowed and stood bright under the high water oaks and the cabbage palms, so that a light boat could go anywhere under them. In the clear water all the light under the wet trees was green. Lower down, the more tropic green stood in solid jungles to the reflecting water. The rain water went east and west of the lake, but most strongly along the great course of the Everglades.

Often the rainy season finds its terrible climax in September or October, in the crashing impact of a hurricane, the true cyclonic storm of the tropics. July is not too early to expect hurricanes. In the West Indies they have occurred in June. The old jingle that fishermen recite along these coasts tells the story: "June—too soon. July—stand by. August—look out you must. September—remember. October—all over." Officially in Florida the fifteenth of November closes the hurricane season but farther south these storms occur in November and even in December.

The hurricanes make up, although no man has yet seen the actual beginning of one, as far east as the Azores, where the hot air rises all along the line of the equator as the Northern Hemisphere cools toward winter. Their enormous high-spinning funnels, moving always counterclockwise this north side of the tropic belt, are begun when the rising hot air is flung into circular motion by the immeasurable spinning power of the world. The velocity of that spin around their hollow centers has been recorded as moving as fast as two hundred miles. But generally the recording instruments are blown away before that, so no one knows their greatest speed. Laterally, they creep westward more slowly, ten to forty miles an hour. They enter the Caribbean at some airy rift between those island-mountains rising from the sea, which are often engulfed by them. They may turn northward and eastward through the Mona or the Windward Passage, or across the Cuban coast or through the Bahamas, to drive on southern Florida. They may go howling up these coasts and north along, to show the Temperate Zone what the roused raging power of the tropics can be like.

Smaller but intense and dangerous hurricanes spring up sometimes in the late fall in the Yucatan channel and thrash the Gulf of Mexico and harry the Texas or Florida coast. They attack the Glades from there. Later still, they become more freakish and unpredictable, like maelstroms of wind gone wild.

But as the northern winter creeps downward, the hurricane season is slowly conquered. The towering clouds of summer are leveled to mild sheets and rolls of gleaming stuff, widespread, dappled and mackereled, or with the great silvery brushings of mares'-tails. Often there are no clouds at all toward the zenith, which has lost its summer intensity of violet and burns now with the bright crisp blue of northern autumns. Then the air is fresh and sweet.

This is the dry season. Officially, no rain should fall. Yet there have been wet, chill winters in which the rains have come down on the edge of a northern cold front while the east winds go around south and west and north, and stand there for three days of cold, or die utterly so that the frost drifts into the low places and at first sun the hoar-rimmed leaves grow black.

In the winter dry season, there takes place here another and gentler phenomenon of the equatorial tropics. In a windless dawn, in some light winter ground fogs, in mists that stand over the Everglades watercourses, the dew creeps like heavy rain down the shining heavy leaves, drips from the saw-grass edges, and stands among the coarse blossoming sedges and the tall ferns. Under the tree branches it is a steady soft drop, drop and drip, all night long. In the first sunlight the dew, a miracle of freshness, stands on every leaf and wall and petal, in the finest of tiny patterns, in bold patterns of wide-strung cobwebs; like pearls in a silvery melting frostwork. The slant yellow sun of winter dries it up in the next hour but all the secret roots are nourished by it in the dry ground.

Then toward what the North would call spring, dryness creeps again over the land, with the high-standing sun. Between one day and the next the winds grow new and powerful. In the Glades the water shrinks below the grass roots. In open muddy places far south the surface dries and cracks like the cracks in old china, and where some alligator has hitched his slow armored length from one drying water hole to another the pattern of his sharp toes and heavy dragging belly in the marl is baked hard.

The saw grass stands drying to old gold and rustling faintly, ready, if there is a spark anywhere, to burst into those boiling red flames which crackle even at a great distance like a vast frying pan, giving off rolling clouds of heavy cream-colored smoke, shadowed with mauve by day and by night mile-high

23

pillars of roily tangerine and orange light. The fires move crackling outward as the winds blow them, black widening rings where slow embers burn and smolder down into the fibrous masses of the thousand-year-old peat.

Then the spring rains put out the fires with their light moving tread, like the tread of the running deer, and the year of rainy season and of dry season has made its round again.

"Look where the sun draws up water," people say of those long shafts of brightness between clouds. The saw grass and all those acres of green growing things draw up the water within their cells and use it and breathe it out again, invisibly. Transpiration and evaporation, it is called; an unending usage of all the water that has fallen and that flows. Sixty per cent of it, over half of all those tons and tons of water which fall in any rainy season, is taken up again. Dried up. The air is fresh with it, or humid, if it is warm. But in the middle of the Glades in the full heat of summer the condensation is so great that the air is cooled and the temperature lowered half a degree with every two miles or so inland. It is not so much the cool movement of wind as standing coolness, freshness without salt, wetness that is sweet with the breath of hidden tiny blossoming things luminous in the darkness under the height and white magnificence of the stars. Such coolness is a secret that the deep Glades hold.

On the west coast there are land breezes and sea breezes. West-flowing winds often sweep out of those cooling Glades down the slow mangrove rivers and out to the islands on the coasts, rivers of coolness among warm and standing airs.

With all this, it is the subtle ratio between rainfall and evaporation that is the final secret of water in the Glades. We must know a great deal more about that ratio and its effect on temperature in all this region to understand its influence on the weather, on frosts and winds and storms.

All this has been caused by other cycles dictated by remote and terrible occurrences beyond this infinitesimal world, the cyclones of heat and shadow that pass across the utter fire of the sun. Or other laws of a universe only half guessed at. Those majestic affairs reach here in long cycles of alternating wet and dry. There have been years after years of long rainy seasons when the Glades indeed were a running river, more water than grass. Or, more recently, cycles of drought, when there is never enough rain to equal the evaporation and transpiration and the runoff.

Because of all this, the high rate of water usage as against the natural runoff, it is clear that rainfall alone could not have maintained the persistent fine balance between wet and dry that has created and kept the Everglades, the long heart of this long land. If Okeechobee and the lakes and marshes north that contribute to it, if rivers and swamps and ponds had not existed to hoard all that excess water in a great series of reservoirs by which the flow was constantly checked and regulated, there would have been no Everglades. The whole system was like a set of scales on which the forces of the seasons, of the sun and the rains, the winds, the hurricanes, and the dewfalls, were balanced so that the life of the vast grass and all its encompassed and neighbor forms were kept secure.

Below all that, holding all that, the foundation stuff of this world, lies the rock.

IV. THE ROCK

To understand the Everglades one must first understand the rock.

The outline of this Florida end-of-land, within the Gulf of Mexico, the shallows of the Bay of Florida and the Gulf Stream, is like a long pointed spoon. That is the visible shape of the rock that holds up out of the surrounding sea water the long channel of the Everglades and their borders. The rock holds the fresh water and the grass and all those other shapes and forms of air-loving life only a little way out of the salt water, as a full spoon lowered into a full cup holds two liquids separate, within that thread of rim. Lower the tip of the spoon a very little and the higher liquid moves out across the submerged end, as the water does at the end of the Glades.

The rock beneath Okeechobee is only a few feet above sea level. The surface of the lake is only twenty-one feet above the level of the salt water. The surface rock below the Everglades dips south at an incline of half a foot to every six miles. The rim of rock that retains it is narrower and higher on the east coast, but in the west it is hardly visible as a rim at all. There it is a broad space of inland swamps and prairies and coastal sandy land and salt-invaded marshes. Yet both hold against the sea.

The rock is not by any means the oldest in the world. It is nothing like the perdurable granite of the ancient Appalachian spine of the eastern continent. The material of it came from the sea. Out of reach of air it is lumpy, soft, permeable limestone, grayish white, unformed. They call it "oölitic limestone" because it is no more fused together than a lot of fish eggs. In the sun and air it hardens in clumps and shapeless masses, dark, or gray, or yellowish, all full of holes, pitted and pocked like lumps of rotting honeycomb. In itself it shows no foldings or stratification, but holds streaks of sand or shells or pockets of humus.

West and east of Okeechobee the rock just below the surface is not so much oölitic limestone as a shelly, marly sandstone. To the east it underlies the Loxahatchee Slough. To the west, under the swamps and flat ponds beyond Okeechobee, the

Caloosahatchee ran strong after the rains, turning from bank to bank in its overflow, carving its way across and into that sandstone plain in the meanders which are the habit of much older rivers. The Caloosahatchee is not so old as that river of Troy which was first called "Meander," but in her curvings and turnings she cut down through new sand into older and older layers of rock and of pure shell fossils. Some of the greatest layers of fossil shells in the world were cut into and crumbled, and cut into again as every year Caloosahatchee changed her banks.

In spite of what the early scientists believed, and people still repeat incorrectly to this day, this lower Florida is not an old coral reef. It is oölitic limestone, with broken bits of staghorn coral or shapes of brain coral embedded in it. "Miami limestone," they call it.

The fresh water from Okeechobee moving south on the long course of the Everglades has in these thousands of years worn the soft rock in a broad longitudinally grooved valley. Along the east coast the rock rim may be seen in long south-curving ledges, worn by the action of the sea. The rock rims emerge farther south still as beaches and peninsulas beyond half-enclosed salt rivers and broad opening bays. East, the sunken reefs stretch to the abrupt edge of the Gulf Stream itself, where the brilliant lime-green, surfless shallows drop off into the blue, deep surge.

South of the last peninsula, which makes Biscayne Bay, the ridges stretch below water to make the long spiny curves of the Florida Keys, turning southwest as the Gulf Stream came, all the way to Key West and the last Tortugas. Other lesser known rims of rock curve within the southeast mainland in a line of high rocky islands. These are called the Everglades Keys. They became legendary. The early white people believed they contained caves into which all the Indians disappeared before hurricanes, warned by the "blossoming of the saw grass," as if

27

the saw grass did not blossom every year, and as if the broken ledges of rock in these inland keys could hide anything except ferns and coral snakes and roots.

On the east coast, the rivers from the great main saw-grass stream broke through the rock rim in a series of low waterfalls or rapids. The rock stood as a constant natural dam between the fresh water of the Glades and the heavier invading tidal salt, which in dry times creeps up the bottoms of the rivers and would destroy all living fresh-water forms above the mangrove line.

The St. Lucie and the rivers running into Jupiter Inlet and the Mouth of the Rat, the Hillsborough, the New River with its two branches, Little River and Arch Creek, had their shallow falls. The Miami River from the Everglades brawled over twenty-five feet of rapids in the North Fork, with a fall of over six feet. Snapper Creek had its ferny, rocky dam, above which the fresh-water springs bubbled clear through all the higher rock.

The water of all these rivers was clean and clear, perhaps faintly brown from mangroves, but with no Everglades humus in it to stain the bright sand bottoms. The water of the bays was clear, tinted by the light shimmering in water over sand reefs, and sea gardens, and acres of clean green weed.

All that rocky barrier in fact was threaded with springs. All these rivers were known to the early sailors as "sweet water rivers," not a name but a description. The springs bubbled up and filled the great ancient pot holes in the rock which the sea had whirled into and worn smooth and deserted, thousands of years before.

The limestone tips very gently downward to the south until at the end it disappears below the surface and is overlaid by a fine, white calcareous marl that muffles all the shallow water of the Bay of Florida. There are blown sand beaches at Cape

28

Sable, the French word for "sand." There are deposits of leafy humus here and there over the marly meadows, and brackish lakes are set like mirrors among the mangroves, and the wandering watercourses are more salt than fresh. It is a marl laid down by infinitesimal algae. There are bits of seashells in it, bleached by the sun and abraded by the tides. The ripple shadows in the marly water are blue, in a liquid like thin cream. To wade out into it is to sink to the hips in ooze, in faintly scratchy white mud, warm as warm milk in the sun-warmed sea water over it.

All this end of the peninsula is a country that the sea has conquered and has never left. Beyond, westward, it is a pattern of curved shapes solid with mangroves cut out by salt water. There, from Cape Sable northward again to the lonely point of Cape Romano, lie the Ten Thousand Islands. They are the sunken tops of sand dunes the winds and the hurricanes piled up from the shallower Gulf. The mangrove covered them. They are edged on the west by fine, hard white sand beaches that are changed in shape with every hurricane. The passes become filled with sand that the mangroves and salt shrubs hurry to make solid, and then new passes are cut swiftly where the driven salt water rages.

On this coast, south of Cape Romano, the rivers move silent and enormous from the saw grass to the mangrove, and so to the sea, linked by innumerable streams and cuts and channels, utterly bewildering, never completely known. The fresh-water Turner River comes down from pineland and cypress to a dozen channels among mangroves, and so to Chokoloskee Bay. Chatham Bend opens out of Chevalier Bay like a great inland brackish lake. Some rivers above the tides are fresh water from the Everglades, many channeled and intricate; Lostman's River with its sand bars into the Gulf and Rodger's River and Harney's River. Then with impressive opening and far inward reaching among saw-grass plains, there is the Broad River known only to the multitudinous flights of the birds at sunrise and sunset, crammed with fish, and once boiling with crocodiles; at noons it lies glaring, soundless, solitary, untouched. South of that is Shark River carved in the rock, and the Little Shark in all their branchings and windings among mangroves, opening inland in channels that lead behind the three capes of Cape Sable, more inlets than rivers, lakes, lagoons, all sun struck, sea invaded.

For the retaining shape of the rock that holds in the western curve of the saw-grass river, one has to go back to the cape and the angle that Caloosahatchee makes with it, a rough right angle, subtended by the long line of the outer coast. Up in that angle, as if it was the western armpit of that country, there is an unseen dome of limestone which makes a watershed for all this. It is not the edge of the true Glades, but it shows where the rock lies nearest to the surface, about at the place now called Immokalee. Water in the rains runs north to Caloosahatchee, west to the seacoast, in some of those small rivers like the Estero and the Imperial, once called Surveyor's Creek, and the Corkscrew River, and into Trafford Lake and Deep Lake, and others. Blue water stands in deep, round cups of the rock. East lies a strange country that borders the Glades sharply. The northern part is called the Devil's Garden, a broken scrubby open land. South is the mass of the Big Cypress, by which for a long time the saw grass curves.

All this again is drained by a bright green swampy, grassy trough called the Okaloacochee Slough, which leads southwestward into the Fakahatchee Swamp, half salt marshes and fresh water, which leads in turn into Fakahatchee Bay behind the mounded islands above the Allen, now the Barron, River.

So, in the middle of the narrow east coast and the broader west coast, the Everglades curve grandly in the limestone.

30

The rock is still strange stuff. The fresh Glades water wore it horizontally from north to southwest in a long valley, never smooth, but a series of long uneven ridges and troughs that hold the muck and the southernmost marl. It was porous stuff to begin with. And then all that fresh water wore and seeped down into it through the cloaking vegetable decay, charged with the strong organic acids that ate and gnawed and dissolved chemically the penetrable limestone. The acid water worked and tunneled it, so that it is honeycombed and fretted and pocked, under the layers of the muck, into something very like rocky sponge. All but the hardest cores and spines of limestone were eaten out downward many feet below the surface in an infinity of grooved strange shapes.

If all the saw grass and the peat was burned away there would be exposed to the sun glare the weirdest country in the world, thousands and hundreds of thousands of acres of fantastic rockwork, whity gray and yellow, streaked and blackened, pinnacles and domes and warped pyramids and crumbling columns and stalagmites, ridgy arches and half-exposed horizontal caverns, long downward cracks, and a million extraordinary chimney pots. Under the sun glare or the moonlight it would look stranger than a blasted volcano crater, or a landscape of the dead and eroded moon.

Nothing of that limestone shows above the surface in the northernmost Glades. For sixty miles or so south of Lake Okeechobee the river of the saw grass sweeps wider than the horizon, nothing but saw grass utterly level to the eye, a vast unbroken monotony. The grass crowds all across the visible width and rondure of the earth, like close-fitting fur. Clouds and the smoke of fires stand far off and are sunk in it, like the smoke of ships at sea. This is the Everglades at their greatest concentration, a world of nothing but saw grass. Nothing seems to live here but a few insects, hawks working a few acres, buzzards soaring

31

against the piled snow of a cloud, a heron flying its far solitary line.

The saw grass sweeps about halfway south, where the whole course begins to arc a little to the westward. There the muck is not so deep, less solidly packed over the limestone. The hardest rock began to show at the surface its ridged top in hundreds and thousands of places. In times of drought the soil subsided around this rock which the new rains and the suns eroded and wore off level. And the surface water around the exposed rock under the surrounding grass shaped and pointed it in the direction of the currents in islands like anchored ships swinging all in the same direction, fleets, flotillas, armadas of stranded island shapes. Southward the islands crowd more thickly in the thinning muck.

Plants seized upon these rocks, hardly less avidly than the saw grass, carried by wind or birds or water, and needing only a pinch of humus, some cranny more hospitable than the all-choking saw grass, in which to send down their first threadlike roots. The enormous machinery of the sun drew up the sprouts, the stalks, the trunks of trees, the covering leaves. Every island, almost at once, reached a tropical struggling life in blossom and quick seed.

These islands are, like the saw grass, the particular feature of the Glades. Small or great jungles, they loom out of the brownness of the saw grass in humped solid shapes, like green whales and gray-green hangars and domes and green clouds on the horizon. They look like hummocks, and many books persist in calling them so. They are called also "heads" and "strands" and "tree islands," but the right name is "hammock," from "hamaca," an Arawak word for jungle or masses of vegetation floating in a tropical river. These are the hammocks of the saw-grass river. No man has explored all of them, or could. They are too many. From north to south there is a changing vegetation on them, by which they can be characterized. Some have known history such as men make. Some hide marks of deeds that few men remember. Some have not known one single human thing, only the beasts and snakes and birds and insects that know nothing else since their time began.

That is not all, for this rock has a shape greater than this visible one of the peninsula. Westward it makes a great shadowy sunken plateau extending far out into the Gulf of Mexico in shallows that drop off abruptly into the midmost deeps. On the east coast it is gouged deeply by a stream of warm water over one of cold, with a current greater than the Mississippi that separates the American continent here at Florida from the Bahama Banks, two hundred fathoms deep, moving four to five miles an hour. It is the enormous oceanic river of the Gulf Stream.

The whole structure of this rock is known as the Floridian plateau. Still, to understand it, one must know how it was made, in time's forward-pushing inexorable years.

V. THE RIVER OF TIME

THE life and death of the saw grass is only a moment of that flow in which time, the vastest river, carries us and all life forward. The water is timeless, forever new and eternal. Only the rock, which time shaped and will outlast, records unimaginable ages.

Yet, as time goes, this limestone is recent. The earth itself is so much older that time grows faint about it, in those hundreds of millions of years which, in its cooling and wrinkling and rising and wearing and changing, might have been but a single day. The mind of man has no way of holding so vast a concept. He has devised symbols to spare himself the agony of trying to think what that awfulness was like.

33

The earth was shrunken and old, the continents almost as we know them, already split and re-formed and taking shape within the all-encompassing ocean, when the Floridian plateau was still a part of the floor of a warm, tranquil, equatorial sea. The Appalachian Mountains to the north already had been thrust up and worn down again by the friction of centuries and still the sea lay here, wrinkling and glittering in its moon-enchanted tides. There was a stump at the south of that continental mass like the beginning of north Florida. Or perhaps it was an island. But that was all.

There came one last heaving and changing, some huge undersea faulting and pinching up, and in long slow centuries the Floridian plateau rose a little, only a little, the east edge of it a little higher, the west sloping back gradually to the sea again. The sea water ran off it as if it were the rising shoulder of some huge sleek beast. The ridged shelly oozy bottom of the sea broke into the sunlight for the first time and as the waters within what we now call the Gulf of Mexico felt the narrowing pinch of the land, they began to pour out irresistibly, as the earth turned, in the Gulf Stream.

They say that was late in the earth's history, a mere geologic yesterday. The Pliocene, they call it, which is only a way of bunching together an unbelievable section of centuries in one word that can be handled without too much thought. They think it was nineteen million years ago and that the period lasted millions of years.

Life had taken shape on the earth long before, long, long before, the top of this Florida rock rose above the sea. Shapes of growing things which this land still bears in the Everglades and the coasts are so much older than the region itself that thought grows dizzy contemplating them.

Eight hundred million years ago there were growing on the warm lands then far north palmlike plants called cycads. They grow on the borders of the Everglades now. The ants were already fixed in their selfless habits of busyness, as they are today. The first reptiles, shaped like the small green lizards on the sun-warmed stones, had taken to the air and learned to fly, having changed their scales to wings, one hundred and fifty-five million years before there was any Florida at all.

The little scorpions that crawl out of rotted wood on cold nights and hang on a wall like perfect small lobsters, whose species have the longest history of any air-breathing thing, are older than any of this rock of which the Floridian world is made. The sponges, the corals, the shellfish, some of the crabs along these coasts, the tiniest shell forms that turn up in the muck below the oldest saw grass, are older than the whole shape of this land. There are forms among these hammocks more ancient by a hundred million years. The most recent dragonfly that crawls from its larval state to dry and stretch its glistening fine wings on the tallest saw grass was shaped and formed so many centuries before the whole contour of the Everglades began that one looks from the insect to the wideness of this grassy world with a feeling that understanding of permanence is, like an understanding of time itself, impossible.

Only yesterday, then, they say, the Floridian plateau was lifted up, long after the quails and the swifts and the flamingos, the warblers and the water snakes, the owls, the woodpeckers and the alligators had assumed their present forms and habits.

The north of Florida may have been a part of the north mainland before the West Indian islands rose in the fire of their own volcanoes from the edge of a huge fault in the ocean bottom that skirts the inmost deeps. The questing shadows of sharks ranged freely throughout all the oceans, east to west, before Central America was an isthmus. There were monkeys in the world and gibbons and that brooding incalculable new thing in the other continent, this shambling figure with the

spark under his thick skull that was the beginning of all thought
—man. The Everglades were not begun before him.

But in that farthest age of the recent they call the Miocene,
when the shape of the Florida plateau was forced up out of
the sea, it was the last such rising movement, or so most of the
scientists think, that occurred here.

There are no loopings and foldings of this rock, no tilted
broken strata here. There is only, far below the surface, the
evidence of that old, old first movement, a slow, smooth, regularly marked ancient dome. The top of the dome, the anticline,
is highest north of Okeechobee, near the center of north Florida
at Ocala. From Ocala southward, like the slopes of a deep-
hidden hill, the strata flow downward, farther and farther below. The oldest, the Cretaceous, which first existed one hundred
twenty million years ago, is the lowest, sweeping down ten
thousand feet below the southern rim of the Everglades and
of the sea. The Eocene lies above that and the Oligocene above
that, and the Miocene curves from north to south under Okeechobee and the Everglades from ninety to nine hundred feet
below the surface. The surface itself, this oölitic limestone,
lies from the surface to ninety feet down under the southern
mangrove rim.

All those strata, from the dome at Ocala, sweep down and
farther down in regular flowing layers. So that what is on the
surface in north Florida, the water-bearing rock that makes
the lovely north Florida springs and cavernous rivers "measureless to man," is hidden under the Everglades by a thousand
feet. From that rock nothing reaches up to the surface here.
That is why only the surface rain water that flows into Okeechobee makes the Everglades and seeps into and frets the
rock. There are no upgushings from deep subterranean rivers.

It proves again that, since the Miocene, those nineteen million years ago, there has been no change in the larger shape of

the Floridian plateau itself. What happened, to surface that hidden dome with limestone and sand and marl and muck and peat, was the phenomenon of the polar ice.

Ice that had formed at the poles, in a world then tropic almost to what we now call the Arctic Circle, in an age of warmth began to move slowly downward in enormous encroaching glaciers, huge mile-high cliffs of ice that scraped and tore and gouged away rocks and mountains in their courses and sucked up water from all the oceans as they froze, in a slowly chilling world. Perhaps the mountains had been thrust up too high, so that too much snow had fallen. Perhaps there was less sunlight, from the tornadoes of shadow that pass across the surface of the sun itself.

At least, the scientists are sure of the ice. It moved southward, in the Northern Hemisphere, killing the forests, shoving the changing forms of living things all southward, scarring and grinding the face of the world. It never reached Florida.

Then, after an interminable cold and shadowy time, the warmth came back. The glacial polar ice melted and retreated, and all that released water flowed back into the seas. The sea rose up over the edges of that new shape of the Floridian plateau, warming and washing it gently, moving north of Okeechobee in a long curve over the once-risen land.

Four times in that measureless age of ice the glaciers froze and formed again and crept grating and jarring southward, in the fogs and glacial mists, beyond the Great Lakes and New York State and New England. Again freezing, they drew up the waters of the earthly seas. When they melted and left the deep gouged lakes and the ice-worn rounded hills and the glacial moraines, they gave back the waters to the sea again. But in some places there had been faultings and enlargings in the ocean's undersurface, and huge lakes were left filled with water so that each time the sea rose back over lower

37

Florida it never reached its earlier levels. Each time the curving waterline was lower.

Okeechobee was left then as a great inland fresh-water lake, a swampy amorphous depression. From this, the powerful rains leached away the salt. On the east coast the lines of retaining ridges were left as they may be seen today, all parallel, north and south but each lower, as between the glacial stages the sea each time did not stand so high.

The slow retreating waves dropped their silt between the great glacial periods. Below the waterline there was water erosion, holes in the shoreward rocks smooth scoured by the sand and the tides. The marl at the south accumulated softly. The fresh-water limestone was established. By the lines of shell fossils geologists can today trace the old sea levels. A last glacier took up the water and the sea shrank back and the fresh water from Okeechobee flowed out and down the slow incline. The western rivers swept farther out along the soft rock than they do now, dropping the scoured silt and sand in outer peninsulas and bars and wind-swept dunes for the sea to shape.

Then that last glacier melted and retreated farther north than it ever had before. It is there now, the north polar icecap, the glaciers, the ice fields of the arctic, the thick ice over Greenland and inner Alaska and northern Siberia. Not all the water was returned to the sea. But there was enough to change again the changing shape of lower Florida. The sea crept back up the mouths of the western rivers, filling and submerging the outer shape of Caloosahatchee, creeping up toward the Everglades in all those shapeless, spreading, wandering tidal rivers among the mangroves, filling up the sand dunes so that they became the Ten Thousand Islands.

On the east coast, along that highest rim of rock, the south-swinging current that edges between the Gulf Stream and the land laid down sand in bars and peninsulas, filled up some of the mouths of rivers like the Loxahatchee, and laid the sand again along the ridgy shapes of the keys. On the south the sea crept over the marly shallows and kept the currents between the keys open, and they filled the Bay of Florida, and laid down the sand of Cape Sable and worked the standing salt ponds and lagoons of the Everglades delta shore.

The sea had risen. It is there now. The shape of this land was established. The long flow of time seems to have slowed to its humdrum working of day to day. Yet if this is the end of the ice age, or if the sea is still rising and the ice melting, if there will be other ages of ice and sunlessness when the seas are taken up and the moist hidden caverns of the lower deeps again revealed, who can guess? Time never stops.

So down the valley of the Glades the fresh water crept in its recent shape, recent by centuries unrecorded except for the rock. The saw grass, one of the oldest forms of green life on the already aged earth, thrust up here its first sharp, resilient spears.

After it, in the earth now seeming so long established, the forms old and new of plant and animal and insect life hurried to take their hold.

Time moves again for the Everglades, not in ages and in centuries, but as man knows it, in hours and days, the small events of his own lifetime, who was among the last of the living forms to invade its shores.

VI. LIFE ON THE ROCK

THE saw grass and the water made the Everglades both simple and unique. Yet bordering and encroaching on that simplicity, fighting for foothold on its coasts and islands, a diversity of life lives upon the rock that holds it. The saw grass in its es-

sential harshness supports little else. It repelled man. But on
the rock the crowding forms made life abundant, so that between the two the chronicle is balanced.

One begins with the plants.

If the saw grass here is four thousand years old, many other
of these plant associations may have been here almost as long.

In the time of which I write, toward the end of the past century when everything was as it had been, the southern vague
watery rim of Okeechobee was bordered by a strange jungle.
The crusted wave foam was washed down among windrows of
dead reeds and branches and rotting fish. In that decay a wide
band of jungle trees sprang up.

Southwest it was all custard apple, a subtropic, rough-barked,
inconspicuous tree, with small pointed leaves and soft fruits.
It grew fiercely, crowded on roots that became gnarled trunks
or trunks twisted and arched into bracing roots in the drag
of the water. The spilth and decay of the custard apple, the
guano of crowds of birds that fed on them, whitening the leaves,
built up in the watery sunlessness below them an area of rich
black peat, denser than muck, two or three miles wide and six
or eight feet deep.

The earliest Americans on the lake called this area "the custard apple bottoms." It was edged with tall leather ferns and
Boston ferns and knotted with vines, which no man could get
through without axes or dynamite. Lake water crept darkly
below.

The southeast was edged with a less tropical jungle, scrub
willow with its light-green pointed leaves and yellow catkins
and the ropy brown bark of elderberries, bearing out of their
lacy plates of white blossoms the purple-black fruit about
which the blue jays and the mockingbirds, the great black-
glinting Florida crows, the grackles and the red-winged black-
birds in their thousands set up a flapping and creaking and

40

crowing and ker-eeing. Bees and bright flies and yellow butterflies hovered when the blossoms were sweet. Under their shadows ground rattlers moved sluggishly. Winds carried to them from the reedy lake clouds of feeble white insects lake people call "chizzle winks," which breed and die in myriads in a short few days.

These were the willow-and-elder bottoms, which fought shrewdly with the saw grass for every rocky space. The dark-brown peaty muck they left went east up the lake edge between the sand ridges and the saw-grass arms.

Over all this thick jungle region climbed and hung down in moving green curtains the heart-shaped leaves of moon-vines. In the luminous unseen dark of the night the moonflowers opened acres after acres of flat white blossoms, cloud white, foam white, and still. Northward, lake water moved darkly under the tiny pointed reflections of the stars. Below the region the moonflowers and the moon made their own, with no man's eye to see them, moved the enormous darkness without light of the saw-grass river.

East along the curving Everglades borders and west by the farther coast stood everywhere in their endless ranks the great companies of the pines. Where they grew the rock was highest—"high pine land," people called it. Their ranks went off across an open slough in a feathery cliff, a rampart of trunks red-brown in the setting sun, bearing tops like a long streamer of green smoke. Their warm piny breaths blew in the sun along the salt winds. They covered here, as they did everywhere in Florida, interminable miles.

Some southern longleaf, "common yellow pine," with its taller trunk and bushier branches is scattered south from the Caloosahatchee and down the east coast to the New River. But below there, wherever it could find foothold in high rock, and up behind the western mangrove to what is now Gordon Pass, which is the area of West Indian vegetation, grows the Caribbean pine. It stands everywhere about the borders of the Caribbean. It is called slash pine. But in Dade County from the first it was called Dade County pine.

Its trunks are set thick with rust and brown and grayish bark patches, which resist fire. The patterns of its skimpy branches people find strange, or beautiful. Dying alone, as they often do away from their great companies, killed by lightning or the borer that instantly finds injured bark, these pines stand dead a long time, rigid gray or silver, their gestures frozen. The young fluffy pines start up everywhere about them, bearing long pale candles in the new light of spring.

With the Caribbean pines, as they do with other pines of the South, always grow the palmettos. These are saw palmettos, silver-green, blue-green, or in dry times magnificent tawny-gold across vast open savannas. Their spiky fans cover all the ground beneath the pine trees, on unseen spiny trunks. If they are burned, with a great oily popping and seething, only the blackened trunks are left, writhing like heavy snakes.

The small brown Florida deer step neatly at the edge of pine forests like these. The brown wildcats know them. The clear light falls mottled through the branches faintly green over endless fan points. Inconspicuous wild flowers grow in the wiry grass between palmettos, faint blue chicory, or yellow tea bush, or the tiny wild poinsettias with their small brush strokes of scarlet. The quail pipe and their new-hatched young run like mice with their small cheeping, at the edge of such pineland, and the brown marsh rabbit with small ears and no apparent tail nibbles some bit of leaf.

A diamondback rattlesnake may push out here slowly after such a rabbit or the cotton mice, or lie after shedding his flaky old skin to sun the brilliant dark lozenge marks on his almost yellowish new scales, slow to coil or rattle unless angered. Then in a blur he draws back in quick angles that wide-jawed head with the high nose balanced over the coils, his slitted eyes fixed and following his object, the forked tongue flicking through the closed jaws, tasting the disturbed air. His raised tail shakes the dry rattle of its horny bells. His strength, his anger, engorges that thick muscular body, ruffles his barky scales. If he strikes it is at one-third of his length. The jaws open back so that the long fangs strike forward and deep. His recovery is quicker than the eye can see. Or he lifts tall that kingly head before he lowers it in retreat, holding himself grandly, with the same dignity that has made him the king among all these beasts.

All the woodpeckers in south Florida yank and hitch and cluck and rap their way up these great patched pine trunks, all with red heads, the downy, the hairy, the red-bellied, and that diabolical creature with a red and white and black head like a medieval battle-ax, the pileated, which the early settlers called so truly "the Lord God Almighty." But in those early days the even more impressive ivory-billed, which we shall never see again, startled these pinewoods with his masterly riveting.

Even in the middle of the saw-grass river, where an outcrop of old rock is the only evidence of preglacial times, the pines grow tall to show where the rock lies. The buzzards and the black vultures, their ragged wing tips like brush strokes of India ink, sail and sail and rise on the upcurrents and soar in their pure flight, turning about some old roost they have always kept and returned to year after year. Their piercing glances watch for the glint of flies' wings over carrion they crave, the most valuable birds in the world. Or from the muddy water holes about the pineland the brown-black water moccasins slide their wet ridged scales. Startled, they coil to retract those open, white-lined jaws, like a queer white flower to anything peering down. Death is there too.

43

Where the pines are thin, the Indians found their first source of life. There grow foot-tall, ferny green cycads, plants older than this rock, with yellow and orange cones for flowers and great thick roots. This is the "coontie" of the oldest Indian legend. Its root is grated and squeezed and sifted to flour to make the thick watery gruel "sofkee," which was always the basis of the Indians' diet here. The Indians' legend came partly from the Spanish fathers. They say that once there was a great famine here in Florida. The Indians prayed to the Master of Breath, who sent down His Son, God's Little Boy, to walk about at the edge of the pinelands and the Glades. And wherever He walked, there in His heel marks grew the coontie, for the Indians to eat and reverence.

Sometimes it is called compte. The early white men learned of it and grated it to make starch and knew it as arrowroot. By the pinelands north of the Miami River, the Indians camped often, so that their women could gather it in what was called the Coontie grounds.

The dragonflies on iridescent wings dart and hang in squadrons by the open air of pinelands. Below among the grass roots stirs all the minute dustlike activity of the ants.

In the summer hosts of big red-and-yellow grasshoppers, with heads shaped like horses', will descend and eat holes in all the softer leaves. Walking sticks fly like boomerangs. Shining brown leaf-shaped palmetto bugs scurry like cockroaches. Spiders like tiny crabs hang in stout webs. The birds snap at small moths and butterflies of every kind. A blue racer, the snake that moves across the cleared sand like a whiplash, will with one flick destroy the smooth, careful cup of the ant lion in the hot sand. The whole world of the pines and of the rocks hums and glistens and stings with life.

But if, on these rocky outcrops, the pines and the palmettos were destroyed, by lightning or the old fires of Indians, another great tree took its place and gradually changed, with its own associated forms, the whole nature of the place. This was the live oak, the first of the hardwoods. They made the first hammocks at the edge of rivers or on the driest Everglades islands.

The warblers in their thousands migrate up and down the continents, spring and fall, South America to North America and back, enlivening the oaks with their small flitting shapes and tiny whisperings; palm and pine warblers, the myrtles, the black-throated blues, the amazing redstarts, the black-and-whites—oh, it is impossible to name all the warblers that pass here.

Dozens of other birds are there in their seasons in the live oaks, among the red splashes of air plants and the patches of lichens. Green lizards puff out their throats like thin red bubbles in some unhearable love call. The eternal cardinals raise their first trillings before dawn, "Pretty, pretty, pretty—sweet, sweet-sweet." A mocking bird, all one whirl of gray and white, flips through those aging branches chasing a small brown owl or flinging him in the sun from the topmost twigs to fling up his modulated lovely spray of words. The small tree-frogs pipe there in the gray before rain and the yellow-billed cuckoo croaks, and the almost invisible rain-crow. In the first tender dark the little owl comes out from his hole where the mocker chased him to begin his low, liquid bubbling, the velvet secret voice of the night.

South in the lower hammocks in a live oak, frowsy with dry Resurrection ferns that the first rain startles to green life, some pale green slender stalk with minute gold eyes will seem to grow along a branch, poking upward on its own thoroughfare, high and higher in the leafiness, a small green tree snake. Such little snakes achieve the sun among the topmost leaves to be spied on by one of the loveliest bird-shapes of all, the free-fly-

ing, easy-soaring, easy-turning swallow-tailed kite, that lifts
and ranges and swings in whiteness above the tree-tops. One
stoop and the free bird slides upward on the wind, dangling the
small tender green thing in pure sunlight to its airy and exalted
death.

A huge ancient line of live oaks stands along the westernmost
rock edge of Okeechobee, deep with moss, looking out over
miles and miles of shallow reeds between them and the mirage-
like glitter of that inland sea. There in open, sunblasted country
the black-and-white caracara, that the Mexicans take for their
national eagle, cries harshly from a bush top, his round, gold
glance avid for lizards on the ground. A king snake, brave in
yellow and fine black in the dust, snaps back in zigzags the
speed of his fighting body. Grackles in thousands, creaking
their interminable wheels of sound, hang in the reeds their
thousands of pouchlike nests. Life is everywhere here too, infinite and divisible.

The live oaks, like dim giants crowded and choked by a
thrusting forest of younger hardwoods, made that great Miami
hammock, the largest tropical jungle on the North American
mainland, which spread south of the Miami River like a dark
cloud along that crumbling, spring-fed ledge of rock. Here
where the leaf-screened light falls only in moving spots and
speckles to the rotting, leaf-choking mold, the hoary ruins of
live oaks are clouded by vines and resurrection ferns, their roots
deep in the rotting limestone shelves among wet potholes green-
shadowed with the richest fern life in the world—maidenhair
and Boston ferns and brackens and ferns innumerable. At night
the mosquitoes shrill in the inky blackness prickled through
with fireflies.

About the live oaks is waged the central drama of all this
jungle, the silent, fighting, creeping struggle for sunlight of the
strangler fig. It is one of those great trees people call rubber

46

trees or Banyans. They are all *Ficus,* but the strangler is *Ficus aurea.* A strangler seed dropped by a bird in a cranny of oak bark will sprout and send down fine brown root hairs that dangle and lengthen until they touch the ground. There they grip and thicken and become buttresses. Over the small hard oak leaves the thick dark-green oily strangler's leaves lift and shut out the sun. Its long columnar trunks and octopus roots wrap as if they were melted and poured about the parent trunk, flowing upward and downward in wooden nets and baskets and flutings and enlacings, until later the strangler will stand like a cathedral about a fragment of tree it has killed, crowning leaves and vast branches supported by columns and vaultings and pilings of its bowery roots.

The stranglers are only the most evident and dramatic of all these crowding tropical jungle trees; smooth red-brown gumbo limbos, ilex, eugenias, satinwoods, mastic, cherry laurel, paradise trees, the poisonous manchineel, the poisonwood, the Florida boxwood and hundreds more which the hurricanes brought over from Cuba and the West Indies.

This was the jungle that people thought the Everglades resembled. Birds flit through it only rarely. The little striped skunk leaves its trail. The brilliant coral snake buries its deadly black nose in its loam. The false coral, the harlequin, with its yellow nose, is hardly less hidden. Spiders stretch their exquisite traps for pale insects. Small brown scorpions move on the rotting logs. And far up among the tufted air plants the small native orchids are as brown and pale yellow and faint white as the light they seek.

Everywhere among these branches moves imperceptibly one of the loveliest life forms of these coasts—the pale-ivory, pale-coral, pale-yellow and pale-rose, whorled and etched and banded shell of the *Liguus,* the tree snails. Their pointed shell bubbles are found chiefly on smooth-barked trees in the dry

47

hammocks, but every Everglades island-hammock has its own varieties, subspecies developed in countless lifetimes in a single unique area, varying with an infinity of delicate differences. They came from the tropics. They are a world in themselves.

Moths move in and out of the light at the jungle edge, the twilight hawk moth, seeking the pale-flowered vines, and the rose-colored tiger moth. There is a day in the spring when myriads of white butterflies drift over the whole land, moving out to sea inexplicably. They are caught and die in thousands against the jungles.

But here especially the strangest of the butterflies quivers silently in the bands of sun in the green light of leaves, the only one of its tropical kind on this mainland. It is the *Heliconius*, named for the sun, barred black and pale yellow as the light and shade, wavering always in companies, which no bird will touch. The *Heliconius* drowse of nights in colonies, delicately crowded and hanging on a single small tree. When bright moon light reaches them they have been seen to wake and drift about, filling a leafy glade with their quivering moon-colored half-sleep.

About the rivers of the west, north of the tropic vegetation line, grows the water oak. The water oaks grow taller and more regular than the live oaks. Their longer pointed leaves drop off the bare boughs in a brief winter and put on their new light green long before the rusty live oaks renew themselves, in that misty river country. Both crowd down to the glossy water and make landscapes like old dim pictures where the deer came down delicately and the cows stand, to drink among their own reflections.

In the great Miami hammock, along the banks of almost every river, bordering the salt marshes, scattered in the thinner pineland, making their own shapely and recognizable island-hammocks within the Everglades river, everywhere, actually, except in the densest growth of the saw grass itself, stands the

Sabal palmetto. To distinguish it from the low shrubby saw palmetto, it is called the cabbage palm. With its gray-green fans glittering like metal in the brilliance, its round top bearing also branches of queer blossoms and hard dark berries, the cabbage palm grows singly or in dramatic clumps over stout round trunks. The basketwork of old fan hilts is broken off below as the trunk grows tall and smooth. Ferns and vines and air plants and lizards and spiders live in that basketwork. They are often engulfed by strangler figs. They bristle on the banks of fresh-water rivers among the oaks. They make dense islands in the saw-grass river.

They are a northern growth, unrelated to the tropical palms, to the coconut palms that rise above the outer beaches and are set everywhere in cities, or the great royal palms that tower among the Everglades keys and in a few magnificent hammocks of their own toward the west coast. The Spaniards introduced the coconuts to Panama from the Philippines, the royals are native West Indians. Their nuts were blown over from Cuba and germinated in the rain-washed debris of some tropical cyclone. Other delicate palms, like the silver palm of the lower mainland, came the same way.

Then there is the enduring cypress. There are many cypresses in the world but the Everglades region has two: the short, often dwarf, pond cypress and the tall fresh-water river cypress. It is the river cypress that is tall, to 125 feet, silver gray, columnar, almost pyramidal on its broad fluted base, whose curiously short branches lose their leaves in winter and stand ghostly and gaunt among the hanging Spanish moss and red-tongued air plants. Spring draws out from the ancient wood the tiny scratched lines of its thready leaves, the palest yellow-green darkening to emerald. It is a fine timber tree. White and green, over brown water, against an amazing blue and white sky, it is most strangely beautiful.

The cypress that grows in muddy water has that curious accompaniment, the rootlike extension into the air, like dead stumps, called cypress knees, which are thought to aerate the mudbound roots. The dry-land cypress does not need them. It grows up rivers of both coasts and about the lake. But in its greatest area, a vast dramatic association of river cypress and pond cypress marks the west bank of the saw-grass river, and forms the Big Cypress Swamp.

The Big Cypress extends south from the Devil's Garden, a wilderness of pine and scrubby stuff and bushes, near that dome of land in the angle of Caloosahatchee and the lake, south in great fingers which reach to the headwaters of the Turner River, as far down as the salt water and the mangrove. The rock below it is uneven and ridgy, all hollows and higher places. It is called "swamp" because in the rains the water stands in it and does not run off. It is not moving water, like the saw-grass Glades. It was called "the Big Cypress" because it covered so great an area.

The river cypresses stand there in wintertime in great gray-scratched heads, like small hills, towering above the dense and lower pond, or dwarf, cypress between, thinly set in the wetter hollows of wire grass, starred with white spider lilies and sedges and, in drier places, milkwort in saffron-headed swaths. Red-shouldered hawks cruise the low cypress and the marsh-lands, marsh hawks balance and tip, showing white rump marks, and far over at the edge of a thicket a deer feeds, and flicks his white-edged tail before he lifts his head and stares.

From high in a plane at that time of year the Big Cypress seems an undulating misted surface full of peaks and gray valleys changing to feathering green. East of it, sharply defined as a river from its banks, move the vast reaches of the saw grass.

The brown deer, the pale-colored lithe beautiful panthers that feed on them, the tuft-eared wildcats with their high-angled hind legs, the opossum and the rats and the rabbits have lived in and around it and the Devil's Garden and the higher pinelands to the west since this world began. The quail pipe and call through the open spaces. The great barred owls hoot far off in the nights and the chuck-will's-widows on the edge of the pines aspirate their long whistling echoing cries. The bronze turkeys, the most intelligent of all the birds or beasts, feed in the watery places and roost early in the thick cypress tops, far from the prowlers below. And the black Florida bear, which sleeps even here his short winter sleep, goes rooting and grumbling and shoving through the underbrush, ripping up logs for grubs and tearing at berries, scorning no mice.

The bears move to the beaches and, like the panthers, dig for turtle eggs. They catch crabs and chew them solemnly and eat birds' eggs if they find them, and ripe beach plums. The panthers prey most on the range hogs of the settlers, and so they are hunted with dogs, and fight viciously, killing many before they leap into trees and, snarling, never to be tamed, are shot.

Here in the cypress pools—but for that matter, everywhere in the watery Glades, from lake to sea—lives the Glades' first citizen, the otter. Like the birds, he is everywhere. The oily fur of his long lithe body is ready for heat or cold, so long as it is wet. His webbed hands are more cunning than the raccoon's. His broad jolly muzzle explores everything, tests everything, knows everything. His quickness is a snake's lightning quickness. He has a snake's suppleness and recovery, but not the snake's timidity. His heart is stout and nothing stops him.

The otter has been seen to swim and flirt and turn among a crowd of thrashing alligators, from whose clumsy attack he has only to dive and flash away. He knows how to enjoy life in the sun better than all the rest of all the creatures. He is gay. He is crammed with lively spirit. He makes a mud slide down a bank, and teaches his cubs to fling themselves down it and

51

romp and tumble and swim upside down in the frothing water. He is fond of his female and plays with a ball and has fun. His ready grinning curiosity and friendliness betray him to the hunter and trapper. This is his home.

On the scanty dwarf cypress the gray Ward's heron stands rigid. The big black-and-white wood ibis, like a stork, which flies so high and so far in such grave and orderly squadrons, slides downward on hollow wing and lights with a great flapping and balancing that makes the tree look silly under its teetering grip as it stares down its great curved beak for a frog there below. It is as though all the life of the Everglades region, every form of beast or bird or gnat or garfish in the pools, or the invisible life that pulses in the scum on the pools, was concentrated in the Big Cypress.

The dwarf cypress has its area, perhaps the most fantastic of all, far toward Cape Sable, south of the live-oak jungle that was called Paradise Key, where the royal palms stood high overhead like bursting beacons seen across the sloughs. Men have said they have seen panthers here, not tan, but inky black. There southward, under the even more brilliant light, as if already the clouds reflected the glare from the sea beyond, the small cypress, four or five feet tall, stands in the rock itself, barely etched with green. These trees seem centuries old, and they are very old indeed, in spite of fire and hurricane. Even in full leaf their green is scant. There are moccasins around their roots out of the standing clear water, and high, high over, a bald eagle lazily lifting, or an osprey beating up from the fishing flats.

Lake jungles, pine, live oak, cabbage palmetto, cypress, each has its region and its associated life. As the islands in the saw grass pointed southward in the water currents, their vegetation changes like their banks, from temperate to subtropic, to the full crammed tropic of the south.

52

The northernmost are dense with pond apple or willow and elder and those charming border shrubs, the silver myrtle, with its spring flowering of silky silvery pompons, the day jasmine, with the dark berries the mocking birds clamor for, salt bush, bay, and dozens of others. There are hammocks centered about live oaks or cabbage palms, crowded and screened with bushes. There are cypress hammocks hung with moss over a deep brown pool where a single heron waits and the blue flag and the water hyacinth and the green arrowy lilies catch a great shaft of light. Beyond lies all that broad, open, windy level of the Glades.

So, at the end of the saw-grass river and its bordering coasts, begins the mangrove. It shows itself in short tufts first, in green leggy rosettes far south where the saw grass is shorter over thinner muck and the emerging rock. There are higher hammocks of mangrove beyond. The saw-grass river goes on around them. In the rainy seasons the current is visible, rippling and bending the grass tops as it flows nearer the sea. The draining fresh-water rivers begin far above the highest salt tides.

Glaring under the sun or bleak in the rain, flat, with patches of scrub and bright salt weeds, this is the country of the birds. The man-o'-war birds from the keys float and tumble over it in their effortless flight. Thousands of sandpipers and sanderlings rise in clouds from the water meadows. The ducks paddle in every stream end. In some great inland bay of salt water, two or three hundred white pelicans, like a snowbank on a reef, wait for the tide to drive the small fish into their scooping beak-pouches. They are ten feet from wing tip to wing tip. When they rise, fraying out, peeling off, in a slow roar of aroused wings, they float high up and sail and turn in great concentric circles, white against cloud dazzle.

The headwaters of these fresh-water rivers are covered in the season with the stick nests of herons, the least blue and the glossy and the Louisiana and the solitary great white heron, the stalker of these shallows. The roseate spoonbills, with their queer bills and delicate, flame-stained pink feathers, have gone through their ridiculous stick courtships here. And drifting down from the saw-grass reaches come the white ibis, in a huge sweeping, turning, flashing circle, tilted groundward so that the lower birds stop and stand with outstretched necks before they are caught up again in the wheeling flying, the rare pattern of their nuptial flight.

Like the otter, raccoons are everywhere about the Everglades, but here in the south by the mangrove they have lived in thousands. Their wonderful small black fingers find the crawfish and the sea grape and the coon oysters hanging on the mangrove roots. They stand on their hindquarters with their hands on their furry chests to snuff at every wind with those sharp curious noses, peering at everything strange with those black-masked bright eyes.

Within the salt meadows here at the end of this world, green with thick-stemmed waterweeds glowing yellow and coral

about the white marly water, the round-nosed dark alligators
find their way along fresh-water inland streams, after their
fierce matings, to make their nests.

There must be heat and wetness for the porous thirty or more
eggs the female alligator lays. She works together a great mass
of waterweeds or grass, mashing it down and letting it rot and
grow compact, and brings new stuff in her toothy jaws to pile
on it. When it is settled and steaming she pushes the top off
and makes a hole and lays her eggs and covers them again. It
may take eight weeks or more, with the sun heat and the fer-
ment and the moisture, to incubate them.

When the young squeak in their shells she comes back and
pushes the stuff from off their lively tails and bright eyes and
tiny jaws, ready, direct from the shell, to snap at minnows.

But the crocodile, the narrow-jawed, clay-colored faster
beast, goes no farther inland than the warm beaches to dig a
hole in dry sand and lay dozens of eggs that any moisture may
destroy. Their clay-colored slitted eyes watch unblinking
among the mangrove-stained watercourses, vicious, intractable,
and vanishing. This last is their country.

So, fringing the salt marshes or the higher saw-grass meadows
of the southeast, where the deer make their paths, there begins in earnest the dark mangrove wilderness. It is a world as
monotonous, as unique, as the saw grass. It looks as if there was
nothing here but mangroves and the mud stinking with vegetable rot and saltreek and the moving sea water.

Mangroves exist in many places in the tropics. But this area
is the most magnificent mangrove forest, and the greatest, in
the American hemisphere.

Two kinds of mangroves dominate this association, the black
and the red. It begins on the last peat with tall hammocks and
forests of buttonwoods, called "white mangrove," not a true
mangrove at all but *Conocarpus*. Then in the first level of the
high tide stands deep-rooted the black mangrove, the *Avicennia*

55

nitida, not tall, but thick, which often sends from its submerged roots up through two or three feet of mud and water the curious pneumatophores, like thousands of sharp bristling sticks, most difficult to wade through. They are breathing organs. The dark-green leaves above them often exude salt crystals. The roots stain the water brown with strong tannin.

Beyond that, marching out into the tides low or high, and rooted deep below them in marl over the rock, goes the great *Rhizophora,* the red mangrove, on its thousands of acres of entwined, buttressed and bracing gray arches. The huge trunks, often seven feet in circumference, stand as high as eighty feet here, one hundred in the drier spots. Their canopy of green obliterates the sky. In the shadowy light over that world of arches over water all is clear gloom.

Entering wave ridges are beaten down, here. The foam washes in all the flotsam of the sea, the accumulated drift of the shallows. The thick leaves turn yellow continually and continually fall. The decay rises among those arches and the younger growths slowly march seaward across it, holding and building the land.

From the high branches long hairy ropes swing and hang down to reach the water and branch into roots. Some have few fruits. Some are heavy with long seeds like small thin torpedoes, which fall and stick in the mud under low tide and grow. But more commonly they float and are carried endlessly on sea currents that bring them upright and alive, ready to root, on other far mangroveless tropic shores.

Where these mangroves came from, to this young mud over the older rock, cannot be guessed. This may be one of the great parent forests from which seeds have been carried as far as the South Pacific. Nobody knows.

The mangrove here is at least as old as the Everglades, of which it marks the end.

2

The People of the Glades

THERE is no place on the American continents to which one can point and say, "Man began there."

To the white European who found man in the New World and promptly misnamed him "Indian" it was sufficient that he was here, where the Lord must have put him. It was centuries before white men began to realize that the Indian who had been here so long might have come from somewhere else. It is actually within the past few years that archaeological discoveries have added definite proof to that hypothesis.

To try, therefore, to explain how the Indian came to Florida by speaking of the southeastern states of the mainland, or even, as some lingering believers in the Antillean theory like to do, of the Caribbean, is like accepting the Indians' belief that the white man sprang new and whole from the Atlantic Ocean.

We know that the human race did not originate on this side of the world at all, because in all North and South America there is not one trace of the evidence found abundantly in Europe-and-Asia, to show where man first stood up and became a man. A million years ago, they reckon, the piece of skull, two teeth and a thigh bone they found in Java was the first living shape of man about which they know anything. "Pithecanthropus erectus," man-first-standing-up, was not entirely a man yet, just as geologic Florida was not yet Florida. The time of that first man was the early Pleistocene, when the last upheaval began slowly lifting the Floridian shape upward through warm sea water. The glacial periods were still to come.

The history of man himself in this world is like the flow and spread and dividing of a great river. Man became the three races in that movement about the earth which must have taken place before all the land masses had ceased to shift, when the land bridges between Asia and North America, and at the isthmus between the Americas, were being joined and wrenched apart and joined again. The glaciers were still there. A million years ago man first appeared, and in that time, strange hostile parts of the same human whole, reached about the world.

The three races were men of three different colors, living in much the same way, urged by the same hungers. The pinky-tan one was to call himself "white," as he called the yellow-brown one "red" and "yellow," and the charcoal-and-coffee colored one "black."

One group of those Stone Age men moved from the Caucasus and held India and reached to the Atlantic and moved down into Africa. They were Caucasian. The black one, the Negroid, came later to Africa, and in some strange way Australia also, as if even after their beginning one land mass had been broken and shifted away from the other. The yellow-brown Mongolian looked east to the Pacific and crowded all that land from the Malay Peninsula to Siberia. They moved farther into the arctic cold, when they learned to wear animal skins and make and use fire. The descendants of some of those first Mongols would become Chinese, and much later, begin the long process of civilization while all Europe still lived in the Stone Age. As it was, to become Caucasian, Negroid, Mongoloid had taken five hundred thousand years.

They tramped and wandered in family groups, fearing and fighting all others like themselves, surviving the turmoils of glacial time by sheer developing intelligence. When the Mongoloids had reached the northeastern confines of Asia, and looked east still, they had come far, as men.

The beasts had gone that way before them.

Four million years before man, the age of the great mammals had begun. The greatest of the animals, the teeth of which have been found in Florida, began in that early time in Africa as a small river beast that wandered where rivers led, growing big ivory tusks and a nose slowly elongating and becoming flexible. Before the Andes had begun to wrinkle and be squeezed up in South America, this creature was prowling, urged forward not just by hunger, but by a love of wandering and by a curiosity stronger than in any other mammal except man himself. Millions of years later this first of the great beasts, with trunks and ivory tusks, the elephant-kind, had developed many forms. There were the mastodons, bigger than elephants, some with two pairs of upper and lower tusks, and the mammoths.

They were to push their way all over Europe and Asia and fill great areas of Siberia with their buried bones. In a time when a land bridge existed between Asia and Alaska the great-brained, lumbering, curious beasts had ventured over Bering

Strait, into North America. Swaying and plodding forward, peering ahead with small wild eyes, they moved, generation after generation, down into the American continents. No other animal has ever walked so far, except man.

They went south from Alaska and plodded down the long land bridge into Central America, against a tide of animals developed down there and driven north by the antarctic ice. In North America also, as another ice age crowded down from the North Pole, mastodons and mammoths and species that had developed here alone, the Columbian mammoth and the huge imperial, standing fourteen feet high and carrying tusks curving down and up in huge ivory scythes, moved slowly before the cold into the warmth of Florida.

They stood switching their tails and trumpeting and trampling the mud of the early swamps and lakes and rivers of the Everglades region, tearing at vines from the jungle growth of trees, along what was to be the Caloosahatchee, where their teeth, like worn lumps of stone, have been found.

The little horses that, in the Siberian country, ran like rabbits on five toes, and that the flesh eaters found sweet, saved some of their lives by running two toes off. Long before the mammoths, they ran into North America by way of Alaska, or perhaps even by Europe, Iceland, and Greenland, to multiply into great herds on the American plains and develop into a horse called "Equus" which was nearly modern. They were all relatives of a horse called "Hippidion." Some of them went south into South America, before they were all extinct in North America. Some ran down into Florida and to the Everglades and were caught there and were never seen again.

North America had originated some species of its own, as did South America. Camels began here as little hopping creatures which developed larger bodies like deer, with long slender necks and long legs, which ranged in Florida in great herds.

60

There were in Florida two other deer besides the small native one we have now, along with a tiny deerlike creature called "Leptomeryx" and a giant pig like a wart hog, and some peccaries and a short-faced bear, a small rhinoceros from Africa and a heavier one, with no horns, came south from Alaska, an early bison with straight horns, now extinct, and a giant beaver, and many rats.

Up from South America, around by the Gulf Coast and into Florida, came tapirs and huge peccaries and two kinds of capybaras and a giant tortoise-armadillo seven feet long with flexible armor, and a great strange mammal called a glyptodont, with head and tail and feet sticking out of his heavy immovable shell.

These were the peaceful beasts, the leaf eaters. The flesh eaters followed them into Florida. There came an Asiatic lion, yellow as sunlight, and cougars and true wildcats, and a long-legged cat more than half lion. But the most spectacular of all was the saber-toothed tiger, perfectly named "Smilodon." He was a heavy-shouldered thing, named for his eight-inch long fangs that must indeed have given him an extraordinary grin. There was a small wild dog and a big early hyena with crushing jaws. Wolves ran in ferocious packs, dire wolves, larger than any wolf man has seen, howling across the open swamps to the bellowing of alligators and crocodiles, their slitted eyes gleaming back to the same moon.

The freezing northern airs kept the animals in the warm south and in that developing shape of Florida like a sack with no lower opening. Nowhere else in America was there to be a more crowded or richer or more varied animal life. The plains of Africa in modern times have held no more amazing collection of these beasts, solitary or running in herds, creeping, pushing, scampering, lumbering and chasing.

There would never be so great a variety again. Since the first interglacial time no new genus of those vertebrate mammals has ever developed. Not one. After that, whole families, orders, genera, over half or even two-thirds of the animal-kind then existing have ceased to exist anywhere on this earth.

Why so many should have become extinct here, no one knows accurately. Perhaps it was because there were too many of them, too many grass eaters for the grass, too many flesh eaters for the flesh. Perhaps they were overwhelmed by the readvancing seas of interglacial meltings that brought the bones of whales to lie among the deep beds of fossil shells which the Caloosahatchee in its meanderings would reveal. Perhaps the clumsy great things like glyptodonts and giant sloths and mammoths, weighed down by those extraordinary tusks, were caught and sank in swamps where the harrying wolves had chased them. The food of such beasts as Smilodon the tiger with his eight-inch fangs must have been snatched away from him by all the smaller, quicker cats, or perhaps the teeth that had grown so long grew longer and left him, mangy and starving, unable to open his jaws wide enough to kill or even to eat. The soil of Florida in all sorts of places is striated with their bones. The St. Johns and the Alachua plains are rich with them, the Manatee River and the Peace River, and the Caloosahatchee, the overrun edges of the Everglades and the Miami River.

It is only recently that scientists have been able to admit that the one other single factor which may have completed the extinction of all these strangely assembled early creatures may have been man.

They used to say it was impossible for him to have appeared on this continent more than ten thousand years ago. That would have been far too late for the complex era of the prehistoric animals. But startling discoveries made recently at Folsom, New Mexico, and at the Sandia cave, and most recently of all, at Alaska, have pushed back our knowledge of man's life here to nearly twenty thousand years ago. It may have been archaic man himself, nicking a tough hide with flint-tipped spears he learned to throw with whizzing accuracy, with spear throwers the later Mexicans would call "atlatls," and trotting tirelessly after a trail of blood until the beast died of bloodletting, or herding them with fires that may have devastated the early forests and begun the plains, drove amazing numbers of these creatures over cliffs to their deaths.

It is perhaps too easy to imagine archaic man in Florida whirling flaming brands to frighten away old Smilodon himself, famished and slinking into the swamps beyond. But man, the most destructive of all creatures at the beginning of his long career, may have been to some extent the death of them.

It is not considered scientific to put any faith in the myths and dreams of present-day Indians, as proof. But it is strange that in many of the old tales handed down to Indians today, as the fathers and mothers tell stories to sleepy children, and so carry on that extraordinary verbal racial memory of the Indian people, something like those shapes of vanished prehistoric beasts are outlined. There are tales that describe and refer to tigers and lions and elephants. There is a series of myths that seem to be about mammoths. Strange creatures give names to Indian diseases, and crowd Indian dreams with the forms of ancient nightmares. They were described by tellers of dreams and tellers of tales, from the oldest times.

Perhaps it means nothing that they speak of creatures with great crossed tusks or low creeping shapes, shadowy and vast and dangerous. There are tribes to the west that have stories of great animals with four legs and another leg that moves from a shoulder. There is that curious tale of the southeastern Indians, a nightmare or a myth that is known now as not much more than a ribald story to be laughed at about a hunting fire, of an enormous creature that drags a penis that can be moved

63

as high as the treetops. But what else would those shapes be but the memories of mammoths or of elephants with trunks for which the Indians would have no other words than such as their gusty humor gave?

They dream and that is not evidence. But the fears that a race has known lie deep and lasting in the dregs of the mind. The stories of ancient peoples are the unwritten records of memories and thoughts too old to be described accurately. Old shapes of incredible danger are made into stories for men to laugh at, or familiar words by which children are eased of fear of the dark, and so in comfort put to sleep. So a stouthearted people might deal with horror they once outfaced.

But if the animals came and became extinct, as the Everglades took shape out of the receding waters, it is certain that no animal life could compare with the wealth of the fish life about the newer coasts.

East, in the pale-green inshore currents the hordes of fighting fishes ran, the sharks and the barracuda, the mackerel, the bonito, the wahoo, the kingfish and the amberjack, moving in from the deeps to spawn and feed in the shoals. They crowded the bays and rivers. The silver mullet jumped before them among hissing acres of minnows as the big fish drove and ravaged behind them. Overhead the crowded sea birds screamed and swooped and fed. But south in the Bay of Florida and west up the coast over the shoals of the sunken Florida plateau trooped millions of other fish in long processions: the striped mullet, the snook, the snapper and the pompano, moving north and so around the shape of the Gulf of Mexico. The bays and passes were thick with fingerlings of every kind and the laughing gulls and the terns and the constant pelicans and the heavy mergansers preyed on them.

The green turtles of the outer sea came plowing heavily ashore to lay their eggs, which the bears and the panthers dug up. Out of the slow western mangrove rivers the small tarpon moved in the spring and grew huge and traveled east and west, rolling and exploding upward from night-colored waters in unbelievable bursts of crystal and silver under the whiteness of the tide-swelling moon.

If the fish were dense past belief, so were the shellfish. To this day, from that hidden floor of the western undersea plateau, where the sponges grew, the tides heap the western beaches with windrows of shells, ivory and yellow and rose-tinted, and crimson and orange and cream and mother-of-pearl, billions of shells. Tiny horns and delicate boats, and turrets and scoops and twisted ribbons and small brittle paws and blunt stars and crescents, they are piled up perfect and uninjured every day from that vast shelly sea-meadow. East coast too, among the gardens of branching corals and sea fans and sponges and black urchins and delicate anemones, where bright ribbons of small angelfish and parrot fish and moonfish stream and slide through green watery twilights, the shell creatures are everywhere.

There is a long reef south from the high dunes of Caxambas on the Gulf coast, which from the earliest known time was covered with miles and miles of the great thick-shelled clam that is called quohaug in the north, from which the New England Indians made their wampum. They are good eating too. On the arched mangrove roots of the west coast, which the tides cover and uncover, the small tasty mangrove oysters grow in clusters. Fine oysters grow there in bars beyond the mouths of lower rivers that bring them their food and the fresh water they must have.

More important were to be the great families of the conchs. They have always grown and been scattered up on these coasts, thousand upon thousands of great creamy whorled shells, like basket hilts of swords under the fluted apex, tapering to a long

65

grooved shank around the central spine, the columella. They house a solid fish-creature, footed like a huge snail, through the aperture that reveals the shining pink or yellow porcelain lining of the lip. Their gaudy china-satin has always caught the eye of sailors in warm seas. The garden paths and mantel-pieces of New England coast towns have long been decorated with them. These were the wreathed horns of Tritons of classical antiquities, and they are still the shells that teach listening inland children the faraway roaring of the sea. There is no end to the supply of them out of that brimming sea treasury.

They are called horse conchs, and king conchs, and queen conchs, but the Latin names are clearer. Everywhere there is a *Busycon perversum*, a brownish-white left-twisted fulgur. There is a *Strombus gigas*, the one with the wide gaudy pink lip. There is *Fasciolaria gigantea*, the great horse conch, sometimes as long as twenty-four inches, one of the two largest known shells in the world, univalve, solid as stone.

One of the most important sources of food, especially inland about the saw-grass river and the island hammocks, were the turtles. There were several fresh-water turtles which crawled also on land, the box turtle and the snapping turtles. But most important of all were the land turtles, the tortoises which pushed everywhere in the dust and ate grass, and much later were curiously called "gophers," and lived in holes.

Here they all were then, or forms like them.

There was man in Asia, crowded into the northeast limits, staring out in some time of the last ice age, wondering where it was out there that the food animals went.

He may have followed across ice the dripping blood trail of a mammoth he had wounded, and so struggled to another land, utterly unaware of the great step he took. Perhaps there were two or three hunters in a skin boat, who dared rough and gusty waters because behind them there was hunger. Not one of them was timid or satisfied to stay in crowded places. They were the boldest, the strongest, the most self-reliant of their kind. Of all those yellow-brown Mongolians they left, they were the most fit to be the first Americans. They were among the first of modern men.

They went east, and others followed them, in a long wavelike migration of people in small mobile groups, brown-faced people, with broad facial arches and straight black Mongolian hair. Their black eyes bore the Mongolian folds. Knowing nothing of what lay ahead, they pushed forward.

It is now thought that they must have penetrated the continent from some coastal bay like Kotzebue Sound and so into the valley of the Mackenzie and south to the broad plains and lakes of Saskatchewan, which lead south into the American plains. There they lived for more centuries than man knows, burning off the forests to drive the beasts and so increasing the plains area, developing some of that enormous variety of language groups known throughout the American hemisphere.

They were the archaic people, river dwellers, when they began to be known again, who came into northeastern Florida and lived along the St. Johns. That may have been even before the last of the interglacial water had been drawn off the south peninsula and the Everglades begun, into which they may have driven the last of the great prehistoric beasts. Their descendants lived there when the New World was discovered, calling themselves by a name which sounded to the Spaniards like "Timucua."

Centuries later, from somewhere west of the Mississippi, a movement was begun of people who spoke one of the languages of the greater speech group called "Muskogean." Some tribes of these made a slow way east along the Gulf of Mexico and the coastal strip of west Florida, and so down to the western shore of the Everglades and the tropic sea.

They were not archaic people, as the early Timucuans had been. They were the forerunners of the Indians of lower Florida. Long after they were established here, the Archaic Timucuans expanded westward all the way across the upper Florida peninsula, cutting off completely the strip down which the modern people had come. For hundreds of years the Glades people were cut off from further migration and developed slowly their own unique civilization.

They settled in three obvious main regions about the Everglades. The first, naturally, was the western, from north of the Caloosahatchee down through the Ten Thousand Islands to Cape Sable. Their name sounded to the later Spaniards something like "Carlos" or "Calos," which may have been derived from the Muskogee word "kalo," "black" or "powerful," and "ansha," "man" as far as is known. So that they were called the "Calusa" from the earliest people to late historic times. The people who moved to the great central lake that they called "Mayaimi," from the Muskogee "miaha," "wide," were called the "Mayaimi." Their neighbors in the same culture group who went to the east coast beaches were the "Jeaga" and those whom the Spaniards called "St. Lucie's." The Indians from Boca Raton south to Biscayne Bay and down the keys, are called by the word the Spaniards gave them, who thought they said something like "Tekesta."

We have no other names for them. In their three related divisions, they were the people of the Glades.

Because of the sun, the semitropical nature of the country about the saw grass, they made an immediate change in all their habits of living, like the intelligent people they were. They were to develop a culture completely their own.

The rough hot skin garments were discarded for cooler things in this country of the sun. The moss on the trees made excellent light skirts for the women, who did their work more freely with nothing above the waist. For breechclouts the men made a kind of plaited piece of palmetto strips, on a belt, and tied a bunch of moss on behind, not for decency, but to have something more comfortable to sit on than bare skin and bones. The young bucks presently changed the moss hanks to raccoon tails, very soft, very dashing.

It was a country without flints. It had no metals either, such as the people about Lake Superior had in these long centuries learned to mine and work. But here were the shells.

It must have been almost as soon as the first of the Glades people had come down to these beaches that a man wading in the warm clear shallows picked up one of those great left-handed conchs. The simplest way to get at the flesh would be to knock a hole in the side. But before he tossed the shell away empty, perhaps he balanced it thoughtfully in his hand. It was heavy as stone. If he could make another small hole in it he could take a stick of heavy mangrove wood and put it through the two holes, front and back, and lash it to that central spine at the right digging angle. If he ground the point and the lip sharply he would have a pick as good as any stone pick he ever used.

One of those smaller conch shells with the side cut off straight and the inside columella cut out would make as good a drinking cup as any gourd. A piece of one of those great shell lips ground sharp on one edge would make as good an ax as any stone. A hammer could be ground down from the heavy central column of the heaviest conch. Adzes for hollowing out logs for boats, chisels, net sinkers, heavy fishhooks, almost any kind of tool either men or women needed here could be picked up on those beaches. To grind a shell with sand and a piece of wood was slow work. But it was at least as easy as chipping flint.

They set their houses, mere open platforms on cabbage palm posts, roofed and thatched with the palmetto, in the sheltered water of inlets, at the mouths of rivers, and by streams from the lake and on the edges of the Glades. Some of the Calusa

houses were built on pilings out in the water or high on dunes
in the winds. The roofs often covered two or three bedlike
platforms between which they could walk and under which
they could build smudge fires against the mosquitoes.

They gathered on dunes and sandbanks and beaches for great
feasts of boiled and roast meat, because they were still flesh
eaters, and some fish and oysters. They found sweet and tangy
the cocoplums and beach plums and the wild grapes festooning
the tall trees of the Caloosahatchee, and learned to eat the black
massed berries of the palmettos. There were elderberries and
sparkleberries and cabbage palm hearts to be cut. They did
not at first bother with vegetables.

The brown, healthy, almost naked people, smeared with fish
oils to keep off the mosquitoes or the sandflies, laughed and
joked about the great cooking fires. Their careless hard heels
trampled into the sand and ashes the bones, the discarded
shells and all the leavings of their untidy roving lives. They
came back again and again to the same feasting places. The
piles they built up through centuries are called kitchen middens,
refuse heaps which in time became accumulations of rich black
dirt, with broken bits of their pottery and pieces of shells and
bones. Some of these mounds are partly shell and partly black
dirt, like the very early group of middens at Gordon's Pass,
which marks the beginning of West Indian vegetation on the
west coast, or at the headwaters, by the edge of the Big Cypress,
of Turner's River.

In these easily worked first middens they also buried their
dead. Human bones and teeth may be found there, two or three
feet below the present surface, in the steaming, hard-packed
and black lower earth.

It is believed certain now, although no one can be sure how
long ago these people came into the Glades country, that they
lived here somewhere around A.D. 900.

The pottery they made has told the story of their years more completely than anything else, to modern archaeologists. Pottery was for a long time the only expression of their real artistic ability. Their first pots were more like the sand-tempered ware of the Gulf region through which they had come, but they were smart enough to use local material with which to make their own. They shaped simple bowls by coiling over a flat base rolled ropes of soft clay, tempered with quartz sand, which John M. Goggin has named "Glades Plain," the earliest type of a long series called "Glades Gritty Ware." The pieces of such ware are still dark and heavy and gritty to the touch. No one bothered to decorate them.

When after many years the potters began to use decoration, the Calusas covered the whole rim with an over-all pattern of variously related, finely feathered lines. The Tekesta craftsmen about the Miami River, with hands growing firm and sure, dressed theirs with crosshatching, or bold repeated loops, or scallops cut with a swift thumbnail.

Then the east coast people used a new kind of paste to make the first of a series called "Biscayne Ware." It is called "chalky" because it has a smooth chalky surface which seems to rub off.

A third new ware, now called "Belle Glade," was developed by the Mayaimi Lake people. It was plain and very hard, marked only with the broad, unsmoothed strokes of a tool.

All such vessels, mouth down, were piled over with wood, and so crudely fired; red and brown and cream color and smoke-black.

Finally they stamped chalky ware pots, often colored with the red ocher they found in a place between what is now Fort Myers and Estero, with a paddle carved in a checked pattern, to be called "check stamped," which was carried far over the area and up the coasts.

It was about that time that they found hunting harder work

than fishing. It was easier to scoop up the fish that crowded the inlet-fishponds or herd them with a great yelling and shouting and thrashing of water and thumping of canoe sides, into the first fish weirs. They used three times as many net sinkers. They had more time too.

The last great period of the Glades culture began then, perhaps about A.D. 1200, when the developed skill of the craftsmen on the sound foundation of their ancient and individual culture blossomed in new freedom, an artistic renascence, of eager and elaborate experimentation. Everyone must have shared that expanding sense of new life.

It really began when someone invented a knife. He set sharks' teeth, the sharp, inch-long blades, into a wooden handle. It was a knife far superior for exact and delicate cutting to anything any Indian had ever used. The handles also were finely polished and carved at the upper end, with involved circles or rayed rosettes which might also have served as stamps. Other shark-tooth points were set at the side of carved handles the width of a palm, or two palms, for adzes. They made quantities of fine bone chisels and awls. They had rasps of sandstone and of sharkskin.

With the knives the craftsmen shaped something that delighted everybody: bone hairpins, three to ten inches long, with which to pin up their hot black hair. The pins were elaborately pretty, highly polished, carved with graceful designs, with carved wooden beads stuck on the ends inlaid cunningly with tortoise shell.

The Glades people from that time on had a lot of fun setting off their shapely brown bodies with all sorts of ornaments. They made pottery still, or perhaps the women did, but pots were dull things. The new art was not only an expression of their love of design, but what a man wore made him feel fine and attracted the girls.

They began to make and wear pendants, a unique Glades

fashion. They carved and perforated bones, deer bone and turtle bone and even human bone, perhaps the bones of a powerful enemy. They polished beautifully carved shell pendants to hang from their belts. They made large round shell ornaments to hang about their necks, and pierced also the occasional fresh-water pearls, or the curious vegetable pearls of the hammocks. They set wooden ear-plugs in shell rings, inlaid at the end with tortoise shell that looked like huge fish eyes. They bored holes in bits of pink and orange and mother-of-pearl shell lining, and bright red seeds, and shaped ivory columellas of conchs.

All those bright things clinked and winked and rattled and glittered on the oiled, shining copper bodies of those young hunters and warriors and fishermen, their black hair pinned up with pins and stuck with arrows. Their raccoon tails switched behind. The dark eyes of girls must have watched them from the house shadows as the self-conscious young men went by on the white sands, walking like dandies.

The social life around the seacoasts must have been a hearty and gay and colorful thing, among all those easy-muscled, graceful, assured people, bronze and dark in the whiteness of the light, with their great feasts and their songs that echoed from the canoes over the dark lagoons, and the laughter in moonlight, and the border wars that kept them tough. All these, the Calusas and the Mayaimis and the Tekestas, must have seemed to have been at home here forever.

Now after centuries, and before this time of the Glades renascence, the archaic river dwellers across the peninsula of Florida had become like the others to the north. Around Tampa the Spaniards later called them "Tocobago." Except in time of war, the canoes of the Calusas could now pass there in friendliness to northern trading places. They carried pottery and shell-work and bone pins, and their valuable pigment, red ocher, to barter for northern flints and galena and other pottery and some copper.

But most of all, the most intelligent among the canoemen, the quickest minded, the shrewdest observers, or perhaps some man already set apart as a priest, brought back ideas. Nothing was ever more contagious or spread more quickly across that continent of Indians than styles in ideas, in religions, in religious cults, introduced by a messiah-figure. What the canoes brought back now was an increased attention to the burial of the dead.

From the beginning there must have been fear of the dead, developed with the developing subtlety of the human mind. The death of a man, that incomprehensible stoppage of the breath, was an evil which must be caused by evil from those forces by which in every living moment he was surrounded. So there must be ways of dealing with that evil, as men had found ways of meeting other sorts of danger.

The care of the dead was related to the beginning of his belief in the soul, a small struggling center of power in him, more carefully to be guarded than his life. Everything he saw about him in nature had a soul, a center of power, from which his own soul was in peril.

74

They had great courage. They came of people who had lived hard and savage lives and their children were not weakened.

For that reason, very early in the history of the Indian, wherever the unknown stood ranged about his life, wherever birth was, and death after all, and every chance and change that can come to man and woman in their progress between the two; and against all unexplainable things, the fall of stars in the night, and lightnings, and the cry of birds, and the terrible force of the sun, and the wind that is the breath in a man's nostrils, and the spirit in his body, there this puny and naked creature who walked erect among the beasts and knew himself as something other than they, set up his beliefs and his rituals. It was the beginning of his religion.

It was concerned flatly with good and evil toward himself. It had nothing to do with morality or ethics. By words, gestures, sacrifices and appeasements, by the council of wise men nearer to the great powers than common, he was determined to seek safety. If in his progress in time and in the world he groped toward a sense of Power beyond all thronging minor powers, it was still a groping, something the ordinary man could not approach, or speak of, or try too closely to understand.

So the care of the dead grew important.

It must have been a thing for which the Indians' minds were ready. The dead were not now to be covered up and forgotten in old kitchen middens. They were buried farther away from the villages of the living, in mounds devoted entirely to burial. Such mounds were made of the local material, shells on the far islands by the mangroves of the west, sand by the lake and the moonvine-covered jungles, and rock by the wide bays of the east coast, and rock down on the lower keys.

The bodies were buried straight, as they always had been, or they were tightly flexed, knees to breast and arms crossed and head bent, a position a man takes in utter weariness, the

75

position he held, unborn, in the oblivion of his mother's body. Or, finally, in a most curious new fashion brought here in long, slow stages from the Gulf coast, the flesh was boiled from the bones, and the bones tied together and buried in the rising mounds, above the bones of older generations.

Only at the northern edge of the Glades, where the people learned the habits of those neighbors, were there many "grave goods," the pots and spear points the dead might need. The burial mounds of all the rest of the Glades were filled with nothing but bones. Growing trees might thrust up a skull, the tender bones of a child's rib. That was all.

They heaped the mounds higher, with those heavy conch-shell picks, especially about the coasts where the high moon tides came gleaming and lipping about the house pilings, and the storms drove the white water foaming through the villages. They had already begun to dig ditches or channels across sand between sea and inlet so that a man could paddle his canoe almost to his own house platform, or so that the fish or turtles might be driven into ponds, like corrals, later a "crawl," to be caught at leisure. Such fishponds, silted up with debris and dead fish, offered rich soil for their first vegetables. There is an ancient name for "fishpond," which later was thought to mean "vegetable garden."

In this region within the sea and the lake the power of single chiefs must have grown greater. They were absolute rulers. A sort of caste system developed: chiefs and warriors, priests, craftsmen and people. The weak, the less intelligent, the handicapped, the captives of the constant border raids, were used as slave labor.

They were set to building an elaborate new system of mounds, courts, plazas and canals set apart for religious ceremonials on some important site. A round mound would be separated by a plaza from a mound curved about it in a long crescent. Or there would be numbers of round or oblong mounds with canals between. Their tops would be surmounted with altars or temples, of cabbage palm posts, probably, roofed with the inevitable palmetto thatch. Log steps would reach up to them, or there would be long ramps of the regional material, sand, or shell, or rock, where priestly professionals in torchlight would move from the massed dances on the plaza to the sound of drums.

Pine Island in the wide sea mouth of the Caloosahatchee was such a site, and the sixteen major mounds and ramps of Big Mound City near Canal Point, now on the lake. North of the Ortona Locks, among the dark pines that have grown up about it, there is a huge ceremonial moundsite. At Naples, where some of the first middens were, there was a mile-long canal across the beach.

The sweating slaves with picks were put to digging other canals, unbelievably straight, bulkheaded with cabbage palm boles, which led across islands, or from one inner channel of a mangrove river to another, so that the long canoes could go swiftly and in shelter about the coasts. Many of the later Indians kept these canals open for their travels. They were from one to six miles long, and may be traced now in half-obliterated indentations.

The Glades people had been expert woodworkers from the first, felling and hollowing cypress logs for the canoes that made their way of life possible.

Now for the ceremonials, which must have been carried on by different clans, like secret societies, perhaps each to its own mound in a group of mounds, each with its totem figure from which to gain special magic power, the woodcarvers made wonderful things. They carved animal masks for the heads of the priestly dancers, heads with movable ears and jaws, painted, with staring shell eyes. Some were stylized human faces, some were brilliant elaborated heads of wolves and turtles, cormorants and pelicans, sunfish and bats and wildcats and bears.

77

With these masks the dancers often wore polished hollowed antlers of deer.

Smaller figures like the masks were made to be kept in the clan lodges or the houses of cult members. They were delicate and beautifully carved sitting figures, half animal, half human, and bird effigies on posts.

More striking still, they carved and painted two-foot long wooden plaques with geometric patterns superbly adapted from the totem figures. These were made with tenons by which they were set on high posts around a temple at the top of a mound, or about a whole village devoted to a particular alligator or bird cult. There were painted ceremonial tablets to be hung on the temple posts, with designs of kingfishers, or alligators, or spiders. Some were carved with long human thigh bones, which may have been the totem of one of the new death cults. Such a cult must have used the single bowl from a lakesite, carved from the top of a human skull. It would be a thing of the greatest possible magic by which a man would gain power, as a warrior might eat the heart of a valiant enemy and so take to himself new strength.

They engraved stone to make large totem figures, like the turtle of a Tekesta clan that lay so long in a garden overlooking Biscayne Bay, and small ones, polished and carved like alligator-eye bumps.

It was only after the Spanish treasure ships began to be wrecked on the keys, or the east coast beaches brought them the white man's soft, fine copper and silver and gold, that the craftsmen adapted their old skills to metalworking. They hammered thin gold and silver plaques with incised or embossed designs, to take the place of the wooden ones on the high posts on the mounds or about a village, shining gloriously in all that sun. Sheet gold and silver was cut out and incised for small alligator tablets. They hammered out ribbons of silver for headbands, and rolled thin strips into long beads, and made concave embossed disks of gold to hang around their necks among the pierced blackened pearls and shell pendants.

The Glades people were the only ones anywhere to take a broad Spanish silver coin, cut a hole in it, and patiently hammer it into a small tube, or barrel bead, to be hung with the other things.

Seven beautiful gold, silver, and copper ornaments, like thin paper cutters cut at one end into the profile of a bird, have been found, of which six came from the Glades area, where the best craftsmen lived west of the lake. They may have been the work of a single master craftsman, for a single and very limited cult. Those were all that ever have been found. One came from a mound in Glades County, from a skull bound with a silver headband, into which the long silver thing had been struck.

It was not to be expected that among the goods from the Spanish wrecks, souvenirs sent home from Spanish conquests, the gold ornaments of South American Indians would not have been snatched up by the men of the Glades. They used hollow embossed gold beads from Ecuador and articles of gold and silver from Panama and Peru. A cast gold figure from the Rio Magdalena turned up in a Glades mound. They treasured the gold turtle shells with small pendant rattles such as have been found at Oaxaca in Mexico. All those things came from the ships.

The metals marked the end of the old time.

Before that, before they knew gold and silver, in this southernmost place of the north continent, which the easterngoing man from Asia had made his own, the westgoer and the eastgoer met face to face. Each had come half around the world, in a diversity of progress that no one understands fully, in an extent of time which no one will ever comprehend.

Far away in the sun over the blue-bright waters eastward or southward some brown man. must have stared and pointed, seeing for the first time that utterly new thing, the glint of a far white sail.

3

The Discoverers

THERE is no reason to believe that the Indian world was not aware of a great change impending before news of that first sail went hurrying among the Florida coastal villages. It may have stirred, as a sleeper stirs on his bed before dawn, with half-open eyes. Because for a longer time Europe, across the Atlantic, a world grown too small, had been tossing with dreams of unknown islands west beyond the blank peril of Ocean-sea. Already between the continents so profoundly unknown to each other had moved the signs of change.

It is not too strange to believe that in the land not yet called America, among the men who had gone as far eastward as they could, a rumor came from the north, carried by the slow contact of tribe with tribe, a tale told by a captive, a myth of pale wing-headed men beaching their hollow boats from out the northern sea. Not gods, but men, the tale must have made clear, whom the warriors of that place drove away. That they should have heard this at long last in Florida is not more strange than the truth that it took almost four hundred years for the same rumor to spread from Iceland to England, and so in Bristol ships to the ocean harbors of Portugal.

However it was told each side of the Atlantic, the fact was the venture of Lief, the son of Eric the Red, who from Iceland and Greenland turned his shield-bulwarked ships west again, and so came to a fair land of islands and rivers and meadows and fine-growing grapes. There they saw mounds and men in skin canoes and killed some and fought with others, and so went away. That was in the year one thousand and two after Christ's birth in Bethlehem and the land was North America. In other years the Northmen went back across summer seas to that fine country where they would have lived except that now those people there, swarthy, broad-cheeked, coarse of hair, fought them off ferociously. The Northmen never went back. But slowly, slowly, the tale spread.

That was far away from Florida and the year 1492. But it was a part of all that slow awakening of Europe from the Dark Ages. Man there, who had but recently forgotten Rome and Greece and Egypt, man the westgoer who may have left Asia long before the man who was to trudge fifteen million miles into the Americas, had gone farther.

Out of his maggot breeding that had filled the Mediterranean world, out of his wars and crowded lusts and treacheries and insatiable desires, he had also made the Pyramids and the

81

Parthenon. Half mad, self-destructive, diseased, self-tortured, ignorant, still he had recorded the Ten Commandments and the Roman Law and the Sermon on the Mount.

But now in the night of Europe, where the Saracens had thrust their power, the mind of the white man was stirring again. The Crusaders had come home from Palestine with changed eyes. Marco Polo returned from Asia with wonderful tales of the riches of Cathay and India and Japan. The caravans to the Black Sea brought gold and pepper and spices and silks. The rumor of riches worked among the busy European city-states, as the routes to Asia were cut off by the growing power of the Mongol Turks. They had taken Syria and the Balkans and captured Constantinople, and there was no more pepper in the shops. The rediscovered Greek language and new scientific knowledge broke the ecclesiastical domination that had sought to turn man's curious mind from this world to the next. And men who gave not a fig for new ideas craved spices to hide the flavor of overripe meat. Asia was suddenly of vital necessity to them.

There was this rumor going about, this idea in the universities, that the world was round.

Claudius Ptolemy, the Egyptian geographer, had said it, as Aristotle and Seneca had written it long before. In England the Venerable Bede had restated it, and, more recently, Roger Bacon. In 1410, a cardinal of the Church itself, Pierre d'Ailly, put all this down in a book, *The Image of the World,* in which he said in plain Latin for any man who could read that by crossing the Atlantic westward, the east of Asia would be there for any man to reach.

Henry of Portugal, in his castle that stood breasting the foam of the Western Ocean, gathered the knowledge of all the geographers of Europe, including Pierre d'Ailly, the maps and instruments which the Knights Templar brought back, and placed the vast resources of the Order of Christ in the hands of his sea captains. "Henry the Navigator" he would be. He was certain that the world was round.

He died in 1460, but already Portuguese ships had discovered Senegal and Sierra Leone south along Africa, had colonized the Azores and Madeira and brought back to Lisbon slaves and Guinea gold. The ships of Alfonso V and John II went southward still along that huge bulk and named the Cape of Good Hope and reached northward on another wind into the vast blue Indian Ocean. The Portuguese would set their colonies in Asia before any other Europeans.

But there was no magic in that course for the men who argued that Asia lay across the Western Ocean.

While the men of books pored over the first flat maps on which the Mediterranean world was ringed with fantasies of the Outer Sea, in every harbor and quayside wineshop along the grim Atlantic there were tough sailoring men who knew nothing and cared less about learned arguments. They knew what men had seen.

These were not the men of the Mediterranean galleys, the long narrow ships that went mincingly on the tideless inner sea, from headland to known headland, by the banked oars of slaves. These were free men of that limitless, turbulent ocean, the men of the bucking, hardy cargo carriers, the round ships, broad of bow and beam, that thrashed forward only before the wind in their single, clumsy square sails. They came about only by a miracle and could hardly beat to windward at all. Many a ship and crew was blown far out into the unknown and disappeared under the unturning, savage, westgoing wind. Not that that mattered. There were men in every port eager to follow them. Their concern was not safety. Their concern was going out. Sailing. Finding out. Seeing. Never mind the coming back.

By the round ships and the tough men who slowly mastered them came the development of the magnetic compass, the cross-staff, and the slightly less crude astrolabe, by which the height of fixed stars or the sun could be taken and distance established by some sort of latitude to help out their dead reckoning. Longitude was reckoned only by timing with a sandglass the unreeling of a knotted line on which a chip was dragged over the side, or by watching the speed of spit alongside. They could measure, after a rough fashion, space, but not time on the sea, where water clocks were no good and pendulums changed with every degree of distance nearer the equator. They had no maps that amounted to anything, ships that were sailed only with the greatest difficulty, and no knowledge of what actually lay out there. There was nothing they were sure of but themselves.

West there was something. That they knew. Sailors from Bristol got drunk on sour Portuguese wine and boasted of the ships that had gone to Iceland and heard the Northmen's stories of the land beyond. The Canaries and the Azores were outposts staring over the seething Atlantic wastes. It was from them that the first few proofs came from the west. Something was there.

Men and ships blown far off their courses struggled back by north-swinging currents, saying they had seen islands like clouds. Perhaps they were only clouds like islands. But the word "islands" grew in magic with every tongue. The legend was born of a single large island out there, which men swore they had seen. Its name was "Antilia." There was another island spoken of often by Breton and Irish and English sailors called "Brasil." It lay out there, west by northwest of Portugal. Or a bit more south. But out there, surely. For seven years the merchants of Bristol, who had sailed regularly to Iceland with their English cloth and tinware, sent out two or three caravels every year, looking for the island Brasil. It was not where they looked. It must be westward.

84

All these were names and tales of islands to stretch the wind eye of the oldest salts and turn the hearts of listening boys wild for the venture, sick for the sea.

The stories grew. There was the tale of the seven bishops who were thought to have sailed with their congregations from Portugal for that Antilia. There, among the rejoicing of the inhabitants, each founded a great city, so there were now seven Christian cities each under its bishop, each richer than the last, blessed and beautiful.

But the mapmakers began to draw Antilia on their maps and some drew near it the island Cipango that Marco Polo had written about, Cipango that was Japan with all Asia beyond it, and India and Cathay. Peering daylong and nightlong beyond the foaming dark rollers, lookouts on those small ships found it was not hard to believe all those places lay there under the heaped ivory clouds, the burning sunsets of that one horizon. West.

Branches of trees had been blown ashore at the Canaries, their leaves strange to Europe. Pieces of wood were found floating, strange wood, strangely and well carved, but not by edged metal. Canes jointed and hollow were picked up, and once a stranger thing, a canoe made of a hollow log, empty, which rode from under the sunset. There was a greater marvel. Two dead bodies were cast up on a beach, two men like none in Europe, copper-brown bodies, black hair, broad faced. Men of what islands? Where? The west?

A map has recently been discovered, made in 1435 by one Beccario, which shows as plain as if some sailor had described them four islands far to the west. They are labeled "Antillia, Reylla, Salvagio and I in Mar." "Antillia," the "Island Opposite," could be only Cuba. "Reylla," "The Kingly Island," looks like Jamaica. "I in Mar" might be one of the Bahamas, but "Salvagio," divided from Antillia by a narrow strait, the "Savage

Isle," "The Isle of Savages," could be nothing but Florida. Yet they are vaguely placed.

The very next year, 1436, a mapmaker named Andreas Bianca made a map that showed the island of "Antilia" seven hundred miles west of Lisbon. That's but halfway. All their ideas of distance were queer. But on that map "Antilia" stretches east and west as Cuba does, and in the map's corner, northwest of "Antilia," is drawn the southern part only of a curiously familiar pointed paw of land. It is labeled "Isla de la man Satanaxio." What he meant, no one knows, or if he made it up or remembered something he was told. It looks exactly like the tip end of Florida above Cuba, just as it lies. No one knew it then, or could have known. Or could he? Could some man on a west-driven ship have seen—it is useless to imagine. But there it is on the map, "La Isla de la man Satanaxio."

Then Martin Behaime made a map that was round, the first globe. Anyone, schoolman or sailor, could look and see what people could not get through their heads before, how by sailing west across the Atlantic there would be the east.

Then came the year 1492 in which Ferdinand drove out the last of the Moors from Granada, and from a Spain saturated for so many centuries with Moorishness. Spain was reborn, in power and in faith, not yet feeling the ills that would come from having cast out the Jews and their nonecclesiastical learning. Already Torquemada's Inquisition, in the flames of burning heretics and marranos, was tempering that passion and that power into a single sword.

The Moors were gone. The lands of Spain lay ravaged, war stripped and lawless, ranged by brigands. The Spanish lords, hidalgos, grandees, with triumph lifting their proud armored hearts, went home after eight centuries of battles from the last bare hills and rocky valleys that had been their forts. All the fighting energy of those centuries, in which they had had no experience but fighting, had now no outlet but impoverished castles in barren lands. There was no future for the knightly soldiers of Spain.

So it was an extraordinary thing for a unified and peaceful Spain that in the same year 1492 Admiral Christopher Columbus, in his three small cranky caravels under the banner of Castile and Leon, sailed west.

It was curious that it was not Portugal that accepted Columbus' offer to share the Asiatic kingdoms that he meant to discover. It was Portuguese knowledge and maps that had been available to Columbus as a young man, because his first wife was the daughter of one of the great sea captains of Henry the Navigator. But the mind of the Portuguese court was fixed on Africa and Asia as known quantities. If Columbus did reach Cathay and claimed land, how could Portugal avoid political difficulties with the Great Khan? But most of all it was felt by careful John II that this Columbus wanted too much for services a half dozen other captains could accomplish at half the price. Indeed, a caravel was secretly dispatched westward, but it did not sail far enough. The sailors were discouraged too soon and returned reporting nothing but empty ocean.

So Columbus, knowing not a great deal more, actually, than many other captains of that coast, but fusing all that knowledge, rumor, fable, superstition in the white heat of his imagination, his shrewd ambition, his piety and his consuming will, took his vision and his demands to Spain. The new-made, triumphant court of Castile and Leon knew nothing of the sea. Ferdinand had come too freshly from the wars to be receptive to outlandish ideas. Isabella's imagination alone took fire at thought of what the farther conquest might mean for Spain, victorious and still hungry. Isabella called him back after his first rebuff. Neither she nor the excited court officials nor Ferdinand knew enough to barter with Columbus about the terms of his grand prize. And Columbus, for all his grasp, did not know enough of the fierce possessiveness of the Spanish crown to realize that no matter what he asked and they agreed to give he would never get it.

He sailed, as everybody knows, and made his landfall in the Bahamas, taking possession of those, and other islands, by flag and sword and cross. Everywhere the respectful brown-faced people, Arawaks probably, brought him fruit and cassava bread and trinkets that he seemed to like especially, such as silver and pearls and gold. He knew now that this was not Asia. Asia must lie beyond these scattering islands somewhere. These were different from his dream, but not bad. The great island he called "Hispaniola" seemed very rich indeed, and he hopefully set there his first colonists. Back home, at his news, at the sight of the gold and pearls and the first Indian slaves, all Spain rose in a single flame of excitement, one mind, one roaring mouth.

It was this Spain, not Columbus, that was to be the conqueror, administrator, spiritual lord and temporal master of the new world only slowly coming into view. In fact no king or kingdom in all Europe of that day could so instantly have grasped that revelation with such strength, such ability, such instant, organizing intelligence. No other country was so starved and braced for empire and for glory, so perfected in will and energy and want, as Spain was then. Her concentrated passion, in which church and state were blended in one power, at that spark roared up in a fire of Spanish genius. Its light was to eclipse every other, blind every other, in that other world, for hundreds of years.

Columbus' ships waited in Cadiz harbor for his second venture as the words "gold" and "islands" and "slaves" went drumming up the pulses of all Europe. In every port of the Atlantic captains of other nations stared at the west. A mutter ran all over Europe, and England, whom this meteor had struck awake. But the Spanish crown had been awake first.

In 1493 Pope Alexander VI was graciously pleased, at Spain's insistence, to promulgate the great series of bulls which gave Spain the lion's share of all that still unknown world. Portugal, which had done so much to pioneer the outer ocean, could not be ignored. But Spain, having done nothing but grasp the chance, was now in a position of supreme and extraordinary power.

The Church saw in one glance new hope for winning souls in the west, cut off as she had been in her spiritual conquest eastward by the rising power of the infidels. There was nothing else the pope could do but give Spain what she wanted, which was to exclude all men and kingdoms but Portugal from that new land, whatever it would turn out to be, forever. In addition, he granted Ferdinand's demand that the crown control all ecclesiastical patronage, all churchly administration, every detail of every missionary effort, down to the latchet in the least lay brother's sandal.

Soon the organizing genius of the Spanish crown would be established in those two ably conceived institutions, the Casa de Contratacion, the Royal House of Trade, by which the commerce of the New World was to be dominated, and the Council of the Indies, for the governance of every island, country, city, colony and man. Nothing was to be left to individual enterprise but the initiative, the expense, the daring, the wounds and the deaths of further discoveries and conquests. Whatever was gained, the crown would have the largest share of it. It would be centuries before time could loosen and the driving force of men other than Spaniards pry open that portentous grasp.

Cadiz in that time of Columbus' second venture must have been jam-packed like a fair, wineshops overflowing, the crowds jostling to stare at the wagons jolting by on the cobbles with casks and boxes, and livestock and arms for the admiral's ships, at the drunken faces of sailors who had seen those ultimate islands, at the horses, the armor, the blowing cloaks and flags, the servingmen, the priests, the high-nosed fighting nobles whom Columbus had chosen, and the crown had permitted, to join him. These had left their wives and ladies, pledged their rat-ridden castles and their untilled fields, melted their last plate, to set their faces to this staggering venture. They must have heard only vaguely the crowd's tumult as they paced through it, their eyes fixed upon the ships.

There among the stately armored figures, the groups of shabby grandees, went Juan Ponce de Leon, chosen as among the most worthy to administer some new tropical city for the crown. For generations the men of his noble house and blood had fought the Moors under this same banner of Leon. An elder relative had once been Duke of Cadiz. As for Juan Ponce, he had been a soldier since he was thirteen years old. Now he was over thirty, a married man with two young daughters for whom there was no dowry. Penniless, threadbare, long nosed, proud, his eyes now steel-pointed at Fortune, he had had time before this for a good long look at a future that, in Spain at peace, held nothing at all.

Perhaps all those men about Columbus who were to take over new landfalls and storm mountains and rule kingdoms now unheard of, with the same contempt for the suffering of others which they had been brought up to have for their own, seem to us now, all of them, to have looked alike, the lean, savage, courtly Spanish gentlemen, with their noses fixed like thin vanes to the new wind, over their tight, starved mouths. Their eyes in the old portraits have that same round dark hawk's glance which stares fixedly outward and inward at the same time, lost to everything but greed and glory and gold and God.

So, for the second time, the Spanish ships sailed from Cadiz. They would all soon go a little mad because of the easy riches, and the greater riches for which they would always hunger. There would be more cloud-piled islands, more strange brown people to be enslaved, more gold to be taken. Men would for a while believe that the straits that led to Asia were still west there in that hazy mainland from which some hints were already coming of fabulous stone cities in the mountains. Already in Hispaniola the gold of the few streams and mines was being worked out. For men who could settle down to it there was greater money to be made in cattle and canefields. There, too, slave labor was the fundamental necessity. So, very soon, along with the search for gold and new countries raged the hunt for slaves.

They were a wealth to be squandered without limit to make more wealth. The docile Arawaks of the first islands died like flies. The fiercer Caribs of Cuba were being hunted, brought in in long chained files to the mines and the fields and exterminated. They died too readily, unable to bear the unremitting toil, the lash, the starvation, the overcrowding, the disease, but most of all slavery. When they revolted or tried to escape or seemed lazy they were burned to death, wrapped in straw in the market places, beaten to death or torn to pieces by dogs. The demand was always for more. And the curious part of it was that they could not be brought in and sold on an island without a license from the crown and the payment of high customs duties. So with that silent struggle against the domination of Spain and her officials which was at once set up among the colonists, traffic in Indian slaves became a lucrative smuggler's business. There is no record of the number of small slaving vessels that slipped in and out the obscure bays of those island coastlines with their loads of stolen men and women. There are only hints of how far those slave ships ranged

91

for their Indian cargoes. Next to the search for gold itself, the hunt for slaves became the second most important enterprise in the New World.

Now, the idea of human slavery itself was not unique to these insatiable adventurers. It was a basic fact throughout the then world. Greek and Roman civilization, Egyptian civilization had been built on slavery. The Dark Ages had increased serfdom throughout Europe. The work of Asia and Africa was carried on by slaves. Fifty years before Columbus Portuguese captains had brought the first Negro slaves to Europe from the coasts of Africa. Human lives were part, then, of the wealth of almost every nation.

So it was perhaps inevitable that the Indians should have been enslaved. But never before in history was a whole people so destroyed, and by so few. A year, two years, three, after Columbus had opened up the New World, island after island of Indian people, by slavery, torture, hard work, homesickness and disease, thousands after thousands of men, women, chiefs, children, priests, fishermen, warriors, had been blotted out.

When Juan Ponce de Leon came ashore in Hispaniola the people of Haiti were already dying. In Santo Domingo groups of the stronger ones had taken to the hills. Juan Ponce, commanding a detachment of soldiers under the leader Ovando, was so successful in capturing and killing them that presently he obtained leave from the governor to cross over into the untouched island of Puerto Rico, where, it was reported, there were thousands more docile people and much gold.

There, having sworn himself blood brother to the chief of that island, he took all the treasure and killed or made slaves of all people who did not submit. He was rewarded in 1509 by the governorship. At last he was rich and powerful. He was satisfied. He built towns and more colonies, sent for his wife and daughters, and established himself as his position and name warranted. Westward, other leaders were discovering a tremendous mainland. It did not matter to him. This land was fine, rich with cattle and growing cane and many Indians to labor in the blazing sun. When one died, there was another, so like the first that it must almost have seemed that these people did not die at all. When they escaped, there was much sport, hunting them with dogs.

In fact, life was very pleasant. Governor Ponce de Leon had a dog of which he was more proud than almost any other of his possessions. The historian Herrera, described it in detail. Juan Ponce "had a dog called Bexerillo, that made wonderful havock among those people, and knew which of them were in war and which in peace, like a man; for which reason the Indians were more afraid of ten Spaniards with the dog, than of one hundred without him, and therefore he had one share and a half of all that was taken allowed him, as was done to one that carried a crossbow, as well in gold and slaves and other things, which his master received. Very extraordinary things were reported of this dog—at which the Spaniards much admired."

But in Puerto Rico also there began to be an end to the man supply.

So that first white sail seen from some Indian mound village of the lower Florida coast was probably a slaver's. And the Indians knew it. The word of the coming of strange white men to the Bahamas and to the southern islands was carried with amazing rapidity by the great sea-going trading canoes that slipped along the coasts. Directly after Columbus' first discovery, Spanish coins were found to have circulated to great distances in the ordinary way of Indian trade. Uneasy news of captures and killings must have traveled even faster. No Indian of Florida was to be as innocent as the Bahamans had been. The first Spanish slaving ships that tried to land on the keys or either of the coasts were met by the roused fury of a fighting people.

They saw the sails of the small light vessels appearing and

93

disappearing after storms. They found ships smashed on the unseen rocks and coral humps of the keys and they swept out and took everything, killing white men or taking them prisoner. Nobody knows what ships or how many men. Long before that land was named at all, the white man and the white man's nature was well known. And prepared for.

In five years after Columbus, England, believing with all Europe that Asia still lay west beyond the constellations of the Spanish islands, was bitter at that single slash by which the pope had cut off all English chance at India or Cathay. Englishmen, captains and navigators, and sailors and merchant adventurers, with that passion for trade and trade routes as authentic as Spain's for empire or for soul-saving, which long ago had made familiar the freezing whale paths to Iceland, saw with the same excitement the possibilities of a northwest passage.

There was an able sea captain, a shrewd and very distinguished Atlantic navigator by the name of John Cabot, a naturalized Venetian, who saw the same chance. But Venice in those days had no stomach for the outer sea. England, the seas eternally beating up her high white bows, was the place for him.

Master John Cabot was sent out in a well-found Bristol ship, with his young son Sebastian and a crew of eighteen men, in that time in the northern summer when east-blowing winds are quiet and the northern Arctic Current flows smoothly from east to west.

There is no end of controversy about John Cabot, and about Sebastian, his son, and about what was discovered. You can get into technical discussions of sailing distances. You can build up all sorts of theories. But the truth is that when you argue about latitudes as then recorded you must realize that no figures for that time are exact because the instruments of navigation were completely inexact. It was a long time before the mapmakers checked their latitudes to correct the grave error that they all made about the Tropic of Cancer when they ran it south of Cuba at least fifteen degrees off its actual position. Nor did they have a practical knowledge of magnetic deviation. So that all the records of all the early voyages, when given in latitudes, are widely in error. But no errors exist wherever a man described actual land masses by which he sailed, which can still be recognized, and currents which ran then exactly as they do now. So, for John Cabot's voyage and discovery we have the words spoken by Sebastian, his son, to the writer Peter Martyr, his familiar friend, testimony which cannot be controverted.

On his first voyage John Cabot sailed southeast and touched probably the land of Carolina, and, still moving south, came down to the coasts later to be known as Florida. What Sebastian Cabot told Peter Martyr about his father's voyage, set down again by that indefatigable water-front reporter, Richard Hakluyt, was as follows:

"So coasting stille by the shore, that he was thereby brought so farre into the South, by reason of the land bending so much southwards, that it was there almost equal in latitude, with the sea Fretum Herculaneum. He sailed likewise in this tract so far towards the West, that hee had the Island of Cuba on his left hand, in manner in the same degree of longitude."

So in 1497 the sails of John Cabot's ship stood down the east coast of Florida, past the Cape of Florida at Biscayne Bay and down farther south until "hee had the Island of Cuba on his left hand" and then, as certainly, turned and came back again, standing well out in the Gulf Stream and making excellent sailing time. Think of the eyes that watched that Bristol ship, of men peering from the tops of mounds or the tropical scrub of the long east coast beaches. Watchfires may have burned at night and canoes slipped along the mangrove-hidden canals to report the wonder.

John Cabot knew well enough he was trespassing in Spanish

waters. But he saw that it was good land and he described the seas boiling with fish which he called "tunnies" because they were tunnies as he had known them in the Mediterranean, although the prosaic English historians had to call them "cod" to make their number believable. The fish of all kinds were so many that you could let down a weighted basket and catch them, said John Cabot, and again Englishmen and scholars ever since have thought the captain was pleased to jest, not realizing at all that Florida waters were crowded with fish just exactly as he said, thick enough to catch in baskets. Certainly it was the Florida coasts he sailed by. In England it was always held that this part of America was discovered by the Cabots.

The English ship of John Cabot moved down these waters and dimly and briefly in the history books, like a kind of ghost, as other English ships, with blue-eyed sailors and crammed with cloth and tin plates and other trade goods, were to appear and disappear in Spanish ports of the Caribbean like bolder ghosts, slipping in and out under the noses of Spanish officials to spy out the harbors and straits and currents and anchorages. Later that knowledge would be put to real account. But Spain's protests were so violent and powerful that for a long time English ships would not venture there.

For fifteen years now, in Puerto Rico, Governor Juan Ponce de Leon and his wife and marriageable daughters had lived their excellent life. He was fiftyish, not actually old, but old enough to enjoy what he had and not envy the younger men who were already subduing richer kingdoms. Probably he would have been satisfied to grow old and die in his respected office, in that city named after him, having little to complain of but the difficulty of getting enough slaves to work his canefields.

Now suddenly he was removed from office, because the powerful Admiral Diego Columbus wanted the place for one of his own men. Ponce de Leon was not by any means rich enough, without the governorship, to retire. He had lost none of his driving energy, the initiative and the administrative ability that had brought him as far as this. He must make himself rich again, he saw, and not by joining other men's conquests, but by searching out some new island that would be his own, with gold and treasure if possible, but most of all with Indians to be taken as slaves. He heard of a rich island called Beniny. It was his.

It was Charles V, the Holy Roman emperor, who now wore the crown of Spain among many others. It was Charles who gave Ponce de Leon the long detailed and businesslike patent, according to the law, that authorized his expedition, aware that the English were already venturing down from the north and that it was high time to take possession.

There is nothing in the pages of that patent, nothing in any records of the voyage or contemporary reports of that time, to indicate that Ponce de Leon had the slightest idea of that curious story which was to follow his name and make it picturesque to this very day. The story of the Fountain of Youth was written only many years later, as we shall see, by a young Spanish captive in Florida named Fontaneda, who repeated some Caribbean legend about a fortunate river in which, if a man bathed, he would regain his youth. Now the historian Herrera, who later told Ponce de Leon's story, a man who liked a dramatic tale better than any dull fact, found that legend in Fontaneda's manuscript. We know he did, because there are notes in the margin in Herrera's own handwriting, showing how he meant to use it. Fontaneda therefore, and Herrera especially, pinned that fountain legend on Ponce de Leon after his death. It has no basis in any discoverable fact.

Probably no power on earth will ever free the name of Ponce de Leon from that legend. It is the first and most deathless of all American myths.

Nothing in the Everglades could have given rise to it. Only

the springs of northern Florida could possibly have been the origin of such a legend. If, as Fontaneda says, a village of Arawaks left Cuba to settle in Florida because of a river, or fountain, of youth, that is just a vague story too. It certainly in no way fits that ambitious, fiftyish, shrewd, able and certainly ruthless man, Ponce de Leon. It is only a frivolous tale, such as a storytelling historian like Herrera could not resist repeating, which many a later real estate man would snatch at.

Otherwise, Herrera is well enough. "Seeing himself rich, and determined to do something with which to gain honor and increase his estate," Herrera wrote of Ponce de Leon, "and as he had news that lands were to be found to the northward, he resolved to go to explore toward that part."

He sought the island of Beniny. The patent of Charles V granted him the title of adelantado and jurisdiction over the island and its treasure for life, subject, of course, to the yearly and increasing per cent of income the crown must always have. He must fit out his own vessels and men-at-arms. The native Indians on that or any other islands he would conquer would be divided under the "repartimiento" system between himself and the other members of his party, whom the king should designate. The crown, as usual, risked nothing and got almost everything.

To gain this authorization Ponce de Leon went to Spain and then returned to serve another year in charge of the fort at Puerto Rico and in fitting out his ships, two caravels and what was then called a brigantine. So that it was not until Tuesday, March 3, 1513, that he sailed from Puerto Rico northwest by north among the Bahamas.

In eleven days he reached Guanahani, the island first discovered by Columbus. The course of the voyage thence, which Ponce de Leon made, has long been argued and arguable. The day-by-day description given by Herrera has been very difficult to reconcile with the famous Cantino map, long considered to be the only one available for these coasts. But a more recent discovery of an Italian map by Ottomanno Freducci in 1514 or 1515, obviously drawn from Ponce de Leon's own charts, makes Herrera's undecorated text clear and valuable at last and removes from that voyage ambiguities which historians have never been able to explain.

Thanks to that map and that text, therefore, we know that on Easter Sunday, of the year 1513, Ponce de Leon was still at sea, running northwest past an island at which his three ships did not stop. From there he sailed almost due west and came at last to the mainland of North America.

According to the correction of Herrera's errors in latitude and to the Freducci map, it is now understood that Ponce de Leon landed on the Florida coast much farther south than was generally supposed. We shall never know the exact spot. It could have been a little north or south of Cape Canaveral.

Nor was it on Easter Sunday that the famous landing was made, but in the days after Easter which are considered the Easter season. "And thinking that this land was an island they named it 'La Florida,'" Herrera wrote, "because they discovered it in the time of the flowery festival." Pascua Florida: "flowery Easter."

That coast was not flowery, even in that season, although many a historian has labored so to describe it. The careful historian Woodbury Lowery borrowed, as he said himself, all the flowers which Bartram the botanist found blooming in the northern part of the state, to make the name fit what he thought Ponce de Leon should have seen. Actually, Juan Ponce did not care a rap for flowers. Like most Spaniards, he had no eye for the description of natural features. What he wanted here was slaves and gold. He found neither. He named it from the churchly calendar and made not one single gesture in a hunt for fountains.

The beach that Ponce de Leon hardly noticed, and certainly

99

never described, is there still, just as it always was, cutting the world in half, from north to south, with the living sea to the east and all that flat, inconspicuous, curious land to the westward, not much farther north than the northern limits of the unguessed Everglades. Except perhaps for a few houses now, if we knew where the exact place was, bathers here and there, or a man surf fishing, perhaps a dog running happily, this beach has hardly changed in essence throughout all the centuries, although not so very far inland between towns, billboards, filling stations and tourist cabins now runs that amazing highway U. S. 1. The beach may still be blank where Ponce de Leon and his gentlemen knelt to take possession, with the sun making a brightness of the banner of Castile and Leon, the swords and the armor and the cross, a little patch of brightness and of color lost in that endless-reaching wideness of the earth and of the sea, under that sky.

The long wave-scalloped sand is there now, as he must have seen it with proud eyes a little blind to anything but his thoughts. Across that beach there is almost always a kind of embankment, which the storm tides piled up and hollowed out over a ridge of rock the sea had put there thousands of years before in a geologic time of which those Spanish gentlemen knew as little as they knew of the years to come. The sandbank is held by the tough roots of massed palmettos and the mounded gray-green sea lavender and gnarled sea grape and cocoplum, with beach grasses against the sky and sinewy sand-clutching vines.

It is humanly inevitable that Ponce de Leon scrambled up that bank, getting sandspurs in his silk hose and certainly sand in his velvet shoes because it was as high up as he could get. So he must have stood there, tall and armored, frowning under his hand to look westward where he would have seen only the sun glare on the steely palmetto spikes going on and on, or

100

scrub trees leaning away from the wind, and beyond that the unending feathery cliff of the pineland. The morning-glories covering the sands would have been purple for him, even in the afternoon, and there would be lavender goatsfoot blossoms and yellow stiff black-eyed Susans and perhaps a patch of white periwinkles in the monotonous silver-green, blue-green, rust-and-bronze-and-shadow-green of all that massed beach growth by the sand's whiteness. The same sun would have flashed on the white flashing sea, the white-fringed dazzling blue sea, frothed and petaled, a more burning blossom than anything on the dull-colored land that would be called "flowery."

The light made it festival, if there were few flowers to do the Easter glory. "It had a very pretty view of many and cool woodlands and it was level and uniform," is about all Herrera could say for it.

The Spanish gentlemen stalked at last back to the boat at the shining waterline, having no eye for the iridescent violet bladders of the jellyfish we call Portuguese man-of-war, or the brown pelican that just about then must have flapped along overhead, three or six or eleven in a line, flap, flap, and sail, flap, flap, and sail, with their elderly chins tucked into their breasts, and not one solemn glance below to the lords of Spain getting into their boats.

The sea filled their last heel marks before they were back in the ships, working a difficult way south beyond the pale-green line of reefs. The tide, or the wind, or a crawling vine would cover the marks in the sand of Ponce de Leon's bony knees and the prodded hole of the banner staff. There would be no other marker ever.

Probably they saw nothing else along that interminable shore that was different or could interest them. They found and marked on their charts the Rio de Canoas, which was Indian

River Inlet, and felt the force of the current, which astonished them and separated their ships, the barkentine standing out to sea, the other two anchoring.

There were huts and Indians on shore, not innocent, humble, surprised people such as Columbus had found in Guanahani twenty years before, but alert and hostile warriors who tried to take their boats. A seaman was struck and a fight started in which the Indians resisted so well with their spears and arrows tipped with sharp shells that two more Spaniards were wounded. Ponce gathered his men and went south to a stream he called "La Cruz," probably Jupiter Inlet, which sixty angry Indians tried to prevent his crossing. He took one of them, violently, for a pilot, regaining his ships.

Farther south, on May 8, a Sunday, they found the current running stronger than the wind "and did not permit the vessels to go forward although they put out all sails." So they doubled the "Cape of Corrientes," anchored behind it at a town called "Abaioa" by Herrera and "Abacoa" by Freducci, which must have been Lake Worth Inlet, and stood southward still, passing and marking Hillsboro Inlet and New River Inlet, and came down to the great bay later to be called "Biscayne" and the place called "Chequescha" or "Chiquiche" which we know was also called "Tekesta," the Indian village where Miami now stands.

From there they stopped for water at Key Largo and ran along the keys. "And to all this line of islands and rocky islets they put as a name 'Los Martires' because seen from a distance the rocks as they raised the view looked like men suffering." That was the way Herrera put it. Whether they looked it or not, these low sand beaches backed by darker trees, with the jagged limestone covered by the clear sea water, were still well named. Men had suffered there already, and would suffer.

The Freducci map marks the name "Canbei" along the

northern keys and "El Nirda" at the present Barnes Sound, and it may be that the ships lingered along there, perhaps sending out the boat to see whether there was a passage or channel to the westward through the shallows. But the ships went on to the end of the line of keys, where probably Key West is now, at a place marked "Archecambei," and from there they sailed westward to the Tortugas and then northward, along the line of the deep water.

Herrera writes baldly, without flourishes, the rest of the story:

They continued sailing, sometimes to the north and other times to northeast, until the 23rd. of May, and on the 24th. they ran along the coast to the south (not going forth to see that it was mainland,) as far as some islets that extended outward in the sea. And because it appeared that there was an entrance between them and the coast for the vessels, in order to take water and firewood they were there until the 3rd. of June, and careened one vessel that was called the San Christoval. And at this time Indians in canoes repaired there to reconnoiter the Spaniards the first time. Seeing that although the Indians called them the Spaniards did not go on land, wishing to raise an anchor in order to repair it, they thought that they were going away. They put to sea in their canoes and laid hold of the cable to carry away the vessel; for which the bark went after them and, going upon the land, they took four women and broke up two old canoes. The other times that they repaired there they did not come to a rupture, because they saw no preparations before they traded skins and pieces of guañin.

On Friday, the 4th., while awaiting wind for going in search of the Chief Carlos, as the Indians of the vessels said that he had gold, a canoe came to the boats; and an Indian who understood the Spaniards, who, it was believed, must be from Española or from another island of those inhabited by Span-

103

iards, said that they should wait, as the chief wished to send
gold in order to trade. And while waiting there appeared at
least twenty canoes, and some fastened together by twos . . .
and began to fight. An armed bark went to them and made them
flee and abandon some canoes. They took five and killed some
Indians and four were captured. Two of them Juan Ponce sent
to the chief in order that they should tell him that notwith-
standing they had killed a Spaniard with two arrow wounds
he would make peace with him.

The following day the bark went to sound a harbor that was
there, and the party went on land. Indians repaired there who
said that next day the chief would go to trade (but it was de-
ceit). Meanwhile the people and canoes came near, and so
it was that on the 11th. eighty men behind waistcloths went
upon the vessel that was nearest. They fought from the morning until the night without hurt to the Spaniards, because the
arrows did not reach, whilst for the cross-bows and artillery
shots they dared not draw near, and in the end the Indians
retired. And the Spaniards, after having stayed nine days, on
Tuesday, the 14th., resolved to return to Española and to San
Juan, with the intention of exploring on the way some islands
of which the Indians that they carried gave information. They
returned to the island, where they took water, which was
named Matança, from the Indians that they killed.

This Matança was undoubtedly Cape Romano, which juts
boldly south, at the head of the Ten Thousand Islands, mangrove and sand and sea water clear to Cape Sable. Romano had
been a landmark for the seagoing canoes between Florida and
Cuba. It is marked clearly on the Freducci map.

From there the expedition moved to another harbor which
may have been northward again near the mouth of the Caloosahatchee, where they stayed nine days. They returned to
Tortugas on their way home.

"In one short time in the night," says Herrera, "they took,

in one of those islands, one hundred and sixty tortoises, and might have taken many more if they had wished. And also they took fourteen seals and there were killed many pelicans and other birds that amounted to five thousand." Most historical writers, commenting on Herrera, say emphatically how much Herrera was in error, since of course no one in that time, they thought, could have taken so many birds. Actually, anyone who ever saw Bird Key, of that Tortugas group,

at the time of year when the birds nest there, knows well that five thousand were not too many for three ships' companies to have knocked in the head, of those amazing white-winged tens of thousands.

They ran south from the Tortugas and reached land that they guessed was Cuba. But they were not interested in Cuba then, so they went north again along the keys recognizing the places they had passed before and stopping again at Chequescha in Biscayne Bay, there to fill their casks with the water in the spring along the rock cliffs south of the river. The village and the great mound must have been empty of people, because nothing is said of them, or of the clear, pale reaches of the bay, the whispering and chittering of the hundreds of green parakeets among the tall trees, or the manatee moving up the river, or the cormorants everywhere flapping their black lines.

It was long thought that from this place the records were confused. But it is clear that from here they could sail straight across the Gulf Stream to the Bahamas, as boats go today. In the Bahamas, called then "the Lucayos," from which already so many sorrowing slaves had been taken, they stopped again for water at an island where they found not one living soul but an old Indian woman, who must have looked at them with strange and terrible eyes.

"In the beginning," as Herrera goes on to write, "there could not be learned by the discoverers the name that La Florida had, seemingly, because, seeing that that point of land projected so much they considered it an island, and the Indians, as it was mainland, told the name of each province, and the Spaniards thought they were deceiving them: but in the end, because of their importunities, the Indians said it was called 'Cautio,' a name that the Lucayos Indians put upon that land because the people of it carried their private parts covered with palm leaves woven in the form of a plait."

They had not yet, then, found that island of Beniny which Ponce de Leon had gone out to seek. Now it was supposed to lie in the western part of the archipelago. Long afterward the name of "Bimini" was given to the small island across the Gulf Stream from Miami, where the Spaniards found the old Indian woman whom they called "La Vieja." They found the northwest Providence Channel and many other islands of the Bahamas, and wandered about. They were caught in a storm and lost a small vessel and finally, on September 23, sailed home to Puerto Rico, having found no treasure or made conquests that seemed to be of any particular importance, or taken any slaves.

No single man of them all had any idea of what they had discovered.

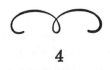

4

The Adventurers

I T WAS years before Juan Ponce de Leon made his second attempt to settle the land he had named "Florida."

He was sent to fight the Caribs of Dominica and Guadeloupe and after three years he had not conquered them. His money was gone. He returned to Puerto Rico to recoup his fortunes and found the cities almost depopulated of Spaniards gone to seek the greater riches of Mexico. Only Ponce de Leon was interested in Florida now.

The slavers who had stripped the Bahamas of people kept the Indians of lower Florida alert and angry, ready, like the Caribs, to risk any death to maintain their freedom. They watched the ship of Diego Miruelo sail north along the coast in 1516, to get a little gold from the washings of Georgia. Three great ships under Francisco Hernandez de Cordoba, in the next year, were blown in a storm from Yucatan to a bay on the lower west coast which the pilot recognized as "Ponce de Leon Bay." The angry Indians fought those men back to their ships, killing many.

Pedro de Quexos, a licensed slaver, joining a caravel of Ayllon's, swept northward from the Bahamas to the coasts of Carolina, where they took one hundred fifty slaves, who died in Santa Domingo of hunger and homesickness.

Word of all this came to Ponce de Leon in Puerto Rico. He must act now, if ever, he saw. "I will return to that island, if it please God's will, to settle it," he wrote to Charles V in February, 1521. But he went obviously with the hope of taking many slaves, as his asiento gave him the right, "that they should come to the knowledge of the Catholic faith, to obey and serve as they are bounden . . . or if they seek not to obey the contents of such requisition [to the Faith] . . . you may make war upon them and enslave them."

He set sail for Florida in two ships, with two hundred men and fifty horses, quantities of domestic animals and agricultural implements, as well as weapons. He had priests with him. The expedition moved toward and up the lower west coast with the dignity of colored sails and brilliant banners.

The caravels stood in to their anchorage, Spaniards swarming onto the brilliant sand. The small boats rowed back and forth across the shallows from the ships. Goods were piled on the beach.

Then there came that curious twang of a released bowstring, and in the next instant the thlock of an arrow reaching its mark. They stared at a man spinning and clutching at his throat, with an arrow sticking through it, stared as he fell and flopped like a fish. Then they were all shouting together as the air thickened with hissing arrow shafts that found throats or joints or splintered and slashed like glass through chain mail to the vulnerable flesh. Spears came in fast and sure, spiking a man clean through before his blood could burst out, red as the flags, on the trampled sand. The first group of men about the shelter were down, and men shouted and ran up from the boats drawing their swords and cursing, or only too late, tried to aim their arquebuses at the racing brown forms darting safely among the mangroves.

The Indians stayed behind their trees. They shot their heavy bows with arms around·the trunks, pouring in those deadly shafts which gleamed like horizontal rain as the Spaniards fell and died. From the boats more Spaniards came pounding up the sand. The Indians darted out to swing a spear from a spear thrower and retreat, drawing the white men nearer the shadows of the trees. Ponce de Leon himself, the conquistador, the great general, the stately figure in beautiful armor and cloak and helmet, rallied his men around him, his eyes flashing with the old light. There must have been a great sense of conquest surging up in the men about him, a great shouting and cheering as the adelantado strode up the sand, his sword drawing light.

An arrow hissed and struck deep in a joint in his armor. So Ponce de Leon bled, and his blood was the same scarlet as the blood of all of them spilled on that trampled whiteness underfoot. That was all he was ever to give Florida, besides her discovery and her name. She gave him his death for it.

They struggled back to the boats, picking up the dead and wounded, and dodging fearfully the last vicious arrows. Juan Ponce de Leon was alive still, turning his head from his deck to look at the long monotony of the mangrove wheeling and sliding away behind. He was taken ashore at Havana, and there in a few days more he was dead: a great, ambitious and courageous man, a hero to everyone but those obscure and resolute Floridians.

It was a long time before any other such ships were to move in to those beaches, east or west. The Indians of those coasts had at last taught the white man what they were. The word went everywhere in that Spanish world that those lower coasts were filled with lean men as raging fierce as hornets, cannibals, and worshipers of the devil. More important, richer lands were being discovered farther north.

Up past the keys, up past the Cape of Florida, up past the long outer beaches, other ships moved steadily, far out from those low deadly shores, in the river of the Gulf Stream. The news was surely carried along the waterways, the hammocks, the most hidden villages of the river of grass.

Ayllon with a great fleet went north to found a colony on easier coasts, with the first Negro slaves and Dominican priests as missionaries to the more tractable natives. Estaban Gomez went by from the north southward in the coastal current, capturing what Indians he could and always seeking that passage to Cathay. The roving slavers went by for the easy victims of the Chesapeake.

The Florida straits were as dangerous as the Florida Indians. There were the unmarked low rocks and reefs and sand bars of those keys, and the extraordinary danger of hurricanes in the tropic latitudes, that could blow up almost without warning from June to November, gray screaming whirlpools of wind more than a hundred miles an hour, dragging in their centers a mound of sea water and blowing before them the high ungovernable ships like dried leaves onto that deadly line of reef and rock. Yearly, even monthly, the wrecks piled up along those shores, but it was the only possible outlet from the Caribbean.

The Indians of the key villages learned to look for broken

casks and bales and boxes and chests, or bodies washed ashore. There were living men and women to be taken for slaves, and for the yearly sacrifices on the altars. The Indians quickly learned to value the fine steel knives, the hatchets and axes, the strange gold coins, the bars of gold, the bars of silver, the bags of jewels, the rings, the altar furnishings, the Spanish loot of Aztec and of Inca. The trading canoes came and went down the canals, carrying the salvaged stuff to the dominant chiefs.

Everywhere, in Spain and in the towns of the Spanish New World, men talked about the wrecks and hazards of "Los Martires" and prayed that it would not be their lot to be wrecked there. It became more and more a concern of the crown that something be done.

There was a one-eyed, lean Spanish captain, redheaded as Columbus, and redbearded as well, a grandee of Ponce de Leon's very stamp, bred to hauteur and hunger and endurance and proud faith, poverty stricken at home, but after twenty-six years in the New World, and in the intrigue and drama about Cortez and the Mexican conquest, grown immensely rich in gold mines and many head of Indian slaves. He was Panfilo de Narvaez, who had seen the great thing it was to be a viceroy of a country like Mexico and was thereby whetted for conquest of his own. He had heard the marvelous tales that Lucas Vasquez de Ayllon and that Indian of his baptized Francisco Chicora had brought back from the expedition to the Carolina coast; tales of tall kings bred on special food and from their cradles kneaded and massaged to make them into giants, and of the vast wealth in gold and pearls that was there. There was mystery, and mystery meant treasure to any Spaniard.

Narvaez was given the right to discover, conquer and people all that land from northern Mexico to the end of Florida. He was to bear all expenses, found at least two colonies, build three forts; for all of which he was to be governor and captain-general at a salary of 250,000 maravedis, to be paid out of the revenues of the country, and as high sheriff receive four per cent of the tax levies and ten leagues of land for his estate forever, as well as the profits from the sale of all rebellious Indians.

The patent was the usual thing, except in this. For the first time the dreadful things that had happened and were happening to the Indians in the Spanish New World had been made clear to Charles V. It had taken all these years for the shocked and protesting voices of truly Christian men, humble priests, Benedictines and Franciscans, but especially the dauntless Father Bartolomé de Las Casas, who had been forced to witness horrors that made them sick, to work some change.

A furious royal order denounced the atrocities visited upon the Indians. It stated clearly that they were to be free men, not to be taken from their houses or put to work against their own free will. No Indians were to be subdued until after they had refused submission to the Spanish king and the Christian faith.

Whether that new clause in the patent would change the usual habits of these conquerors was another thing.

Narvaez sailed from Spain with a great fleet of five caravels, six hundred men, soldiers, colonists, Franciscan friars, Negro slaves, which, curiously enough, de Las Casas had suggested be introduced into the New World in place of Indian labor, and a band of noble gentlemen appointed already as mayors and officials of the cities Narvaez would build. The treasurer and high sheriff of the enterprise was a man who had been king's treasurer, another descendant of those impoverished Moor-fighting families, distinguished, courageous, truly honest, truly religious, and possessing uncommon common sense. He was Alvar Nuñez Cabeza de Vaca, by whom Narvaez's expedition was to be made famous.

The fleet sailed west to Santo Domingo from Grand Canary, on the long cramped miserable verminous ocean journey. They spent the winter in Cienfuegos and, sailing for Havana, were caught up suddenly by storms and blown to the lower west coast of Florida. That was April, 1528. On Holy Thursday the pilot, Diego Miruelo, nephew to that earlier pilot of the same name, looking for the bay of Espiritu Santo, found an inlet between beaches, and within, overlooking clear bay water, the thatched roofs of Indian houses by an inland mound.

The ships went on slowly. The next day, Good Friday, they found a pass through which they could sail into sheltered water. They called it "Baia de la Cruz."

The village in the distance was empty when Narvaez's men marched upon it, swords glistening and crossbows ready. The men ransacked the thatched huts, rummaged among the pots, the fishing gear, the shell ornaments. But everybody crowded to see when some man shouted and held up a trinket made of gold. That settled everything.

On Saturday, the day before Easter, fifteen years after the season of Pascua Florida when Ponce de Leon had found and named this land, Narvaez took possession again. The Spanish flag was raised and the friars set up the cross. All the stately Spanish gentlemen, in order of their rank, paced up to bow before Narvaez, to present their commissions. These he endorsed and gave back, bowing. The governor's act of possession was then signed and witnessed before a notary, who had set his little table there in the light on the sand to add to every document his signature and his seal.

The most curious part of this legal and religious ceremony was the reading of the king's requisition to the Indians, by Governor Panfilo de Narvaez himself: "In behalf of His Most Catholic Caesarean Majesty of Don Carlos, King of the Romans, and Emperor ever-Augustus, and Doña Juana his mother,

113

Sovereign of Leon and Castile, Defenders of the Church, ever victors, never vanquished, and rulers of barbarous natives, I, Panfilo de Narvaez, his servant, messenger and captain, notify and cause you to know in the best manner I can, that God our Lord, one and eternal, created the heaven and the earth, and one man and one woman of whom we and you and all men in the world have come"—the elaborate phrases must have seemed strange there, blowing on the wind—"but because of the infinity of offspring that followed in the five thousand years and more since the world was created, it has become necessary that some men should go in one direction and some in another . . . All these nations God our Lord gave in charge to one person, Saint Peter . . . and he commanded him to place his seat in Rome . . . One of the Popes who succeeded him to that seat and dignity of which I spake, as Lord of the world, made a gift of these islands and main of the Ocean Sea, to the said Emperor and Queen, and their successors. . . . Wherefore as best you can, I entreat and require you to understand this well which I have told you, taking the time for it that is just you should, to comprehend and reflect, and that you recognize the Church as Mistress and Superior of the Universe . . . And their Majesties, and I in their royal name, will receive you in love and charity . . .

"But if you do not do this, and of malice you be dilatory, I protest to you that . . . I will enter with force, making war upon you from all directions, and in every manner that I may be able . . . I will take the persons of yourselves, your wives and your children to make slaves . . . doing you all the evil and injury of which I may be able . . . it will be your fault and not that of his Majesty, nor mine, nor of those cavaliers who came with me."

In that silence, no Indian replied. Again the notary, head bared to the sun, goose quill squeaking on the heavy parchment, wrote out his statement that the Requisition to the Indians had been read. This again the witnesses paced to sign and the notary attested with his signature and seal.

The next day the priests set up an altar and celebrated a Solemn High Mass of thanksgiving. Suddenly, a group of Indians walked angrily out from behind the houses making threatening gestures. They went away slowly, turning their backs to all those staring Spanish eyes.

All this happened some miles south of the great expanse of Tampa Bay, which, presently, exploring bands of Narvaez's men discovered. It is only remotely connected with the Everglades. But, like the sails going up the Gulf Stream, word of it and of strange men and stranger animals, was carried among the alert villages.

Narvaez commanded an exploring party going northward by land. The ships went along the coast to wait for him at a meeting place that was never found. The three hundred men of the company, priests, officers, and forty horses with their riders, the banners, the sound of Spanish voices, the clank of armor and the plodding feet of many foot soldiers moved off, out of our region completely, into death and history.

Behind them for a while the waters were empty of sails. Then, in the southwest, there was seen a pinnace moving uncertainly northward, standing off and on again, as if looking for a landing. The twenty-five or so Spaniards who had been sent out from Havana by the wife of Governor Panfilo de Narvaez, after his ships returned from the rendezvous without any news of him, finally recognized the bay and beach where Narvaez had gone ashore. There was nothing to be seen but thatched roofs and two or three Indians standing motionless. But they did see something that a white man might have left, a cane sticking in the sand with a thing like a letter in its split top.

Sailing nearer in the shallows they made signs that the Indians should bring the letter out to them. The men there motioned the white men to come ashore.

There was on board a young man named Juan Ortiz, from Seville, nobly born like so many, and like so many, poor, who had come here first with Narvaez but had gone back to Havana on the ships. He was crammed with life and courage and enthusiasm, good-looking, sure of his fate. He could not wait to go ashore and get that letter. But only one other man would go with him in the small boat. The others argued with him, warning him of the known ferocity of these Florida people. Nothing about that peaceful shore stopped Juan Ortiz.

He rowed the small boat gratingly up the sand and jumped out. It is probable that Juan Ortiz ran gaily toward the letter, his hair blowing, grinning to himself because he was ashore at last and because the sun shone and the world was new. So that when he was stopped short by a crowd of tall dark men standing there impenetrable as trees, who grabbed him with arms as hard as tree limbs, he must have been more surprised than angry or frightened. Perhaps he stood half grinning still, looking eagerly at the men about him, tattoo marks over strange colored skins, stern faces, arrows pinning up black hair, their bright strings of beads and pearls. He smelled for the first time the Indian smell, oily and a little fishy, with some pungence in it of herbs he did not know. At any rate he did not struggle, only jerked around against the hard hands when he heard blows and saw the other Spaniard break loose and run and then stumble, struck down from behind by a man flipping a great wooden club as if it had been a light stick; that man who had been as eager as he going down on the sand and lying there given up to it, face in it, blood soaking it, in one blink dead as mutton.

Juan Ortiz may have struggled then, but it was too late. He was made to walk forward, although he must have strained to turn his head to keep on looking back where the pinnace with her sail shivering in the wind was desperately rowed toward the sea.

There was the village before him. The dark-faced, dark-bodied painted people swarmed out from the houses on pilings along narrow waterways, running and shouting at him over the littered earth, old women and naked young boys screaming,

in a curious burst of hostility that must have shocked him as much as the hard hands wrenching him along. In a sort of square cut out of the brush there was silence, and a group of men sitting on logs under a thatched shelter at one end, about a great brown chief, a man absolutely still, his face like magnificently carved weathered wood, the blue tattoo patterns on his skin shining like oil. The men there spoke quietly, hardly glancing at him as he was held before them. He watched the hands relaxed and dangling over their knee bones, jerking a little now and then in an easy gesture. The old women, the young boys were quiet behind him, massed at the entrance to the Square Ground.

It had happened so quickly—it was so strange—young Juan

117

Ortiz must have looked about him slowly with his bold Spanish glance dulling a little, at the silent crowds ranked about him, men stern and silent on each side, the women peeping and whispering behind, old women with faces like withered nut meats, handsome quiet mothers with babies, and girls comely and smooth as doves, with great shy eyes. The noise of the crowd was stilled for the deliberate murmur and stop, and murmur and stop, of the voices of the council. It was dreadfully hot and glary, Juan Ortiz's skin prickled under his heavy Spanish clothing and a chill sweat ran down his spine. The painted faces, with eyes half shut, imperturbable as turtles, hardly turned to him.

He could hear flies buzzing in the silence. Then with only a turn of the chief's wrist the talk was over. He spent the night tied in a hut, listening still, only half believing the strange night noises under the quiet of that world new as a dream. It must still have seemed like a nightmare when in daylight men walked Juan Ortiz across the trampled sand to low posts that were set over old ashes, and tore his clothes from him, so that he stood there naked, his flesh white and shining strangely in that whiteness of the light, with those brown crowds staring beyond. Poles were laid in a kind of grid, lashed to the corner posts over which, when they had tripped him and stretched him as easily as they would a split fish, he was bound with thongs hand and foot, spread-eagled, as helpless as a man could be. A proud boy ran with a blazing stick from another fire and Juan Ortiz heard the quick crackle beneath him and smelt smoke and stared in anguish unbelievable straight up into the blinding blue sky and knew that this was no dream, but pain— and death. So soon—so soon—sun and fire—Mother of God!— he screamed then as a man must, the full-wrenched utter scream of protest, that life should prove so quickly only a torture and a cheat—that life should end so—Mother of God!—pain from

118

which his cringing muscles could not pull away stabbed deep in his back—his flesh fried . . .

Perhaps he thought his cry had been heard by the Blessed Virgin. Suddenly they were scattering the flaming sticks and cutting the sharp thongs that had numbed his feet and hands. He was jerked roughly to his feet and pushed stumbling, blind with sun and agony, to face again that heavy brown man and the others at the log seat.

Vaguely he saw that one of those girls he had thought comely was standing there also, speaking quickly. She was brown and bare and soft above the waist where her moss skirt fell to her shapely knees, and she wore bright ornaments about her neck and was graceful, shaking back her long black virgin hair. Presently the chief moved his head to look him over as Juan Ortiz had seen Spanish slave buyers look over an Indian on a block. The chief nodded and he was taken away, twisted with the pain growing in his burned back. But he understood now that he was not to die and that the girl had saved him. He was to understand later that she and the other women had thought him too young and too good-looking to be destroyed and had insisted to her father, Chief Ucita, that it would even be a proud thing for him and for the tribe to own a white captive.

Some old woman on the plank floor of a thatched hut put salve on his back and brought him water and food, and so presently Juan Ortiz stood springy and hopeful on his feet again, breathing the bright air thankfully into his lungs. He learned to eat with relish the Indian food, fish and shellfish roasted in the fires, and the sharp palmetto berries and hearts of palm, and deer steaks broiled and savory, and the good meat of queer little animals the Spanish had thought were dogs. He went without all clothing but a breechclout, and turned brown in the constant sun, and learned Indian words

119

and the skills of the fish spear and net, and worked with the women at their tasks of pottery making and skin scraping and woodcutting, and constant carrying of water.

That young girl who had saved him looked at him kindly, and it may have been that she slipped into the thatched hut where he lay of nights and comforted him in the way of love, as it was not improper for young Indian girls to do before marriage. She brought back to him not only his life and his desire of life, but his pride and his courage, so that he could walk as a Spaniard should among indifferent people, speaking their language, feeling the logic of their ways less strange.

Soon it was not enough that he join in the women's work around the village, like those curious, long-haired creatures, half-men, half-women, the berdaches. Juan Ortiz was taken far out beyond the village where the pines and palmettos stretched far eastward, their fine tops black lace against the moon, green lace against the pink sky of morning.

There was a place beyond where logs were piled up in crude shapes like tombs, and he understood that this was the way these people exposed their dead, and that the new, small pile covered a dead child, a chief's son. It was an evil place, the Indians felt. For four days and nights the small body must be guarded, not only against wild beasts, but from its own small second soul that would come whimpering about in the nighttime, seeking to do evil.

Juan Ortiz's good Catholic scalp must have crawled, for the souls of the recent dead are fearful things, but he prayed, calling on his saints and the Blessed Virgin, and in this bad place commending his soul to God, who had surely kept him safe until now. He had a great fire to watch by, when they left him alone, and he sat by it and thought of his father's house and the street corners of Seville. About him in the trees he heard small, throbbing, murmuring voices and loud hooting cries, and farther

120

away sharp voices calling, and farther off still, but rasping enough to loosen his hair again and start his prayers whispering, some great harsh screaming like the souls of the damned.

He was young still and scared to death, knowing nothing of the little owls and the great barred owl, and the chuck-will's-widow, and a panther winding and shrieking his love beyond the bushes. But Juan, holding tight to his faith, slept when he should not be sleeping, in the depths of the Florida night when the great stars that have smoked up from the east turn at the top of the enormous vault and slope imperceptibly westward, and the crickets have stopped, and the cold dews drip from the cold unseen boughs of the pines.

When he woke, in such a moment, there were stealthy sounds of dragging among leaves. A stick cracked. Beyond the embers of the firelight slant green eyes glared at him and went out. He ran with his heart pounding and slammed his spear at the thrashing in the bushes. Straining to listen, he heard nothing else. The dark grew darker all about him and he went back to the eye of his fire and called upon his saints and slept. Very early, in the first shadowless light like clear water slipping through the trees pearly with wet, he woke with a start and saw the shape of the small piled logs wrenched apart as if by some great paw. The child's body was gone.

The cold dew was no colder than the gooseflesh roughening his skin. Some birds began to cry harshly above the gilding boughs. This would be the death of him. Presently men stood about him and he saw the dark hating face of the father of the child. The old scars on his back stung as he tried to tell them what had happened. Men went trotting where he pointed, just before they began to bind his wrists.

But there was a shout. They were coming back carrying high the little boy's body, and behind, dragged by a leg and the tail, a great dead grinning wolf with Juan Ortiz's spear fast

121

in the throat. That was the luckiest blow any man ever struck, Juan Ortiz must always have thought.

The three years after that in which Juan Ortiz lived in the favor of Chief Ucita must have been good enough years for a young man, living more and more as an Indian and a warrior, binding up his long hair with arrows, scraping off his beard with sharp-edged shells, moving lightly and easily in no clothes but a breechclout, his oiled skin deeply tanned, eating with relish the Indian food, and even letting himself be tattooed and initiated into a clan. The Indians gave respect and courtesy to any man who could hold his own among them. He shared food and laughter at the cooking fires and did not lack for girls to warm him on his plank bed of nights.

Then from the northwest, where between the Caloosahatchee and the Kissimmee the slow streams of the rainy season move through great open plains of palmettos to feed Lake Mayaimi, came the chief of another tribe and his warriors, Mococo, as far as Juan could reproduce his name, in one of those quick border raids, and burned Ucita's town and took prisoners, so that Ucita and his people only just escaped to another town of his, farther south, on another of those long beaches. It was clear to Ucita that the evil that had come to them had been caused by some failure to do service to the Sources of Power. Looking about him, as the priest muttered by his shoulder, he saw the white man, who for these years had been let live as an Indian, a pledged and promised sacrifice. Naturally, the evil lay there.

That night, as Juan Ortiz slept, the girl, the chief's daughter who had saved him first, slipped to him in the dark, whispering that her father meant to have him killed in ceremonies of expiation tomorrow, that the luck of his people might be changed. He must get up and go now, at once, to the victorious Mococo. There was some talk that she fled with him in spite of being

122

pledged to marry a young chief. But the first narrative has it that she only went halfway, to show him the path.

In the morning he came to a river and two of Mococo's men fishing. When he tried to talk to them, they ran away and roused the warriors, who would have killed him except that he shouted at them and someone understood. Then came Mococo himself, pacing out to see this Christian who had fled to him from his enemies. He received Juan Ortiz with generosity. Ortiz promised to serve the great chief truly, who in turn pledged his word that if any Christians ever came in a ship to that coast he would be free to go with them.

This was the dramatic story of Juan Ortiz and his rescue by a chief's daughter, which was first noted by a Portuguese gentleman of the town of Elvas, who had it from Juan Ortiz himself later. The Gentleman of Elvas included it in the clear and authentic narrative of the De Soto expedition which he wrote largely from memory, and published in Portugal in 1557. It is a curious parallel that in the year 1616 Captain John Smith published the story of his romantic rescue by Pocahontas, the second version of his account of experiences with the Indians of Virginia in 1608. Captain Smith's first version made no mention whatsoever of the Pocahontas episode. Some historians consider the Gentleman of Elvas's narrative the true origin of the great American tale of the white captive and the rescuing Indian maiden.

But whether or not Captain John Smith brought fame to this story by appropriating it, there was Juan Ortiz making the best of his years among the Indians in the swampy plains and slow rivers set about with palmettos and cabbage palms north of the Caloosahatchee.

The day came when Mococo told Ortiz that Spaniards had landed on the coast where Ucita's village had been, and that he was free to go there.

This was the greatest expedition of all, under the greatest leader the Florida coast had so far seen, the adelantado Hernando De Soto. They had been allowed to land.

The amazing tale told by the man Cabeza de Vaca, survivor of that expedition of Panfilo de Narvaez which Juan Ortiz had been sent from Havana to try to overtake, had set Spain afire again for conquest. Years after Narvaez had disappeared and Juan Ortiz had begun his life among the Indians, Cabeza de Vaca and three companions had survived the hardships of a truly extraordinary journey on foot north and west along the Gulf of Mexico, and west and south again into Mexico itself. The tale he told and wrote and repeated was a record of utter misery, of barren coasts and unfriendly and impoverished natives, and no riches of any kind.

No one believed what he told of the poverty of those coasts. They thought he was concealing vast new riches for himself.

The man who caught up and focused all the excitement and mystery in what de Vaca did not say, was Hernando De Soto. Like Ponce de Leon, he was noble on all four sides of his house. With nothing of his own but his sword, he had been a West Indies venturer and had married the daughter of Balboa. In the incredible conquest of Peru he made a name for himself as one of the twelve supreme conquistadores. Enormously rich therefore, magnificent as a lord of the Inca Empire, when Hernando De Soto returned to Spain at the head of a glittering train of men-at-arms and slaves and servants bearing unbelievable gifts, it was inevitable that anything he wanted he would be given.

He wanted the governorship of all that vast region of Florida, with Cuba thrown in. He was given it. He was to have twelve leagues square of that country for his own. He was to share with the crown half of all treasures, of temples, burial places, palaces, one-sixth the ransom of all chiefs and rulers, and un-limited rights to take slaves.

Nobles of every kind, rich and poor, soldiers, sailors, colonists, farmers, struggled to join his ships. Fortunes were spent in equipment. Men impoverished themselves, selling their lands, pledging inheritances, to be of that company. Ten loaded ships of De Soto's set out for Cuba with twenty ships moving toward Mexico, in one glorious fleet.

At Santiago, and again at Havana, the great undertaking, the trampling of horses, the crowds of men-at-arms richly provided, loud talking in the streets and boasting in the wineshops, the shouting and feasting and trafficking in supplies flooded the quiet Cuban towns with new excitement, and the one word "Florida."

There was to be nothing casual about De Soto's venture. A pilot, Juan de Añasco, was sent on two voyages to the lower Florida coasts, seeking harbors and any Indians he could pick up to be held as interpreters, hostages and slaves.

Nine great ships De Soto commanded, higher ships than ever, more like the great castled galleons that were still to come, their great square sails colored and stretched tight, their raked lateen sails, their high painted bows and gold-tricked and painted sterns all taking the light like clouds, under the pennants and banners streaming in crimson and gold of the unsurpassed Spanish pride.

Sunday, May 18, 1539, they set sail. In the calm air the sea swelled and stood like polished steel, in which white clouds and empty sails alike were dazzlingly reflected. The ships stood like pictures, moving only a little. It was seven days before De Soto's vessel had sight of that low dark-green coast and for three days all the ships crawled northward along it, looking for the bay where Narvaez had landed.

From the first moment that they sighted the low west coast

of the land called "Florida" they saw in brilliant daylight the
smoke of signal fires lighted and keeping abreast of them all the
way. The smoke went up in thick columns, creamy brown and
white with purple shadows in the sun. At night the constant
fires rose straight from every moundtop in that enormous dark,
as if the flame-lighted pillars of fires rose out of the sea itself.

The men of the nine vessels, six hundred lancers and crossbow men, went ashore with the supplies, the two hundred
thirteen horses, the dogs trained to pursue Indians and tear
to pieces escaping slaves, the cattle, the swine, the forges, the
carpenters' tools, and all the churchly equipment of the
Dominican friars.

Again, as with Narvaez, when they found Indian villages
they were deserted. The two captive Indians slipped away
easily. On June 3, with the most formal and elaborate ceremonies of church and state, De Soto took possession of the land
that was only a strip of sand between the sea and the unknown.

Word came that far away in the interior there was a captured Spanish Christian who knew the country. An expedition
came back with the man Juan Ortiz, who had gone to meet
them. He stood among them brown and naked and tattooed
like the other savages. He moved with the ease and poise of
an Indian but his eyes stared with incredulity at the hordes of
men about him. It was some time before his Spanish came back
to him. But presently, clothed and in armor again, which must
often have seemed intolerable in that hot sun, sitting on a
horse, everyone but he forgot those years of his when he had
hunted and danced and made love as an Indian.

Juan Ortiz told them boldly that there was no gold in this
part of the country, and they were willing to believe him.
There might be some north and east, he thought, although he
had never been there, but he had heard that the way was more
open and the going better for both horse and foot. De Soto

sent some of the ships back to Havana, with some noblemen. So on August 1, 1539, under the full blazing sun of a Florida summer, leaving behind him a small garrison that presently would retreat to Havana, De Soto with his horses, his foot soldiers, his men in armor, and his supply trains toiled off across that land as Narvaez had done. With months and years of wandering they would venture farther into the new country than any others, and reach and christen the Mississippi. Many, especially De Soto himself, would die. Juan Ortiz, whom the Indian girl had rescued, would find his death also, drowned crossing an unknown river, weighted down with Christian clothing and armor. Others, after hardships like Cabeza de Vaca's which they had not believed, would struggle down into Mexico. With them also went many Florida Indians, the men taken for beasts of burden, the women for cohabitation, some of whom would survive in Guatemala and some make their way back to Florida after many years.

But no Indians from around the Everglades were so taken.

There, where the last rumor of that noisy, glittering confused caravan of strange men and stranger beasts had passed, the silence of the untouched land was absolute. The palmettos and the quick clawing vines grew across the swaths they had made. The bones of the stolen cattle that had been killed and eaten were covered.

There were young warriors telling the tales of these latest white men at a dozen campfires, who had been born long after the first white man had come to Florida, who heard only as tales told by the old men how it was in this world before there were any white men at all. That menace and their vigilance had now for nearly fifty years been a part of the life of every family, every tribe, every clan, every man, woman and child in the whole country of the Everglades.

It had kept them free.

5

Captives and Martyrs

THE triumphant Indians of south Florida made very clear to the Spanish king and all his officials and gentlemen that they were not to be made slaves of. There was nothing else of any value to outlanders in that flat country of theirs, only sudden death in the sun.

It is true that the whole direction of the incredible Spanish energy was set westward. In ten years Santo Domingo city in Hispaniola, San Juan de Puerto Rico, San Cristobal de la Habana de Cuba, Santiago de Cuba were built and flourished and left behind. Before Santiago de Cuba was finished Balboa discovered the Pacific. Mexico was taken in 1519 and in 1520

Magellan swept down South America and around into the Pacific. The deadly glittering tide of Spanish conquest surged into Central and South America. The dominant cities were San Juan de Ulloa, that would be Veracruz on the Mexican coast, Puerto Bello on the Isthmus, Cartagena on the Spanish Main called "Tierra Firme". The long Spanish arm reached to the East Indies and the Philippines and linked the world into one empire.

In Europe the wealth of Spain's new world had already roused the envy and greed of every other nation. They were stopped by the pope's bulls creating the Line of Demarcation, and by the still overwhelming power of Spain. But as the loot of empire, the melted-down gold of temples, the jewels, the silver bars like cordwood, the rich gains in hides and dyestuffs and pearls and sugar went jolting in the king's wagons from Cadiz to the Spanish treasury, the envy of sovereigns exploded in the energy of lawless independent men.

Every Atlantic seaport was by now crowded with mutinous sailors, thieves, cutthroats, gutterscrapings, desperate landless men, nobles who hated Spain, in whom the rumor of that wealth worked like fever. No imaginary line on a map or fear of the pope's hell, threats of Spanish galleys or the fires of the Inquisition already burning for marauders and heretics could prevent a seepage into the crannies of the Caribbean of such individuals of every blood and mixture of blood ravenous for gold.

Presently from the stronghold of Tortuga, north of Hispaniola, certain such men engaged in the curing of meat, stolen probably, and became buccaneers instead of "boucaniers." Freebooters, thieves and smugglers of everything including slaves, drove their small open fly-boats against single ships rich with treasure, and captured them. The days of piracy began.

By 1547 French pirates, with nobody knows how much actual backing from the French government, boldly stormed Chagres on the Isthmus, invaded Honduras and captured nine treasure ships within sight of Cartagena. Spain's long dreamed of immunity ended there. She knew now that she was ringed with invaders who feared her less than they craved her enormous loot.

The problem was wholly geographic. The great arc of islands making the Caribbean's east wall was not a bulwark. Spanish ships could enter the enclosed sea only from the south, between the volcanic islands. Their natural course was straight across from the Azores, helped by the equatorial current and the unfailing winds. They could not go back that way. They could get out of the Gulf of Mexico only north of Cuba, and so up along the Florida keys and the coast between the mainland and the Bahama banks only as the majestic river of the Gulf Stream carried them. They had already abandoned the old Bahama passage, north of Hispaniola, a dangerous journey, wrecking too many ships. The Gulf Stream, to its blending with the Atlantic anywhere between Bermuda and the northernmost Bahamas, became the great Spanish corridor toward home.

All the goods and supplies of every possible kind, which Spain in jealous monopoly sent to her colonies, were shipped into the Caribbean between Dominica, Martinique, or St. Lucia, or the channel north of Trinidad called the Galleons' Passage.

For the dangerous return voyage from Havana up the Florida Straits a concentrated fleet system was established. At first only a few merchant ships crawled along together, but as the attacking pirate horde increased the Council of the Indies ruled that all ships must go in convoy. At Veracruz in Mexico and Cartagena in South America, once a year on the arrival of the fleet from Spain, were held the great fairs from which all goods, licensed and inspected and taxed, went out to all the posts of empire. Cartagena and Veracruz were the great storage points of goods and treasure for the return voyages. To Cartagena were directed the mule trains from the mines of Potosi with their

loads of silver bars to be stacked up about the market place of
the Great Fair, unguarded. Ships brought the treasures of Peru
to the Isthmus, and later the cargoes of the galleons from the
Philippines were unloaded and transshipped to Cartagena.

The first ships were open caravels, like the ships of Columbus
and Ponce de Leon. Then shortly the galleon was developed,
the most powerful fighting vessel known until then, many
decked, long beaked, with high castled poop, fore- and main-
masts lifting courses of colored and embroidered silks, topsails
to catch the highest wind, lateens on the mizzens for quick
maneuvering. They were mounted with forty or fifty guns and
towered among their humbler convoys of thirty or forty ships at
a time; brigantine-rigged pataches, caravels, lumbering Mediterranean galleasses with oars as well as sails, with chained and
beaten pirates laboring at them, galleys and roomy hulks and
howkers and the fast luggers with sails so angled they could
outsail and outpoint them all, and two-masted pinks with
lateen sails that gave them raffish wings. The pinks and luggers,
with their swiftness and their ease in steering, were ideal for
pirates.

There were two fleets. One was the flota, under an admiral
and convoyed by a galleon or two. But a fleet of four or five
galleons sailed yearly to Cartagena and Puerto Bello to gather
a larger convoy of homeward-going ships, called "the galleones,"
commanded by a captain general and sailing under sealed
orders. Havana was the assembling port. The galleones from
Cartagena took a northward course past Jamaica and the Isle
of Pines, rounded Cuba's westernmost cape and sailed east to
Havana. There the flota from Mexico joined them. There the
general of the galleones broke the seal of his last order and
learned how far north beyond the Florida coasts, and how near
to the Bermudas, he was to sail all that motley collection of
ships.

They made a great procession past the keys, past Biscayne

131

Bay, past Canaveral. In Havana at the great cathedral the captain-generals and the admirals and the captains had crossed themselves and burned candles, commending their souls to God, against all the perils of storms and hurricanes, of deadly rocks and of waiting Florida Indians.

No one seemed to realize that the months from June to December were the months of hurricanes. The galleones were frequently ordered to sail from Havana in September. Sometimes they waited there for the Mexican flota until October, so that again and again a howling gray tropical cyclone, in one day tore that blue world to raving gray and white tatters and scattered and sank and ran aground that great array of ships. We shall never know how many wrecks there were, overwhelmed in the sand and white ooze of innumerable shoals, with the green bland waters hiding everything.

The Indians of the coasts and keys were ready for them. They must always have been sea watchers, staring out over the incredible, pale sea for the shadows of fish or the fins of sharks, or the floating shapes of turtles. After the ugly storms had passed, the Indians came back to poke over the mile-long windrows of sea stuff from the outer depths. They were born wreckers before the first ship came driving in somewhere in the lashing white salt murk over the cruel lumps of brain coral, the harsh spikes of coral antlers, the rough limestone gouged by sea and wind and set with every shape of knife-edged barnacle and shell, where in one terrific sea a keel might be lifted and broken as a boy snaps a stick.

In another morning the sea breathed calm and smooth again where the broken ship hung, and drowned men floated, their drowned hair waving with the waving weeds. The canoes came out from a beach among the mangrove bays, slipping over the bright water and the mossy rocks and the sea gardens. The ship was rifled and the corpses stripped. Boxes and water-logged casks would be broken open on the sands, and the brown curious people would poke in wonder at the white man's strange things.

The casks and boxes broken on the white coarse sand under indifferent Indian heels would spill out a round yellow shine of gold coins. Gold in bars would be picked up and dropped. Great casks of silver ingots from Potosi would be left carelessly for any boy to toss about. The small skin bags of emeralds, the necklaces thickset and blazing, rings, bracelets, the runlets of pearls, might have appealed to them more, sifting them through their brown fingers in the sun's blaze. Silver plate, candlesticks, silver and gold cups and trays and crucifixes, flagons for wine, tall jeweled combs, all the trophies of Montezuma not already melted down, rayed suns and strange tablets and ceremonial vessels, gold dust in small sacks, and the queer rough wedges into which molten Peruvian gold was poured, lay and were scattered, and the fat brown Indian babies played with them while the chiefs and wise men made up their minds what was to be done.

If there were white men, women, priests, children alive among the floating planks and boxes or dragging themselves ashore half-drowned, they were herded in groups, fed and guarded. They would be slaves and sacrifices at the yearly festival of the sun, led up the ramps of long ceremonial mounds to the fires and burned, as men were everywhere in those days, white or Indian, Christian or heretic, tied to a stake and screaming in the flare. The gods were different, the suffering was the same.

Among the men who floundered or swam ashore, and stood panting and staring about them at the Indians closing in, from a wrecked ship that sailed from Cartagena in 1545, was a boy of thirteen named Escalante de Fontaneda. His father was an official of that colony, of sufficient wealth and consequence to send his two sons to Spain for their education. They had with them twenty-five thousand dollars in pure gold. The elder boy, with most of the crew, was lost.

Escalante and the other captives, with the clothing and gold and other loot from the ships, were eventually taken before Carlos of the Calusas, the greatest leader among all the early Florida Indians, who was to dominate all these tribes and make history for many a Spaniard to come.

With his boyish quickness Escalante had been able to pick up a few Indian words from those of his captors who had a few words of Spanish. When the chief ordered him abruptly to sing and dance, to make a little sport for the dark-faced elders, Escalante was quick to strike up some sailor's song and shuffle about in the sand and snap his fingers. It saved his life.

He was allowed to help the women until he was accepted as just another boy, going off deer hunting with the other men or "shining" alligators at night up the dark rivers leaping with fish or paddling a canoe in the shouting, foaming excitement of the seaward chase of the manatee. But he was always on watch for the long yells that announced the arrival of another gang of fear-stiffened Spanish captives. He had seen many a head bashed in with a war club because the white man could not understand the guttural Indian orders.

The chief asked him, one day, why the Spaniards were so obstinate that they would not do what they were told. Escalante convinced him that they knew not one single Indian word. After that some man who spoke a little Spanish always went with the guards of such a group of castaways. So Escalante Fontaneda saved many lives, for the fires or for rescue.

After seventeen years of living in Florida Fontaneda was himself rescued, probably by the French on the upper east coast. Later he returned to Florida as interpreter with Menendez and in Spain he wrote down everything he remembered in a clear and vivid narrative which is the first written source we have of that early time about the Everglades.

What he wrote supplements the later knowledge of the archaeologists, that the country was held by the Calusas, the Tekestas and the Mayaimis about the lake. Of these last he said especially that there were many towns of thirty or forty inhabitants each, and there were many more places where only a few people lived, setting their fish weirs in the shallow fresh water far from land, living on wide-mouthed bass and great trout and eels and alligator tails and things which disgusted the finicky Spaniards because they thought they were rats or dogs, which we now know to be opossum, and turtles which the Spaniards thought were reptiles, like the snakes which the Indians always found savory. They had the coontie flour, the staple food of all these Everglades tribes, except in great flood season when the lake villagers took to their mounds and their canoes and lived on fish alone.

Chief Carlos, when the Spaniards first knew him and called him that name, which he accepted when they told him it was the name also of a great white king, had dominated his area by the force of his own military might and mother wit and personality. His father, Senquene, had been chief before him. Power was increased in Carlos, young, lean, imperious. He had it in mind to bind all the tribes about the Everglades in a peaceful federation which he would control, and from which he would receive tribute.

Fontaneda lists the towns he knew of that day subject to Carlos's rule, and they furnish almost all that is known of that lost Calusa speech. The meaning of some were given by Fontaneda, and some have been shown by later scholars of Indian linguistics, Buckingham Smith and John R. Swanton, to be similar to Choctaw.

Fontaneda's list of towns includes Tampa, "a large town," which was not Tampa as we know it today but the principal town of Carlos below Charlotte harbor, and Tomo and Tuchi and Soco, translated later as the Choctaw "muscadine grape";

135

No, "the town beloved," Sinapa, the place of snake eaters, Sina-esta, Metampo, Sacaspada and Calaobe, "deep spring," Estama, Yagua, Gueva, Muspa, which was probably not far from Cape Romano, which on Herrera's map was marked "Pta de Muspa"; Casitoa, Tatesta, which may have been Tekesta, Cayovea, Jutun, Tequemapo or "women's bowl," Comachica and Quisi-yove. Inland on Lake Mayaimi, the towns Fontaneda remembered were Cutespa, Tavaguenve, Tonsabe, "the swallow-tailed hawk," Enempa, "where we eat," and twenty others.

Down the keys Fontaneda says there were two important towns subject to Carlos, Guarungunve, "the town of weeping," and Cuchiyaga "the place of suffering." The first was said to be on Matacumbe Key which may be Spanish for "mata hombre" or "kill man," which would again have been a translation of the original Indian "Cuchiyaga."

North of the Calusas on the west lay the province of another powerful chief and tribe called Tocobago, inhabiting the mounds and well-populated islands and shores of Tampa Bay. On the east coast, north of the Tekesta country, there were the Jeaga and Ais Indians.

They were more closely related to the Calusas than the Timu-cua Indians of north Florida. They paid Carlos tribute, for Fontaneda saw his men arming to go to the Ais country and returning with great store of treasure from the shipwrecks of that coast, which Carlos traded with northern tribes.

With all his years of living among the Indians and his knowl-edge of them, Fontaneda never lost the deep-seated bitterness that a captive learns. Thirty years later, writing in Spain, it was old hate that lay behind the treatment he recommended for the Indians.

"I hold it certain," he wrote in his crabbed Spanish, "that they will never be at peace and less will they become Christians. If my counsel be not heeded there will be trouble and matters

136

worse than they were beforetime. Let the Indians be taken gently, inviting them to peace; then putting them under deck, husbands and wives together, sell them among the islands and even upon Terra Firma for money. In this way there could be management of them, and their numbers diminished."

Fontaneda's ideas were the ideas of all Spanish officials. With every year the fleets grew greater and carried more treasure, and not only jewels, silver, melted and reshaped gold, but the new wealth of hides and sugar and indigo and chocolate. There were more captives. It was desperately important that something new be tried.

Now, the province of Guatemala had been found to be peopled with tribes no less ferocious than those of Florida. Their remote mountains made them as independent as the Glades people. But in Guatemala a different force had prevailed.

Long before Fontaneda's day, the Catholic Church in the New World had voiced its outrage against the Spanish treatment of the Indians. Father Bartolomé de Las Casas carried that protest to the king himself. As a result, the Guatemalan tribes were brought peaceably and quietly under the domination, not of soldiers, but of devoted priests.

The man who so triumphantly proved the claims of peace was a Dominican friar, Father Luis Cancer de Barbastro. He was an Aragonese who founded a great mission in Puerto Rico, and in 1505 went into the Guatemalan mountains. For five years the missionaries excluded every other white man from that country. The king pledged these people freedom forever. They settled in villages and gardens, never far from the sound of church bells, and developed their fine handicrafts in peaceful centuries.

What Father Cancer had done in Guatemala, it began to be said on his visit to the Spanish court in 1547, might be effective with those unregenerate heathen of Florida, those worshipers of the devil, cannibals, child murderers, workers of abomination. Father Cancer was eager to make the attempt.

So that early in 1549, from a small ship from Veracruz, with no soldiers, but only four peaceful and devoted priests and an Indián woman interpreter, Father Cancer looked with eyes as brilliant as any conqueror's at the long low line of the southwest mangrove barrier.

There could have been little outward difference between that great churchman, organizer, leader and power among thousands of other Spanish conquerors except for the coarse habit and the tonsure. There was the same thin long nose in the dark face, the tight control of the lips, the look of race, the purpose, the will. There was the same courage. He was driven, as they were, by a great and single hunger. But there the difference began. They strove for the single prize of this world. This man's goal was everlasting life. It was the one other purpose for which the genius of Spain, at its greatest age, burned with a continuing flame.

The other men with Father Cancer were his close friend, Father Gregorio de Beteta, and Father Diego de Tolosa, Father Juan Garcia and Brother Fuentes.

They had with them in their small vessel, the *Santa Maria de la Encina*, very little but the vessels and vestments, the molds for making wafers for the Mass, the incense, the crosses and candlesticks of their worship, as well as many small trinkets such as the Guatemalan Indians had liked. The Christian slave woman who had been baptized Magdalena in Havana had been caught as a child on this coast. She must have looked strangely at the land rising in a dark-green line widening beyond the shallower sea.

Father Cancer's thought, for after all he was a practical man, was to have landed far north on the east coast of Florida where the Indians were supposed to be more docile; but Captain Juan de Araña sailed them to the west coast north of Cape Romano.

Father Luis Cancer and Father Juan Garcia, rowed by sailors in a small boat, ventured in and out among shallow islands and inlets. The glittering water, the line of sand and inlet and bay and mangrove were empty of people.

Captain de Araña, impatient about the harbor, went ashore the next morning, and Father Luis Cancer, Father Diego de Tolosa, Brother Fuentes and the Indian woman went with him. Within a small bay they saw signs of Indians. Father Diego and Brother Fuentes begged to go ashore. Father Luis Cancer, with some reluctance, gave his permission, and the small boat was held just off the shallows by the oarsmen, so that he could watch the men, and the Indian woman Magdalena, wading in and moving slowly up the beach. Father Diego crossed the sand and climbed a tall tree to stare about him. And then the men in the boat cried out sharply to him because they saw a naked brown man slip out from the underbrush toward the tree, and behind him another, and another, until there were as many as twenty.

Father Diego looked suddenly, saw them, and slid down and stood with his back against the tree as the Indians drew around him. The other priest ran toward that place, shouting. The woman Magdalena, in her Spanish clothes, moved toward the Indians and spoke. They listened, grim and still. Father Luis Cancer suddenly leaped from the boat to sink deep in the soft mud and water as he floundered ashore.

On the dry sand above high-water mark he fell on his knees and prayed. The Indians turned their heads slowly toward him. When he got up he moved at his stately full height and they stood waiting, as still as animals. Again he knelt and prayed. He moved slowly nearer the tree, his face brilliant and serene. He took from his wide sleeves handfuls of the small bright gifts he had brought and smiled that good smile of his.

139

The rosaries, the strings of round bells, the small gleaming knives brought them toward him, snatching and fingering. So Father Cancer got through between their relaxed ranks to the priest whom they had surrounded, who embraced him, a little pale, breathing fast. Then the Spanish priests knelt down, and the Indian woman too, while the other Indians turned and watched them as their voices murmured the litanies and the prayers. Some of the Indians knelt down also, which Father Cancer saw with a great throb of joy. Some squatted. All watched.

Now they seemed friendly enough and Father Cancer and the others went along to a hut with them to ask about a harbor. Father Diego and Brother Fuentes asked to be allowed, with Magdalena, to go by foot to reach that place. Father Cancer was not yet satisfied with these brown men, their stillness, their watchfulness, their blank faces, the heavy voices wheedling for more presents. He would go back to the ship and get more, he told them, and they let him go.

But when Father Cancer had come back he could see nothing of the white men or the Indian woman. A few Indians came down to the water's edge and held out their hands. One of the sailors asked if he might take them the presents, and again Father Cancer agreed, but reluctantly. He watched the sailor wade ashore and the Indians snatch at the things in his hand. And suddenly their hands were at his neck and tight on his arms, and even as he shouted Father Cancer saw him forced to a half run up the sand beyond the bushes. No one was left on the beach.

Until the enormous west coast sunset had faded, the distant greens glowing and darkening, the herons flying inland, the pelicans flapping away, the cormorants moving in trailing black ribbons of wings, the pink afterglow in the east fading, the purple night smoking up from the western water and hazing the world; long after sunset, until the sands shone faintly across water in the starry light, Father Cancer had the small boat rowed up and down, peering and calling anxiously. No one came. It is likely he stood on the ship's deck late in the night looking over at Florida and praying. In the morning the world of water and far sand and mangrove was empty of human forms.

For eight days that small ship sailed and anchored, while the

small boat rowed in and out among the islands and the passes. The dark shapes of fish darted below. The wind shook the leaves. Their hope was that those they had lost would be there before them at that harbor.

On Corpus Christi they found a bay reaching inland. Father Cancer celebrated Mass on an empty beach. The next day, all day, they rowed. Late in the afternoon they saw on shore an Indian carrying a staff topped with silvery palm branches, and another who cried out to them in Spanish, "Come here—come here—sword no—sword no." Father Cancer called out quickly "We are good men" and their far voices echoed "We are good men."

Father Cancer tried to make them understand that the three Spaniards and the woman must be brought back. The Indian smiled and nodded and went away.

The next morning Indian men and a woman waded out to the boat, holding out fish and begging for presents. The woman, bare above her moss skirt like the others, was Magdalena. The very look on her face was changed.

The whole Indian country along that coast was aroused, she said. They expected a Spanish invasion, although she had tried to tell them that there were only four men of peace. The three Spaniards, the father, the lay brother and the sailor, were prisoners in the house of the chief.

That the men were alive was good news. But on board there was a strange Spaniard, Juan Muñoz, who had been captured by the Indians from De Soto's expedition ten years ago and had just escaped to them. He said the Indians had killed Father Diego de Tolosa and Brother Fuentes. He had seen their scalps drying. The sailor was still alive.

The dreadful news plunged the fathers into great grief and dismay. Things were not well on the ship either. Sailors were ill, the meat and fish were spoiled, and the drinking water had given out. The ship was leaking badly. The always contentious captain was anxious to get away. The fathers decided they must go back to Havana for a better ship. All, that is, but Father Luis Cancer.

Father Cancer must have stood a long time, looking over at that shore. His lips moved in prayer. He had no intention of leaving, he told them slowly. That land had been dedicated by the blood of his brothers. He would do the work he had planned, or die under the martyrdom for which he had hungered. It was in the hands of God.

Nothing they could say made any difference. His face was prepared and serene, his glance withdrawn as if to the great moment for which his whole life had been the preparation. One day he spent putting his reports in order. The second day the sharp brightness of the sun, the dark line of coast, were obliterated by gray rain blowing in a sudden storm. The wind still blew hard on June 23, so that the waters were churned bright yellow flecked with white and streaked with plum color, and the distant sand flashed white.

The men got the small boat toward shore with Father Gregorio and Juan Muñoz staring ahead with the greatest anxiety. Only Father Luis Cancer was unaffected, his eyes brilliant and even happy. An Indian climbed down from a tree as they drew near, running back to a mound beyond massed foliage, where other Indians threatened them with clubs and spears.

There was nothing but menace in the sight. Father Gregorio in despair begged Father Cancer not to make the attempt. He called out to the Indians, but they shouted back only, "Is the slave there?"

Juan Muñoz, knowing well the slow death they would give him, stood up in the boat and shouted, "Here I am but you'll never get me. We know you only want to kill us as you killed the others."

Father Luis Cancer said to him quietly, "Be silent, brother. Don't provoke them." Father Gregorio said, "Nobody in the world could be more enraged than they are now. For love of God, wait a little. Do not land."

But Father Cancer, already standing in the bow of the boat at his full height with that look of exultation, stepped overboard like a sleepwalker. He sank and rose up and then went steadily shoreward through the soft mud and water. The boat followed him as far ashore as it could get, but he went on up the oyster shells and the rising sand without once looking back. The Indians moved farther back under the trees.

He walked toward the mound quite slowly and steadily. Once he stopped and went down on his knees and remained rigid in a passion of prayer. When he got up he went forward serenely with the same pace, in the same direction. The men in the boat saw the dark men on the mound staring and motionless.

143

One of those naked figures suddenly darted from the shadows. He held out his hands to Father Cancer, and Father Cancer took them and was embraced and embraced the other also. Then the Indian took him by the arm and hurried him forward, and another ran and seized him, and then others, so that he seemed surrounded.

The helpless men in the boat saw with horror a great wooden club raised and brought down and saw Father Cancer fall, and heard a single great word that he shouted, and the dull sound of the blow. Then his body was hidden by a mass of Indians striking and striking.

Even while the men in the boat stared and crossed themselves and wept, a great hissing flight of arrows came at them from Indians running on the sand toward the canoes. The rowers started from their trance of horror and rowed frantically, frantically gaining the deep water and the ship.

That was the end. Father Gregorio de Beteta, alone of that devoted group, finally got back to Mexico, bearing the news of the death of those others, and of the deliberate and courageous martyrdom of Father Luis Cancer de Barbastro. "Holy Fray Luis," "Blessed Fray Luis," he was called in *The Triumph of Martyrs,* and by the great bishop of Chiaha, Father Bartolomé de Las Casas. He died, truly a martyr, but not more by the savagery of the Indians than by their inability to understand how a Spaniard could be anything but dangerous to them. Father Cancer fell also at the hands of all those other Spaniards who had shed the blood of so many thousands of Indians, in wanton defiance of his own belief that all men are brothers.

That death shocked all the Spanish world, confirming in them the opinion of the treachery, savagery, and ferocity of the men of Florida. No one else would venture to conquer or even approach those Indians, for years after many years.

6

The Conquerors

Tʜᴇ Spanish crown and the increasingly unwieldy colonial organization became aware of threats graver than the Florida Indians.

Piracy was growing to alarming proportions. Reckless men of every nationality and color, French, English, Portuguese, Greek, Mohammedan, white, black or mulatto, in their fast boats harried the Spanish ships. Spain wreaked an individual vengeance on every man, especially Lutherans, who fell into her clutches by all the methods of the Inquisition, as ingenious for torture as the Indians, prison and slave iron and galley, rope, lash, rack and fire. It had no effect. Ships were taken. The cities of the Main were ravaged, citizens were tortured, robbed, murdered, women were ravished, churches looted while the bells tolled horror.

The attack and burning of Cartagena by French pirates brought to a head all Spain's fear of invasion from Europe. In a three years' war Spain defeated France, achieving nothing but promises.

In 1562 the Spanish ambassador to France frantically warned the Spanish crown of a fleet of six ships loading at Dieppe under the command of Master Jean Ribaut, with the encouragement of the Huguenot admiral Coligny, and of the queen mother and her court. But Jean Ribaut and his ships were away before Spain's protest, sailing as no one had ever dared before, straight across the Atlantic, straight across the Gulf Stream, straight to Florida. At Port Royal, a little north of the present St. Augustine, Ribaut founded his colony, which lacked every means of survival.

There was no help for him in France, torn by the great civil war between Catholic and Huguenot. Ribaut fled to Elizabeth of England for aid secretly given even as she had him jailed. A Spanish ship went from Havana to destroy Port Royal, but already its hungry garrison had vanished.

Philip and the Council of the Indies, remembering the Florida Indians, had been reluctant to attempt another Florida colony. If France, impoverished after her civil war, had not turned her thoughts again to the riches of the west, Spain would have done nothing more about that mainland. But Coligny sent René de Laudonniére to build Fort Caroline at the very top and outcome of the Spanish voyage through the Florida Straits.

At once that harbor was crowded with pirate vessels of every kind, swarming out like hornets against every Spanish fleet. English John Hawkins, with his ships crammed with Guinea

146

Negroes to be smuggled to the labor-hungry Spanish islands, made that a harborage.

Spain could ignore it no longer. Even while Philip made formal protests to the French court, a great armada moved out of Cadiz for the Florida coast. At Port Royal, hungry Frenchmen shouted at the far gleam of sails. It was the captain-general adelantado Pedro Menendez de Aviles, for the king of Spain was moving against them.

In all that Spanish empire, for more than half a century now dominated by the graft-ridden power of the Casa de Contratacion, there was no more brilliant or able or honest figure, no more loyal subject of the king's person, than this great seaman, great lord, great fighter, great leader, Menendez de Aviles. He had been one of those restless and fiery boys of an impoverished noble house whom the astonishing drama of his times had made precocious. At eight, he was so restless to be off to a career that they had married him to a girl of another old family, two years older than he. When he was fourteen, lovely Maria de Solis could hold him no longer. With his own vessel he defeated the fleet of the pirate Jean Alphonse. His youth, his boldness, his great quality of leadership brought him vividly to the king's attention, and so to the hatred of the Casa de Contratacion.

The king saw in Menendez a perfect weapon against the corruption of his colonial organization. He took the lucrative control of the whole fleet system away from the Casa, and in 1554 named Menendez as captain-general over both flota and galleones, and all the New World trade. For that honor, the Casa threw him in prison on false but serious charges. The king got him out.

In courage, in force and in commanding ingenuity he showed himself the equal of the great leaders who had preceded him. His eyes were as bright and dark as theirs, his brows as heavy, his noble mouth as firm over his thick brown beard. But unlike them, there was no greed in him. He was to carry on the New World commercial empire, not by cupidity but by organizing genius. He would die a poor man.

Doña Maria de Solis had borne him three daughters and a son, Juan, who grew quickly to a like ability. In 1563 Juan was sent to Mexico as admiral of the year's fleet for Spain. From the crowded harbor of Havana his father must have watched with pride his son's ships move out on the homeward voyage on that curving sea that seemed to swell toward the horizon northward and northeastward from the Cuban coast, and burning to an enormous purple jewel under the long sunset light. The sails stood out there, catching the afterglow. They were never seen again.

Perhaps the key Indians saw the ships blown like birds in a storm. Perhaps their bones were picked clean in the roaring black night of the Atlantic. Nobody knows.

His father's one hope was that Juan might be alive, a slave in Florida. That intruding French colony to the north must also be destroyed. So Menendez as adelantado of Florida sailed from Spain in command of a great armed fleet. His asiento gave him absolute control. He might import Negro slaves or take Indians, as he chose. Of course, he paid for everything and the Spanish crown had not forgotten how to drive a shrewd bargain.

On August 28, 1565, Menendez went ashore from his flagship at the mouth of a northern Florida river and took possession and named the place St. Augustine. He had encountered the French fleet under Jean Ribaut sailing to the relief of Fort Caroline. He took Fort Caroline, killed or took prisoner all the people of the fort, marched with difficulty by land to St. Augustine, fought Indians, captured a group of French from Ribaut's fleet, and had all but about eighteen Catholics among them killed. There was not food enough for both conquerors and prisoners.

Menendez was now master in the north. All the French had been killed except a group that had escaped southward.

When Menendez looked about him at his new country he was enthusiastic. "The province of Florida," he wrote to the King, as if he was the first of all Florida real estate developers, would "bring enormous profits from vineyards, sugar, cattle, ships stores, pearls, timber, silk, wheat and endless supplies of fruit."

"And I assure your Majesty," he wrote, "that in the future Florida will be of little expense, and will pay your Majesty much money and will be of more value to Spain than New Spain or even Peru."

He marched next against and subdued the French who had built fortifications southward near Canaveral. This time, because he had food enough for all, no one was killed. He even spared Huguenots. Spanish and French marched south to the land of the Ais Indians, where he was received cordially, and from there, in two open boats, he shoved off for Havana.

Yet in Havana his old political enemy, the governor, refused him further aid. To finance that venture on which his heart was set Menendez was forced to borrow money where he could. Months were wasted. The ships sent to St. Augustine and the newer colony at Jupiter Inlet returned with news of Indian uprisings, death by starvation and disease. The Jupiter colony had managed to survive by moving south to a river and village they christened Santaluce or Santa Lucia to be called by the French St. Lucie, as the name is today. Still he had not explored the southwest coast nor found a harbor, nor his son.

It was 1566, the 10th of February, that the great captain-general was able at last to sail out of that harbor of Havana with a fleet of seven vessels and five hundred men. He found

149

the channel running northward between the Dry Tortugas and what we call now the Featherbed Banks. There he left the fleet and went forward swiftly in one or two light vessels which could draw more closely inshore to the changeless coastal mangrove.

The water was foamy yellow and the sky ahead was streaked with long mauve banks of cloud as a norther beat down on them. The greater ships were forced to stand far outside as the smaller vessels clung to the lee of some high mangrove island. The boats went on as the hot sun brought the colors burning through pearly morning fogs.

They stared then at the first sign of anything living. A canoe, paddled by a brown naked man, came out of a river mouth. Spanish words cried across water, as thin and clear as the mewing of the gulls, "Spaniards and Christians—Spaniards and Christian brothers—welcome—"

Spanish eyes stared down into an unmistakable Spanish face, cured dark. The words were choked: "God and St. Mary told us you would come. The Christian men and women here—alive —sent me to give you this letter."

He stood naked on the deck, staring and panting. To Captain Amaya he gave not a letter, but a small worn crucifix. "To beseech you, by the death suffered by Our Lord for our salvation, not to pass by but enter the harbor and rescue us from this chief and take us home."

To Menendez in the other boat the man said that they were only twelve men and women left of two hundred people cast ashore. His son had not been one of them. Their own turn at the fires was soon to come. Menendez heard again about the Indian king called Carlos.

The harbor indicated by the captive may have been any of those deep-drowned river mouths of the west coast from Cape Sable to the Caloosahatchee. It may have been Pine Island.

Menendez drew near among the shoals to a beach. The Spanish captive went ahead to bear gifts from Menendez. They could see plainly the Indian chief, "cacique," the Spanish called him, "king" as they held him to be, come down splendidly to the shore in a litter carried on the shoulders of slaves with long floating hair, and surrounded by three hundred breechclouted bowmen.

The eyes in the painted face of that chief, taller than his tallest warriors, pearls and carved shell beads around his neck and arms, his high head tossing with dazzling white egret plumes, stared into the face of the Spanish lord. Menendez stared too. This man was young to have attained such power. His face was keenly intelligent, mobile, except for its proud control. The Indian flowed to his knees in a splendid formal gesture.

He held out his arms before him with the hard palms up, as a man addresses the Beings of Power, until Menendez de Aviles, router of pirates, terror of the French, came pacing slowly to put his two hands into the Indian hands.

Standing among his priests and bowmen, the chief received his presents, a shirt, a pair of silk breeches, and a fine velvet hat. There were trinkets for the women and white Spanish bread, jars of honey and jugs of resinous dark wine. All the Spanish faces turned like one face as a man of Carlos brought forward one heavy small bright bar. Silver from Potosi. There were some handfuls of gold coins, objects beaten out of gold, some pearls, blackened by the fires that had opened the oyster shells, and the sparkle of a few jewels broken from their settings.

Carlos said to the Spanish captive, who translated, that the food he had been given was not enough. They were invited to dine on the flagship. Twenty warriors, as cautious as antlered deer, stepped to the boats behind Carlos. As the sails were swung and filled and the bow headed for the open gulf the Indians started up in anger. But there came the platters of food and flagons of wine and the interpreter reassured them. The ship was put about and let drift. They were free to go ashore, Menendez announced, as soon as Carlos promised to deliver all his white captives and give full friendship to the Spanish.

Carlos promised everything.

That night on shore five Spanish women, weeping quietly because of their Indian children left behind, and three men eagerly leaving their Indian wives were pushed over to the white men in exchange for more presents. The adelantado was invited to pay a visit to Carlos in the great town up the river. But the men who had so long been slaves of the Indians, perhaps through his interpreter Escalante de Fontaneda, warned him that Carlos meant to capture or kill them all.

Menendez was quite prepared to believe them. Next morning a great crowd of singing unarmed Indians came down to the beach to carry the adelantado and his men on their backs to Carlos's village. "Such honor," the adelantado sent back word, "was not for them." So he sailed north again in his small boats, studying the coast. On his return to the bay of Carlos, the great fleet under Captain Las Alas had arrived, and the whole place was swarming with Spanish soldiers already bartering everything they had for Carlos's visible store of gold and silver bars.

Nobles or soldiers, they were all on fire with the rumor that Carlos had hidden somewhere near by a treasure equal to more than a hundred thousand ducats. The Indians had not the slightest idea of its value, the white men argued. They would readily give up a great piece of gold chain set with emeralds, for a common knife, or bars of silver worth hundreds of ducats, for a silk handkerchief or a playing card. A committee of hard-breathing Spanish gentlemen waited upon Menendez to beg him to take Carlos captive and hold him in exchange for that fabulous wealth.

He had not come here, Menendez said, to make anyone rich. He had come to make peace with the Indians and settle the lands for the king. It would be the gravest disaster to ruin everything now.

Carlos observed the swarms of armed men thick as mosquitoes after the summer rains. He could not fight this man. It would be wiser to bind the strange new power to his own. Carlos had a sister, older than he, an unmarried woman, not even beautiful as those small rounded dovelike Calusa women could be, but long-nosed and tall and dignified. He would give her as wife to this great Spanish leader. He said as much to the adelantado. But first the adelantado must visit the chief's town and dine with him.

In the stately text by Menendez' brother-in-law, the writer Gonzalo Solis de Meras, whose sister had been the girl married to the boy Menendez, there is no indication that Menendez took seriously at first this extraordinary offer of Carlos's. He was absorbed in the problems implied in this visit. He would go, but he was not a man to walk blindly into ambush.

When the adelantado landed on the grassy upriver beach where the canoes were drawn up he saw before him on the rising ground the great ceremonial mound where year after year so many Spanish victims had been sacrificed above one of the great Indian towns of the day. As many as a thousand thatched roofs spread around the greater and higher roof of the council house. The ceremonial plaques of gold and silver glittered on their long posts. The murmur and movement of hundreds of quiet dark people were about him as he walked in his finest armor, as grave as to any audience with the king. Behind him were the correct ranks of two hundred arquebusiers, groomed to the last mustache. Over their progress snapped and rolled the heavy scarlet silk banner with the royal arms of Castile and Leon.

Before him, between the Indian crowds, walked Menendez' personal extravagance, his musicians, playing gaily through the sun and sweet wind: two fifers, three trumpets, one harp, one guitar played with a bow, and two drummers sending the long rolling white man's drumming above the trumpeting. But startled Indian eyes followed the strutting of Menendez' small ugly dwarf, making dreadful faces at the squeaking Indian children.

Over the white glaring sand to the shadows of the great central house with its polished raised floor, sweet smelling with new thatch, the white men marched. The crossbowmen took their places all around, facing the crowds. Menendez stepped with his heavy tread up on the raised flooring, and twenty gentlemen in velvet stepped behind him.

Before him on a higher platform he saw the Indian Carlos with a crowd of men about him, and lower down a tall Indian woman, with many small, half-bare brown women shy about her. Under the great peaked roof the light was soft and shadowy, the waiting faces with eyes politely looking away. Beyond the fringed thatch the adelantado could look out on the heads and shoulders of his men, a wall against the glare.

Carlos rose tall and cold to receive, gesturing the Spaniard to his own high place, stately, composed and still. Menendez sat and motioned the chief toward him, who slipped easily into the kneeling position of respect. As his cool palms slid from Menendez' great hairy hands, all the men and women followed him in a long graceful procession.

After that, a crowd of young women with their round arms high in ceremonial gestures and girls whose black, maidenly hair blew about their lovely backs and breasts began to sing. Men began to dance, old men of dignity and young men. The noise rose in long shouting chants, the long line of stamping dancers outside passing and repassing in light and in shadow.

When it stopped, the crossbowmen outside shifted on their

154

hot feet, their eyes blinded. Menendez had prepared a speech written in the Calusa language. He read slowly and carefully the strange words that praised the power and friendliness of Carlos and the beauty of his wife.

There was a ripple of something, perhaps even amusement. Carlos led Menendez to the stately woman he had addressed.

"She is not his wife," the busy interpreter said after Carlos

spoke. "She is his favorite sister, whom he gives to you for your wife."

The burned ears of the arquebusiers, sweating under their armor in the sun, must have heard it. Even Menendez heard it now. But the man who had fought the pirates at fourteen and defied the Casa de Contratacion and wrenched support from the king himself certainly would have revealed nothing now of surprise or discomfiture. He took Carlos's sister by the hand and seated her beside him and went on reading his speech. Everyone saw how the woman's dignity and composure were equal to his own.

The adelantado requested that Carlos's wife be brought in also, and this was done, although now for a moment Carlos seemed a little uneasy. She was a lovely little brown thing, very young, with delicate wrists and ankles and a beautiful body all but naked, except for a moss apron and a great collar of pearls and shining carved stones.

Seeing the Spanish eyes upon her and possibly also upon her pearls, she blushed and drooped her head. Carlos frowned. The adelantado only bowed and asked that she might dine with them. Then quickly the presents were brought in. Menendez with his own hand unrolled the fine linen chemises and bright velvet gowns, and had the interpreter tell the laughing women how to put them on. He gave them small mirrors and watched the tall sister smiling at herself. There were knives and round hawk bells and more mirrors and machetes and hatchets, so that all the formality was broken up as the Indians admired and compared.

Then the food was brought in: fish roasted and boiled, and, a great rarity, a hundredweight of hard ship's biscuit and jars of honey and bottles of wine. The adelantado had his own table linen to make a greater show, and napkins and silver plates and cups and everything elegant in the Spanish manner.

Outside, Spanish trumpets tossed up their high, silver notes, blowing away over the far thatched roofs and the sun on river water. Inside, the fifers and the drummers and the harp and the guitar, which was played with a bow, made music for the feasters, and five or six Spanish gentlemen stood and sang, the long drawling nasal quavers the Moors had left them sounding strange in this primitive remote place. But the eyes of the adelantado, chewing his hard biscuit beside the quiet, erect woman, must have been narrowed as his mind darted here and there for a way out of this extraordinary situation.

The Indian girls outside began their songs again. Carlos sent to tell them, sharply, not to go on. The white man's music was better. But when another Spanish song was over, Menendez rose. He had come. Now he would go.

The Indian's glance must have met his like a knife. There was no need that he should go now, and in the full heat of the day, Carlos said. Now, after feasting, was the time to rest. There was a place prepared for the white lord where he might take his ease. Carlos's sister would join him there, since she had been given to him for a wife.

The adelantado stood very still, with all his gentlemen stiff around him. He must not have glanced at any of their faces, especially his brother-in-law's. In the silence the murmur of all those hundreds and hundreds of Indians surrounding the thin line of crossbowmen rose loud.

Carlos's assured glance glittered a little as it shifted among their faces. He said composedly there were more than four thousand people out there come to see the white man do honor to their chief. They would not endure his contempt.

Menendez spoke slowly. "Christian men," he said, "do not sleep with women who are not Christians."

It is not impossible that many of those gentlemen, and Solis de Meras, his writing brother-in-law, let go their breaths a little.

The Indian gesture that followed was lordly, suave and just the faintest degree condescending. "Naturally," Carlos said, "but since he had taken the white lord for his brother, naturally, he and all his people were Christians also. One blood, one heart. There was no difficulty."

The adelantado drew himself up. It was not so easy as that to be a Christian, he said to the dark face listening politely. "To be a Christian means this . . . " He spoke out of his sincere and firm belief, in full voice and authority. The interpreter's voice, in the necessary pauses, stumbled in its work of translating the rolling Spanish phrases into the so different meanings of Indian words.

At the end Carlos said, "Very well." He had been observing

all the customs of the Spanish. They were superior. Their music and their food were superior. Undoubtedly their religion was superior also. He would adopt it. He had given his sister to the Spanish lord once. Now he gave her again, that she might be taken away and instructed in this Christianity.

Menendez bowed and gave her his hand out of the shadows of that place, down between the ranks of the Painted People, to the Spanish boats at the water's edge. The trumpets were clear before him, the drums thumped hollowly, the dwarf pranced. Menendez marched stately by the tall, half-naked sister of Carlos, her women slipping along behind, toward what unimaginable future.

On the beach of the island where the Spanish brigantines were drawn up, the tents were stained bright orange by the sunset. Fires sparkled against the lavender night before the council of Menendez and the captains reached its conclusion.

The question he put to them directly was, what should he do with this woman? The only aim he had here was to settle the land and make it peaceful, and see that all the Christians were saved from the Indians, and the Indians baptized. To that end, as they knew, he had impoverished himself, had aroused the enmity of powerful persons, had bitten his nails in prison, and had gone deeply into such debts that if the venture failed he was forever ruined. If he ignored this woman now and sent her back slighted— He may have paused then, remembering the fixed ophidian eyes of Carlos.

The bearded faces of his captains may not have been so solemnly perturbed as his own. There had been women more comely in the retinue of the chief's sister. Certainly the face of his brother-in-law, who records this scene without a hint of protest, remained bland.

A captain said bluntly that it was fitting that every attention should be paid to this—lady, and to all who came with her.

Let a great feast be given to them all. Let the lady be baptized and let the adelantado sleep with her. It was a thing absolutely essential to the welfare of them all.

Menendez stood there, a big man suddenly awkward. Was there nothing else to be said? Nothing was said by anyone, nothing at all by the brother of Maria Menendez y Solis.

"Speak to the women then," the adelantado said. The Spanish women who had been captives went to the Indian woman with their arms full of clothing from the ship's chests. They helped her bathe and put on a fine linen chemise and a long velvet gown and pinned her hair high with pins and a great comb, and put a fine gold necklace around her neck. Her women also were dressed in silks and velvets. They came from the tents and paced the sand by the great fires to the place where Menendez and his captains sat, ruddy with wine, the sternness gone from their faces, all the men-at-arms and the Indians who had come silently to the feasting, amazed at that woman's still, tall handsomeness.

The fires blazed. The wine casks were broached for everyone, the scent of broiling meat came on the wind. The music sounded as men's voices roared old drinking songs. Men and women ate together, and drank and laughed.

Far out beyond the Spanish fires the night lay dark over the unknown land. The night of the sea stretched westward beyond the lights of the Spanish ships, low and yellow as the lowest stars.

Whether or not it was a true priest who made the sign of the cross over the kneeling velvet figure of Carlos's sister, we do not know. When she rose up she was greeted as Doña Antonia because Menendez prayed to St. Anthony that he might find this place and make a good beginning of his endeavor. The relaxed Spanish captains caught at the waists of laughing Indian girls.

159

There was a tent for Doña Antonia and tents for the Indian women, and presently there was an end of feasting and only the sentinels paced along the darkened beaches beyond the embers of the fires where the musicians and the crossbowmen and Indians and the dwarf lay and snored, and only some solitary priest prayed beyond.

Afterward, long afterward, Menendez made a good act of penance for that sin. But the Church, which excuses the Matanzas massacre of the French, does not forget this night as a blot upon Menendez' Christian record.

In the days after that, Doña Antonia's plain face was radiant as she looked after her lord with eyes luminous and soft as those of any other bride. She had fallen in love with him, whom she believed implicitly to be her husband. She would be a good wife to him in the Indian manner, humble, affectionate, modest and, in public, mute. All her small women were happy too. Carlos seemed satisfied, stalking watchful as a heron at the head of his troop of bowmen, watching his men feast and reach freely for more, as in the camps of kinsmen.

Menendez told him he must have a great wooden cross erected, that every morning Carlos and all his people, as well as the Spaniards, might go to worship. And now, Menendez said, raising his voice a little, Carlos must give up all his idols to be burned and worship only the Christian God.

The interpreter had a little difficulty trying to make clear the word "idols." Carlos looked at him in silence. The cross, yes. That could be built. But—idols? Perhaps the white man meant the carved masks of the clan dance rituals hanging in the council house, the fine carved and painted deer masks, the fox masks, the wolf masks; symbols of the greatest possible power. The white man offered only this cross to take the place of the proved and ancient things, the pipes, the drums, the rattles, the posts of the ball games, the secret magic bundles of the priests that held all the strength of the sun and the

lightning, the earth's force and the wind, by which the evils of
the natural world were made into good. All reverence might
be given to the cross also. But to destroy all these other things—
The richly stocked subtle mind of the Indian must have stared
aghast into an empty world of evil and darkness. No, these
things had been given the Indian long ago by the Strong Ones
from the Sources of Power. Could a man put out the sun? No,
he said strongly. No. His eyes, which had seemed asleep, revealed themselves in a jetty look that Menendez met with
shock. These things would not be given up.

Carlos was suave. Let his sister go with the white lord to
be instructed in the way of Christians. When she came back
she could tell him what he must know and do.

Menendez saw that was as far as he could go then. The cross
was set up and he and all his Spaniards knelt before it, crossing themselves in companies. The sound of their prayers whispered like locusts in the sun. Doña Antonia and her women
knelt behind. Carlos knelt, never quite bowing his erect head.

The adelantado and all his men, the captains and the musicians, the dwarf and Doña Antonia and her Indian women, and
the Christians who had been captured and released by Carlos
went on board the brigantines to go out to the waiting ships.
But at the last minute three of the Spanish women would not
go. They had been sobbing all night long because of the children
they had left behind with their Indian husbands in those remote Everglades villages. Now they stared with scalded eyes
as the last Spaniards shoved off the boats. The three would
never see Spain again. But they sobbed no longer.

For Menendez, on board his flagship, there was bad news
of hunger and sickness, and mutiny even, at his colonies of St.
Augustine and San Mateo. Ais Indians of the east coast were
attacking Santa Lucia. While the busy decks resounded with
the noise of hoisting anchors and creaking blocks, he was absorbed already with Esteban de Las Alas over the papers,

letters, lists, mounting records of indebtedness. He must be off at once in the fastest brigantine to the east coast, leaving de Las Alas to take the ships to Havana, beg the governor for money, and send a ship for supplies to Yucatan if necessary, if the Florida venture was not to fail.

Let the Indian woman be turned over in Havana to Regidor Alonso de Rojas and his wife, to be instructed in Christian doctrines. Perhaps at the last, remembering his manners, he strode hurriedly to bow his farewell to Doña Antonia, watching with that look of a recent bride still on her plain face. He would see her in Havana.

It is perfectly certain that the adelantado never gave her another thought. If the friendliness of the Indians was secured by what was at best a mock marriage, it was well enough. He would have been startled to know how completely the Indians, and especially Doña Antonia, believed it was real. He would have been dumbfounded to learn that because of that belief of hers all that part of Florida below the great Lake Mayaimi, the east and west about the Everglades, was forever lost to him and to Spain.

Up that monotonous long length of east coast above the Head of the Martyrs he sailed, the coast he was to pass and repass so many times, in anger, in impatience, in necessity and in frustration, but never with any less courage or eager will. His thoughts were busy with plans to bring in settlers and cattle and farmers to make gardens, orange groves, fields of barley and sugar cane to feed his garrisons. There must be a way across this incredible peninsula, by some of those waterways the Indians and captives spoke of, so that he could go quickly from the west country of the Calusas to the northeast colony.

But first he would make an expedition northward into the country called Guale, to establish forts against the French Lutherans. Oh— and let the Frenchman be murdered secretly, who had escaped him before and was inciting the Indians to outrages against the Spanish at the cape called Canaveral.

In June he was in Havana again, desperately in need of supplies. He was refused again by Valdarrama, licentiate of the Royal Council of the Indies, and Asorio, the governor of Havana. They looked with pleased, cold eyes at the dismay of this bustling man who had dared to go over their heads to the king. His letters repeated over and over his conviction that Florida must be held, that "The souls and natives thereof may be saved and his Majesty's purpose be furthered, which is to prevent the Lutherans from setting foot in that land, and to endeavor to implant the gospel therein."

But then from Spain arrived his faithful brother-in-law, Solis de Meras, with money he had raised privately, and some friars and soldiers, and letters, along with money, from his gentle and patient wife, who prayed for his success and his safe return.

The dark Indian woman also waited with increasing sadness for her lord's return. She had done everything she had been told. All the ladies of Havana had been amazed at her proud, grave demeanor and her discretion. She had learned the prayers and doctrine quickly so that she had been baptized a true Christian. It happened, as it did often to those Indians who came from clean waters and open living in Florida to the filthy, crowded Havana streets, that all but two of her people had died. But when she learned that the adelantado had returned she was happy again.

It was a serious thing about the death of those Indians, Menendez felt. If anything like that happened to her, Carlos would be sure she had been murdered and there would be hell to pay. He must get her back to Florida at once.

So that presently, with his captains, and the musicians playing before him, in his best gold-embroidered suit with the great star of the Order of Santiago blazing on his shoulder in the torchlight, he went to call upon her, making a great noise and stir in the narrow stone-paved streets. In the little room in the light of the candles, he saw her. Her eyes were turned away, the look withdrawn, dark, Indian.

The gowns and glittering laces he brought her she received with dignity, unsmiling. She spoke only a few words, intense words, to the interpreter's question. She wished that God might kill her, because the adelantado had not sent for her when he first returned, to take her to his house, as a husband should, to eat and sleep with her. The adelantado thought for a moment, standing blazing there in his own light, his hand upon the great cross on his shoulder. "Knights of that cross," he told her, "when they returned from an expedition against their enemies, could not sleep with their wives until eight days had passed." He said also, thinking only of the look on her face at that moment and never once of the time to come, that he wished the eight days were over because he loved her much.

She laughed then, with tears in her eyes, and was happy for an hour while he sat beside her, listening to his musicians and drinking wine. He told her they would soon go to her country.

That night, when the adelantado was asleep in his own bed, Doña Antonia, with a Spanish woman who told the guard she had been ordered to bring her there, slipped into his room. The adelantado woke, startled to see her there, holding up the candle so that her great eyes were in shadow.

He said, "What's this, sister?" to the white woman. Doña Antonia spoke softly, but fiercely. She begged him to let her lie in a corner of the bed, not touching him at all, but so that she might tell her brother Carlos that they had slept together. For without that he would know that the adelantado laughed at her, and his anger would be unforgiving.

The adelantado called his servant and sent her away with presents and, he thought, satisfied with the glass beads and the mirrors and the chemises. But it is clear that the Indian woman truly loved him and desired only friendship between her people and the Christians. He never understood that.

In the morning, in the dancing light over the sea, they all embarked for Florida. The small patache went quickly in the fine wind and in three days they had come again to the villages about that bay of the Caloosahatchee. The adelantado did not dare land, because of the few men he had with him. But he promised her that he would come back and build a house and live there among them and they would all be Christians. Perhaps then the Indian woman may have looked long at his face and known finally that he never once had intended to be a true husband to her.

Carlos came to meet them in a barge made of two canoes lashed together, tall in the full panoply of his pearls and feathers. He and his sister greeted each other formally, but the families of the Indians who had died in Havana went away weeping.

After a fine dinner on deck, and more presents, Menendez asked Carlos if he was ready now to cut his hair and be a Christian. And if he would give up now all the Christian captives he still held, here or across the Everglades in the Tekesta country.

Carlos asked leave to speak apart with one of his chiefs When he turned back he said it was impossible for him to do so now or his people would rise and kill him. But after nine months let the adelantado return and it might be done.

Menendez then suggested that Carlos's nearest relative, who was also his heir, with two more young Indians might go with him to Havana to be made Christians. The word "hostages" was not used, but Carlos understood perfectly. The young men might go.

The desperate condition of his other colonies took all Menendez' attention. In Havana, for all his begging, he got nothing. He was forced to sell his gold-embroidered suit for five hundred ducats with which to buy a little meat and cassava roots, and pay sixty-five men to sail with him in a captured frigate back to those north Florida forts. But at St. Augustine he was rejoiced to find a great fleet from Spain with supplies and soldiers sent because of the rumors of a Lutheran invasion gathering in France.

His days thereafter were crowded with all sorts of activities, but he had time to make an exploration up the St. Johns River to discover some possible waterway to the country of Carlos.

He was to return only once more to the country of Carlos, where he had sent his Captain Francisco de Reynoso with thirty soldiers to erect a blockhouse on the Caloosahatchee, and to explore it to the lake. Reynoso returned with Carlos's heir, who in Havana had been baptized Don Felipe, and took Doña Antonia and five or six chiefs back to Havana. Perhaps for the last time the poor woman went with a lingering hope of her great lord's return. She was not with child by him and Carlos's restlessness and suspicion increased.

Menendez did nothing to allay it. On his last visit to Carlos he sailed north again with them to the bay of Espiritu Santo, which we call Tampa, for the purpose of finding a cross-country waterway to St. Augustine, which was so much in his mind. He made friends with Carlos's worst enemy Tocobago, the chief of that wide landscape of islands and villages and beaches. He gained the release of some of Tocobago's Calusa captives and established a garrison. But by his friendliness to Tocobago he gained Carlos's final and undying enmity. And Doña Antonia's bitter reproach.

It had been his intention to take certain Tekestan captives of Carlos back to Biscayne Bay, but bad news called him to Havana. The captives were freed and made their own way across the Everglades to the headwaters of the Mayaimi and waited his coming with renewed friendliness.

166

After that, there were no more quiet days for Menendez. War had broken out with the Indians beyond St. Augustine. In France a storm of protest had been raised at the news, only just arrived after much more than a year, of Menendez' massacre of the French. The north Florida forts were temporarily destroyed by de Gourgues. Menendez was raised by the king to the rank of captain general of the west, with a personal fleet of twelve galleons, two thousand soldiers, and two thousand ducats as a grant in aid.

All his grandeur, all his ability, all his leadership in that Florida which he had hoped to make particularly his own had failed. Long after, he wrote to Pedro Menendez Marques, who was to take the place of his lost son Juan as his heir and administrator: "After the salvation of my soul, there is nothing in this world that I desire more than to see myself in Florida to end my days saving souls."

But before he died he had lost all hope of it. He was convinced at last of the relentless hostility of those southern Indians.

There was only one course left to be taken with them. "They are so bloodthirsty . . . that war should be made upon them with all rigor, a war of fire and blood, and that those taken alive shall be sold as slaves, removing them from the country and taking them to the neighboring islands. And if this be done, no Indian will be living therein, and if any vessel shall be wrecked, the people can easily go in safety to the fort at St. Augustine and take safety there; and this will arouse fear and be a great example among the friendly Indians."

But after Pedro Menendez de Aviles was dead, there was no Spaniard left who could succeed where that great captain, lord of the fleets, confounder of pirates, scourge of the French, had so completely failed.

So, after all, there were no conquerors here, but the Indians themselves.

167

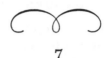

7

Three Hundred Quiet Years

THE work of Menendez went on in southern Florida a little while after him, before the Indian world, like a rising tide, engulfed all trace of the defeated white men. There followed three hundred years in which history was the wind running over the enormous waves of the saw grass. Men and women were only small, far-off figures, rarely glimpsed, forgotten and unknown.

Such a glimpse gives us a picture of what was probably the first settlement of white men in all south Florida. It was along the shore of that great southeastern bay called "Viscaino" or "Biscayne" according to Fontaneda, because of the wreck there of a ship owned by the man called El Viscaino from the Spanish province of Viscaya. There within the key called "Cabo de los Martires" and later "Key Biscayne," the sun-glistening sea opened to the south.

Along the mainland ridge in ferny potholes, springs gushed and brimmed, from which, since the time of Ponce de Leon, coastwise Spanish ships had filled their water casks.

At the sandy end of Key Biscayne, at Cape Florida, the Tekesta Indians had a favorite feasting place. On moonlit nights, they roasted the turtle eggs laid in the sands and the fish they speared in the westward channel and the crawfish from the weedy shallows. Fires there gleamed often in the nights. A Spanish ship which in his first year Menendez had sent to the relief of San Felipe in north Florida had been seized by sixty mutineers who sailed her south. In a hurricane they were lucky to find shelter in the lee of Cape Florida. The canoes of the friendly Tekestas found them hunting for food along the sand. At the village of thatched huts by the Miami River, among many smiling brown faces, a tall chief awaited them, speaking a few words in Spanish.

News of the honors paid the great Spanish lord who had taken Carlos's sister to wife had come long since to Tekesta by canoe, through those intricate ways threading the saw grass which no white man would learn for hundreds of years. Tekesta gave his heart in friendliness to the mutineers.

The Spaniards were feasted on coontie flour cakes and broiled venison. They ate also huge broiled steaks of manatee, tasting like the best beef, which these Tekestans hunted with great excitement, as was described by the Spanish cosmographer, Lope de Vasco:

> "In winter, all the Indians go out to sea in their canoes, to hunt for sea cows. One of their number carries three stakes fastened to his girdle and a rope on his arm. When he discovers a sea cow he throws his rope around its neck and as the animal

169

sinks under the water, the Indian drives a stake through one of
its nostrils and no matter how much it may dive, the Indian
never loses it because he goes on its back. After it has been
killed they cut open its head and take out two large bones,
which they place in the coffin, with the bodies of their dead,
and worship them."

The Spaniards learned with surprise that there was a village
of white men a little farther south, and there they at once made
their way along the paths winding through the dense hammock.
They came out from green twilight to sunlight on a fine bluff
where to the east the sea opened and were greeted by white
men who lived in thatched huts with comely Indian wives. They
were the mutineers from San Mateo who had worked their
way south along the beaches and by the kindness of Tekesta
allowed to settle here. They meant to stay.

The Spaniards from the ship sailed without them. We know
nothing more of these first white settlers.

In San Antonio a blockhouse had been built for Captain
Reynoso and his men. Indian women came amiably to live with
them. But because of the Indians' distrust Reynoso was unable
to get on with his explorations up the Caloosahatchee or obtain
the promised release of white captives. The Indian women began to whisper to their white lovers that Carlos intended to
have Reynoso killed.

Menendez had still one last hope of conquering Florida, the
Christian Church. To his mind, there were no men so capable
of enduring the dangers and sacrifices of Florida as the members of the Society of Jesus.

Now, no Jesuits had ever been sent to Florida, chiefly because
of the hostility of their general, Francisco Borgia, to the supreme ecclesiastical power assumed by the Spanish crown.
When Menendez asked for twenty-five priests, Borgia permitted three to make the Florida attempt. Of these, in a ship-

wreck north of St. Augustine, Father Martinez was promptly murdered by the Indians. The other two, Father Jean Rogel and Brother Villareal, sailed again from Havana with Menendez on his last visit to Carlos. In San Antonio a chapel was built for Father Rogel, who was able to teach the Indian children the four great prayers, the Credo, and the Ten Commandments only so long as his supply of Cuban corn meal held out. The more the father saw of the customs of the Indians, plural marriage, blood sacrifices, the worship of idols, the more vehemently he preached and protested against them. So that Carlos and his priests became openly enraged.

In broad daylight a great ceremonial procession of priests and cult members moved from the Council House to the fort. The masked and stamping dancers surged to the very gateway of that Spanish stockade. Father Rogel in his vestments walked out to face them, raising high the cross. He would have been torn to pieces if Captain Reynoso and his soldiers had not rushed out, to put themselves between that mob and the priest, and to hit furiously about them with their clubbed lances. The leader went down at Father Rogel's feet and the others fled.

Therefore, on another day when Carlos in his full paint and plumage was carried out in his litter on the shoulders of the berdaches, a single Spanish crossbowman put an arrow through his throat. The figure of the Indians' greatest chief lay dead in the sun. The crying of his women raised shrill as sea gulls. The long burial ceremonies beat like pulses through the appointed nights.

Reynoso had expected Carlos's heir, the young man educated in Havana and called Don Felipe, to be friendly. But when as chief, Felipe announced he would marry his own sister, Father Rogel threatened to refuse him baptism. It made no difference to Felipe. The wedding went on. The priests and the people were openly hostile.

171

The end had come. Reynoso and Father Rogel and the garrison gave up San Antonio and returned to Havana.

On the east coast, Brother Villareal, who had spent his first days in Florida with Father Rogel in San Antonio, studying their language with the Tekestan captives, was left on Biscayne Bay by Menendez on his way north. The chief there, receiving with joy his people freed from Carlos, readily agreed to allow three young Tekesta Indians to sail with Menendez on the long voyage home to Spain. These young men, the first from Biscayne Bay to be taken to Europe, attracted much attention at the Spanish court by their intelligence and their dignity and their fine manners.

But on the Miami River Brother Villareal was left with a few soldiers to begin his mission. We have a letter from him, the first, as far as we know, ever written from the village that so many centuries later was to be called Miami. It was written in January, 1568, to Father Rogel while he was still in San Antonio, on the west coast.

My reverend Father in Christ:

. . . I and all of us here remain in good health, glory to God who helps us to endure in this land trials which would appear insufferable in another place. I say this for we have had for the past three months or more a plague of mosquitoes so bad that I spent several days and nights without being able to sleep an hour. On top of this we suffered some days for lack of food. At this time a majority of the Indians went to an island a league from here to eat coconuts and palm grapes. No more than thirty remained here . . . I have been teaching the doctrine to the Indians up to fifteen years of age, the others will not come to the lessons although I believe there is none who does not say he wants to become a Christian . . . There are many here now because some of the nearby villages have come in to help in building a house of the chief. They now have food from the whales [manatee] they kill and from fish. With

172

all this the young chief is very fond of the Christians and it seems he will become one. He had a sick child and brought it to me saying through the interpreter that he didn't want them to do witchcraft over 'it but wanted me to pray and make the sign of the cross over it. In another day it was well, thanks to God.

I need to have your reverence inform me the manner in which I can explain to these people the immortality of souls and also the manner I must use in baptising and whether there are not some doubts or difficulties in administering this sacrament, also whether I should go and visit them when they are sick because then they readily consent to become Christians and I am in doubt whether they do this in fear or in lack of understanding or whether they do it to get some meal of corn. . . . These Indians take matters with so little seriousness that I am frightened.

. . . I live in a house with a soldier and we get along well, thank God. We hold fiestas with litanies to the cross. We have put on two comedies, one on the day of St. John when we were expecting the governor. This play had to do with the war between men and the world, the flesh and the devil. The soldiers enjoyed it very much. Some of them, however, have resented my not going to Havana to obtain them more supplies.

I have tried to make the Indians like me as your reverence commanded and bought a little corn for this purpose, for as I said I live apart and they give me a nation little larger than that of the others so that up to now I have had nothing to give them and when there is nothing to give them I believe there is little friendship. . . . From Tekesta, January 29 of 1568, from your reverence's unworthy servant in the lord.

Francisco

The trouble between the brother and the soldiers went back to that old quarrel between the Spanish crown and the Jesuits. They refused to abide by the wise and peaceful counsels of Brother Villareal.

173

While the Indians crowded twice daily into the square where the cross was set up for worship, the soldiers went among their huts and seized what food they could find and offered such indignities to the people that they were roused to an anger which Brother Villareal could not quiet. The soldiers killed the uncle of the chief. The Indians rose then in earnest, tore down the cross, burned their thatched huts, and took to the dense hammocks south. When the Spaniards from the garrison attempted to get to the springs the Indians ambushed and killed them in such numbers that only a few, with Brother Villareal, were able to escape up the outer beach to St. Lucia.

There was trouble, hunger and fear in all the remaining colonies of Florida. Some time after April, 1569, the adelantado sailed for Florida for the last time. Father Segura, the vice-provincial at Havana, was left at Tekesta with that brother of the chief of Tekesta whom Menendez had taken to Spain. With his safe return the friendship of the Tekestans was temporarily restored. The crosses were set up again and the people came quietly along the paths from the hammocks or down the river in their canoes to the landing to worship there. Yet that could not last. The priests could neither tolerate nor understand the Indian ways. They tried to put a stop to the cheerful roughness of the ball games, at which ribs were broken and heads cracked. They preached and threatened against the custom of child sacrifice at the deaths of chiefs, the strange burial customs, and all that complicated magic which the white men held was the worship of the devil himself. The Indians had no patience with these tiresome white men who did not bring them enough presents and were always interfering with important things. The mission at Tekesta was therefore given up and the fort abandoned.

All the forts Menendez had with such difficulty and care established, St. Lucia among the Ais Indians above Canaveral,

Tocobago at Tampa, San Antonio in Calusa Bay, which was to have been so important, and this one at Tekesta, were gone. The Spanish power in all this region vanished, leaving only a few words of Spanish and a keener understanding of the white man among the Indians.

North Florida was still to be Spanish for a long time. The Spanish fathers went on baptizing and teaching the Timucuans soon to be docile farmers, fruit raisers, cattlemen and ingenious idlers, oblivious of the fact that in the Caribbean, as in Europe, the power of Spain was rotting at the core. The tribes of the lower coast, which now no longer were held together strongly by Carlos and his chiefs, lived their scattered, primitive and satisfactory existence, hunting and fishing and watching for wrecked ships down the keys and along the coast.

One heritage only the coming of the white men left with them which was to affect them more deeply than any invasions. From time to time, from the wrecked men they captured on the sands came contagion, or it was brought down from the Spanish country to the north where they went on long trading expeditions and raids for stealing the Timucuans' Spanish cattle. They were ravaged by the white men's diseases, by yellow fever and smallpox and measles, all of which killed them off like flies. Their dismembered bones were heaped in mass burials of as many as five hundred at a time, only hastily covered with scattered earth at the tops of burial mounds slowly piled higher, far beyond the once populated lagoons. The ashes of villages were scattered.

The great heap of bones which gave Key West its name, from "Cayo Hueso" or "Bone Key," was not so much evidence of a battlefield, as has been claimed, but proof of the death by disease of a whole village or villages. There were fewer people up and down these coasts. And so there were fewer wars and no more blood sacrifices.

175

The New World was changing fast. The French had taken islands in the West Indies and held the mouth of the Mississippi. England was entrenched in Jamaica and northward in America, land-hungry men worked their way inland, beyond the great holdings of the English kings and their favorites, seeking land.

But for long years the Indians of the Florida keys still watched for wrecks. The Spanish treasure fleets were less and less imposing. English or Dutch or French merchant vessels wallowed

under full sail up the indigo Gulf Stream. From the Bahamas and the shallow inlets and lee of the keys, the last of the pirates harried them. Piracy as an organized affair was slowly broken up by tacit consent of the English, French and Dutch governments, now that they also owned property in the New World. Only the frowsy, disreputable lesser ships of the last of the pirates lurked in these waters. Pirate crews lighted fires at the tip of Key Biscayne, known also to English navigators as Cape Florida.

No one knows exactly when that site became a camp for white men, refugees, wrecked sailors, drunken pirates. Probably it had existed among the ashes and potsherds of Indian cooking fires off and on since Menendez's mutineers. It must have been there in 1696, when the barkentine *Reformation*, Joseph Kirle commanding, was storm-blown beyond it in the dangerous month of August, from Jamaica on a voyage from Philadelphia. On board, besides sailors and Negro slaves were five passengers, notably Jonathan Dickinson, a Quaker, and his wife and baby.

The ship was cast ashore upon "a wilderness country looking very dismal, having no trees, but only sand hills covered with shrubby palmetto." But even in August, because of the hurricane, there was wind and very cold rain, and the survivors huddled about a fire in the gray day.

There the Indians of that coast found them, Indians earlier called Ais or Santaluces. The careful description we have from Jonathan Dickinson is all that we know of them in this century. They were naked as always, except for breechclouts of plaited straw, were very "furious and bloody," and carried the invaluable large Spanish knives we now call machetes. Everything the white people had and the supplies from the wrecked ships were taken away.

Some Indians were hostile, but the chief was kind. Dickinson and his people asked about St. Augustine and St. Lucia. The Indians tried to persuade them that both lay farther south. But Dickinson insisted, and slowly they were taken north on that difficult journey.

The Dickinson party suffered not only from the Indians but from the country itself. There were mosquitoes and sand flies and at night it was extremely cold. The Indians shared with them, finally, the food they always ate, oysters and clams and fish, sea grapes and cocoplums in abundance. But of the palmetto berries which were offered in quantity, Dickinson wrote: "But not one among us could suffer them to stay in our mouths;

177

for we could compare the taste of them to nothing else but rotten cheese steeped in tobacco." Dickinson was the first to bear testimony to the untidiness of primitive Indian living, the dirt and flies and vermin.

He saw something of their ceremonies, the long drumming night after night on a skin stretched over the top of a pot and the shaking of rattles and the animal howling of the Muskogee hunting dance.

> This day being the time of the moon's entering the first quarter, the Indians have a ceremonial dance, which they begin about eight o'clock in the morning. In the first place comes an old man and takes a staff about eight foot long . . . and in the middle of this staff is fixed a piece of wood shaped like unto a thigh, leg and foot of a man, which is set fast in the ground standing upright . . . Then another old man comes up and sets up a howling like unto a mighty dog; withal making proclamation. This being done the most of them having painted themselves some red, some black, some black with red, having their sheaves of arrows at their backs and their bows at their hands, being gathered about this staff; six of the chiefest men in esteem amongst them, especially one who is their doctor, and much esteemed, taking up the rattles makes a hideous noise, standing around this staff, taking their rattles and bowing without ceasing, unto the staff for about half an hour . . . Then they all begin a dance, violently stamping on the ground for the space of an hour without ceasing.
>
> Thus often repeating the manner they continue till about three or four o'clock in the afternoon; by which time many were sick and fainty. And then being gathered into the Cassee-key's house they sit down, having some hot casseena ready, which they drink plentifully.

But the most important testimony Dickinson gives of the forces for change already at work on the Indians relates to their friendly attitude toward the Spanish and the transference of all that ancient hatred of theirs to the English. The Catholic fathers to the north had worked well. Their kindness and the prosperity and freedom of the Christian Indians were well known now all over Florida. Even the unbaptized south coast Indians were now tolerant of them.

The only English words Dickinson heard an Indian use was "English son of a bitch." "For I do believe," he wrote, "that they had had some of our nation in their possession, of whom they had heard such an expression."

Undoubtedly they had been sworn at by many English captives. But it is even clearer that they hated the English who lurked about the lower coasts or drank and howled by the fires at Key Biscayne, because they were not only petty pirates but aggressive and ruthless slavers, selling every Indian they could lay hands on in the West Indian plantations.

By the latitude worked out by the *Reformation's* mate, we know that they went aground five miles south of that inlet called "Jupiter" where the St. Lucie River makes the northernmost outlet of old swamps and watercourses which eastwardly drain Lake Okeechobee, a kind of northeast shoulder of the Everglades. The town of the Jeaga Indians, then, according to Dickinson, was "Hoe-bay," derived from "Jeaga" which the Spanish called "Ho-ve," and the English again made it "Hobe," as in "Hobe Sound." "Jove" to the English also meant "Jupiter," so it is "Jupiter Inlet" to this day.

The wretched little party worked their way northward and out of any coast that could be said to be near the Everglades. That is the only glimpse we have of the Indians of that day.

Far to the north, Carolina plantation owners grew more and more enraged at the constant escape of their Negroes to the Indians and to the Spanish domain. New men clamored for rich Indian lands. There was trouble on the border between Spain and its Indian allies and the Carolinians and theirs. A new colony of Georgia was established along the seacoast, as a buffer state. The slaveholders overran it. The settlers pushed into the deep Creek country and spoiled Indian hunting grounds. The Creek Indians in their restricted country saw their prosperity going and tribe turned against tribe like dogs in a too-small kennel. English and French and Spanish set their Indian allies against one another, destroying settlements, scalping and raiding and burning, with all the horrors and hatreds of Indian and white border warfare.

In 1702 Captain James Moore of Carolina with his allies the warlike Yemassee of the coast made war upon their neighbors the Creeks. They were paid so much a head for Indian captives, to be sold as slaves in Charleston. In 1704 the Yemassee decimated the Timucuans of Florida and made long raiding expeditions through sparsely settled Spanish Florida, capturing every escaped Negro slave they could lay their hands on and taking Indians also. There was a great slave trail which the Yemassee followed down the St. Johns and the Kissimmee to Lake Okeechobee, and so down the Caloosahatchee, where they enslaved many peaceful Calusas. They came down the east coast and destroyed the last of the Ais and the Jeaga and moved down to Biscayne Bay and got drunk with their friends, fellow slavers and small-time Bahama pirates at Key Biscayne. Thousands of Indians from the Everglades region were taken into captivity.

On the lower west coast, however, Spanish traders from Cuba were welcomed among the last villages of the Calusas. They sailed up the winding green Caloosahatchee to the plains about Fisheating Creek, the herds of half-wild cattle were butchered and their hides shipped to Havana in a profitable trade. It is not likely at all, as has been stated so often, that these cattle were descended from the few stolen from De Soto's expedition, so long before. What cattle there were, and hogs along the east beaches of Okeechobee, had been stolen and brought in from the northern Spanish missions.

Spain still held Florida in spite of the claims of Carolina. But the Spanish crown was at last aware that it must make some additional effort to strengthen its hold on the east coast if the wrecking, the piracy, and the slave raids were to be curbed. Yet now Spain was powerless to control by violence. If a settlement and fort were to be established on Biscayne Bay, which dominated the keys and the coast, it must be by the peaceful strength of the fathers of the Church, and a handful of soldiers to clear out that camp on Key Biscayne.

In June of 1743 an expedition of priests and soldiers was therefore ordered by the ranking head of the provincial government in Cuba to sail from Havana. They discovered the key Indians were friendly and learned much about Indian ceremonials without understanding any. They took for an idol a carved wooden ceremonial tablet of the Fish clan and remarked upon the magic arts claimed by the chief who was also the priest. And the Fathers noted that these Indians were in the habit of getting roaring drunk on the white man's alcohol. At the moment, they were at war with the Tekestans, by whom many had been killed.

The fathers went often between Havana and the villages on the keys, the chief of which was near Matecumbe Key, where the mounds of the elder Indians still stand. These Indians, like the others of the area, were not interested in the Catholic religion. His Excellency, Señor Don Juan Francisco Gomez de Hercasitas, the governor of Havana, as it was recorded in *La Historia de la Compania de Jesús en Nueva Espana*, "decided that such a situation could not be allowed, that the Indians must become Christians, not only for the salvation of their souls and for the glory of the Church but to ensure the safety of the Spanish ships along the Florida coast."

181

The same record continues the narrative very well:

The padre rector of the college of Habana sent the Father José Maria Monaco and Father José Xavier de Alana, who sailed from Habana on June 24, 1743. . . .

At Cay Frances [French Key] they met a Spaniard who was on a hunting trip who told the fathers that the key Indians together with the Indians of Santaluce had left for Santaluce for celebration, and that the Santaluce Indians intended to sacrifice a child to add to the solemnity of the occasion.

This news saddened the fathers, who at once sent two men in a canoe telling them to hurry and to beg the Santaluce Indians to stop the sacrifice. They arrived only a few moments before the sacrifice and their request was granted without much difficulty by the savages.

On the 13th of July, the fathers arrived at their destination among the Florida keys and went to visit the chiefs of four or five tribes, the Maimies, Santaluces, Mayacas, and several others.

They told the Indians that they had come to them at the express wish of the governor of Habana to introduce to them anew the glories of the Catholic religion.

The Indians did not receive them as well as they had hoped. They told the Fathers they had never had any business dealings with the Governor of Habana, nor asked any favors of him, neither had they asked the Fathers to come to them. The Indians were so threatening in their attitude that the Fathers were compelled to return to their schooner, without having been able to get the Indians to accept the clothing, hatchets, knives and other gifts ° ° ° ° sent by the Governor. They deemed it best to wait a few days before approaching them again, thinking if the Indians were given a little time, they might be willing to accept the instructions of the priests.

Finally conquering their fears they went ashore and built a small hut in which they celebrated Mass, sang hymns to the praise of their beloved Father, St. Ignatius, and brought the

182

Eucharist out for a public adoration. Then they waited to see what they could expect from the Indians. A few allowed themselves to be baptized, but for the most part the Indians said that if they became Christians it would be because they would expect to be fed, clothed and given plenty to drink at the King of Spain's expense.

Father Alana, in the meantime, with the help of the people on the schooner and some of the more friendly Indians built a small fort in triangular shape, with about sixty-nine foot sides, the bulwarks and watchtowers were on the angles and built of rock, the rest of the fort was wood. Each of the angles commanded a view of either the road to the village, the jungle, or the sea. When the embankments and moat were finished, they erected a pole and with very solemn ceremony raised the flag of Spain.

After everything was completed, Father Monaco decided to stay, sending Father Alana back to Habana to inform the governor of their work . . .

Father Monaco kept with him twelve soldiers and a corporal to aid in guarding the fort. He then started to try to educate the Indians in matters of health. Every year many children died of smallpox; drink and smallpox killed a good many men. Father Monaca started a vigorous campaign to ensure care for the sick, and insisted that preventive measures be used to halt the spread of smallpox. He would not forgive remission in anyone, as he wished to assure the safety of the Indians, and he felt that by kindness, patience and care he would be able to convert and teach the older Indians.

However, in a very short time the governor in Havana ordered Father Monaca back to Habana, and a little later ordered the destruction of the fort, as he feared it might be taken by the English or some of the Indian tribes.

It was Spain's last and feeblest attempt to resettle the Everglades coast. In north Florida her ancient hold was weakening. The English of Carolina destroyed the Apalache missions and

183

demanded the return of slaves escaped to the Indians and the Spanish. And although the Spanish governor hotly refused to give up men considered to be free Spanish subjects and armed his Indian allies to raid the English settlements in revenge, Spain's day on the continent of America was over.

In the West Indies a triumphant English fleet ravaged where John Cabot had not dared to go. Spain's greatest stronghold of Havana was captured. Spain was only too glad to give up Florida to get Cuba in return. So that in 1763 Florida became English, and the proud flag of Spain sailed no more past the coasts it had never conquered. The three hundred year list of Spanish governors who had hardly set foot on the shores of south Florida were over. Unless there are more documents in the archives of the Council of the Indies or the records of the Catholic Church, this is all we know.

Except for the coconuts about the coasts, the Everglades were as they had been for four thousand years. Only the people of the Glades were changed.

The Tekestas and the Mayaimis of the lake had disappeared. Only the scattered Calusas were left, ranging throughout the area. It has been repeated often that after 1763 they left for Cuba en masse. I do not believe that there was ever a time when the Glades were empty of villages. I believe they kept to themselves by the islands and the rivers until they were roused again, after three hundred years. Their identity, their very name, would be lost in a new name the white man gave all the Indians here, a name which for all later history would mark the terrible days to come.

8

The Free People

T HE name was "Seminole."

The word was Muskogee to begin with; "iste," man, and "semole," free. In the poetic Indian fashion it meant "people of distant fires." At worst, to the contemptuous white man, it meant "outlaw" or "runaway." But the people most accurately known as Seminole preferred to speak of themselves as "Ikaniuksalgi," "the people of the peninsula."

Americans used the word to describe all those tribes and remnants of tribes, separate, often warring among themselves, who moved into upper Florida, emptied by raids on the descendants of the ancient Timucuans and of the Apalache mission people. South there were only the "Spanish Indians," the last of the Calusas.

Long before the name "Seminole" was used, when the Glades people of lower Florida were still cut off from the rest of the continent by the archaic people of north Florida, a last wave of Muskogee-speaking people came from the west. They were a valiant and energetic lot whose legends described their long migration as if they had emerged from caves in the western mountains, "the backbone of the world," and walked toward the rising sun. They crossed the Mississippi and dominated the earlier tribes already living in what is now Alabama and Georgia. In the centuries to follow all these people who lived along those innumerable creeks and rivers running from the hills to the Gulf and to the Atlantic were by the English called "Creeks." There were Upper Creeks, near the mountains, and Lower Creeks, near the Florida border, when the Spanish fathers eventually Christianized the Timucuans.

There had been always in the Creek country two main language groups. There were the Creeks and the others who spoke Muskogee. There were other tribes who spoke a language called "Hitchiti." Between these two there were memories of old wars and ancient bitternesses.

The most independent and fiery of the Hitchiti-speakers were a people called "Mikasukis." Before 1750 the Mikasukis, feeling the pressure of the whites and at war with the Muskogees, moved down into Florida and settled for a while about a lake near Tallahassee spelled still in the old way, "Micoosukee," before they drifted south again, hunting even to the Caloosahatchee. It was their Hitchiti word by which the old Calusa name of the lake, "Mayaimi" later became changed to "Okeechobee," "Big Water." Their able chief, in the days to come, would be Arpeika, called "Sam Jones."

The Muskogee-speakers who would be the nucleus of the

186

later "Seminoles" came into Florida from the northeast. They were led by a man incorrectly called "See-coffee the Cow-keeper," whose name was Chipacasi or Se-pe-coffee. His father had been the brilliant "Emperor Brims," the leader of what he planned would be a general uprising of Indians against the British of Carolina, but which failed for lack of co-operation. Chipacasi and his people moved down into the safety of Spanish Florida. Some of the defeated Yemassee who were Hitchiti-speakers, it is thought, came to Florida also, and later fused with the Hitchiti-speaking Mikasukis.

There was a tribe of Talasis, Muskogee-speakers, whose lands were taken for the new capital of Florida Territory, and their name adapted to "Tallahassee." They moved south to a town on the Hillsborough River. Later their great chief would be Tiger Tail, or Thlocko-Tustenuggee, a suave man who knew white men thoroughly from the time when, as a boy, he had begged on the streets of Tallahassee. He also learned to lie. His own people thought him important. His brother, Nethlok-Emathla, was a greater war captain, both honest and intelligent. But he could never sway the young men as Tiger Tail did.

There were odds and ends of other Indian tribes roving about the Florida country, a few Yuchis from the northeast and some Choctaws from that independent republic of lower Mississippi whose language is thought to have been so similar to that of the Calusa, with whom they had trade relations.

Last, a group of Upper Creek warriors under King Philip worked their way down to Florida. They lived completely by themselves at first, under that sensible elderly chief who wanted peace but had every intention of dying, if he could not live, in Florida. His two sons were young then, Octiarche, silent and stubborn, and brilliant mercurial young Coacoochee, the Wild-cat, who from boyhood led his own band of fiery young gun-men.

187

In the Alachua plains the village of the chief Micanopy was the wealthiest of all in horses and cattle stolen from the whites and in the nominally held, very useful escaped slaves. Micanopy's right-hand man would be Jumper, a talkative man, a plausible orator, and shrewd. Little Cloud, brave, cruel and bitter, would be his boldest war captain.

There were over eighty villages in all of Hitchiti-speakers or Muskogee-speakers keeping to themselves, raising cattle, hunting or fishing. There were a number of villages of Negroes. There were the last of the Calusas still, far south. Near them was a chief of sound judgment and ability who had been exiled from his own tribe, possibly of Mikasukiś, who moved down below the Caloosahatchee. He married a woman of Spanish blood and was a link between the old Indians under their watchful chief Che-ki-ka and the others who were to move down into the Everglades.

These, then, were the people in Florida, whom the white men were to call "the treacherous Seminole." All used the Muskogee titles of war rank and peace rank, which the white men often thought were their own names: "micco" was chief; "tustenuggee," subchief; "emathla," captain; "heneha," top warrior or lieutenant. Inspired medicine men were "hilis-hadjo." The titles of honor achieved in battle were "hadjo," reckless, "fixico," heartless, "ya-ho-lo," black drink hallo-er. Their old men were "beloved."

All of them lived by the old customs of the Muskogee-speakers until they moved far south and adapted their ways to the practical living habits of the Calusas, the centuries-old dwellers of the Everglades.

They were all people of more practical political ability than they were religious. Their leaders were hereditary if they showed ability, but more often they grew to higher rank by proving their ability in peace or in war. They were bound by the relationships

188

of family and clan and tribe, formalized, exact and mannered. Descent and clan were always on the mother's side. They spoke to their elders in fixed terms of respect and were informal only within their own age groups. But religion still played a most important part in their living. Their priests, or medicine men, were important chiefly as they were effective. They must be good men, in the Indian sense, if they were to inherit the powerful medicine bundles of the highest rank, the "yaholi." They had to go through years of preparation of prayer and fasting and study with their elders until they became plain doctors or "medicine grandfathers." In some cases, for practical work with childbearing, women were also doctors.

The doctors were supposed to be able to heal, with brews of herbs, sweet bay, willow, cedar leaf, snakeroot and all the others, by chanting or sucking evil from the patient's forehead, such Indian diseases as the dog sickness, the rat sickness, the mosquito sickness, the fever caused by dreams of fire or of the bear or the distracted wandering that is the giant disease.

Their magic had to be strong and protect warriors in battle and bring weakness to their enemies. The people must be strong in peace, obeying the rituals. If they failed, new magic must be attained.

They were, they are, a hearty people, with a great gusto for living. They loved feasts and dances. There was the harvest dance in the fall when they paid respect to the flesh animals by which they lived, imitating the way they moved and shook their heads, or howled, or bellowed. They danced then, along with the deer dance, and the wildcat dance, and the men's feather dance, with sticks topped with white egret plumes, the old bison dance of the Mississippi Valley. They dance it now.

In the moons of spring when the corn was growing in the corn patches they gathered for the dances that preceded the great season of the "Buskita," the fast, of the green corn dance.

In Florida the corn ripened earlier so that in the Everglades the bundles of sticks by which the days were counted were sent around to all allied tribes for the full moon in June.

Then in a great cleared place called a "Square Ground," set with logs at the four quarters for the Old Beloved Men, the priests, the warriors in their prime, and for the boys glassy-eyed with long fasting and prayer before their coming manhood initiation, the priest kindled the New Fire. Old things had been destroyed. Old fires were quenched. This was the time of forgiveness and renewal, of trials and punishments, of marriages, of the conferring of honors, and of the long secret councils of the elders.

The chief ceremony of the green corn dance, and of other festivities requiring purification, and religious exaltation was the "black drink." The Indians called it "asi." It was a strong concoction of herbs which the yaholi brewed in a big pot, chanting and blowing tobacco smoke. It was composed chiefly of *Ilex cassine* or *Ilex vomitoria* which grew everywhere in Florida except very far south, or the common button snakeroot. As the strong tealike stuff boiled, gourds were filled and consecrated youths raced to serve first the elders and the chiefs. The young men stood before them as they drank to give the black-drink cry, held until the gourds were empty, the long shout, the "Asi-ya-ho-lo."

The black drink was so quickly emetic that the men walked from the Square Ground to vomit, that habit which all Indians seem to exercise with ease. Herb drinks were passed to the women crowding with the children beyond the lighted square.

The councils went on for three days, or another three days: the songs, the long prayers, the exhortations. Men who were to be punished for murder or adultery or for marriage within a clan were exiled or sentenced to death, or with the guilty women were given the "long scratch" that with snake fangs or garfish teeth slashed them deeply down the back from neck to heels.

Boys to be initiated bore without flinching the test of splinters stuck under the skin of the arms and lighted. Some clans initiated the girls also. A long line of men moved forward to the medicine man to hold out their arms for a lesser scratching, so that the evil blood might run out and they would be cleansed for the new power.

Then in the nights the long lines of the dancers, men, or men and women, or women by themselves with turtle-shell rattles on their ankles, stamped and moved and wove patterns about the fire, to the buzzing of rattles, the squealing of wooden pipes, and the hollow thudding of skin-and-pot drums. After that they ate the new corn and feasted and rejoiced in the new year.

They all played the fast exciting Muskogee ball game. A consecrated post like the one to which victims had once been tied was topped with a mat which must be hit with a stuffed ball of sewn deerhide, by rackets of looped wooden sticks laced with skin thongs. Men in two teams played the double-racket game, a furious and reckless competition, with no rules, in which rival villages joined, in a kind of substitute for war, betting and yelling in excitement over victory or chagrin in defeat. There was a shouting rowdy game between men with rackets and women playing with the flat of the hand, at which the watching people screamed with laughter.

But to gain honor the young men went on raids across the borders of their enemies, to steal cattle and attack from ambush, and take scalps in ancient Indian war fashion.

These were to be the people of the Everglades. They were not all allied in friendliness. Until they fought the same war, under their own leaders, against their common enemy, the Mikasukis and the Seminoles always hated each other.

191

Among them now, and none the less "Seminole," the true runaways were the escaped Negro slaves.

These were the tall fierce black men of the most warlike tribes of the West African coast, taken only in war by the great slave-trading nation of the Dahomeys, their enemies, sold to slavers supplying the West Indies and the continental colonies.

The most intractable among them were the Ashantis of the Gold Coast, called then Coromantees, whom especially the French and Spanish of the Caribbean learned not to buy, pre-ferring the more docile slaves of the Niger. There were other fighting men among those slave cargoes from the African bar-racoons later not taken through the West Indies at all, but straight by the Middle Passage to the American coast, the rangy round-faced Senegalese from Dakar, the Ebos and the Egbas.

These were the men, especially the Ashantis, who in Jamaica and the British West Indies were the first to revolt, called Maroons from the Spanish word "cimarron" meaning "outlaw." It has been suggested that there might be some remote con-nection between the words "Cimarron" and "Seminole," al-though historians do not approve of it.

These men were called Maroons in America also. They began that endless series of uprisings and escapes which put the fear of the black man into the white man's heart and gave the lie forever to the white theory that the Negro was happier in chains.

There had been an immediate understanding between the tall hardy blacks, soot-black, brown-black, blue-black, and the Seminoles. The Mikasukis and the Calusas had little to do with them. But the others shared that innate love of liberty which was not exclusive to the colonial white man. They had similar customs. Both were used to communal ownership of land, worked for the good of the whole tribe. Both believed in plural marriages, a modified matriarchy, and a close, extended family.

192

The uses of drums and rattles, of priestly magic, of ceremonial headdresses and face painting, were not dissimilar.

The hardheaded realism of the Negro made him prompt to adopt the obviously superior gods of the conquerors and he blended his beliefs cheerfully with those of the Indians. His rich culture of animal myths and folk tales was to take its place among the Indian stories. It is hard to say whether "Br'er Rabbit" was first Negro or Indian, since the trickster tales occur with both. The obi superstitions among the Ashantis and their. kind, not the vaudou of the Dahomeys, which was to remain in the Spanish and French West Indies and enter America only in Louisiana, fell in easily with the Indians' store of magic and taboo.

Besides, the Negro had a great deal to add to the Indian way of life, especially his agelong preoccupation with agriculture, which made him always a harder everyday worker, on his own land, than the migratory hunting Indians. The Negro's never sufficiently recognized legal shrewdness, which in Africa had produced his system of tribal courts, with his practical gifts of gab, argument and windy eloquence, which the Indians call "nigger wit," were to serve for well or ill the councils of his Indian allies, masters and relatives. He fought more fiercely even than the Indian. He had more to lose.

The effect of that alliance between the two enslaved peoples was to be felt ultimately to the remotest depths of the Everglades.

All these Indians and the escaping slaves had been forced down into Florida by the continuing pressure upon them of the white man, French and British, and later the even more aggressive American. The Creeks in their prosperous old country had at first welcomed the traders from the colonies. But as the sound of white men's axes grew louder from the advancing clearings the Indians began to learn how they were hemmed in.

Landless white men looked greedily at Indian hunting grounds and fields. All the wiles and diplomacy of leaders of the Creeks like McGillivray who tried to make alliances with French, British and American, in turn, deals that would offset one another, were helpless before the long slow avalanche of white encroachment.

The white men wanted land and they wanted slaves with which to work it. The Indians who gave safety and freedom, or a nominal slavehood, to escaping Negroes and loyally refused to give them up to the slave catchers, had both. That was the whole story.

Spanish Florida gave all Indians and escaping slaves freedom and citizenship. By 1654 there was trouble because of that between Florida and the British colonies to the north, each claiming land far into the other's borders, each raiding and harassing the other. This would go on for a century. War broke out between England and Spain. England captured Havana and in 1763 Spain was glad to exchange all Florida for her great central port in Cuba. Then war between the English and American colonies was inevitable. At the end of the Revolution England exchanged Florida for the Bahamas and Spain was given control over Florida again.

In all this time, no matter who won, it was never the Indians. The Upper and Lower Creeks had not been able to achieve any sort of solidarity among themselves. They had allied themselves with the various warring white governments. Their people were scattered and killed; their country, their ancient prosperity, broken up. The movement begun long before of Indians and Negroes down into the Peninsula was accelerated. But at the end of the American Revolution men of the new colony of Georgia swept over the Florida border and down into the

Indian country, stealing cattle and slaves. Spain was too weak to prevent it. It was the Indians who fought back against the Americans then, in whatever ways they could.

The British Tories defeated in the Revolution left for the West Indies, especially the Bahamas, with their slaves and some Indians. They established immediate relations with Key Biscayne and the east coast by which they supplied the Indians with free powder and arms against the Americans, just as the Cubans supplied ammunition to the lower west coast.

The British attitude toward emancipation increased the fury of the planters of Georgia and Carolina. Already in the Bahamas the smaller plantation owners gave their slaves every opportunity to buy their freedom as farmers and fishermen. All slave ships that put into Bahama ports were impounded and their cargoes freed. All escaped slaves reaching these islands from the Florida coasts automatically became "free men of color." It was a great encouragement to runaways.

It was at this time that a group of Seminole Indians of some Negro blood escaped the slave catchers and sailed for the Bahamas from Cape Florida in canoes. They settled at Red Bay on Andros, which may have been named for them. Their leader was Scipio Bowlegs, an Indian medicine man. There is still a Bahama song about "Bowlegs in the Trees." They took with them corn, peas and pumpkins, and kept themselves apart from the Negroes on the other side of the island, whom they called Congas. It is said there is no evidence now of their Indian blood, but until recently they used bows and arrows and lived in American-type log cabins.

In Georgia the Americans were more determined than ever to have the Indian land. Some of the chiefs were cajoled or bribed into signing treaties: the Treaty of Galphinton, the Treaty of Shoulderbone, the Treaty of New York, which promised definitely that no more land would be taken from them. Still the white men were not satisfied.

In 1808 the importation of Negro slaves into the United States was forbidden. Slave prices, the value of escaped Negroes and of Indians with Negro blood, rose enormously. Spanish Florida was at once invaded again by bands of slave catchers. After Andrew Jackson had defeated the British at New Orleans in the War of 1812, he moved into the Creek country against a great Indian religious uprising called the "Red Stick War," led by Prophet Francis. After Jackson's terrible victory at Horseshoe Bend, the broken tribes of Georgia and Alabama were forced to move to the forbidding lands west of the Mississippi, which the white men thought they would never want. A few Creeks who had been American allies were allowed to remain.

At the insistence of the slave states Florida was purchased from Spain in 1818. And although the Treaty of Cession had explicitly stated that the inhabitants of His Catholic Majesty's Territories should enjoy all rights of the citizens of the United States, that was never understood to include the Indian, who had been a Spanish subject.

Slavery again, as it had from the first, brought history to the Glades. Andrew Jackson, first territorial governor of Florida, who truly epitomized the freedom-loving frontier American, saw the Indian as the frontiersmen's bitter enemy. He said that all the Seminoles, by which he meant every Indian in Florida, should be removed to the West. The Negroes who had been free among them, and their free-born children, must be returned to the slave gangs.

There was no way by which the new territory of Florida could round up and ship off the Indians; short of war. But if they were roused to acts of desperation the American government might send the army. This was the announced intention of the Legislative Council. Border toughs moved down among the Indian villages, stealing cattle, destroying crops, taking Negroes. Many of the Mikasukis and some others began to move quietly down near, or into, the Glades.

They lived there much as the Calusas and the old people had done. Their thatched huts, the chi-kees of the Calusas, were cool and comfortable in the hot weather. In cold northeasters they put up skin or cloth windbreaks. They built their cooking fires under high thatched roofs, logs set like spokes of a wheel to be pushed in as they burned. They ate what everybody around the Everglades had always eaten, turtles in great numbers, fish boiled or broiled, venison, ibis, fat young deer, and turkey. For vegetables they had beans and squash, a little corn ground in a tall log mortar with a long wooden pestle, palm cabbage, and above everything, ground coontie, or compte root, grated and sieved and made into cakes or boiled to a soft gruel called sofkee. This was drunk from the communal wooden sofkee ladle. They raised bananas and knew where the sour orange trees and limes grew, planted from Spanish seed.

The Americans who began to settle middle Florida thought there were still too many Indians. It would be easier to herd them all south, to those unknown swamps which nobody wanted.

Seventy chiefs and warriors were collected at Camp Moultrie near St. Augustine and made to sign a treaty which required the Indians to move south of the Withlacoochee River on the west coast. Five million acres would there be provided for them with "protection against all persons whomsoever and to restrain and prevent all white persons from hunting, settling and otherwise intruding upon their lands." The sum of $15,400 was to be divided among them for their property in north and west Florida and they were to receive annuities for twenty years.

197

The United States acknowledged the Indian rights to Florida lands with the Camp Moultrie treaty. The settled opinion of the Supreme Court of the United States was that "the Indian title is certainly to be respected until it be legitimately extinguished." The treaty was not in any possible legal manner ever extinguished. It was merely forgotten.

The Indians got out of their ancient locations and the flood of frontier settlers moved in at their heels, and over into the new Indian lands. It was an overt violation of the treaty to which no one paid attention. Yet, by an act of the Florida legislature, the penalty of thirty-nine stripes of a lash on the bare back was imposed on any Indian who violated it.

An army officer writing from Camp St. Johns in December, 1837, wrote that the treaty of Camp Moultrie "was maintained by the Seminoles with the greatest integrity."

The white men began to think that the new Indian lands to the south might amount to something after all. It would be simpler just to ship the Indians west and forget them. In May, 1832, although the treaty of Fort Moultrie had several years yet to run, a group of chiefs were gathered together, by threats and promises, at Payne's Landing on the Ocklawaha River to sign a newer treaty. This promised them an equal amount of land in Arkansas. They were to be paid annuities and $15,000 for their stolen cattle, but they must pay $7,000 as an indemnity for the Negroes whom they refused to give up. Seven chiefs· were to be permitted to visit the West and return with a report.

Micanopy, fat old hereditary chief of the main group of Seminoles, refused flatly to sign, as did his subchief King Philip and the great majority of the others. Only fifteen of the chiefs were induced to sign the Payne's Landing Treaty, including old Billy Bowlegs, or Bolek, from some remote French ancestor "Beaulieu," Alligator from Tampa Bay, Jumper and Charley

Emathla. There were many more tribes and villages in Florida which were not in any way represented.

Among the young Indians present was one described by an army officer as being of striking appearance: "His eye calm, serious, fixed; his attitude manly, graceful, erect, his thin and close-pressed lips . . . his dignified and composed attitude, his perfect and solemn silence except during his sententious talk, the arms firmly folded on the protruding chest." He had burst into a passionate speech against immigration to which the old men listened as if they saw in him the very Source of Power finding tongue for them at last.

This young man was Osceola. His name was not Powell, as has often been said, although his grandfather was a Scotsman. He was born a Lower Creek on the Tallapoosa River and he was never a chief by descent, but only a brilliant and natural leader. His name was derived from his title "asi-yaholo" or "black drink Hallo-er."

The seven Seminole chiefs who went west reported that the lands assigned to them were occupied by their old enemies, the Lower Creeks. The conditions of all the displaced Indians were deplorable.

Of that seven one was a Negro, Abraham, typical of those Maroons for whom and with whom the Indians fought. Abraham had been owned and freed by Chief Micanopy, who had the highest opinion of his shrewdness and his fighting ability. He must have looked a good deal like that other famous Ashanti, Toussaint L'Ouverture of Haiti, lean and withered, very polite. But here even Abraham's wits were not sharp enough. The seven men, while in Arkansas, were induced to sign a so-called "Additional Treaty" promising immediate removal, for which they had no authority whatsoever. To the Indians in Florida it was only another instance of American bad faith.

The United States itself did not approve the Treaty of Payne's Landing until two years later, which further confused everything. General Wiley Thompson, the Indian agent, called a meeting in October, 1834, with the principal chiefs and sub-chiefs at Fort King, which is now Ocala.

The somber chiefs assembled in council all night long about the council fires. They agreed not to emigrate, and to resist. They also agreed to treat as an enemy any man of any tribe who accepted the white man's terms. This was probably the greatest single council attended by the greatest number of chiefs representing the greatest number of assorted and scattered tribes then in Florida. It was perfectly clear from their action that the Treaty of Payne's Landing, which the government was still thrusting upon them, was never formally ratified by them.

Their spokesman before General Thompson was now that rising young leader Osceola.

He spoke. It was the desire of his people to abide by the Treaty of Fort Moultrie, he said, by which the Indians had promised, and had kept their promise, to remain south of the Withlacoochee. Eight years of that agreed and ratified time had not expired. The chiefs assembled, Osceola said, "did not intend to give any other decision."

It must have been a singularly impressive sight, the young man, his brown hard body half-naked, a few feathers in his hair, beads around his neck, and the chiefs behind him with their impassive faces, the picture of a great race dying, and fighting its fate.

The keen dissimilar faces of the Americans, officers in good uniforms and gold braid, must have been the greatest possible contrast. Perhaps they never looked full into the Indian faces. Perhaps their eyes looked beyond them with the white man's

passion for the future, for land and slaves or power and un-
limited progress.

The intelligent Governor Eaton of Florida and many other
prominent Americans argued that right and justice was on the
side of the Indian, that the treaty could hardly be legal, that
to remove them by force meant war. But Benjamin F. Butler,
the attorney general, held that the treaty, although not yet ratified by president and Senate, was valid. It provided for the removal of every last Indian in Florida in three lots, in 1834,
1835 and 1836.

General Clinch of the army and the Indian agent, General
Wiley Thompson, insisted it could all be done at once.

"Let every measure short of war be taken," wrote the secretary of war to the general. The transports were already waiting
at Tampa Bay, to take the Indians to Arkansas.

The Indian council of the largest group of tribes met and
fasted and prayed and smoked their pipes, while their priests
called upon the Ancient Powers. It was the Everglades and
the Beings of Power of this sun and this earth and this grass
and this water that had given them strength before. To abandon
them now was to render the Indian naked and defenseless.
To cling to the past, to defend themselves here, to fight, to resist,
were the only ways they knew.

General Thompson called another meeting in April, 1835.
He swore that if they refused to emigrate they would be driven
out by force. He insisted that each chief now present should
come forward and sign a paper acknowledging that the Treaty
of Payne's Landing and the Additional Treaty of Fort Gibson
were both binding to the entire "nation."

There was a long silence. Eight chiefs, either impressed or
promised beforehand good prices for their cattle and slaves,
came forward to make their marks. Others, called on by name,
only shook their heads and sat or stood like stone. Among these

201

were the old chief Micanopy, Jumper, Alligator from Tampa Bay, and Arpeika called Sam Jones, the intractable Mikasuki. Osceola, when his name was called, walked forward deliberately. As the eyes of his elders followed him, fixed in shock, he said clearly, facing the table, "The land is ours, we want no

agent." He moved his arm in one lightning gesture. The Americans stared at his knife quivering a little, stabbed into the table, through the long white paper.

The chiefs behind him let out their breaths in a long grunt.

"That is the way I sign," Osceola said and pulled his knife out and turned his straight brown back on the red face of General Thompson.

The general shouted. Aides got the irons on Osceola and hustled him to the guardhouse.

At the end of four days, still refusing to sign, Osceola was set free.

The Indians were given until January, 1836, to prepare to leave. They tried to get powder from the agency store. General Thompson refused to sell. Osceola, curiously enough, as if still believing he had rights and that the general could be convinced that this alone was an act of war, tried to argue with him. The general had him thrown into jail.

Osceola was told he could go if he promised to bring in seventy warriors ready to go west. When he nodded, or grunted, and they accepted that as his word, they must not have noticed that his face, which had been young and eager, was now set in flint.

Already, along the borders beyond the Withlacoochee, crowds of settlers waited to take possession of lands they had once considered worthless. Slaveowners came down to look over and claim surrendered Negroes.

Then Charley Emathla, who had started to bring in four hundred of his people to Fort Brooke, to go west, having on his person a handkerchief full of gold he had received for the sale of his cattle, was ambushed and killed. The gold was scattered about his body. The Indian council had ordered what Osceola did. There was a general drift of Indians into the Everglades. The entire number still in Florida, including the Negroes they refused to give up, was about three thousand. Against these General Clinch's seven hundred regulars were thought to be enough. War was taken for granted.

General Thompson himself was the first man to die. Walking with another officer about a mile beyond Fort King, in the pleasant sunshine of December 28, 1835, they were both shot and scalped, and their scalps cut up and divided among the attacking Indians. The store was burned and other men killed. The soldiers of the fort stoutly returned the Indians' fire. A man escaped to give warning. Osceola, who had led them, left them firing at the fort to gallop his lean horse to another attack.

Major Francis L. Dade, with eight officers and one hundred two soldiers, had already been on the way from Tampa to reinforce Fort King. They were guided by Louis Pacheco, the slave of a Tampa woman. They had not imagined that his sympathies would be with the Indians who freed his kind. Louis had sent word to Osceola.

Major Dade and his men moved at the pace of the oxen drawing his six-pound cannon. The morning of the fifth day, December 28, along a trail through pine country, a deadly fire blazed from the palmetto clumps. Major Dade was killed instantly. Half his command died with him.

The rest rallied quickly under the shouts of their officers. "There was a little man, a great brave," Alligator said admiringly afterward, "who shook his sword at the soldiers and said 'God damn!' No rifle could hit him!" Yet he died.

Cannon balls passed over the heads of the leaping, yelling Indians. The men who loaded them were shot. Six survivors had thrown up breastworks. Their powder gave out. The Indians came screaming over and killed them. Two other severely wounded men had managed to crawl away and reach Fort Brooke with the alarm.

By four o'clock, on the scene of the massacre, all the dead were scalped. Old Micanopy, who had been forced by Jumper and Alligator to fire the first shot, was moving back to his camp when, late in the day, Osceola bucketed in from the Fort King attack. He brought many goods from the looted store, but took nothing from the Dade Massacre, no·money or watches from the white men's pockets, but only the scalps and Major Dade's uniform.

That night in the Wahoo Swamp, Hilis-Hadjo, the medicine man, dedicated with full ceremony the ten-foot sacrificial pole, to which the drying scalps were hung. All night long about the pole and the sacred fire, with drums and rattles and the white man's scalding liquor, they danced the wild, stamping dances of the first victory.

9

War in the Glades:
Fighting Retreat

THE word was "war."

It blazed all along the white settlements and echoed in panic as far as Georgia and Alabama, carried by frantic, galloping men. Fright and anger took the place of the jubilation with which the frontier people had waited across the border for January, 1836. The Dade Massacre was the single act by which the whole wrath of the American nation was detonated, like a chip knocked off a shoulder.

Everywhere in sparsely settled middle and north Florida log cabins and plantation houses were deserted. Men hurried with their wives and children to the small "forted up" settlements, to stand about armed and angry on the street corners in the dust of later-coming ox carts or racing horses or hoofs of cattle under the shouts and shotlike cracking of "cracker" whips.

Seven days before the massacre the Legislative Council of the territory was to vote on dividing off a large portion of Monroe, the single county of south Florida, to make a second. Mr. Richard Fitzpatrick, of Biscayne Bay, president of the Legislative Council, had proposed that it should extend from north of Bahia Honda Key to a line running to the coast from the then Lake Macaco. The county seat would be at Indian Key, but sometimes the court would sit at Cape Florida. At the news of the massacre, the new county was named Dade County. There were only eighty-five white people in the whole region.

In the Everglades, Indians were hastily planting new crops, drying deer meat and grating coontie root. A little meal stirred in hot water over a secret gleam of fire was all that a man needed, half fed, half fasting for the warpath. They were ready for the long plunging trips to ambush.

Now they attacked. Sixteen plantations in east Florida were destroyed in January, cotton gins, stores and houses and crops were burned, men and women shot at and killed. Fort King was still surrounded. All the tribes had put aside their old grudges against each other to fight under their several tribal leaders against the common enemy. They were thought to be at most a force of 1,661 warriors and 250 fighting blacks.

Congress called out the troops. Southern states called for volunteers. Brevet Brigadier General Duncan L. Clinch, Brevet Brigadier General Eustis, Brevet Major General Edmund L. Gaines, General Smith, Lieutenant Colonel Twiggs, com-

206

manded regulars, militia and volunteers. There was haste, confusion, a divided command, and no planning whatsoever.

There were battles about the Withlacoochee, some won by Indians, some won by the Americans. Congress passed a law to provide rations for the white settlers driven from their homes, which for years to come would keep the settlements crowded with idlers who would oppose any measure by which the war might be stopped. Claims for damage would be paid to over eight hundred people in thirty-two settlements from St. Augustine to Tallahassee, and as far south as the Manatee River, in supposedly Indian country.

South on Key Biscayne in 1825, a Mr. Walter (or Waters) G. Davis had purchased land in the name of his wife, Mary Ann Davis, from the Vargas grant. Three acres at the southern end had been deeded to the United States government, which had erected there in 1827 a lighthouse called Cape Florida Light. The Davises hoped to bring down a colony of "respectable wreckers" for legitimate aid to wrecked vessels and to prevent the running of powder and supplies from the British to the Everglades Indians.

Strange white men were here too. Two men came up from Key West and stole skins from an Indian camp and murdered the Indian owner as soon as he got drunk on their whisky. These were the "Spanish Indians," the remnants of the Calusas.

One day thereafter, John W. B. Thompson, the lighthouse keeper, as he was going to the dwelling house, heard a slight noise behind him, turned, and saw Indians. He shouted to his old Negro and ran toward the light. The Indians shot, hitting his hat, but he and his Negro slammed the door just as the first running Indian reached for it.

Thompson had three muskets which he shot from an upper window. The Indians yelled and fired back until dark. Then they set fire to the door and the flames spread in the oil that ran out from bullet holes in the lighthouse tanks. He retreated to the top of the light with the Negro as the flames roared up the inside stairs.

The two men, already singed by the flames, went out of the lantern tower and lay down on the two-foot platform. The lamps were on fire, the glass bursting, the flames running along the planks. Their flesh was burning in their burning clothes. Mr. Thompson threw down the shaft a small barrel of gunpowder he had carried up with him, thinking it would put them out of their agony. It exploded and damped the fire but it blazed up again. The Negro was wounded and lay presently dead, half roasted. In the intense heat Thompson had to sit on the balcony with his feet outside, and these were at once struck with many bullets. The staircase was burned so that the Indians could not get up it.

In the light of the waning fire the Indians began looting and sailed off in Thompson's loaded sloop. He lay bleeding and helpless with a burning fever as the sun rose and beat on him all next morning.

Boats from the U. S. schooner *Motto* rescued him by firing twine made fast to a ramrod from their muskets, by which he hauled up a tail block and a rope and two men, who got him safely down. He was taken to hospital in Key West and for a while, until it was restored in 1838, the lighthouse was a smoke-blackened wreck.

The war went on. Then came summer, when white men could not fight. The Indians went back to the Everglades, hunting, harvesting, and under the glaring summer moons, in the Glades' cool breath, held their green corn dance.

General Scott was relieved, complaining about the difficulties of this outrageous country. Governor Call took over. The troops idled about the settlements. The settlers idled on government rations.

They sent down Major General Thomas J. Jesup who had just put down the last uprising of the Georgia Creeks. He commanded ten thousand men, the largest concentration of the U. S. troops in the country.

Coacoochee, the valiant son of old King Philip, with his own band of dashing young Indian desperadoes, attacked Fort Mellon. General Jesup drove him off, followed him, as he thought, into a big swamp. A lot of warriors went south over the Caloosahatchee, driving with them their herds of cattle.

Jesup got hold of Alligator from Tampa Bay, made him agree for the "Seminole Nation" to leave Florida. He ordered that their hostilities be stopped and that the chiefs meet him at Fort Dade.

Many chiefs met with General Jesup at Fort Dade. The question was, Were they ready to go west? The chiefs stated that they could not discuss the question until they had been guaranteed their Negro allies would go with them free to that new country.

General Jesup felt that would be all right. The fifth article of the capitulation read: "Major General Jesup, in behalf of the United States, agrees that the Seminoles and their allies, who come in and emigrate to the west, shall be secure in their lives and property; that their Negroes, their bona fide property, shall accompany them to the west, and that their cattle and ponies shall be paid for by the United States at a fair valuation."

It was only an agreement between them and General Jesup. They would meet at Fort Brooke.

In the next few weeks eight hundred Indians and Negroes visited Fort Brooke and registered for removal. The southern Indians, and Arpeika and Osceola, did not come. Coacoochee came in occasionally, but promised nothing. Twenty-six vessels lay in Tampa Bay to take them to New Orleans.

On March 26, General Jesup announced that the war was

over. The War Department approved his agreement with the Indians.

But not the people of Florida and Georgia. There was a tremendous outcry from the slaveholders. Armed night riders and raiders crossed the now peaceful borders and many Negroes were taken, with no redress.

General Jesup was forced to amend his agreement to make "an arrangement with the chiefs to deliver up the Negroes belonging to white men, taken by them during the war."

The Indian council announced that General Jesup's addition to the agreement released them from all necessity of abiding by it. General Jesup was furious. He sent messages to Osceola, through Colonel Harney, that he meant to send exploring parties into every part of the Everglades to take all the Negroes belonging to the whites, "and I intend to hang every one of them who does not come in."

Overnight the encampment of Indians at Fort Brooke vanished like smoke. But ninety Negroes were not quick enough. General Jesup caught them and sent them to jail in New Orleans, where there was the greatest possible uproar on the part of hundreds of avid slaveowners. The courts decided, with General Gaines testifying for the Indians, that Negroes found in the service of the Seminoles and speaking the same language were not escaped slaves. They were sent to Arkansas.

The government began to object to the constant payment of rations to the white settlers, as they put off from season to season the planting of their crops, arguing that the frontier was still in danger of Indian uprisings so long as there were any left in the country.

In September, 1837, General Joseph M. Hernandez and his men found and attacked a band of twenty-one Indians on the Halifax River bank of Port Orange. Seventeen Indians were captured and imprisoned at St. Augustine, notably old King

Philip and his son Coacoochee. General Jesup let Coacoochee out to take a message to Osceola, to come in with captive Negroes to arrange for King Philip's release.

Coacoochee came back and said that Osceola and one hundred men were in camp eighteen miles south and were coming in. Osceola sent in seventy-four Negro prisoners. General Jesup, not knowing this, secretly ordered Lieutenant R. H. Peyton to seize them all. They had a flag of truce. General Hernandez surrounded and took them all prisoner.

It was the first time in Florida, but not the last, that a flag of truce was ignored, under orders, by an officer of the United States Army.

The truth was that the people of Florida and the adjoining states wanted war and Indian removal or extermination.

Osceola, in prison, sat down stonily to his fate. Coacoochee and one or two others escaped.

It must have been a complete surprise to General Jesup that many newspapers throughout the country, many leading citizens, and even men and officers who had fought in Florida began to protest against the dishonor of his methods. Time after time thereafter, and later in his life, he found it necessary to try to justify his action.

Delegates from the Cherokee nation in Arkansas were brought to Florida to talk with the chiefs in the Everglades. They advised the Florida Indians to lay down their arms and go west. Again, as seventy-one Indians came in under a flag of truce to meet Jesup at Fort Mellon, he had them all surrounded and arrested.

The Cherokees were furious. They were allowed to go to Fort Marion to talk with the Indians there and convinced them they had had no part in the treachery.

General Jesup's war went on. He ordered campaigns to be carried on in every part of the country at once.

On the east coast, Lieutenant Colonel Pierce, under General

Hernandez' command, moved south along the Indian River and put up a stockade called Fort Pierce, and continued south to Jupiter Inlet. Everything inland was green and watery and marshy and difficult to penetrate, except by the shallow-sliding Indian canoes.

There on the sand dunes a small band of Indians tried to fight off a landing party of eighty men who came ashore from a navy vessel in Jupiter Inlet. The Indians were driven away.

But the most spectacular campaign was fought by Colonel Zachary Taylor, a young man still, and eager, who was to become Old Rough and Ready, the hero of the Mexican War and the twelfth president of the United States. He was at Fort Gardiner on Lake Kissimmee when his orders came. He moved south with twelve days' rations and 1,032 men, horse and foot, and broke a trail through pine and cabbage palm country down the west side of the Kissimmee and erected blockhouses. He picked up some Seminoles he thought were friendly, who told him that a large body of Mikasukis were camped twenty miles away.

At the crossing of the Kissimmee, about fifteen miles north of Lake Okeechobee, he laid out "a small stockade work" to be called Fort Basinger and left the whole of his heavy baggage, the artillery and a company of men, and hastened eastward around the lake.

In the afternoon he reached a dense, gray cypress swamp through which they worked, spending the night on its edge. The next day was Christmas. The word came that besides the Mikasukis there was a large body of Seminoles.

They marched again that sunny morning and found the Seminole camp abandoned, and came to an open grassy prairie set about with round dark cabbage palms where two to three hundred Indian ponies were grazing. A mile away, across a brown level of saw grass was the dense dark green of a great hammock

212

of cypress. Some man picked up a palmetto leaf, on which had been scratched, by some defiant Indian hand, two rifles opposed point-blank. There were the Indians.

But there was the saw grass, between the prairie and the hammock, extending east as far as the eye could see, five feet high over depths of black muck and water.

No horse could cross it. The horses and supplies were left behind in a stretch of pineland, under guard.

The men were ordered forward in two lines, volunteers under Colonel Gentry in the first, the regulars in the other. They went in holding their rifles over their heads as they sank up to their knees or deeper in the sticky muck among the tough grass clumps, half wading, half crawling. The sun beat down. Their hands were bleeding where they grasped at the edged blades. The line of volunteers crawled forward raggedly.

The ground rose. A stabbing rifle fire crackled out from the cypress. Many a north Florida boy went down, shot through. As they dropped and rolled to cover under the grass clumps and began to fire, the Indians' fire came steadily from the bushes and high in the trees. Colonel Gentry, shouting his men ahead, fell, mortally wounded, and his son also. The volunteers broke and set off crawling backward. Many a wounded man could not lift his face from the black muck, where presently the bubbles stopped breaking.

Colonel Thompson and his regulars had gone on steadily.

The Indian bullets clipped the saw grass, cutting down every head that was raised. Colonel Thompson was killed, and his adjutant, Lieutenant Center, whose names would be given to forts on the Caloosahatchee and on Fisheating Creek, and Lieutenant Van Swearingen, for whom Colonel Taylor would name another fort to the east. Every other officer, but one, and most of the noncoms were killed or wounded. Five companies were so cut up that of one only four men remained. Yet they retreated

213

only to re-form, in all that grass and bloody muck, and crawled forward again with steady and orderly courage, firing as they came.

Here and there a man could see along his rifle barrel into the aisles of the great moss-hung cypresses, where in a slant of sun an Indian flitted, and so fell. In the saw grass many a man was hit from the treetops and grunted and lay still.

When the Americans leaped into the cypress, the Indian fire grew ragged. But they met often in such close, point-blank shooting, such a welter of shouts and shots and smoke and clipped leaves and shadows among the gray cathedral trunks and the cypress knees in green-scummed water, that here and there a soldier clubbed his rifle and struck at a naked brown man slipping up with a knife. Two white men were found dead and scalped. Yet the Americans drove forward.

In two hours the Americans saw sunlight ahead. They forced the mass of Indians out to the open sandy beaches of the broad lake. The Indians broke and fled south.

Of the Americans there were twenty-six killed and one hundred twelve wounded. It was still Christmas Day. They had won the battle of the Okeechobee.

General Jesup himself, in the meantime, moved with five hundred men across the state from Fort Taylor to Fort Pierce, and camped at the St. Lucie. Farther south at Fort Jupiter he was joined by General Eustis and with twelve hundred men marched south and inland to meet the fire of about one hundred fifty fighting Seminoles and Negroes at a crossing of the Loxa-hatchee.

There General Jesup was slightly wounded. Seven white men were killed. The Indians slipped away among the green and watery mazes. It was considered a victory for the whites.

Now General Eustis and Colonel Twiggs, with the agreement of many other officers, came to the general to ask that he write to the secretary of war to ask that the remaining Indians be allowed to stay in the Everglades. General Jesup thought it was an excellent idea.

He wrote to Secretary Poinsett: "My decided opinion is that unless immediate immigration be abandoned, the war will continue for years to come and at constantly increasing cost."

At the same time General Jesup sent word to the chiefs in the near-by Everglades that they should come in for a talk. Already about that great camp of soldiers seven hundred Indians of several tribes and many free Negroes had come to trade and wait word of the new peace. The general had already sent word to several near-by leaders, notably a Mikasuki chief called Tuskeegee, a lieutenant of Arpeika, whose camps were between the headwaters of the New and Miami rivers. There was no response.

The secretary of war wrote that no compromise with the Indians would be considered. The war must go on. At once that casual camp of Indians began to disappear back into the streams threading the green and lilied sloughs. The troops surrounded 513 Indians and 165 Negroes, of whom 150 had been born in Florida, free, and spoke only the Seminoles' Muskogee language. They were all sent to Tampa for emigration.

Back in St. Augustine, General Jesup, stating that he feared an Indian attack on the fort, sent all his prisoners, Osceola, Micanopy, King Philip, White Cloud and Alligator, who alone had made the original agreement with Jesup, with 116 warriors and 82 women and children, to prison at Fort Moultrie, South Carolina.

Osceola, broken by imprisonment and homesickness, died there and was buried under a stone on which was carved "Patriot and Warrior." As a dramatic figure he had already caught the attention of people everywhere and was to epitomize for future history the highhanded injustice of his capture. In

Florida, as time was to go on, a county, a town, a lake, many streets and avenues, many people, both Indians and whites, would be named after him; a very handsome snake, *Osceola elapsoidea*, and a U. S. torpedo boat destroyer also bore his name.

From Fort Moultrie the others were sent to the hardships of Arkansas, where old King Philip died at once. The word was brought back to Coacoochee, his son, no longer a dashing youth, but an angry, bitter, and desperate leader. Arpeika the Mikasuki sent word to General Jesup that he had never made a treaty with him and he never would, and that he and his most independent people would fight it out forever. Che-ki-ka, the chief of the Old People, watching from the lower Glades, said nothing at all.

At the bad news of the failure of General Jesup's plan to let the Indians stay in the Everglades, the now always smoldering wrath of the Indians broke at once into action.

As early as December 27 in the year 1825, a donation grant on the New River, affirming a grant in 1796 from a Spanish governor, had been issued by the United States government to a man named Frankie Lewis.

There were no settlers on the Lewis grant by the New River where the Indians came to camp, until a man named Colee, with his family, came up the east coast from Key West some time after 1835 and cleared land for a garden and put up a log cabin, and called it Colee Hammock. It must have been he who planted coconuts along the river, because an old map of 1845 marks this place "Old Cocoanut Grove."

The Indians had been bitter at the loss of their old campsite. There is a story that a young Indian boy hung about the clearing every day until the Colees, busy and unafraid, gave him some of their corn pone and fried fish and let him help with the work of clearing the garden. They called him Charley.

216

Word had come of the battle of Okeechobee and General Jesup's capture of the peaceful Indians at Fort Jupiter. The subchief, Pahosi-Micco, and the warriors, having painted their faces, stamped out about the campfire the long dances that bring the power of the warpath hotly rising to the heart. The boy Charley slipped away to warn the Colees, but already Mr. Colee and one son had left in his sailboat for the long trip to Key West for supplies, and Mrs. Colee and the others paid no attention.

That night late the canoes slipped down the flowing black glass of the river. At dawn, perhaps, Mrs. Colee woke with a start because the cicadas, which even now along that river all night long sound their dry incessant "cric-crac, cric-crac," were deathly silent. Then the war whoop ripped dreadfully through the dewy greenness and freshness, and she learned with what agony fear becomes real. The log cabin was attacked. The woman and the boys fired desperately but they were shot and scalped and their bodies left to burn, and for a while over the ashes the little flames whispered.

It is believed that the Indian boy was sentenced at that year's green corn dance to have his ears cropped and be exiled from his tribe. Such an Indian, crop eared and silent, stumping in rags about the streets, is said to have lived there until he was an old, old man.

The man Colee and his son sailed in from Key West to stare in dazed horror at the blackened timbers of their cabin, stooping to pick up something and let it drop, a child's blue bead, a trampled pewter spoon. Then they sailed grimly up the coast looking for soldiers.

General Jesup had ordered Major Lauderdale, with a company of artillery and two hundred Tennessee volunteers to explore the country south and set up forts. Mr. Colee and his son reached Jupiter after Major Lauderdale was on his way, but word was sent after him. Lieutenant Colonel Bankhead was ordered to reinforce him with a strong detachment and Lieutenant Powell with his navy vessel. Among those live oaks by the New River they set up a stockade that hummed now with the activities of the soldiers. It was named Fort Lauderdale.

A small detachment under Lieutenant Anderson took by surprise forty-seven Indian prisoners and found supplies from the Colee cabin in their camp. And scalps.

Lieutenant Colonel Bankhead pushed up the river to the Everglades looking for Chief Arpeika himself. Under the hot sun, through the sticky black muck and glassy cutting blades,

they waded and floundered and pushed those boats, foot by foot. They worked forward in an agony of heat and sweat and pricking midge bites.

Far ahead there was the dark-green coolness of a hammock, an island, stranded in that grassy waste. There were Indians watching in a tree. A white flag was sent forward. Sweating officers and men were furious when the white flag was fired upon. They pushed forward, firing. Spurts of rifle fire stabbed at them from the trees. When they had reached the rocky sides

218

of that hammock and the coolness through the surrounding bushes of silver myrtle and willow, the Indians were already moving their canoes, slipping easily along known watercourses westward.

The exhausted and sun-blistered men returned to Fort Lauderdale, where Lieutenant Colonel Harney replaced Bankhead. Harney was to be the dramatic figure in all later Everglades work, a shrewd student of the country, an unrelenting fighter and excellent leader. Now he carried forward the attack at once, moving by boat down to the great open, sun-misted waters of Biscayne Bay and landing his men on one of the few shelving beaches of the mainland some fifteen miles south of the river, from which the ancient trails moved to the pineland of the Great Hunting Grounds.

Across a grassy open swale they saw naked Indians dodging, and dropped to cover and fired. A stinging considerable fire crackled out at them from the distant pine ranks. The Indians were Arpeika's Mikasukis. They moved away, firing, carrying their wounded, drawing Colonel Harney's men after them. A messenger brought orders he was to meet General Jesup in Tampa.

General Jesup had been called to Washington. On May 15, 1838, already busy with the explanations he would write and continue for many years to make on the question of his handling of Osceola and the flags of truce, he left Florida. The war was no nearer being over than when he had taken his command.

10

War in the Glades:
The Undefeated

Zachary Taylor, brilliant as a soldier and already a man of statesmanlike judgment, was now in command of the army in Florida and sole interpreter of the government's Indian policy. From the moment he assumed command the war in the Glades became a different thing.

His orders were that no white men would be allowed to come into the war zone and inspect and claim as slaves the Negro prisoners of war.

All through the Everglades the word flashed that the Negroes were to receive the same treatment as the Indians and that General Taylor thought they should go west. As this was what most of the Seminoles and Creeks and Yuchis were fighting for, numbers of them, war exhausted, eager for peace, began to give themselves up at Fort Brooke on Tampa Bay. In less than a year of General Taylor's control more than four hundred Indians and Negroes were sent to Arkansas.

But behind them the Mikasukis and some of the Tallahassees, many of the Seminoles and Creeks, and certainly all the descendants of the Calusas, remained defiant in the deep Glades. They meant to stay in Florida, or to die there. The man called the Prophet, who had fled here years before from the religious uprising of the Red Stick War, was making powerful new medicine that would deflect the white man's bullets and make a warrior invisible and invincible. He gathered the young men in secret rituals. It was like a pulse quickening and throbbing there, beside the dark reaches of the saw-grass river.

The year 1838 was the great year of Zachary Taylor's peace. White men began to move back to the older settlements. The navy began its several years of co-operation with the army. Key West grew steadily.

Indian Key was headquarters for the east coast, a small island of some twelve acres east of Lower Matecumbe, which in 1819 was cleared by Captain Jacob Houseman, shipbuilder and trader, and undoubtedly the leading wrecker of all those men who ranged these coasts to pick up salvage from vessels in distress on the reefs or claim salvage. Captain Houseman built a house and docks, and a store for trading with the coastwise sailing vessels or with Indians in their canoes.

It was at Indian Key that John James Audubon, the great ornithologist, arrived in April, 1832, in the revenue cutter *Marion* to study the great flocks of birds living in the shallow waters and flatlands between here and about Cape Sable.

In the war more houses were built, and docks, and the naval hospital that was the first along all these coasts. With its neighbor Tea-Table Key, Indian Key became full of bustle and activity. The island air that has no echoes was full of the sound of hammers and the creaking of blocks, the shouts of children playing, and the voices of women calling them to supper under a great sunset.

It was headquarters also for what would be called the Florida Squadron under Lieutenant J. T. McLaughlin. There was the schooner *Wave,* the sloop *Panther,* the schooners *Otsego* and *Flirt,* and *Phoenix, Madison* and *Van Buren,* the revenue-cutter schooner *Campbell* and some barges. From 1839 a detachment of marines would be based at Indian Key and later, in 1842, at the newly built Fort Dallas on the Miami River.

But at that time Key Biscayne, called also Cape Florida, was the other most important settlement on this coast. Title to the land had existed since 1805 in a grant from the Spanish governor to Pedro Fornella. At Fornella's death title passed to his stepson, Raphael Andreu, from whom in 1824 Mrs. Mary Ann Davis, wife of W. G. Davis of St. Augustine, had bought 175 acres.

In 1827 three acres on the southeast point were deeded to the United States government for a lighthouse. A keeper's house was built behind it. In that work many things came to light out of that ancient trampled sand, the ashes of old fires, broken Indian pots, worked shells, and ancient fishbones. It is said a coffin was dug up containing a complete skeleton.

Here in the year 1838 of Zachary Taylor's peace, and in the years of later expeditions into the Everglades themselves, Lieutenant Colonel Harney had his base near the Davis house with a large detachment of troops, who whooped like boys dashing into the long slow creaming surf in the sunsets before mess call.

The energetic Colonel Harney and W. G. Davis walked and

talked often along the path from the tents to the lighthouse. Behind the lightkeeper's lodge they often stopped to look at the more than a hundred boxes of plants which Dr. Henry Perrine had shipped from Yucatan to the lighthouse keeper, Mr. Dubose. The blossoms of orange, lime and shaddock trees already sweetened the salty air.

Enjoying all this freshness and brilliant light and peace, Colonel Harney or Mr. Davis had a great idea. Why was not this the perfect place for a small tropical city? The climate was fine. There was the promise of these fruit trees, all the fish in the world, good hunting on the mainland. And most amazingly, those miasmas or bad airs, which in the swamps of north Florida struck down such a high percentage of soldiers with the dreaded swamp fevers, seemed not to exist here. In those days, when malaria was one of the greatest scourges of the American South, this was supremely important.

That night in the lamplight they made an outline map of the Key and marked it with streets and building lots. Nothing ever came of it.

Colonel Harney had some of his hardest soldiering ahead of him. Other men ventured to make clearings about the lower coasts. Most notable of all, Dr. Henry Perrine arrived from Yucatan by way of New Orleans to Key West, and so to Indian Key.

For ten years Henry E. Perrine, M. D., had been United States consul at Campeche, Yucatan, but he was an enthusiastic practical scientist, and his insatiable energy, even in the tropics, had turned him avidly to the study of tropical botany. He had already advocated the still little known use of quinine for malaria. It is said that he discovered that a man named Smithson had died in England, leaving a large sum of money to establish a scientific institute in America. The courts had not released it. With Richard Rush, secretary of the treasury, Dr.

Perrine went to England. They were fortunate in securing the money that founded the Smithsonian Institution. In Yucatan he not only survived yellow fever and cholera by methods of his own, but saved the lives of many people in the villages about.

Dr. Perrine's greatest career began when Richard Rush sent a circular letter to all consular officials to encourage them to collect and ship home plants for propagation in the United States. Dr. Perrine was the only consul who threw himself with enthusiasm into the work. His monumental reports to Congress on the values of tropical fruits and spices and dyewoods and fiber plants were the first of their kind. He asked for a grant from Congress on the new lands just acquired from Spain in Florida, which would lie unemployed and useless for many years.

Congress delayed action while Dr. Perrine wrote articles for American newspapers. He explored Yucatan trying to buy seeds. But the local officials looked on him with such suspicion that they had all his seeds carefully boiled. He despaired until the people of the villages heard that the American doctor who had cured them wanted live seeds to grow in his own country. They brought him quantities of viable seeds as gifts, which in a big chest he shipped to Indian Key.

The state of Louisiana offered him a grant on La Fitte Island for a nursery of Useful Tropical Plants. But Dr. Perrine, from his long correspondence with Mr. Charles Howe, postmaster and customs officer at Indian Key, was convinced that only in South Florida were the conditions right for tropical plants. In 1838 Congress granted him and his associates, James Webb of Key West and Charles Howe, a township of land, almost twenty-four thousand acres, on the mainland of lower Biscayne Bay, halfway between Cape Florida and Cape Sable. It was the first grant for plant introduction ever made by the United States. The Chapman Field Plant Introduction Station of the

Department of Agriculture is now located near the original grant.

This tall keen-eyed energetic man, then, on Christmas Day, 1838, brought his family to the big house with balconies and cupola on the water's edge at Indian Key, and became the most famous citizen of the new Dade County.

At Indian Key the settlement of Jacob Houseman had been increased by the families of James Webb and many workmen. It had already been planted with a great square of coconut palms about which the smaller buildings were grouped. Sea grapes and gumbo limbos were left within the rocky ledge to the south, and everywhere were growing the trees Dr. Perrine had already sent from Yucatan, lemon and orange and lime trees, an avenue of trees called Paradise and Pride of China, and fig trees and tamarinds.

The list of plants he was anxious to try here was a long one: yams, ginger, cassava, indigo, sugar cane, pimento, tea, orange, shaddock, lime, citron, sugar apple, banana, plantain, pineapple, sapodillo, soursop, avocado, mango, mamey sapota, olive, boxwood and ship timber, spice and medicinal plants, and the white mulberry for silkworms.

His greatest interest lay in the introduction of sisal for hemp from the two species of agave which he introduced here, setting them out in the potholes on the mainland. One still bears his name, *Agave sisalana Perrine*. He sailed with his son Henry to the tip end of Florida where Charles Howe was interested in building a settlement. Presently the shallow-draft sailing vessels from the keys began to put in there and Cape Sable began to look like another thriving south Florida village.

On the lower west coast the small Spanish vessels had always moved between Cuba and the beaches north of Cape Romano and made similar settlements on the white sand dunes south of Marco Island, where there had always been springs of fresh water the Cubans called "caxambas." The prehistoric Indians had drunk from them, and frowsy pirate vessels and Che-ki-ka and his watchful men.

The year 1838, the fine year of Zachary Taylor's peace, ended. His policy of fairness had lasted as long as it could. The commander in chief of the army of the United States, Major General Alexander Macomb, came to Florida to negotiate "a new treaty" on the terms General Jesup had suggested, without success, to the secretary of war. Messages were sent throughout the Everglades that the government had concluded to let the Indians stay in Florida.

About fifty chiefs assembled at Fort King, with eager and pathetic hope. The government, through General Macomb, promised to let them alone in part of the Everglades. They were allowed to believe that they would be let alone in Florida forever.

There was no signing, there were only promises without guarantees on the part of the United States, hope on the part of the Indians. "Nor did I think it politic," General Macomb wrote in May to the secretary, "at this time to say anything to them about their emigration, leaving the subject open to future arrangements."

Again, the war in Florida was declared over. Yet again the people in Florida and Georgia were furious. What about their escaped property, the slaves? What about the loss of army rations to families who had so long lived on them? What about those civilian workers who depended on the army?

In St. Augustine angry citizens held a mass meeting in protest against General Macomb's treaty. The secretary of war replied, "I am of the opinion that the arrangement made by General Macomb will lead to the pacification of the country and enable me to remove the Indians from the territory much sooner than they can be done by force." The newspapers of the day, especially in St. Augustine, printed long wordy editorials arguing that the treacherous red man must be driven from Florida or be exterminated.

The Indians could not read, but they did not need to. They understood at once that the white man, his officers and his government had lied.

Now at last the Indians in the depths of the Big Cypress and the Ten Thousand Islands were aroused also. They had arms which the Spanish by the west coast and the British through the east had furnished them.

The Mikasukis met for the green corn dance at the full moon of that peaceful June. And the man called the Prophet, having brewed the black drink, moved into the firelight and spoke. Behind him on the seats of the elders drowsed Arpeika, whom the whites called "Sam Jones," worn by age and old despair. The Prophet watched the faces of the younger men, the warriors, the new leaders who had fire in their hearts, Chitto-Tustenuggee and Halleck-Tustenuggee, who had represented Arpeika in talks with General Macomb and Holatta-Micco, called Billy Bowlegs. Overhead, the great moon flared in the blanched and inviolate sky as he made new magic.

What the Prophet said was something like this: In the old days the white men had come like beggars to the powerful lodges of the old people. They returned in multitudes like angry wasps with lies in their mouths seeking the Indian's lands. The Indian had forsaken the old ways of the elder people, the ways of power and of peace, and had followed the evil ways of white men until their strength was gone from them. Now even this last land which the Great Spirit had given them the white man wanted also.

Only by return now to the ways of power, only by prayer and fasting and meditation, would the hordes of the white man be driven into the sea from which he had come.

227

"Purify yourselves, strengthen your hearts," the Prophet's long harsh and howling voice sounded over and over above the silent listening men. "Let the warriors unite and prepare."

Many Indians had not listened before. Now the remnants of tribes, the last of the Yuchis, the Tallahassees, the few Choctaws, and the determined and resolute Mikasukis, were deeply stirred. They watched the patterns of his ritual by which they were made invincible. The young men ran with the black drink and the elders were made clean. The drums sounded and there began the dances that would last until dawn and the dawn prayers and the baths and the feasts.

And now at last Che-ki-ka, giant Che-ki-ka, who had waited so long, began to move. He was the leader now, among all these councils. His allies were Hospetarke, who had lived here so long beside him in friendship, and Holatta-Micco. They had two hundred fifty dedicated warriors.

In spite of all the agitation of the citizens of Florida, the orders of General Macomb still stood, that the boundaries of the Indian country should be at least half the Everglades south of Charlotte Harbor. There were to be Indian posts along the border, for the profitable trade in skins. Lieutenant Colonel Harney now moved toward Charlotte Harbor with twenty-six dragoons and two sutlers and a large supply of goods. The detachment camped on the Caloosahatchee River, in a great grove of oaks.

The white men slept without sentinels. At dawn, out of the mists only faintly lighter than the gray-green moss, the Indians struck, firing from the bushes, screaming that scream which curdles the heart of a man waking to it. Thirteen men died in its echoes. Colonel Harney in his drawers and shirt leaped into the bushes by the river with one other man, half naked. Eight others swam out to a sloop in the river and slipped with the current beyond the river-dipping trees. Colonel Harney and the other found a canoe and got away. The two boats met at the mouth of the river and hailed the sloop *Jane* from Tampa, on her way to Cape Florida.

But Colonel Harney prevailed upon the men in the sloop to sail up the river again, to rescue any survivors. They found only the trampled ashes of their fire and some corn, and the body of one man scalped and mangled with his entrails torn out and the buzzards heavily flapping up from it.

In a day or two of steady sailing the *Jane* put in at Cape Sable, finding there the schooner *Charles Howe,* which they sent to warn the troops at Cape Florida. The *Jane* proceeded along the keys to Key Vacas, whence the news of the Indian uprising would be carried to Key West.

At the same time from the north came the news of travelers attacked on the road to Tallahassee, indicating that a small band of warriors had moved far beyond the stated boundaries. The word again was "war." The Florida people were in panic. At every stockade or trading post peaceful Indians coming in with skins were captured and sent immediately to South Carolina, and from thence to Arkansas.

Secretary of War J. R. Poinsett reported to the president the real situation in regard to the Indians: "Composed as the Florida Indians are, of the remnants of tribes that had taken refuge there and acknowledged no common head, no treaty stipulations that are not sanctioned by each and every tribe can be regarded as binding; nor can the government consider the country pacified until there has been a general submission of all chiefs of the various tribes inhabiting the peninsula."

Now the territory of Florida, like its citizens, became aroused against the presence of the Indians. The militia was called out to guard the northern settlements.

The legislature also ordered that bloodhounds be secured from Havana to track and pursue their usual prey, the Negroes,

229

who still escaped the slave catchers. Thirty-three bloodhounds were brought in, at a cost of $151.52 apiece, and five Spaniards experienced in slave hunting. The dogs enjoyed their usual bloody meat of calves, but refused to follow any footprints whatsoever. A storm of protest was raised by sensitive-minded northern citizens.

So in April, 1840, General Zachary Taylor asked leave to retire from command of the army in Florida. Brigadier General Armistead was appointed in his place, and government policy was changed again.

Again some Florida Indians, from Arkansas, were brought back to the Glades to persuade the Indians that removal was a good thing. But what these Indians had to say about Arkansas was all bad. Nothing had been prepared for the Indians there as the government had promised. These men had themselves suffered cold and hunger and had seen their old men and their young children die. They had been forced to live with their hated enemies, the Creeks. The secret councils of the Everglades made new laws, that any messengers who came to them from the white men were to be killed.

There had been trouble between Captain Houseman on Indian Key and the young Indians who had gone there to trade skins for liquor. Captain Houseman had had their drunken bodies dumped into an outhouse and the door nailed up. When they were sober they were kicked out. Then Che-ki-ka struck.

Seventeen war canoes full of naked, fasting warriors slipped in the dark of the moon down toward Indian Key.

The houses, the docks, a sloop or two, the trees of Indian Key were only a huddle of black against the starlight and the breathing starlit sea as the canoes slipped to it from the west. They were beached under the line of rocks and one by one the Indians snaked through the shadows to the fence halfway across the open plaza, to lie there silent as logs waiting for the first light.

In a workman's cottage a ship's carpenter by the name of Bieglet stirred and woke, unaccountably, and went to stare out the window. He saw seventeen Indian canoes on the beach and woke his companion. Together, snatching a shotgun, they started along the path to the other houses. By the fence an Indian leaped up and snapped a musket harmlessly in their faces. Both barrels of the shotgun went off and the white men ran in different directions, shouting. Everywhere men and women started from their beds at the shots, the crashing of windows, and the long screaming panther howls of the Indians.

The Perrines, among all the others, were instantly aroused. Mrs. Perrine and the two girls and the boy, Henry, hurried down through the trap door to the slatted bathhouse where the tides ran, and so into a smaller place beyond, walled with rock and roofed with heavy planks and rock, next to the turtle crawl under the wharf. Dr. Perrine had gone out to speak to the Indians in Spanish. One told him they were looking only for Captain Houseman and his family. The store had already been broken into and the Indians were whooping and drinking and loading their loot into the small sloop at the dock. Dr. Perrine pulled over the trap door in the floor the heavy chest of seeds from Yucatan and went upstairs to get some of his papers.

At daylight the Indians were back again, wildly drunk and furious because the Housemans had escaped. They battered at the Perrines' door and, as it crashed, ran about inside, smashing everything. Dr. Perrine retreated through the heavy door above to the cupola. The Indians were a long time breaking the door down, screaming and howling. But the first painted creature to burst into Dr. Perrine's hiding place killed him there.

Mrs. Perrine and the children, crouching in the water below, heard them dragging out boxes and trunks. An Indian lifted a plank over the turtle crawl and peered down into the shadowy place. They could see the dark glitter of his eyes in the stripes of war paint. He did not turn his head in their direction. The plank slammed back.

Soon they smelled smoke and heard fire crackling overhead. Slowly the smoke thickened about them and they heard the roar of the flames as the whole house burned. They could breathe only by lying in the water with their noses out. Fire ran along the planks overhead so that they were forced to plaster their hair with the wet white marl to protect them from the burning embers. Young Henry, half suffocated, said he would rather be shot than burned to death and forced a plank, and to the horror of his mother and sisters made his way to the turtle crawl, and so out to the smoky light.

There were no shots, except from the other side of the island. Mrs. Perrine dug down to the marl around a post in the turtle crawl and loosened it and they got out. The sloop that the Indians had piled with goods lay by the wharf. They found Henry and dragged the sloop out into deep water, where the smoke lay so heavy that the Indians could not see them. They began frantically paddling with one oar, one paddle and two poles, cringing before an expected rifle shot. Twice they grounded on a shoal and waited until Henry jumped overboard and pushed them into deeper water. The smoke was far away now.

Out in the open sea they saw the sails of a schooner. In their marl-plastered nightgowns and their sodden hair they presently stood on the deck of the *Medium*, a schooner in which Captain Houseman and his family had escaped with other refugees—the Charles Howes, a Captain Otis, and Mr. W. C. Maloney, the clerk of Dade County who had lost everything but the great Dade County seal. But Charles Howe's two sons, who had been hunting on the mainland, were never seen again.

It was said that at his house the Indians found some Masonic regalia which they laid carefully on a table and did not harm. They were a people who understood the force of symbols.

The refugees stayed on the schooner two nights, and through a bad storm until they were picked up by Captain McLoughlin in the USS *Flirt*. He conveyed them, wrapped in navy sheets, to Cape Florida, to await the arrival of the steamer *Santee* for St. Augustine.

The *Flirt* returned to Indian Key and rescued several other whites left alive there, and a colored woman and her baby. They buried the many dead. In the ashes of the Perrine house they found a burned body that was Dr. Perrine's, and buried him on Lower Matecumbe Key. The houses were burnt, the trees were burnt, all the plants into the collection of which Dr. Perrine had put so many high hopes, had been destroyed. There is no marker there even now, except Captain Houseman's tombstone, to show where the first great experiment in tropical plant introduction was so patiently and valiantly begun. Only the sisal, the agaves and the century plants, in which he had been so especially interested, were not destroyed. The rocky windy sunny place of ruin was perfect for them. Today the sisal and the cactus have taken all Indian Key for their own. They spread from his plantings and grew wild all over South Florida. They are his monument. A single town on U. S. 1 south of Miami is the only place which today bears his name.

Fifty years later, Mexico put an embargo on fiber for binder twine. The wild sisal introduced by Dr. Perrine provided hundreds of thousands of seed bulbs and saved millions of dollars for American and other planters. A recently produced lemon, a hybrid of the limes Dr. Perrine first planted in south Florida, one of great vigor and fruitfulness, has been named "the Perrine lemon."

The Indians were back in the deep Glades and all General

Armistead's 4,941 men, ten companies of regulars, and 1,500 militia guarding the again-fearful settlements of middle Florida, were paralyzed with inaction. In November General Armistead sent word to Halleck-Tustenuggee, the Mikasuki subchief, to come in for talks at Fort King. The talks were friendly. The Indians brought in their deerskins to trade, had all they wanted to eat and drink, but were evasive about leaving Florida. Then with calico and frying pans and other store goods they disappeared, and the heavy pursuing troops could find no trace of them.

But Colonel Harney at Fort Dallas on the Miami River had not forgotten the Perrine Massacre or that earlier defeat of his own on the Caloosahatchee. He knew a great deal about Indian fighting now and had been training one hundred experienced men and assembling his supplies and boats. The word came that Che-ki-ka and his people were living in some hammocks in the saw-grass Everglades south of the headwaters of the Miami. On December 4, 1840, he left Fort Dallas in charge of Lieutenant William T. Sherman, and with ninety men in sixty long, light Indian canoes, craft which the men handled like Indians, they moved up the pretty river, turned up the South Fork, and made straight west through high water in the saw-grass glades. They kept going in a heavy rain that fell all day long accompanied by a chill north wind.

Still the water was not deep enough to float the canoes for any distance. They had to be pushed, pushed, and pushed again through the hissing scratching grass clumps by crews floundering through the wet black muck. At times it seemed to them that they were completely lost; making no progress whatever in the obstinate brown sere grass that here reached from horizon to horizon.

They saw an island about a mile ahead to which eventually the boats were pushed. That island seemed to be only about an acre of low bushes set in water, but within they found a deserted Indian camp planted with bananas and wild papayas under two enormous strangler figs. The men dried themselves before a great fire and slept well.

At daylight Colonel Harney set out with four canoes. Officers and men were stripped and painted like Indians. They pushed the boats through muck to dry land but found no Indians. Through the slashing chilling rain that shut down around them it was ten terrible miles more to another hammock. Still there was no one!

Next morning early at the first camp Colonel Harney climbed one of the great fig trees and saw two canoeloads of Indians coming up. Four canoes went to meet them and chased them, firing, until the Indians got into the tall saw grass. The Americans captured two men and wounded a woman attempting to escape with a child on her back. In another direction a boat captured a woman, with a girl about twelve, and two small children.

Back at the island Colonel Harney ordered the ropes out and the two Indian warriors were hanged from the top of the fig tree. They swung there, dark and painted, against a great crimson sunset.

The wounded woman died. It was reported that Che-ki-ka was on a neighboring island. The rain began heavily again at nightfall. But in spite of the cold some of the boats with Lieutenant Rankin and Lieutenant Ord were sent out to crawl forward all night long for a daylight attack.

Chilled through, these advance boats waited in the outer bushes of the hammock until the gray light cleared. There was the sound of an ax chopping.

The Americans fired and dashed forward yelling into a camp, where from the thatched huts men and women roused and scattered everywhere in terror. One man was shot dead. Two warriors, one boy, five women, and some children were taken prisoners. The huge form of a man with an ax slipped through the far bushes. Hall, a dragoon, ran after him alone, fired and saw him fall. Hall ripped off the scalp neatly and brought back the dripping bit of hair to Colonel Harney with a wide grin. The man was Che-ki-ka. His tall lean frame weighed, they thought, over two hundred pounds.

Lieutenant Ord followed two other men, escaping to another island, where a white flag was hoisted. But as the Americans came up, they were fired on. They returned to the first island for Che-ki-ka's body. The same evening Colonel Harney had the other two prisoners hanged to the high tree and Che-ki-ka's body hauled up alongside the others.

In the camp they found clothing, linen, calico, tools and powder which had been taken from Indian Key.

They were informed by Che-ki-ka's sister that three Spaniards from the west coast had supplied the Indians with ammunition and urged them on to the attack on Indian Key.

The expedition kept west and then south in ever-deepening water, suffered a ravening horde of mosquitoes, came out to the mangrove rampart of the Glades and found a river running south and west. This they followed, came to the Gulf, turned, and made their way east again and back to Fort Dallas. That river is now called Harney's River. This was one of the first times a body of white men had crossed the great unknown Everglades from east to west. At least now, the army felt, it had shown the Indian that soldiers could go where he went and fight him in his last retreats.

Still the Indians in the Glades gave no sign. Under renewed political pressure General Armistead, in February, was now ordered to prosecute the war with the utmost vigor; $100,000 was appropriated in January and $1,061,816 in March to suppress the Indian hostilities.

There were now the months of February, March, April and May before the spring rains would set in to overflow Okeechobee and start running among the saw grass the great moving mass of clear water.

Many of the Indians, learning again of the government's more rigorous policy, went to the army post then established at Sarasota to talk vaguely about peace and exchange skins with soldiers for what they needed, while behind them, in the hammock gardens, the old men and boys and women hurried to plant the new crops of corn, squash and beans, to dry deer meat and grind coontie flour for the summer. In April all the Indians vanished again into the Glades.

At this time the most brilliant Indian leader since Osceola, the chief Coacoochee, called Wildcat, one who since boyhood had known nothing but warfare with the whites, now a mature and embittered man, attacked a traveling troupe of players and went into hiding. Colonel Worth had taken Coacoochee's young daughter in a raid near Fort Mellon. He sent word to Coacoochee to come in for friendly talks and get his daughter.

Coacoochee came in. Colonel Worth met with a straight face a distinguished group of chiefs, dressed in the theatrical costumes they had looted from the traveling players, Coacoochee magnificently dignified in the rusty black doublet of the conventional Hamlet of that time, and his men in cloaks and helmets, and plumed hats and Roman togas. The meeting went off well. Colonel Worth was able to impress on the leader his own honorable intentions about the Negroes, and the sincerity of his belief that the Indians would be better off to go.

Coacoochee was held in camp for several days. His little daughter was given back to him, on his promise to go out and talk to his people and try to get them to surrender. He would meet Colonel Worth in another month at Fort Pierce on the

237

east coast. In Coacoochee the Indian's sense of fatality burned deep. He said he realized that he must go.

In May, Colonel Worth was appointed general commanding the army in Florida. It was the summer season, when all army activity had always ceased, that was, after all, the greatest ally the Indians had, besides the Everglades themselves.

Colonel Worth determined on a new policy of aggression through the summer, of expedition after expedition, by marines, dragoons, sailors and soldiers, everywhere that boats could be made to go. The high water made it easier, not harder, to get about as the Indians did, in canoes. The orders were, "Find the enemy, capture or exterminate him."

On the Caloosahatchee depots were established, Fort Dulany at Punta Rassa, Fort Simmons and Fort Denaud at the most important river crossing where the wagon road from Tampa went south. Years earlier a Frenchman, Pierre Denaud, had had a store there.

The story of those expeditions has never been completely retold from the reports of the dozens of officers commanding, or of the men with whom they shared every hardship.

Every expedition was like every other in many ways, because travel of any sort through the Everglades differed only between the wet and the dry season.

In wet weather the boats could be poled as the Indian poled his canoe, moving with comparative ease from dripping hammock to hammock. But the men suffered always the discomforts of the thundering rains, wet clothing, clouds of salt-water mosquitoes in the mangrove country, wet food, sleeping in wet boats or on wet ground haunted by moccasin snakes also seeking dry land, and the roaring and thrashing of alligators that invaded the muddy flats. Nights in the drowned glades with a norther blowing on chilled skins and sodden garments were a singularly penetrating agony. In dry weather under the burning sun with the water all but vanished below the grass roots, and the wind cut off by the high swordlike stalks, the men pushed the boats with infinite difficulty through the slimy black muck, floundering to knees or waists in the clinging mud, bleeding from saw-grass cuts, exhausted, and seeming to get nowhere.

The tales of their accomplishments were also much the same. They would come upon a hammock in the heart of which there

was a corn patch and some empty Indian huts, which they burned. They captured a canoe with one Indian, two women and a boy. Or a camp of a few women with stolid faces, two old men and some children, none of whom cried. It was impossible for them again to surprise warriors in camp as Harney had done, because now the Indians kept lookouts in the highest trees. They could only return to their bases on the rivers, on the Caloosahatchee or at Fort Dallas or Fort Lauderdale, having the satisfaction that they had penetrated the Indian country, had destroyed a few crops, taken a few prisoners, and returned. Men and officers alike, soldiers, dragoons, sailors or marines, were sunburned, bitten, mudplastered, and worn out.

It was a source of comment on the part of the navy doctors and medical men, however, that beyond those things, a few wounds and snakebites, the men were completely healthy. The myth about "the deadly miasmas of the Everglades" was forever dispelled.

Only one part of the Everglades was never crossed or penetrated. No boats ventured into it, nor any men. Neither did the Indians, in their entire history. That was the vast unbroken brown expanse of the true saw-grass Everglades, unbroken by any hammocks. There it was, the true river of grass. It extended between the western bank of the Big Cypress and the narrow rock ledge of the east coast, between which the solid current of the grass and water is held, silent, enormous, unimaginable, impenetrable. If there was mystery in the Everglades, it was there.

The exploit of Major Childs in crossing from the coast to Okeechobee, and thence back again, was one of the earliest of these ventures. But Major Childs was also to distinguish himself on his return to Fort Pierce. Having had no opportunity to learn how Colonel Worth had given his word to Coacoochee, he arrested Coacoochee as he came into Fort Pierce as the chief had promised, with his family and many of his tribe. Major Childs shipped them off in the first transport to New Orleans, Coacoochee in handcuffs.

News traveled slowly in those days. But when Colonel Worth heard of this "mistake" he raised a fury of protest straight up to the War Department. He had meant to use Coacoochee in Florida. From New Orleans the ship was ordered back to Tampa. Coacoochee in bitterness saw his own country again. But he kept his word. He persuaded many Indians to come in to Fort Brooke, kept them there with organized ball games and long ceremonials, dances, and army rations, even convincing them, as the women prepared the food they must take with them on shipboard, that the Americans did not intend to get

them out there on that vast unknown gulf of sea water, and
drown them, as they had believed. The men resigned themselves. The women worked and grieved. Many children and
some old men died in camp.

But in the deep Glades and the Big Cypress the Council of
the Prophet buzzed with drums like the warning of rattlesnakes.

A Negro messenger sent them from Coacoochee was kept
prisoner for two years. A chief killed his sister, who wanted to
surrender. Other Indians who despaired were killed. No tricks,
no promises, no friendliness, no burning of camps and corn-
fields could bring them in.

Wily old Hospetarke came into a camp on Peace Creek with
a number of his chiefs, without rifles or women and children.
They bartered deerskins for whatever they could get, leaving
by sundown and coming back by daylight. They stayed cold
sober.

Colonel Worth invited them to a feast on a steamboat on the
river. The old chief and his men went in their scarlet leggings
and their best calico ceremonial shirts, with plumes in their
folded turbans. The most striking figure of that group was
Gopher John, the Negro Indian interpreter, tall and black as
his Ashanti ancestors, bracelets and bangles, shirt and leggings
brighter than any.

After they ate, Colonel Worth spoke. He asked them to go
with him now to Fort Brooke, send for their women and children, and go west in full friendship with the government. He
promised them, and Gopher John in particular, that no Negroes
would be sent back to slavery.

Hospetarke temporized, as he had done before. He could not
go now. Next moon he would come.

Colonel Worth was furious. He said, "Not one of you will
again leave this boat." Before Hospetarke turned his head, the
bugle sounded, the officers leaped to their feet and drew their

241

swords, soldiers stood in the door with drawn bayonets and on shore the long drums rolled. They were all held at Fort Brooke until their wives and children should come in.

The expeditions into the Everglades began again in earnest that summer. Fifty-five cypress canoes had been built. Fort Denaud, at the crossing of the Caloosahatchee, was the headquarters for the Devil's Garden, the Big Cypress, the Okaloacochee Slough, and the western mangrove barrier. Lieutenant Ketchum, Major Wilson, Lieutenant Sibley, Captain Holmes, Major Childs, Captain M. Burke, Lieutenant Rogers, USN, Lieutenant Colonel Clarke, Captain Ker and Captain May were some of the officers in command of many expeditions. Only a lone midshipman, one Preble, who would later be an admiral, writing his own story of an expedition toward Okeechobee from the east coast, recorded the presence of vast flocks of egret and ibis and heron, and of innumerable alligators thrashing the streams to foam.

A naval expedition up the Caloosahatchee to Okeechobee sailed into a lake beyond Hicpochee which no white man had ever seen before. It was named Lake Flirt after the first vessel of the Florida squadron. Rogers' River also was named, north of Harney's River. Stockades and temporary forts were set up, soon to be abandoned. There were Fort Shackleford, on the edge of the Big Cypress on an Indian landing place from the Everglades; Fort Keais; Fort T. B. Adams, across the Caloosahatchee from Fort Denaud; Fort Doane, in the Big Cypress; Fort Harrel, at the southern end of the Big Cypress; Fort Henry, a temporary fort in the Everglades west of Biscayne Bay; Fort Wescott, a temporary camp east of the Ten Thousand Islands. Already established a year or two before had been Fort McRae, south of Lake Okeechobee, in 1838; and Fort Poinsett, named for the then secretary of war, at Cape Sable.

The war dragged on, yet there was a feeling everywhere that

it was almost over. The government could not afford to go on with it. Expenses were curtailed, supplies and numbers of men were reduced wherever possible. Key Biscayne was reduced to six woodcutters for the occasional coastwise steamers.

The Indians still waited at Fort Brooke for the transports. There was for a time a great clamor of slaveowners claiming the Negroes among them. The government adopted a policy that would have saved hundreds of lives and hundreds of thousands of dollars if someone had had the wit to think of it before. The escaped slave claims were tried before a military court. If the owner proved his claim to the Negro, the government paid his claim in cash and sent the Negro to Arkansas with the Indians.

Many more Indians came in, discouraged with white penetration. Then the murder of three white men on a main road in central Florida set off a new wave of excitement among the settlers. Coacoochee was sent off to bring in Tiger Tail at all costs. He failed. It was decided to send all the Indians, including Coacoochee, to New Orleans without delay. He and his chiefs stood on the deck in silence, with stony faces, until the last line of the Florida coast had disappeared. "It was my home," Coacoochee said, "I loved it and to leave it now is like burying my wife and child."

In Florida it was still believed that Tiger Tail had crossed the Everglades and was hiding near the east coast. Captain Burke's noteworthy expedition from Fort Dallas to Punta Rassa, to the lake, and back to the Miami River, reported seeing not one Indian. The Indians in the Big Cypress had had a fine crop that summer, rice, pumpkins, beans and corn. They made no sign of surrender.

An Indian attack on Mandarin on the St. Johns sent the territory of Florida into another uproar.

There was intense feeling of bitterness between the people of

243

Florida and the War Department. The people of Georgia wanted the militia called out to protect their borders. Hundreds of settlers did not want the war to be over. An army officer wrote: "Many of these people are too idle and too indolent to labor for the means of subsistence; many live by hunting and fishing, and hence the distress of these inhabitants and their desire to get into the service for a maintenance. They are but little improved beyond the Indians themselves."

In February two hundred thirty Indians of all tribes were shipped to New Orleans. A battle was fought in the Great Wahoo Swamp and another at Palatka, at which a few more were captured. Tiger Tail was taken. He died later on in barracks at New Orleans.

The whole country was sick and tired of the war. Colonel Worth was ordered to bring it to a close in June, 1842. The army was ordered out. Two small naval vessels were to be left, based at Indian Key, to try to put a stop to the constant illicit traffic between small sailing vessels from Cuba and the Indians of the lower west coast.

Colonel Worth reported to the War Department that a few more than three hundred Indians were left in hiding and could not be got at. There were, roughly, forty-six Mikasukis of Sam Jones, thirty-seven Creeks of the Prophet's, sixty Seminoles near the Kissimmee, thirty-two Mikasukis and ten Creeks in another group, forty-seven Creeks with Coacoochee's defiant brother, Octiarche, and some sixty-nine Creeks, Tallahassees, Mikasukis, and perhaps a Choctaw or two, in the Everglades. He advised that they be left there.

Of the leaders only old Billy Bowlegs could be reached. Sam Jones was senile, the Prophet had lost his power, Octiarche refused to have anything to do with any white man, so old Billy Bowlegs, Holatta-Micco, the last chief, and some of his warriors, reluctantly came in for a last talk with Colonel (now

Brevet General) Worth on August 14, 1842. They were told they would be allowed to remain temporarily. In November, General Worth established the boundaries of the country the Indian might occupy. It lay, in general, south of Charlotte Harbor, west of a line from the middle of Okeechobee south to Cape Sable. In the Everglades there was to be a twenty-mile stretch of neutral country across the state. Billy Bowlegs was informed that he would be responsible for the good conduct of all the Indians, and he agreed. Four months later all troops were withdrawn except for one regiment at Fort Brooke. In November, 1843, General Worth left Florida. The Indians had not failed to remain completely quiet.

Whether the Indians of the Everglades were defeated is often argued. Certainly this last number never surrendered. They had now the peace they had always wanted.

So the war in Florida had worn itself out. It had dragged from April, 1836, to February, 1842: 3,930 Indians and Negroes had been shipped to Arkansas; numbers died on the way. Of the whites, 1,555 men, army and navy, had died, and the loss among citizens, Indians and Negroes was greater than that. The total expense was forty million dollars. It was war in which only the resistance and determination of the Indians, not four thousand people all told, against the whole might of the United States of America, could be called heroic.

11

The Coming of Peace

Peace did not come at once to the last of the Indians who now remained quiet, renewing their lives in the deep Glades. It did not come at once to the southern shape of Florida, which on its transfer from Spain had been considered by the American government to be the haunt not only of these troublesome Indians but also of renegades, outlaws, escaped slaves and cattle thieves, and, along its lower coasts, of smugglers, wreckers, petty pirates, and illicit slave dealers. Of these, now, the Indians were the least troublesome. When General Worth left Florida in 1843 he wrote that they had observed perfect good faith and strictly fulfilled their engagements.

That was enough for the United States of America. The truth

was that much greater trouble was brewing with Mexico over Texas, which had asked for admission into the Union in 1836. It would be a slave state. Antislavery forces in Congress could not put that off much longer. Mexico, with British and French backing, was increasingly resentful. General Zachary Taylor was already waiting on the northern Texas border.

For the territory of Florida, the removal of the army was very bad news. It was more than the loss of all the money the army had poured in during its occupation. It was more than the simple, bitterly resented fact of Indians still left at large in the Everglades.

Evils still followed the accepted evil of slavery. Slaves still escaped south to the Everglades, with the Indians hijacking the gangs of slaves from the West Indies which the smugglers landed anywhere along this intricate coast.

Since 1808, when the further importation of slaves was stopped in the United States, and cotton plantations were spreading everywhere, because of the newly invented cotton gin, the value of slaves had doubled and quadrupled. Men who were worth a dollar a pound brought three and four hundred dollars delivered from Florida. Slavers sailed their living cargoes from the West Indies to land them up the Caloosahatchee or at Charlotte Harbor, to march them north to the great plantations. So the Indians and the free Negroes attacked, freeing the slaves and robbing the slavers. There was no one to record that. Who but they, the nameless shadows, the speechless, could have spoken of shots in the night, the hard cool hands on the knots of their ropes, the standing clear, who but they could have uttered the word as it should be spoken, the word "freedom?" Then white men hijacked the slaves for their own convoys, and freedom died again. The planters of Florida and Georgia were outraged at these attacks on their supply of labor. They were afraid also that the successful revolution in

247

Haiti and the constant slave insurrections in the sugar islands might prove dangerously encouraging. In the Bahamas slaves were rapidly being freed, as well as all the refugees and slaves of all captured vessels. The waters of the Caribbean, the Gulf of Mexico, and the Florida Straits were infested again with pirates, from which honest merchantmen as well as slave smugglers were in constant danger.

From Key West, in 1822, Admiral Porter's fleet had been harrying the main pirate fleets about the coast of Cuba. Small raffish vessels lurked and pounced about the inlets and islands of lower Florida. From these have come the legends of pirates and buried treasure along those coasts, about John Gomez and his kind at Panther Key and Caxambas, Black Caesar in the eastern keys, and tales impossible to substantiate.

The two small navy vessels stationed at Indian Key in 1842 were not enough to soothe the citizens of the territory of Florida, constantly in fear of British invasion. They insisted—and it had been so agreed between Colonel Worth and Billy Bowlegs—that the Indians were to keep themselves south of the Peace River on the west and not to come east of a line due south from Okeechobee to Cape Sable. A border of neutral land was to be drawn about the Indian country, not to be invaded either by Indians or by whites. In addition, the Twenty-seventh Congress was urged to pass "an Act to provide for the Armed Occupation and Settlement of the unsettled part of the peninsula of East Florida."

It provided "that any person, being the head of a family, or single man over 18 years of age, able to bear arms, who had made a settlement south of" certain townships and east of the base line, was entitled to one quarter section of said land, "provided he register and did not already own 160 acres, that he should live in the Territory five years and should erect a house, fit for the habitation of man," and clear and cultivate at least five acres and live there for four years.

The unspoken idea was that a cordon of hardy and vigilant Indian-hating frontiersmen would prevent the escape of slaves southward and prevent the hijacking of slave gangs.

A total of 1,317 permits covering 210,720 acres were issued, but many were never taken up or were sold or abandoned. There were no surveys.

It was then that men from the states of Georgia and Alabama and north and west Florida, on horseback or plodding along with oxteams, began straggling down the Kissimmee valley, driving before them the half-wild cattle the Indians had abandoned.

Grants as far south as the Caloosahatchee were bought up by big planters ruined by the failure of the Bank of Tallahassee, having mortgaged lands and slaves to buy bank stock so that they could borrow more money for slaves and land. For their cattle and their canefields all these people needed slave labor.

On Biscayne Bay, the first "donation grant" of 640 acres was made to people from the keys who called themselves "Hagan," British cockney style. The name was really "Egan" and had later to be so established in court. Along the Miami River, William F. English had bought a part of the Egan grant from his uncle Richard Fitzpatrick and lived there with slaves and orange and lime trees, bananas and pineapples, by the clear river teeming with fish and manatee and crocodiles.

A similar donation grant on the New River was confirmed to Franklin Lewis by a warranty deed in 1843, under the new act. On the Jonathan Lewis grant, in what was later Coconut Grove, a log house was built and lived in by John Harner. Down the keys were already settlements of English from the Bahamas, intelligent and cockily independent wreckers and fishermen.

249

Still there were not enough of these settlers in their small first clearings, or larger plantation owners, to protect this territory. Many of them would remain as they always had been, hardy and simple people who brought to the frontier only a frontier way of thinking, living in log cabins by patches of sweet potato and black-eyed peas, bringing no new skills or knowledge except shooting and hog curing and tracking. There were not enough inducements for other settlers to dare so wild a country.

The question was, Would it not be better if Florida were a state? Territorial finances were in a bad way and a state meant state taxes. The two old divisions of east and west Florida grew farther and farther apart. On the other hand, the territory of Iowa was shortly to be admitted to the Union as a free state. Slavery interests in Congress were much concerned. The resolution of the legislature of Florida in favor of it was finally attested to by a secretary of state who was reported to have delivered boatloads of slaves up the Manatee to the Gambles' sugar plantation.

But in Dade and Monroe counties there were not enough white men to hold an election for representative to that Legislative Council. The latest Dade County census, taken by men in sailboats or walking down the outer beaches, recorded 314 people, of whom 263 were whites, 29 slaves, and 22 free blacks. In Monroe County there were 618 people, or 452 whites, 93 slaves, and 73 free blacks. Nobody counted Indians.

On March 3, 1845, President Tyler signed the bill making Iowa and Florida states; the first, free, the second, slave.

The new statehood was still not enough to balance the constant draining away of the hardiest and most restless citizens to the Mexican War, to Texas and the developing West. The hard-working, intelligent immigrants from an unsettled Europe went west rather than compete with slave labor in the South.

Florida officials saw that they must make an effort to attract settlers by offering them more roads and railroads and canals, and more land.

It was then for the first time that men began to think about the Everglades.

Many veterans of the Indian wars remembered now with pleasure the sea about those southern beaches and the sun glinting along the great levels of the saw grass, the unending openness, the great light, the fine air. They knew well the blackness of the saw-grass muck. The idea sprang up spontaneously that the Everglades ought to be drained. It was an idea more explosive than dynamite, which would change this lower Florida world as nothing had so changed it since the melting of the glacial ice four thousand years ago.

In the same year in which Florida became a state, therefore, the legislature urged Congress "to examine and survey the Everglades, with a view to their reclamation."

The Hon. J. D. Westcott, Jr., wrote the secretary of the treasury and asked him to appoint "an agent to make a reconnaissance of these lands and make a report as to the probable practicability of the work [of drainage] to be laid before Congress at its next session."

Mr. Buckingham Smith of St. Augustine, in June, 1847, was appointed to procure "authentic information in relation to what are generally called the 'Ever Glades' " on the peninsula of Florida.

This was in the same year that a lighthouse was set on Cape Canaveral. The United States government began to set aids for navigation up and down that difficult coast where the wrecks still piled up and the wreckers darted out from the inlets to "salvage" them.

This Mr. Buckingham Smith of St. Augustine was to be a most distinguished if little known citizen of the new state of

251

Florida. He was certainly then and for many years the first scholar and historian of Florida, in a day when more men in south Florida knew how to shine a deer and skin an alligator than to write their own names.

He had come from Connecticut, the public schools of New Bedford and Taunton, Massachusetts, Trinity College and Harvard Law, to practice in St. Augustine for twenty years. He was secretary to Territorial Governor Raymond Reid and member of the legislature. He cultivated oranges, took an interest in the poor of St. Augustine, and wrote the first *Annals of Florida*. His passion was the history of the Spanish in Florida and in this country. He gave his life to it.

He would be sent to Mexico to starve on an almost infinitesimal salary, to study old Spanish records and write home, to people like Daniel Webster, volumes of confidential information. He struggled for an appointment as legation secretary at Madrid because he was wild to go to Spain and work in the great archives of the Council of the Indies. He got there and spent years, half starved, lost in those archives. He sent twenty-five volumes of copies and translations of Spanish documents to Washington. He never had enough money or any support from the American ambassadors, who thought he was cracked. He had the respect, however, of the Spanish officials and their full co-operation. Eventually, his money was cut off and he was forced to return to St. Augustine. With his great work unfinished, he died. "No one before or since," it has been said, "has done so much for Florida history."

This was the man, then, this passionate and unrewarded and unrecognized researcher, who made a trip up the Miami River and into the Everglades to write the great *Report on the Everglades,* submitted in June, 1848, which was printed in full in the Senate *Reports for the First Session of the Thirtieth Congress*. Single copies of this report are now a collector's item.

Colonel Robert Butler was the surveyor general for Florida at that time, more than six-sevenths of which had never been surveyed at all. It was he who made the classic reply to the order to survey: "I now ask your attention to the Everglades, which cannot be surveyed without first being drained." That it would also never be drained intelligently without proper survey and adequate geological study did not seem to occur then to anyone. The main question in Colonel Butler's mind was whether the draining of the Everglades would not conflict with the sovereignty of the state of Florida.

As for Buckingham Smith's magnificently written report, it still contained a number of errors. It records the ancient canals of the prehistoric Indians as Spanish. The water of the Everglades would easily run off, he wrote, once the rock that held it in place was cut through. Beyond some little stench of decaying vegetation, it would be attended with no ill effects and should cost about $500,000, he believed.

But his main contention was still the political one, that a great new state might be formed, which would be a slave state forever.

Mr. Smith printed also a number of reports from officers who in the last Indian war had known the Glades intimately. General William S. Harney was satisfied that, by building enough canals, the Glades would remain dry. "If it succeeds," he wrote, "that region would in less than five years have a population of a hundred thousand souls or more." Many other officers added their cheerful opinions of how simple the whole thing would be.

Only Stephen R. Mallory, the collector of customs at Key West, who would be secretary of the navy for the Confederacy, had a grimmer view: "Whether sound policy and expediency, keeping in view the expense and the lands to be reclaimed, dictate the attempt to drain these Everglades, and whether it be

253

possible to accomplish it to any considerable extent, are questions which a careful examination of the lands and streams, a knowledge of the quantity of water falling per annum, and a connected system of levels can only adjust or solve . . . but I have been in the Glades and about them, from Jupiter to Miami, much. I have ate of its fish, drank of its water, smelt of its snakes and alligators and waded through its mud to my middle for weeks, and am *au fait* upon all these, besides possessing some little acquaintance with its mosquitoes and horseflies, both of which can be recommended. I have also, together with a friend, taken soundings with poles, marked for that purpose, from our boat for miles and miles; all of which labor might as well have been expended in surveying the moon. My own impression is that large tracts of the Glades are fully as low as the surrounding sea, and can never be drained, that some lands around the margin may be reclaimed by drainage, or by dyking, but it will be found wholly out of the question to drain all the Everglades. As the country now is, healthy and mild, with its good lands in small parcels, with water at hand anywhere for irrigation, I think it offers inducements to small capitalists, men with from one to ten hands, to go there and raise fruits. Fruits will grow well there."

The year was 1849 and gold was discovered in California. A tide of excitement throughout the whole United States turned and flooded in that direction. Men shooting alligators on the Florida frontier left for the West. William F. English, on his pleasant plantation by the Miami River, made up his mind to leave at once for the California gold diggings. He meant to make a million dollars and come back and build a beautiful small tropical city on each side of the Miami River, between the rapids of the river and the shining loveliness of the bay. A million dollars of that gold lying right on top of the earth would do it. William English got to California, but he died there.

Then in July, 1849, three men were reported murdered, one on the Indian River, two on the Peace River. The resulting panic emptied the plantations and the clearings as men and women fled north for protection. It was said only one white man remained in all that southern country and he was on the coast, at New Smyrna.

Major General Twiggs was ordered south with several companies of regulars as the governor called for volunteers. Two companies were ordered to the Caloosahatchee to lay out a post. General Twiggs, whose pretty daughter was engaged to one of his dashing young officers, Abraham Charles Myers, the chief quartermaster, had his little joke. He ordered that the new post be called Fort Myers.

It was above Punta Rassa on the broad lower waters of the Caloosahatchee, at the place where Fort Harvie had faced the gold and gray of west coast winter sunsets. There were barracks and officers' quarters and oyster-shell walks about the old parade ground. Officers' wives in long stylish skirts would pass back and forth among the flower beds to the spirited music of the military band. A military watchfulness but fashion too, with its ringlets and bare shoulders and fine slippers, had come to the Caloosahatchee.

Mail came to Fort Myers by sailboat from Tampa, once a week, it was hoped. When the boat capsized with stores for the commissary, there were no more for another week. There was often no milk, as the scrawny, half-wild Florida cows gave hardly any at all, even when captured.

The men fished in the river, hunted deer and great bronze turkeys and quail in the pinelands. The latest Indian war in Florida did not seem very serious from Fort Myers.

Billy Bowlegs was reported to be surly and insolent to such officers as met him hunting. But actually General Twiggs knew no more about the murders or any Indian uprising than he had before.

There was a very able man, an Indian War veteran, who had been made Indian agent with headquarters at Fort Brooke. He had been one of those many officers who had understood and sympathized with the plight of the Indian. He took up his duties at a time when not one Indian would have anything to do with white men. It was Captain Casey's duty to get down into the Indian country and convince them, if he could, that he meant to have friendly and honorable dealings with them.

For all these quiet months he had been busy at that difficult task. As a result, all the chiefs except Sam Jones had learned to give him confidence and would go to see him at Tampa for the presents the government had for them. Sam Jones, very old now, would meet him if Captain Casey would come to some camp of his in the Glades.

General Twiggs was wisely satisfied to leave things to Casey, who sailed up and down the Caloosahatchee for a week, letting himself and his guide be seen but seeing no one.

Then near Sarasota Bay, his guide, Felipe, found a peace token. At the top of a pole was a stick in which white heron feathers were fixed, with a string of white beads and a twist of tobacco. Felipe left a sign that they would be there at the full of the moon. When Captain Casey's small sloop came slowly landward then, three Indians hailed him. On shore, the leading Indian would not shake hands but said, "More good friends do this," and took hold of his arms above the elbows and shook Indian fashion.

They had been sent by Holatta-Micco, old Billy Bowlegs, to say that the murder on the Indian River last July had been done by five reckless young Indians camped on the Kissimmee River, whose leader for some crime had been outlawed by the Indian council and condemned to suicide. He wanted to start another war with the whites. Three days later, the same young men had crossed to the Peace River and killed two more white men there.

Bowlegs had sent a party to bring them in but they had already been captured by another chief, Chitto-Hadjo. Bowlegs was anxious that Captain Casey should understand that the Indian council deeply regretted the whole business and that they wanted no more trouble.

Captain Casey sent word to Bowlegs that he must confer with General Twiggs, and gave his personal word of honor for their safety. The meeting between General Twiggs and the Indians was completely satisfactory. The criminals were to be delivered on October 19. Bowlegs, with twenty warriors in their finest shirts and plumes, came in with the three men and brought

the severed head of a fourth, as proof that he was dead. The fifth had escaped. General Twiggs, and later the president of the United States, reported to the Indian council their full satisfaction with Bowlegs' action.

Yet the roused state of Florida wanted every last Indian out of there. It was agreed that "the tribe" should be bribed to emigrate. The secretary of war authorized General Twiggs to offer them the sum of $215,000 if they would go. At first General Twiggs flatly refused. "To approach them now with an offer of a million of money and all the prairies of the West, and war as an alternative, there would not be a moment's hesitation in deciding on war," he wrote.

Yet the importunities continued, with such orders from the secretary as General Twiggs could not ignore. At a later meeting with Bowlegs, the question of emigration was brought up. Bowlegs and all his men showed such spontaneous anger that the general refrained from bringing up the subject again.

In August, 1850, a white boy was murdered near Fort Brooke. Everybody said the Indians did it. Bowlegs said they did not but that he would see what he could do. He sent in three Indians who confessed the crime to Captain Casey and in jail promptly hanged themselves. "No outrages have been committed," Captain Casey said in a later report, "nor are any likely to be so long as we leave them alone."

The question of reclaiming swamplands in the state of Ar-.kansas, as well as in Florida, was coming up in Congress. That body had had considerable pressure brought to bear on it on the subject of draining large quantities of swamplands still retained by the federal government within the boundaries of a single state.

On September 28, 1850, the Congress approved an act "to enable the state of Arkansas and other states to reclaim the 'swamplands' within their limits. They were hereby granted to said state, on a patent to be issued in fee simple, subject to the disposal of the Legislature." Provided, however, "that the proceeds of said lands, whether by sale or direct appropriation in kind, shall be applied exclusively, as far as necessary, to the purpose of reclaiming said lands by means of the levees and drains aforesaid."

This was the great Swamp Lands Act of 1850, on which so

much Florida history is based. An act so to secure the swamp and overflowed lands from the federal government and provide for all necessary examinations and plattings was at once passed by the Florida legislature. It provided also for the creation of a Board of Internal Improvement for the State of Florida, to consist of the governor, attorney general, treasurer, comptroller and state register of public lands "who shall be for the time being ex-officio members thereof."

All the money resulting from sale of such lands in the control of the trustees was to form a separate and distinct fund, to be called the Internal Improvement of the State of Florida, to be applied strictly according to the provision of the act.

Five hundred thousand acres of swamp and overflowed lands, in general known as the Everglades, thus came under the control of the state of Florida. Now the federal government, in turning over this vast unknown area, had only to make an exact study and authentic description of it as far as possible, with maps, profiles and levels as a basis for future work now thoroughly implemented by the state.

With all these great matters on their hands, the people of Florida were more and more impatient with the Indian situation. The United States Army, the government itself, was doing nothing. The state of Florida therefore authorized the governor to call for a regiment of mounted volunteers to get rid of the Indians. The sum of two million dollars was granted. The secretary of war refused flatly to allow Florida to go to war with the Indians again. But they might try to bribe them to get out.

There was a man by the name of Luther Blake, of Alabama, who had been well paid for helping to remove the Cherokee Indians to the West. In 1851 he was appointed a special agent to remove the Indians of Florida. He was allowed expenses not to exceed $10,000 and $5 a day for himself. He would receive, in addition, a reward of $800 for each warrior and $450 for each woman and child whom he sent west. The government would take care of the transportation and incidental expenses. The idea was that he would pay the Indians some of the money he got, but there was no contract to that effect. It evidently never crossed his mind.

Captain Casey at Fort Brooke knew nothing of this new scheme until Luther Blake, shortly to be known as "General" Luther Blake, presented himself at Casey's office with an order to have all money and supplies turned over to him. Captain Casey moved only as he was forced by his own superiors. Blake sent fulsome letters to the Office of Indian Affairs, saying that he felt quite confident that the Seminoles could be removed this fall and winter, and left for Arkansas to get a delegation of Indians there to go back to Florida and persuade the others to leave. He returned to Fort Myers in March to find that Captain Jernigan of the Florida Volunteers had captured one old woman with a child, since which the old woman had hanged herself. Blake kept on writing the commissioner how friendly the Indians were and how in a few days he would have a talk with Bowlegs, but the truth of the matter was that the Indians stayed hidden in the deep Glades and would have nothing to do with anyone but Captain Casey.

The western delegation, as usual, had nothing good to say about the still bad conditions in the West. Even Luther Blake suggested to the government that if decent living conditions and food were first arranged for, the Indians might go more willingly. "No," the government said; "get them there first. Then somehow things will straighten themselves out."

Bowlegs allowed himself to be talked to but said he wanted the payment of an old claim for stolen cattle. In June fifteen Indians had come in. In September, by a supreme effort, Luther Blake took Bowlegs and another Indian on a long expensive trip to Washington and back, at which he and his party and

"Mr. William B. Legs" and Abraham, the wily old interpreter, were registered in all the hotels along the way, Tampa, Palatka, Orange City, Savannah and Washington, to which they traveled by hacks and horses, steamboats, diligences and trains, fed well and provided with all sorts of things, "not to exceed $600," the commissioner had written. The account included one pair of drawers for Abraham, 7½ pounds pilot bread, 7½ pounds sugar crackers, one pair boots and one plug of tobacco, and for Bowlegs, one pair pants, one pair half-sewed boots, one handkerchief, 6 bottles French brandy, 6 bottles claret and one tumbler. "General" Blake's own account was full of more lavish expenditures, especially for tobacco and liquors.

Bowlegs got back from Washington, evidently much invigorated by his trip, and disappeared into the Glades. Captain Casey had stayed in Fort Brooke speaking clearly and forcefully exactly what he thought. Blake wrote the commissioner long complaining letters that Casey had said that Blake would swindle the Indians out of everything he promised them.

Captain Casey replied, when charged, that he claimed a right to speak of public measures and the official acts of public officers and was not in the habit of mincing his words. Blake wrote the commissioner that Casey had said that the "Honorable Secretary of War was only a pettifogging Louisiana lawyer." Casey had asked to be relieved of his duties at Fort Brooke and that was done immediately.

By February, 1854, Blake had sent west thirty-six Indians, twelve warriors, and the rest women and children, at a cost of $48,025 with $5,000 for transportation. Blake was dismissed and Captain Casey at once reinstated as agent, the first friend the Florida Indians had ever had.

It was the Everglades and not the Indians in them that were of the greatest possible importance to the state of Florida and the trustees of the new Internal Improvement Fund. Impatient of the delay of the federal government in getting on with the necessary work of mapping, the state pushed its own surveyors down the east coast to run township lines to Okeechobee.

There had been surveys of the lower east coast, in a rough sort of way, by the Spanish. During the British occupation of 1763 and 1784, William Gerard De Brahms had made a more careful one. A. H. Jones, of the General Land Office, surveyed a line between Okeechobee and the St. Lucie River. The old military road from the Indian River across the Kissimmee to Tampa was reopened. Fort Jupiter, on the coast, and Fort McRae, east of Okeechobee, once abandoned, were re-established. At this time also were set up or re-established Fort Capron in what is now Brevard County, Fort Casey at Charlotte Harbor, Fort Simon Drum east of Lake Trafford, Fort Thompson up the Caloosahatchee, Fort Poinsett at Cape Sable, Fort Wescott in the extreme south saw grass.

W. J. Reyes, a man of Minorcan descent from St. Augustine, assistant to the surveyor general, ran the Jones line again and established a surveyor's camp in the northeast of Okeechobee, at Chancy Bay, probably the first camp or settlement of any kind that side of the lake.

The Chancy who gave his name to that bay was a Frenchman, a hunter and otter trapper who must have camped there first about the time that Pierre Denaud established his first store on the Caloosahatchee, later Fort Denaud. He had come into Florida the way so many early hunters and settlers did, from the Carolinas and Georgia and north Florida down the Kissimmee to the lake and so to the coast. He and some friends used to go out hunting to Lake Okeechobee from Eau Gallie on the coast in a high-wheeled oxcart.

Once Chancy went out 'gator hunting by himself. A 'gator got him by the leg. The 'gator couldn't bite his leg off, but only hold on and roll over and over, and Chancy knew it. So although he lost a lot of blood he rolled over as long as the 'gator could and got loose and crawled back to camp. They had a barrel of salt for curing hides and he put that on. They asked him afterward if it didn't hurt, and he said it did, but it was better to do that than not to do anything.

W. J. Reyes, who had been surveying in Florida ever since he was a boy cooking for surveying parties, made many trips to the lake by yawl and wagon from the Indian River. The surveyors lived off the country, taking with them only corn meal, rice, beans and salt. They flushed turkeys and ran them down with dogs. They slept on the ground and only sometimes in tents and were much annoyed by the wolves that still existed in Florida then.

Reyes resurveyed all the townships about the east side of the lake at that time, at a cost of $4 a mile. It was considered, as Surveyor General Westcott of Florida wrote, "that a gradual and easy approach by surveys and settlements from the present surveyed lands would be safer for the inhabitants of the frontier and sooner accomplish peaceably and economically the object so much desired [the removal of the Indians] than any other way."

The state of Florida deliberately violated the agreement with the Indians in allowing traders and hunters and surveyors to invade the neutral zone. Casual Indians did not keep entirely clear of it, either. But the surveying parties were the deliberate threat of continued encroachment to come. Billy Bowlegs and the Indian council were perfectly aware of that. Reports were made to Captain Casey of the Office of Indian Affairs, and the War Department hastened to issue a reprimand to the state.

The War Department's Topographical Engineers, under Captain A. A. Humphreys, at last proceeded with the business of surveying and mapping what Everglades they could.

In the year 1855 Captain Dawson made two expeditions, one

263

in a dry March. Their boats dragged through mudholes, and at last were stopped by a vast expanse of saw grass standing in no water at all. The other was in June, after the rains. In December of that year a squad of men under Lieutenant Hartsuff, U.S. Engineers, had pushed a survey into the Big Cypress two miles from the main garden of old Billy Bowlegs. The story as written by Andrew P. Canova, who was one of the party, was that, because the soldiers wantonly destroyed Bowlegs's fine bananas, he next morning attacked the Hartsuff camp and wounded several.

It was nothing so trivial. Bowlegs had done everything possible to prevent acts of war by the Indians. He had waited and watched, year after year, judging perfectly the attitude of the Florida people. Now at this trivial depredation he struck.

It was exactly what the Floridians had wanted. War was declared. Secretly Jefferson Davis asked the governor to call for a volunteer force to supplement the regulars under General Harney. A bounty of $150 on every live Indian brought in somewhat slowed up the general shooting.

All that year the white men went about that country and were fired on by small bands of Indians, a burst of gunfire for an hour, three or four killed and nobody knows how many Indians. It was the same story everywhere: blood on the palmettos and blue smoke drifting off down the pine levels as all the crows flew screaming and the buzzards came in afterward, tilting and dropping down. The Indians met the whites almost where they chose, at Fort Denaud or on the mainland east of Chokoloskee Key, near Bowlegs's village in the Big Cypress and near Fort Doane and at a great Indian encampment in a hammock of royal palms near the present Tamiami Trail. Thirty houses and many acres of pumpkins and beans and corn were destroyed. The Indians who had retreated came back fighting when they smelled the smoke. They overtook the marching

264

column and killed Captain John Parkill, who had come back safe from the Mexican War and left his father's great plantation in Leon County to come down here and fight Indians, and be buried. Five others were wounded with Indian arrows. In December, Captain Stephens with ninety men destroyed another big camp in the Big Cypress and were fired on from ambush and had five men killed.

The only real excitement and color of this last erratic and haphazard campaign was provided by that dashing Indian fighter, Jacob E. Michler. He appeared first to a bedraggled company of Florida Volunteers who had pushed along the flat country from the Caloosahatchee to Fort Center, near Okeechobee. This was in 1857. They were a rawboned, sallow, malarial lot, with long hair over their faded butternut shoulders, riding horses as rawboned and wretched. But the man who walked into the mess room was something to stare at. He was slight, wiry, quick, in a bright blue suit and overalls tucked into high boots. His face under a huge white felt hat was dark and his long hair was black and his long mustache was black and his eyes were black and lively as crickets. He carried a rifle, a shot bag, a hammock, and he was eating an orange.

He was announced as a guide sent by General Harney. He was also a surveyor from St. Augustine and a hunter and Everglades tracker, a dead shot, a dangerous poker player, and an accomplished snake spearer. In the boats, the company worked their way across Okeechobee, up the Kissimmee and the smaller lakes, looking for Indians and seeing none. Michler and the major commanding were ripening a sound mutual hate. One day Michler said that he wanted to go ashore because he had seen Indian signs. The major refused flatly.

Michler pulled out his revolver and forced the officer to have him pulled ashore, where he disappeared. He made his way overland one hundred miles to Tampa, where General Harney gave him permission to raise his own company of volunteers. He appeared later in Fort Myers to his old ragged company in pure-white flannels and a remarkable Panama hat. His own men dashed up on fine horses, tricked out western Indian style in leggings and beadwork. He had sworn to have every Indian out of the Everglades in two months. He brought in a small camp of men, women and children and ponies, from the place where he had gone ashore from the boat.

The Everglades still protected its own.

Jefferson Davis, the secretary of war, stated in January, 1858, that the Seminole "had baffled the energetic efforts of our army to effect their subjugation and removal." Colonel Elias Rector, superintendent of the Western Seminoles, brought a delegation to Florida to try to talk to these people. They managed to get Billy Bowlegs to come in. He was offered $6,500, his four sub-chiefs $1,000, his warriors $500 apiece, and each woman and child $100.

He said he would go. One hundred twenty-three went voluntarily and forty-one who had been captured. Tiger Tail, old Tiger Tail who fought so fiercely, committed suicide on the steamer *Grey Cloud* on the way to New Orleans.

It was considered that only about one hundred Indians were left silent and unnoticed in the Everglades—Sam Jones, senile but indestructible, and his changeless Mikasukis and some Tallahassees. Actually, there were many more than that. They were to live and grow in numbers. They were the undefeated.

The great Ives map, as it was called, was published in 1856, before the war was over. It is a superb piece of mapmaking and etching, the first fine American map of the country.

Another war of so much greater import was brewing to the north of them that for a long time the Everglades would be forgotten. It was slavery that brought it about, whatever other causes there were, slavery that from the beginning of the white man's history had been so great a force in the events that surrounded, like the sea itself, this lower peninsula.

The money that the trustees of the Internal Improvement Fund had collected by the first sale of land went somewhat illegally into bonds of the Confederacy. The Union troops captured Key West and occupied Fort Myers and ravaged the plantations on the Manatee. Only the Florida coasts were busy with blockade runners and the men who ran cattle down from the Kissimmee prairie and hogs from the lake beaches to the hidden inlets and the black boats. John Weeks, a fugitive from Confederate drafts, was allowed to raise vegetables at Cape Sable for the Key West garrison. A man named Wagner grew vegetables up the Miami River for Union refugees at Fort Dallas.

The great war ravaged the South. But in it peace came to the Everglades.

12

White Man's Return

T HE end of the Civil War was a remote happening to the few
white people about the Everglades. The surrender brought confusion and dismay to the landed and now impoverished plantation owners about Tallahassee and North Florida. To the
lower bays and islands it brought some outlaws and refugees
from justice, and a drift of veterans who remembered, from
service in the Indian Wars or the later blockades, the great
teeming sunny solitudes.

The hazy plans for reclaiming the Everglades by draining
them were locked in the state archives. The Internal Improvement Fund's money was lost in interest guaranteed on bonds for

something like four hundred miles of prewar, and now ruined, railroads. Now the bonds were in default. State politics were in the greatest confusion. State Republicans and Republican carpetbaggers were in control, picking up what profits they could find. Internal Improvement Fund coupons for more than a million dollars were held, for the most part, by a man named Francis Voss, a Republican, who in 1869 began suit for interest payments. The value of Everglades land was down to thirty and forty cents, and there were no sales. The minutes of a later Internal Improvement Commission stated clearly that Voss was "a little grasping fellow, with a heart no bigger than a mosquito's gizzard." He was driving the fund into receivership.

The most important thing the Civil War did for the Glades was to free the slaves. It removed forever from the descendants of slaves and of Indians the fear of man catchers. White men to whose slaves the Everglades were a constant hope, forgot them now. They were now moving their families in oxcarts to the lakes and pinelands of middle Florida, to make orange groves and a living in new towns that had been forts.

Yet here was still freedom. A Homestead Act had been passed by the Congress of the United States in 1862. Yet the few people here did not bother with titles.

To the west coast, men rode mules from the home place, or oxcarts, down from North Florida, across the old fords of the Caloosahatchee to Fort Myers, or down the Kissimmee by boat and across the lake. Or again, they zigged and zagged by sailboat up the bewildering mangrove country from Key West, looking along the river mouths and the mounded islands for a likely place. By the seventies there were more people keeping to themselves on the lower west coast than there were anywhere on the east, north of the keys. Many of these people were Cubans who had lived there for several generations, farming some of the old black dirt middens with the help of the remnants of the Calusa Indians. The Indians trapped, with gumbo limbo gum, the bright birds that came through on their long migrations, and sent them to be sold in Havana in cages made Calusa-fashion.

Punta Rassa, where the Caloosahatchee broadens to the gulf, in 1867 saw the first sign of progress. The International Ocean-Telegraph, which one day would be the Western Union, sent a lot of Yankee boys in wagons to string a land line all the way from Jacksonville to Punta Rassa, from which the cable would go undersea to the keys and so to Havana. A few of those boys stayed on.

The company moved its office into the old Fort Myers. The trail down the river from Fisheating Creek and the Kissimmee to Punta Rassa was dusty still with the hoofs of the half-wild cattle. In 1871 over one hundred schoonerloads for Cuba and the Bahamas in that year alone brought in $60,000 in heavy Spanish gold to the pockets of the frontier cattlemen.

Fort Myers grew with it. The ruined buildings about the frowsy parade were fixed up. The Hendrys got into the cattle business. Their name would thereafter be connected with the town and the river and the new county very much later to be created nearer Okeechobee, to be called Hendry County.

The man Weeks who had raised vegetables at Cape Sable during the war brought his three daughters up to the Allen River, now Barron's River, that runs into Chokoloskee Bay. He claimed before he was through that he had settled on every island in the entire Ten Thousand. There were two or three Catholic families on Chokoloskee Island, where even in summer, although the mosquitoes may be thick among the scraggly shell-mound trees, a flood of chill air sweeps from the Glades down Turner's River.

Richard Bushrod Turner himself, who had faced the Indians

270

fighting with bows and arrows in the battle of Royal Palm Hammock, moved up in his boat to clear the land under that tremendous series of mounds which runs back a mile and a half into mangrove, ancient, solitary, silent, utterly impressive. He built a shack and a rain-water cistern, and started some vegetables and a cane patch. He trapped raccoons and lived alone with the owls and the wildcats and the Indians slipping down the river in their canoes from the Big Cypress. They got along all right now.

Captain Hall went up and down to Key West with his schooner, picking up mails and skins and delivering supplies. Cuban fishing smacks put in at Caxambas for water, as they always had. Captain Bill Collier, north on Marco Island, began to put up a store and wharf after his father's boat was wrecked in the storm. There had been a preacher aboard besides the two of them. When the storm came up, his father had given the preacher an ax to cut the main sheet when he yelled. But the preacher dropped the ax and fell to his knees in prayer. The boat capsized, and Captain Bill's father was drowned. Only he and the preacher were saved. Captain Bill claimed to have been an atheist ever after. He'd stop anything he was doing to argue about atheism with anybody, he was so religious about it.

Places up that coast began to get fixed names. Cape Sable was French for "Sand Cape" instead of the Spanish "Punta de Tanche." Cape Romano, the lonely westernmost sand cape north above Ponce de Leon's Bay and what was then called Delaware Bay, or Gallivan's Bay, was named Cape Roman for the British surveyor Bernard Roman, who went by it in 1775. It is spoken of now, Cuban fashion, as Cape Romano. There was an inconspicuous mangrove river somebody named "Pickiune-hatchee" near the Fork River or "Fakahatchee" that the local people still pronounce "Fikahatchee."

271

John Gomez had been a pirate and lived to be 118 years old, he said. He spoke seven languages and couldn't read one, and had seen Napoleon in Madrid when he was a boy, and he also told about how he had been the only one of a band of pirates to escape hanging in Havana, by stealing a boat and sailing to this coast. John Gomez lived on a key where he started a goat ranch, but a panther ate up all the goats, so it was called Panther Key.

North still, Estero Bay, with Estero Beach and the Estero River, shallow and lovely, with the high mound on Mound Key, came from the Spanish word for "estuary." The Spanish "Boca Grande" named the deep pass beyond. At the north end of Pine Island, within the Caloosahatchee mouth, a little landing place had been called "Bocilla" by the Spaniards, which is spelled "Bokeelia" today. Still farther north lie the charming shell beaches of the island called Sanibel, from "Santa Ysabel," and "Captiva," with its somewhat unconvincing legend of the pirate Gasparilla.

Nobody can now remember all those high sand-and-shell islands of that coast where at one time or another a solitary man wanted by the law or a man and his family seeking living room have not lived. There would be no bother about titles. His boat would be tied at the plank wharf, high over the rough black mud and oyster-shell beach, where his fish nets dried on their frames. The shack of sun-silvered boards would stand in a hollow in the lee of the mound, with rusty pipes leading to the rain-water cistern. A few chickens would scratch in the shell soil under his bananas. There would be lime trees and a sour orange someone had planted. There would be an Indian midden of good black dirt higher up, fine for sweet potatoes among bits of Indian pottery and ashes and oyster shells of old feasts. There would be all the fish in the world, and he could

272

sell his catch for a cent or a cent and a half a pound. It wasn't a bad living.

His wife and the children might walk to the place where the high altar or the signal fires had stood on the path curving among tall dry weeds, loud with crickets, and about cactus clumps, and stand on the windy top higher than the trees, looking far and far out over the polished Gulf or, the other way, to the interminable mangroves. There would be one sail over there. The rooster would crow lingeringly in the sunny silence. The bright warblers they call Nonpareils would flutter like butterflies in some scrubby tree for the boy to shoot at with his slingshot until he was old enough to have a rifle.

When the wife could not stand the loneliness any more, a boatload or two would carry all their gear. All they had to do was leave. But at the last minute the man would send the boy back to lean a plank in the cistern so that the raccoons climbing down the walls to water would find a way to get out, and not drown in it.

Nobody on the west coast thought a thing about reclaiming the Everglades, one way or the other.

When the northers blew the water out of Okeechobee across the shallow Lake Flirt and Lake Hicpochee and flooded the swamps from which the Caloosahatchee drained, and the river water stood clear and shining under the live oaks and the water oaks, the crackers had a hard time herding the bawling cattle across.

These were the people who spoke the slurring early English of the old South, who had come in after the Armed Occupation Act of 1842. Their one- and two-room log cabins were made with a hip roof, a porch, and perhaps a "breeze-way." They lived much as they always had under mossy oaks, with chickens in the bare swept yards and a chinaberry tree, a Cherokee rose that the woman had planted, and a hog to butcher for fat back

273

to go with their grits and sweet potatoes. They had a hippy cow or two in the pineland and all the wild hogs and game the men could shoot. Once in a great while there would be a Methodist or Baptist circuit rider and the songs and shouts of the converted would ring through the trees about a camp meeting.

On the east coast they were not thinking so much of drainage as they were of transportation. There were still a few pleasant places up the Miami River where men with a few slaves had raised indigo and cotton and had a sawmill. They brought in governesses for their children, and their heirs started coontie starch factories and complained about how difficult it was to know what was going on in the world.

A mail schooner sailed up from Key West twice a month, but to get a letter and send back an answer from Lake Worth to Miami, sixty-eight miles away, took more than a month. It had to go up the Indian River by steamboat to Titusville, then by railroad to Tampa, by steamer to Key West, and so by the regular schooner to Miami at last.

In the late sixties a man called "Long John" Holman carried the mail all the way down the beaches on foot from St. Augustine to Fort Dallas. There were too many panthers in the palmettos and sometimes bears in the beach plums, so he walked through the long nights pale with stars over the sea always there beside him. In the daytimes he hid and slept. Nobody at all lived between Jupiter Light and Fort Dallas, except at Fort Lauderdale.

The government built the first House of Refuge on the beach north of Biscayne Key to give shelter to people from wrecks. Mr. and Mrs. H. D. Pierce came down from Chicago after the great fire and he was the first keeper. They came overland from Cedar Keys to Fort Pierce by oxcart. Later they homesteaded a place on an island in Lake Worth, which they called "Hypoluxo," the Indian word that meant "Big-Water-All-Around-No-Get-Out."

A man named Bradley and his son Louis took the contract to carry the mail down the beaches for $600 a year. Later Ed Hamilton carried it. Somebody moved his boat to the other side of the inlet from where he crossed. On the way back he left his clothes and the mail and tried to swim, but the swift current drowned him. The man who moved the boat was arrested and taken to Jacksonville for trial but he was let off.

Some time after that the mail came down from Jupiter to Lake Worth by wagon, and then by stagecoach. Uncle John Clemenson was the first driver. Everybody knew him. He used to walk ahead of his pair of mules playing the fiddle.

In Tallahassee a great scandal was growing up about the sale of Internal Improvement Fund bonds and the proposed grants to railroads of over seven million acres of swamplands. A Florida Inland Navigation Company, among which were some of the state officials, ex officio trustees of the fund, tried to sell themselves over one million acres of land, for one dollar. Republican Lieutenant Governor William H. Gleason of Dade County took part in an involved deal which would pay the Internal Improvement Fund with bonds at par which could be bought anywhere for thirty-five cents. He would have made $100,000, which he proposed to divide with Governor Reed. Reed refused. Gleason and others tried to have him impeached. Reed ousted Gleason from his state office, and Gleason retired to his place on the Miami River, held in the name of his wife, Sarah H. Gleason. He began to see a great future for this bay country.

With his partner, W. H. Hunt, also a Republican, he petitioned the Internal Improvement Fund trustees to allow him "to enter certain portions of swamp and overflowed lands and drain them." He set up a company called the Southern Inland

Navigation and Improvement Company in order to claim the free grants of Everglades land given by the Internal Improvement Board. But he was able to sell so little stock, in spite of his energetic salesmanship, that in 1873 he petitioned the board for more time in which to get the canal and steamships started. They gave him until 1877.

That brisk and efficient traveler, Dr. Daniel G. Brinton of Philadelphia, in his *Guide Book for Florida and the South for Tourists, Invalids and Emigrants* had only a little to say about "Key Biscayne Bay" then. Key Biscayne was then the county seat. Travel was possible only by mail schooner from Key West. Brinton wrote that the climate was undoubtedly the finest to be found on the southeastern coast. "It could also be made the most accessible part of the seacoast of Florida. Lieutenant-Governor Gleason," he wrote, "resides at Miami and will entertain travellers to the extent that he can."

In 1871 William B. Brickell, with his second wife, an Englishwoman, and some of the first of his seven children, came to the Miami River and bought land on the south point of the river mouth occupying the Rebecca Egan grant.

Mr. Brickell was already a picturesque character. He had drifted from Ohio to California, to Japan and Australia before bringing his family to Biscayne Bay. He built a house and wharves and a store, where later he kept the post office. Sailboats coming up and down the bay to the store added an air of liveliness to wide tinted waters and the palm trees along the clear river.

Indians in their canoes from the long trip from the Big Cypress stopped at the old campground by the south fork to put on their storegoing early finery, bright cloth leggings and moccasins, and egret plumes in their turbans bound with silver bands such as the Calusas had made. The women sewed by hand the men's fine calico skirted-shirts and their own long

276

dresses, of ruffled calico with a bit of a bertha, which did not cover a bare brown strip of waist. They wore their black hair in tight pompadours over bangs, and strings of beads and many silver coins.

Then the long canoes full of people dark and brilliant as birds swept down to the store, the children's eyes big with wonder in their Mongolian brown faces, the small women shy and quiet and excited.

The Indians brought bundles of raccoon and deer and otter skins and alligator teeth, for which they were carefully paid in silver coins. They would pay the same coins out again for fine-sprigged calico and new kettles and thread and knives and axes, and the new Singer hand-sewing machines the Indian women yearned over. The men would buy liquor. With one man sober to guard them, they would drink themselves into complete torpor under the bushes, while the women and children waited, sitting in bright watchful heaps by the canoes.

Indians who lived near town brought in any amount of vegetables and fresh-killed meat from the hunting grounds, and peddled it among the few houses by the river paths, deer and turkey and quail, so that the white people had all they wanted. Everybody considered them honest, quiet, reliable people, who would walk miles to return a coin overpaid, or a favor, or keep a promise.

The Rev. Clay MacCauley, for the director of the Bureau of Ethnology of the Smithsonian, visited Florida about this time to make a report on the condition and characteristics of the Indians. He reported there were then two hundred eight "commonly known as Seminole," thirty-seven families living in twenty-two camps, gathered in five widely separated settlements, Big Cypress, Miami River, Fisheating Creek, Cow Creek and Catfish Lake. He reported that they were very healthy and should increase rapidly. That they spoke different languages and represented entirely different tribal groups he did not seem to recognize.

White half-breeds did not exist among them, he said, and such an interbreeding would result in the death of the mother at the hands of the Indians. The only mixed bloods were the children of Negroes and Indians.

They shared in the then developing plume trade. The fine white nuptial feathers of the large American egret and of the smaller snowy egret were suddenly worth seventy-five cents apiece in New York, where business after the Civil War was beginning to boom again. The finest egret plumes, called by the stylish French word "aigrettes," came from the egret rookeries of Florida.

In those days the jungles south of Okeechobee, where the moonvines hung heavy in the dark of the moon and the shallow reedy morasses of the lake, were in the season after February one of the greatest nesting places in the world. They were covered with acres of stick nests of egret and glossy ibis and heron of every kind. The reeds in the lake bore fresh-water snails, the ampularia that the long-beaked wading birds and

278

the long-legged curve-beaked ones and the kites of the air came to feed on all through the day.

At sunset with full crops they would move in their white thousands and tens of thousands, with the sounds of great stiff silk banners, birds in flocks, birds in wedges, birds in wavering ribbons, blue and white crowds, rivers of birds pouring against the sunset back to the rookeries. Turning and maneuvering against the winds over their nests the parent birds tumbled headlong down to the right nest in the clamor and squawking and curious yelping, and queer deep grunting of their fuzzy open-beaked hungry young.

When the sun rose the ethereal whiteness of the plumed parent birds shone like frost against the blue, blue sky. They were white in the nights under the moon, or to the torches and firepans of the men with clubs in canoes slipping along behind the lights. A few men with clubs or shotguns rising suddenly by those low rookeries could kill and scalp hundreds of birds in a night. By morning the bloody bodies would be drawing the buzzards and alligators. The great black Florida crows that shed the light like water from their feathers would clean out the dying young. Ants in long lines as fine as pepper would carry off the rotting pieces of their bones.

In four years the Okeechobee rookeries were destroyed. The white ibis they call curlew were shot for food, the flesh salted for the Key West market. The limpkins were killed for food and the Everglades kite would be shot for the fun of shooting. The survivors scattered to hide their future nests in brackish lakes far south.

American women's demand for aigrettes increased. The Havana and South American markets were good. Plume buyers from New York made yearly buying trips to Florida trading posts.

Ornithologists had been coming to Florida for bird study

since Audubon's time. Edward Harris of Moorestown, New Jersey, discovered the Everglades kite in the great lake at the headwaters of the Miami River in 1844, and Dr. Henry Bryant of Boston described twenty-five different species in many trips between 1850 and 1860. Gustavus Wurdemann, working for the United States Coast Survey, beginning in 1856, sent to the Smithsonian the first studies of flamingos and white-crowned pigeons, and terns, and collected the heron named for him, which is believed to be a hybrid between the great white and the great blue.

Charles B. Cory, later curator of zoology in the Chicago Field Museum, wrote the first book on Florida water birds and hunting and Indians, and came back year after year to live on the Caloosahatchee in a great houseboat with wide decks and a grand staircase, which later the actor Joe Jefferson had on the New River where it was a landmark for years. They were the only people to protest the incredible destruction of the plume birds. By 1877 the Florida legislature was made to pass a law against it, to which no man about the Everglades paid the slightest attention.

Before that, Charles Peacock came to Fort Dallas and made a living with a coontie mill up the river until he moved down to the Little Hunting Grounds, where the Frow family lived, who had been lighthouse keepers at the cape, and the Pents. A post office had been granted in 1873 to that village along Jack's Bight, seven miles south of the river, to be called Cocoa-nut Grove. It would be some time yet before Mrs. Kirk Munroe would get them to drop the "a." Charles Peacock built the first hotel anywhere on Biscayne Bay, but until somebody came to board there he went back to making coontie starch for a living. The few houses had been made from timber washed up from wrecks on the outer beaches, and they had many things from the same source, cases of wine and furniture, old ships' figureheads. In their dooryards lime trees and orange trees were dark and fragrant, and the banana fronds thick under the coconuts.

Now out of the welter of politics a figure began to emerge with new hope for southern Democrats and confidence to rich possible investors wintering at Jacksonville and St. Augustine and along the St. Johns.

He was William D. Bloxham. His great-grandfather had come from England to take charge of George Washington's plantation, and his father pushed on to the new Tallahassee to seek his fortune. Young William was born near there on a plantation; his education as a southern gentleman took him to William and Mary College and to Europe on the Grand Tour. He had served in the legislature, and in the Confederate army, a tall handsome courtly figure of a rising young politician. He failed in his first try for the governorship and went back to orange raising, a country gentleman interested in all the new talk of railroads and mindful again of that forgotten idea of reclaiming the Everglades.

He gave as much encouragement as possible to Reverdy Johnson a Washington lawyer, representing an English company, the International Chamber of Commerce and Mississippi Valley Society, southern sympathizers in the Civil War, who were looking to invest heavily in southern lands and might be induced to come to Florida.

The white feeling against Negroes in politics was aflame. William Bloxham hunted out all the meetings of black voters, and by sheer eloquence and charm won them over, promising protection for all Negroes who would vote for the Democrat Drew, who became the next governor.

At that first session of the Democratic convention, "a person hailing from Dade County," who was none other than the ex-lieutenant governor, ex-Republican, William H. Gleason, who had not been elected by any law known to the statute books, presented himself as the member from Dade County. They had to accept him.

The Internal Improvement Fund was still in receivership. Francis Voss was threatening legal action to obtain fourteen million acres of Everglades land for the Internal Improvement Fund coupons he held. National affairs were not better. In the Hayes-Tilden contest evidence was found that the votes of Monroe County, among others, were fraudulent. Or it was claimed so. Dade County had not enough voters for an election. Everywhere the confusion and dishonesty of a postwar period discouraged honest men. Again, that was an excellent background for Bloxham. He was made secretary of state, and in the Democratic convention of 1880 was unanimously elected governor.

Dade County then cast fifty-four votes.

Six days after Bloxham moved into the Executive Mansion in Tallahassee he called to order his first meeting as president of the Board of Trustees of the Internal Improvement Fund.

Hamilton Disston, of Philadelphia, the rich son of a Scottish sawmaker, had been coming to Florida long enough to have observed with interest its vast undeveloped resources. The governor was informed of Mr. Disston's interest.

He left at once for Philadelphia, an imposing figure in his Inverness cape, to approach Mr. Disston with his new gubernatorial silk hat in his hand. Mr. Disston was charmed by the governor as easily as were the Negro voters.

He made the governor a proposition. Conferences, contracts, would still be necessary. But when the governor drove through the neglected streets of Tallahassee to the live oaks of the mansion driveway and kissed his wife in the great hall, with the view of the ruined slave quarters at the back, he must have felt sure that this was the greatest moment of his career, the beginning of new Florida history. He was able to report to the trustees, perhaps waiting upon him after supper in the long Victorian parlor, that Mr. Disston would be glad to buy four million acres of swamplands for one million dollars.

With that, the trustees paid all the Internal Improvement Fund's debts. They were now free to handle the Everglades situation.

The word was again "drainage." Disston and his friends, several of those titled Englishmen of the International Chamber of Commerce, formed the Atlantic and Gulf Coast Canal and Okeechobee Land Company which would drain and improve four million acres west of Lake Okeechobee.

Results to the whole state of Florida were immediate. Henry B. Plant, the magnate of the Southern Express Company, had been buying up bankrupt southern railroads. Plant had spent the Civil War in Europe, but his hair and sweeping mustaches were very southern in style when he approached Henry M. Flagler, the tall mustached cool-eyed partner of John D. Rockefeller, and the man closest to Rockefeller in all the hectic Standard Oil Company history, to organize a Plant Holding Company. For dash, for cold calculation, and brilliant financial acumen, Plant and Flagler were too well matched to remain partners. Both had been poor boys, one from Connecticut, one from New York State. Both had left home when very young to make their fortunes by the practice of the Yankee virtues of hard work, thrift, sobriety, honesty, and the ability to see an available dollar through a slit no bigger than a gnat's eye. It was the time when similar great fortunes were being made throughout the recently confused country by similar dominating figures, and for no altruistic reasons.

In the year 1882 when the Disston Company put to work its engineers, J. M. Kreamer and R. E. Rose, Plant bought for little or nothing the South Florida Railroad from Sanford to Kissimmee and planned to extend it to Tampa. Flagler began to build an elaborate turreted and porticoed hotel in St. Augustine, inevitably called the Ponce de Leon, and began also to look into the Florida railroad situation on his own account.

Only the year before, Thomas A. Edison came on a cruise to Fort Myers, poking about its sunny sleepy streets with his quiet look. He liked it. He would come back and take a house on the river and plant palm trees along a whole city boulevard, and get other people to plant palm trees, although Fort Myers citizens refused his offer to provide a power plant for lighting its streets. They did not want the expense of the poles. He was to spend more and more winters in his laboratory by the Caloosahatchee, experimenting and thinking. To Mr. Edison the reclamation of the Everglades was only a half-heard and unimportant rumor.

Drainage began. The parts of the first dredge were put together at Fort Myers. They started up the broad waters of the lower Caloosahatchee. The big dredge went up easily enough on the high tide but it stuck on sandy curves and great cypress roots. A rope was run forward to a tree on a bank so that it could be warped to the next bank, and so on. It took three months to rope it from Fort Myers to old Fort Thompson, up beyond La Belle. For six months thereafter the dredge worked steadily toward Okeechobee, through the flat swampy basins of Lake Flirt and Lake Hicpochee that Fred Ober, in his expeditions to the lake for the magazine *Field and Stream* back in 1871, had said did not exist, because in the dry season he never saw them. The spoil banks the dredge left behind stuck up across that flatness in long jagged hills of raw dirty white. The water in the Caloosahatchee began to silt up. That canal was the only one Disston had dug.

In 1883 Mr. Disston, and possibly Governor Bloxham, and a party of expansive gentlemen made a steamboat trip up the river from Fort Myers to see the work. There was fine food and champagne on board, and the company was entertained at some of the newer Caloosahatchee settlements under the oaks, by the old fords.

They must have stopped at Alva, homesteaded in 1881 by Captain Peter Nelson, a Danish yacht captain. He named it for a little white flower he found growing there. Perhaps it was the white sultana that still grows in the window box of the old bridge tender's shack in the great tree's green shade, or from the sparkleberries among the shadowy oak and cabbage palm hammocks. The captain was not intent on making money. He wanted a nice place for people to live. He dedicated a parksite by the river, and land on which was built a small white schoolhouse and a small white library, which surely must have been the first public library anywhere, east coast or west, south of Okeechobee. People came there because of the good school and built small white houses, and put out groves that soon bore the fine, too-little known Caloosahatchee oranges, and farmed.

The English Brothers started a grove there, and Raymond Robbins's family. Alva people were always leaders in education, like Colin English, head of the State Department of Education.

The Disston party had come up past Upcohall and Caloosa and Olga and Alva and Fort Denaud and La Belle and Fort Thompson and so on through the canals to the lake and to St. Cloud. The sugar plantation at St. Cloud was shortly to make a record of more granulated sugar per acre than had ever been produced. But later something happened. Either the government bounty was off or the first yield had exhausted the virgin soil. Later, when Florida had forgotten all about the St. Cloud million-dollar company, it went into bankruptcy.

The agent for the Internal Improvement Fund came back to Tallahassee in 1882 and told the governor and the other trustees that the Disston Company's two dredges then at work were not going to be able to drain all the Everglades.

The trustees must have looked at one another with baffled

285

eyes. It was a committee appointed in 1885 to study the Disston results that produced the classic statement: "The reduction of the waters is simply a question of sufficient capacity in the canals which may be dug for their relief."

It had evidently not occurred to Governor Bloxham, or Mr. Disston, or the later trustees, that the problem was not one of getting the fund out of bankruptcy or developing the country, but one based entirely on a scientific and thorough study of the Everglades themselves. That was not to happen until recently, late in World War II. Before that, in all those years of talk and excitement about drainage, the only argument was a school-boy's logic. The drainage of the Everglades would be a Great Thing. Americans did Great Things. Therefore Americans would drain the Everglades. Beyond that—to the intricate and subtle relation of soil, of fresh water and evaporation, and of runoff and salt intrusion, and all the consequences of disturb-ing the fine balance nature had set up in the past four thousand years—no one knew enough to look. They saw the Everglades no longer as a vast expanse of saw grass and water, but as a dream, a mirage of riches that many men would follow to their ruin.

But Mr. Plant and Mr. Flagler went on buying railroads.

The point was that under the Swamp Lands Act of 1850, and the Act of 1855 which set up the Internal Improvement Fund, the legislature of 1879 decided that quantities of swamp land should be given to all railroad and canal companies in addition to the purchased right-of-way. Each parcel of land must be proved to the state as being predominantly swamp, such as could be traveled by boat. There are prodigious tales of land claimed as swamps over which men rode in a boat on a stout wagon. Ten thousand acres of swamplands in alternate sections within six miles were allotted for each mile of construction. Every railroad must then prove it had a certain number of miles of roadbed and rolling stock consisting of at least one locomotive, several freight cars, and a passenger car. There again, it was claimed, many a mile of rails was picked up by a stout crew after the train was moved over it, and laid again ahead of the panting engine. The Jacksonville, Tampa and Key West Railroad was the first to comply with these regulations and acquire the extra lands.

That began an era of intensive railroad building, although many of them were narrow gauge and never reached more than a few miles into the pinelands. There was the Florida Tropical Railroad, the Waldo and Ocala, the Green Cove Springs, the Orange Ridge, Deland and Atlantic, which ran from Cabbage Bluff to New Smyrna. The most famous one on the east coast was the Celestial Railroad, which began at Jupiter and ran through Neptune, Venus, and Mars to Juno on Lake Worth, a sometime county seat of Dade County, where the mailmen started down along the beach to Biscayne Bay. There was a fine confusion and talk of progress.

But Mr. W. H. Hunt of Dade County, who had been ex-Lieutenant Governor Gleason's partner in many railroad deals, reported that the wreckers of Biscayne Bay did not want railroads to bring any more people to the country. There were not wrecks enough, or enough salvage, or enough goods floating in on the beaches to go around as it was. The board, however, declined to rescind a resolution of a former board rescinding the contract with W. H. Hunt for the reclamation of Dade County lands. The land was then worth as much as seventy cents an acre.

The Florida Coast Line Canal and Transportation Company said it would build a railroad from the northeast end of Biscayne Bay to Key West, which sounds a little like the work of busy Mr. Gleason of Dade. That company received patents for 93,156 acres, and the Atlantic Gulf Coast and Okeechobee Land Company 1,174,942 acres.

Mr. Plant and Mr. Flagler bought up these little railroads as they withered and died. Mr. Flagler got the Jacksonville, St. Augustine and Halifax River Railroad. Mr. Plant bought the Gainesville, Ocala and Charlotte Harbor and the Ocala, Tampa and Peninsula. Mr. Flagler got the South Florida Railroad that ran from Sanford and the Indian River to Punta Rassa, and the Lake Jesup, Osceola and Kissimmee.

They were rivals now. Mr. Flagler was extending one long railroad down the east coast as fast as he could, buying old railroad and canal companies and claiming the extra land, to catch up with Mr. Plant, who had tapped the grove and phosphate districts and had built the rococo brick Tampa Bay Hotel with its long lobbies filled with palm trees in tubs and hosts of rocking chairs judiciously interspersed with shining brass spittoons. Mr. Plant was already running steamers, the old *Morro Castle*, for one, to Key West and Tampa.

Mr. Flagler's railroad was now the Jacksonville, St. Augustine and Indian River Railroad. In 1898 it was renamed the Florida East Coast. His crews laying rails south of Daytona in 1892 swallowed up the Celestial Railroad.

That was the year also when Mr. Flagler decided to study the Everglades. He had bought the rights of the Florida Coast and Gulf Railway Company, which was planned to be run from the St. Johns River to Tampa by way of Dade County, if not Miami. He sent his chief engineer, Mr. J. E. Ingraham, with a group of men to cross and survey the Glades as no white expedition had done since the Indian wars.

They started from Tampa by steamer, which stopped at the new fashionable hotel at St. James City on the south end of Pine Island, and so came to Fort Myers, already green with Mr. Edison's palms and with bamboos and the tropical gardens about the neat frame houses. Mr. Ingraham shipped their supplies, two canvas boats and two wooden boats by ox team through the long pinewoods to old Fort Shackleford on the edge

288

of the saw grass. In Fort Myers they were told all sorts of tales about the mysterious interior of the Glades. They were told of a series of deep lagoons, with a large central divide or even a vast unknown lake basin. Whatever they were, everybody now believed the Everglades could be drained and put into cultivation at small cost, to support an immense population.

The Ingraham party found nothing but saw grass. They asked an old Indian woman how long it would take them to get to Miami. She laughed and said, "Indian, two days. White man, fifteen."

They lost track of days. They suffered sore feet and saw-grass cuts. The water was low. They pushed the heavy-laden boats through mud and grass and water and scraped holes in the boats' bottoms over rocks. They pulled themselves out of mudholes to fall into others. They had too many supplies and too much equipment to carry, but they ran out of food and could not bring themselves to eat alligator tails and such. There was plenty of fresh water, but they slept in mud and grass among moccasin snakes. They were exhausted, ill, and lost. They got out finally, because one man found an Indian in a canoe who took him swiftly ahead for a rescue party. They reached the headwaters of the Miami and shot the twenty-five feet of rapids over the rock rim and saw the houses of Miami, and Mrs. Tuttle's at Fort Dallas, with new eyes.

That was the last thing Mr. Flagler ever did about the Everglades, except to keep on acquiring land in it by railroad grants from the Internal Improvement Fund.

The great freezes of the winter of 1894-95 ruined the fine orange groves in Orange County and middle Florida, from which the people, Georgia people, North Florida people, English people, got up and left their houses, doors swinging and food on the tables, and the dark trees ruined on the ground.

The great thing then was to get below what they called the

"frost line." Mrs. Tuttle of Miami made the well-known gesture of sending Mr. Flagler an untouched orange branch, filled with fruit and flowers. Mr. William Brickell, who owned so much land both sides of the river, has never had sufficient credit for donating land for streets and right-of-way. So that Miami, which had been only two or three houses, by the next year had a seething population of two thousand people, railroad men, construction men, a few tourists, with Brady's grocery store, a livery stable, John Siebold's bakery, and Isador Cohen's dry goods store, among others, lining the dusty streets among the pine trees.

Mr. John Sewell, who was to be mayor off and on for years, in charge of the construction of the new Flagler Hotel, had his men begin chopping trees and digging into the great Indian Mound that had stood for so many centuries north of the river mouth. Mr. Sewell collected the long bones and skulls they dug up and had them buried secretly some place else—where, nobody would ever know. That would be the Royal Palm Hotel.

Miami was not a town that Mr. Flagler was particularly interested in, although he gave the usual lots for churches and the Woman's Club out of all the land he held. He and other very rich men preferred an atmosphere more singly devoted to the contemplation of wealth. Miami would not amount to much, he felt. He was angry with the engineer who laid out the gridiron pattern of the streets, not because it was a bad plan that did not take into consideration either the curves of the river or the line of the bay, but because, Mr. Flagler said, the streets were ten feet too wide. No land was reserved to the city for parks, especially on the bay front, where he preferred that the railroad lines should reach directly to the docks. If it had not been for the mistake on the part of a clerk, who carelessly wrote "park" on a blank space, the city would have owned none of the bay front then. It cost millions to buy up more later.

Mr. Flagler was also extremely irritated with the captains of untidy Nassau schooners of the kind that for generations had known that straight plunging voyage across the ink-blue, deep-rolling, white-tossing Gulf Stream to Cape Florida, and up the channel to the river. They had at once gone into the coastwise carrying trade, bringing down lumber and supplies for the street after street of narrow, northern-style wooden houses, steep-pitched roofs and porches and narrow windows, or, on the better streets, all turrets and wooden fancywork about wide piazzas. The schooners kept coming over from Nassau loaded with the tall black men of the Bahama Islands, who were needed as laborers on the railroads, as well as hands in the groves. Their African sense of life hummed in the paths and tiny shacks beyond Fifth Street in Miami as the slums that no man cared about at once crowded the palmettos.

In Coconut Grove the white or brown board houses of the earlier settlers stood on the rock ridge overlooking the broad tinted bay and Cape Florida light. The old Indian trail ran below from springs to hunting grounds, where the Indians still walked. Behind the long strips of land filled with citrus trees, and sapodilla trees and sugar apples, the road that would be a highway was only a dusty cart path where at evening the rich voices of Bahama Negroes going home to a colored town crowded with the same trees and plants from the islands, sounded their "Good ev'nin's"; the singing accents of the Berry Islanders, the soft words of tall round-faced people who had been Senegalese before they had been slaves in America and free in the Out Islands, the more knowing people of Nassau with their British sedateness, their broad "a's" and their dropped "h's." Most of them went back on the schooners every year to pay British taxes on their island farms.

The Grove was completely West Indian still. The green turtles that fed on the grassy shallows were kept in "crawls" before

291

shipping. Every family had its sailboat. Every family had its coontie, or compte, mill, wooden cylinders studded with shoe-maker's heel brads, which ground the roots by horse or hand power under running water, from which the starch was dried and barreled. Five barrels of root made one barrel of starch, or 250 pounds, which brought three to five cents a pound. A num-ber of people worked for reputable wrecking companies. Ralph M. Munroe had settled down to boatbuilding and Kirk Munroe, next door, wrote boys' books about the Everglades, and the Library had been started by them both. The Grove was un-touched by the new excitement of Miami, a long buggy ride to the north, a long sail by boat.

Mr. Hugh L. Willoughby, ex-lieutenant commanding the Rhode Island Naval Reserve, a precise, scientifically minded, if adventurous gentleman, who for some years had wanted to make his own observations of "the mysterious Everglades," re-marked all this change in Miami as he and Ed Brewer paddled down the river at the beginning of his long-planned trip. He had never seen a lovelier place than the entrance of the Miami River into Biscayne Bay, he had often said. The raw beginnings of the hotel on the denuded point, the crowds of workmen, and the clutter and noise and excitement that the railroad had brought dismayed him. He had no doubt the hotel would be fine and the gardens and palm trees beautiful. But he felt that the remote charm of the bay was forever shattered.

However, they continued on the trip down to Cape Sable, and so to Harney's River, with his carefully chosen two canoes, his sleeping bag, his instruments for measuring distance, water flow, temperature; his gun, his weighed rations; his studied costume, knickers, long stockings, canvas shoes, with leggings to strap on if necessary, his hunting knife, his binoculars, and his special straw hat. Ed Brewer, turning the wad of tobacco

292

in his cheek, wore his usual pants, shirt, galluses and hat. He said nothing, as he continued to do throughout the trip.

But it is quite likely that Ed Brewer contemplated the improvements with a gleam in his eye. The town must have looked like a better market for plumes and alligator hides from the Everglades, which he crossed any time he wanted to in his cypress canoe. He was glad to be guiding for Mr. Willoughby at the moment, because he had heard that Captain Dick Carney, the sheriff, was as usual looking for him with a warrant for selling liquor to the Indians. Ed Brewer probably spat with reflective virtue on passing Captain Carney's house on the bluff at Coconut Grove. At least this time he didn't have any liquor on board, though no telling how often he'd wish he had.

Thanks to high water and Ed Brewer's expert knowledge and his own intrepidity, ex-Lieutenant Willoughby made a wandering, not too difficult, and successful trip. He did not scorn alligators' tails as Mr. Ingraham's party had, but found them very delicate. He got burned and cut, and tired of sleeping in the boats or on a rocky hammock with an old Indian lookout place still up a tree, first carefully shooting out the snakes, or on wet ridges. He found out about the stinging horseflies, and how noisy the lower Glades could be at night with shrieking limpkin and acres of guttural frogs. But he really did make the first attempt at a scientific study of the Glades. He found that the flow of the high water was more than four miles an hour, a quite respectable river. He did not think then that anyone would attempt to drain it.

They returned by the South Fork of the Miami River. Mr. Willoughby went to rest from his trip at the Peacock Hotel in Coconut Grove. Ed Brewer went back to the Everglades, probably first picking up some grits and bacon and coffee, and a few gallons of liquor for the Indians.

The railroad got no farther south at that time, for in two

years, while Mr. Flagler's engineers were surveying the lower Glades and Cape Sable, the Spanish-American War blew up. Mr. Plant's railroad got the best of that, hauling the army and its supplies to the hot sands of Tampa, and all the officers in their bulky new uniforms, General William R. Shafter and Lieutenant Colonel Theodore Roosevelt, and Colonel William Jennings Bryan and Lieutenant Andrew Summers Rowan just back from carrying that message to Garcia, condemned now, like all of them, to sit for a month in Mr. Plant's rocking chairs in the Tampa Bay Hotel.

Key West was a jam of overheated Cuban juntas and correspondents like Frederic Remington and Stephen Crane, Sylvester Scovel, and Richard Harding Davis in his high collar and new khaki, riding around in surreys, drinking champagne out of bottles, waiting for the war to begin. Davis was already carrying on his private campaign which would discredit the quiet ability of General Shafter. Miami had troops in tents all over the Royal Palm Hotel grounds and the hotel parks, and horses pranced and bugles blew.

But swashing and roaring down all along that east coast, past Canaveral and Hillsborough Light and Cape Florida, in the inshore current, running without lights to dodge the revenue cutters, the big Jacksonville tugboat, the *Three Friends,* had already gone a number of times with guns and insurgent generals, to be landed somewhere on the Cuban coast. Up on the bridge, a peaked cap shading his sharp bold eyes and his black walrus mustache, his big stocky figure well braced against the chances he was taking then as a neutral, a ready and suitable follower after all those sailormen who had adventured the seas, Cabot or Menendez or Hawkins, wreckers or sea rovers; there, hardly glancing over at the coast that hid the Everglades, went Napoleon Bonaparte Broward, who would drain them.

294

13

Drainage and the Frontier

T HERE would be two more governors in Tallahassee before Napoleon Bonaparte Broward started his roaring campaign for drainage.

The Spanish-American War ended, as far as Miami was concerned, when the camps of returning troops, and the city itself, were shut up fearful and dead, by the quarantine against yellow fever. The first to die, a sailor on a dock, was accurately diagnosed by Dr. Mrs. Captain Simmons of Coconut Grove.

Dr. Mrs. Captain Simmons, one of the first women doctors in the Middle West, had arrived at Key West by steamer and asked how she could get to Coconut Grove. Captain Simmons,

295

who carried the mail and passengers, was down at the docks then. He would take her but he didn't have any other passengers, and it wouldn't be decent for a lady to travel up there with him, alone. It was an overnight voyage.

The upshot was, and they do say that the doctor suggested it, that they went and got married. Captain Simmons's plain brown board house overlooked the fine breadth of the bay in a jungle of bearing guavas and oranges and limes. In a shed at the highway he and his wife canned guava jelly for the tourist trade. She rode a horse to call on patients, with medicines in her saddlebags. The Indians came to her for help.

The yellow fever epidemic put a stop to everything but the beginning activity of Miami real estate. J. A. McCrory, who claimed to be the first lawyer, abstracter, real estate dealer, and funeral director in Miami, sold his first house in the suburb he called Buena Vista, in the quarantine. The two principals and the two witnesses met secretly out in the untouched pinelands, standing ten feet apart in fear of contagion. Mr. McCrory signed the deed and threw it at the buyer, who picked it up and signed it and tossed it to the witnesses. McCrory picked up the man's check for $1,000.

The same sort of activity went on wherever the Florida East Coast Railroad had passed. New towns clustered on it like beads on a string. Besides the old settlements of Hypoluxo and Fort Lauderdale, there were Lantana on the west shore of Lake Worth, Boynton and Delray and Boca Raton. There was Deerfield and Pompano, Hallendale and Ojus, from the convenient Indian word, already part of the Miami vocabulary, meaning "plenty." Dania was being settled by the Danish Brotherhood. Yamato would soon be a neat Japanese village that meant "Japan" not "tomato." Fulford and Arch Creek and Biscayne were old homesteads. Little River, the valley by the old Humbuggus Prairie, shipped now by train the fruit from its old trees. Lemon City, settled by Key West people long before the railroad, was still a deeper water port than Miami. Coastwise steamers docked there. Goods were shipped from there to Miami in small sailboats.

South of Coconut Grove was Larkins, and Cutler, where the Perrine Grant of 23,008 acres was to be confirmed to the Perrine heirs by President Cleveland, and the last village on the bay front where Dr. Richmond had a small hotel called Richmond Cottage. Beyond that, when Mr. Flagler moved the construction gangs south, the railroad would go first through Black Point, Naranja, and Homestead.

The air of expansion and progress hung only over the east coast. The Everglades, under the winds and storms, the rains and dews, and the constant work of the sun, lay unchanged.

The Indians lived there as they always had, only changing very slowly, becoming more and more uniquely themselves. Peace and freedom and health in their own ways were theirs. Their old people lived vigorous long years. In the small houses the husbands built beyond the camps, so that the evil that attends a woman in childbirth might not affect others, their wives gave birth to many square-faced brown, slant-eyed babies that the smiling grandmothers handed out squalling to the medicine grandfathers, to be passed through the smoke that cuts off evil. Two green corn dances every year gathered the Mikasukis and other Hitchiti-speakers to the Big Cypress, the Muskogee-speakers to a ground northeast of Okeechobee, where with the old ceremonies the medicine men each year lighted the new fires.

Since 1879 they had steadily refused to accept any aid the government of the United States tendered them. They needed nothing, and wanted nothing they could not get for themselves.

Since 1891 when the ladies of the Women's National Indian Association had visited the Big Cypress, with Captain Hendry of Fort Myers, the Mikasukis received amiably enough the first missionary efforts of Dr. J. E. Brecht and his wife. The Brechts settled in a log cabin on four hundred acres of land bought by the Indian Association, next to eighty purchased by the government, with a sawmill to cut lumber for a house and an Indian school. Later, through the interest of Bishop Grey, this plant was transferred to the Episcopal Church's missionary district. Dr. William J. Godden, a medical missionary, maintained the Glades Cross Mission until 1914. The Indians were always polite and noncommittal.

In 1905 there were many stores where plumes and alligator hides could be sold, liquor bought and new kettles and beads and fine-sprigged calicoes made up in ten-yard "books." Thirty abreast, the long canoes swept down the New River to Captain Frank Stranahan's at Fort Lauderdale, from the campground where they played the two-racket ball game with the old vigor. There was Wiggin's store at Sand Fly Pass and McKinney's at Chokoloskee, in the Ten Thousand Islands.

Mr. William Brown with his young wife and two children and goods in a four-ox team pushed out from Fort Myers to build a log cabin store at Immokalee, at Boat Landing, near old Fort Shackleford, at the edge of the saw-grass glades. The Indians, five days out of Miami, paddled their canoes to the platform, and tossed up their bundles of plumes and skins, vegetables and sugar cane and bananas from the hammock gardens.

Mrs. Brown taught the Mikasuki women to use hand sewing machines. Mr. Brown sold them their first shotguns. The Browns kept eight yoke of oxen hauling supplies from Fort Myers in the winters. They served Christmas dinner every year to seventy-five or eighty Indians, beef and wild turkey and deer and a week's baking of mince and apple pies.

It was in those days that Mr. Brown bought up some bankrupt stocks of derby hats and fancy vests. Photographs taken in those times show the Indian men standing stiffly proud with

298

high-rounded derbies on black bangs and dark vests over their calico skirted-shirts, which their wives had sewn with broad patches of solid yellow or red, not yet made into intricate stripes.

The white men would have stills hidden in the mangrove where they made the pale "aggerdent" as powerful as Cuban aguadiente, which, at a price, they would share with any Indian.

None of that activity about railroads was known down there on the lower west coast. What was important was fish prices and plume prices and alligator hide prices. Every boy along those mangrove rivers knew as well as any Indian how to "grunt up" a 'gator, a kind of quick squeal deep in the throat with the mouth closed.

When Mr. Lopez, who had lived at Chokoloskee, moved his wife and family up to the untenanted mangrove stream that people grew to call "Lopez River" he used to take the boys off on hunting and fishing trips for days at a time, leaving Mrs. Lopez with the girls and the new baby. She was from Tampa and not yet used to this wild lonely place. She was scared to death that the little girls would be pulled in by those 'gators that lay thick as logs, often fourteen feet long, their deep, throaty hissings, their fighting and bellowing frightening in the night.

One of the Lopez boys would later take ten thousand alligators in one month of night fire-hunting from a lake near Shark River and sell the skins for fifty cents apiece. Everybody said that was about the last of them. It was extermination, savage, instinctive, and profitable.

Mr. C. G. McKinney had come to Chokoloskee from near Alachua, when there were only three other families on it. He caught redbirds and fish for the Key West market, hunted, and sold alligator skins, fifty cents for seven-foot lengths. He started his own store and the Chokoloskee post office. McKinney was a leisurely man, a natural-born good talker. Later he began to write weekly notes about life on Chokoloskee for the *American Eagle*, in Estero. Nobody in all South Florida wrote with more vigor, serenity, and good sense.

He wrote about the last time he went plume hunting: "We ate our lunch and went to the birds' nests a few hundred yards away and began to shoot the mother birds and kill them from their young; then the crows would go and take the eggs and the young birds and carry them away to eat them. I decided that I did not think it was doing God's service and I never went on that kind of a hunt any more."

He wrote about his own experiences: "After a few months more I bought the home where I am now living from Mr. John Howard and went to work getting out timbers in the cypress swamp near Needhelp." That was a place he had cleared and named in the cypress up the Turner River. "I worked many days and weeks there, standing in water from six to twelve inches deep, splitting out boards from cypress logs and hewing out square timbers; then rafted them down Turner's River to Chokoloskee.

"I remember quite well one morning, when I was standing in the water trying to make a cup of coffee. I heard some noise that appeared to be some person knocking on a log. By and by I heard some splashing in the water similar to a person wading. There were high ferns all through the swamp and I took up my axe and stood perfectly still. In a moment or two more I saw the ferns begin to shake and a big black bear stuck his head out coming nearly direct for me. He got up within about 20 feet of me where a palmetto log was lying and he put both of his front feet on it and began to look at the surroundings. I caught his eye looking off from me and I cast my axe at him with all my might. It passed just under his head, and dropped into the water just beyond.

"He thought he might not be welcome so he jumped over

the log and went in a bear trot toward the river. Thus I escaped having a bear fight. If my axe had struck him in the side of the head and stopped him just a little I would have jumped on him with my axe and we would have had a racket right there by ourselves in that swamp.

"Well, some old boys will say, 'Why didn't you shoot him?' Bless your life, boys, I had no gun at all. I just worked all day in that water and tied up a little boat sail I had in a tree, coiled up in it wet at night and slept well; got up before sunrise, made me a little fire on top of a stump to make some coffee, fry some meat and cook some grits. Then I ate my breakfast and went to work on those old cypress logs, sawing, chopping, hewing and riving out boards to cover the house I am now living in and under those same boards.

"When I was trying to sleep in that thick swamp I would often hear strange noises of birds and some coons and other screams which might have been panthers but I had no gun and felt perfectly safe as if home. The hoot owl was great company; he would scream out in the dead silent hours and almost made one shiver to think what fine agreeable neighbors he had. I very rarely saw a rattle snake. I killed a few, just for meanness, when I was about the age of twenty, and used to carry one or two of those rattlers' fangs in my pocket to pick my teeth with; but thank the Lord, I have no teeth now."

In that time, a different kind of people came up the green and winding Estero River from Estero Bay. An old German named Damkohler had homesteaded many acres of high hammock land, with a clearing by his shack almost completely hidden by huge bearing mango, lime, and orange trees. He made a living selling honey, bay oysters, and fish from those teeming waters, by sailboat forty water miles to Fort Myers. It was in December, 1893, that Damkohler met there and invited to see his place an impressive, square-jawed, magnetic man from Chicago, Dr. Cyrus R. Teed.

The nineteenth century in the United States had seen a development of American fortunes based to a large extent on land and railroads. But it had also seen a quiet countermovement among groups of people who were not satisfied with the capitalistic and orthodox way of life. Thinking in original ways, half religious, half scientific, there were many people who wanted to make a better way of life, based not on individual wealth but on voluntary co-operative communal ownership. Many such colonies had grown up in America from the beginning of the century and flourished for many years and are now dead: Shaker communities, the Oneida community, Bethel, Brook Farm, and Robert Owen's venture at New Harmony.

Of all these, Dr. Cyrus R. Teed's ideas were certainly the most original. He had made two attempts to establish co-operative communities in New York State, which had been the birthplace of so many. But it was not until he settled in Chicago in 1886 that his ideas, a new concept of the entire universe, physical and mental, attracted converts who gladly gave up their possessions to the common use of the colony he founded in 1888. Chicago, however, was not entirely satisfactory to him as a community home.

The man who sailed up the Estero River with old Damkohler and looked with his brilliant glance at the lavish green growing things in the tropical light, in all that silence, felt he had found the right place at last. He bought the land and sent down workers who would clear paths and gardens and build their first house, a big log cabin. That was the nucleus of the Koreshan Unity in Florida.

Dr. Teed's name was Cyrus which in Hebrew is Koresh. It was from that he had derived the name "Koreshan." What he wanted for his people was truth, without which equity and justice cannot be established, and deliverance and everlasting righteousness.

To Dr. Teed the universe was one great universal cell with a central nucleus. It was not a "Deific spread-all-overness," as he explained it in that elaborate special vocabulary of his, but the center, heart, and focus of life, "the dwelling place of humanity." It was expressed physically, as he described it in his book, *Cellular Cosmogony*, in a one-celled universe. The surface of the earth was concave, with a curvature of about eight inches to the mile. It was therefore a hollow sphere with a diameter of eight thousand miles and a circumference of twenty-five thousand. The Copernican theory, which stated that the universe was illimitable, was fallacious because if it was infinite it would be beyond the reach of human aspiration and effort. The Koreshan Cosmogony brought the universe within the comprehension of the human mind.

Dr. Teed said other things which seem curiously modern, almost Einsteinian. "Nothing exists without motion" and "The laws of motion conform to and determine the principles and arrangements of organic relation and shape."

The people who followed Dr. Teed to Florida were converts also to voluntary communism, co-operative living, and celibacy. Already in the thousand acres of hammock and pineland where he meant someday to build the city of the "New Jerusalem," the huge brown board buildings were rising among oleanders, eucalyptus, date palms, and bamboos. Everything had to come by boat from Punta Gorda, all those loads of Victorian sideboards, beds, tables, chinaware, and the quantities of books that the members brought to the colony. They had their first sight of it from the Bamboo Landing at the river, where every year on Dr. Teed's birthday a water pageant was held with music and laughter and Japanese lanterns.

Two hundred people at the most filled the big dining hall

for the excellent food from their own gardens, dairy and bake-shop, listened to their own orchestra in the Art Hall, where paintings of superior quality were hung, or moved serenely to classrooms or their appointed tasks. They enjoyed lectures on everything from populism, socialism, and the single tax to religion, mental science, and astronomy. Politically they were liberal and ahead of their times.

Husbands and wives separated to live celibate lives in the brothers' or sisters' dormitories or alone in the cottages by the river or among the pines. Their children went to the excellent school and shared supervised play and circumspect living under special guides. There was money then for colored laborers. Their nursery began the introduction of tropical trees like the cajeput, which has changed the appearance of that countryside, of fine mangoes and of important new forage grasses, among other things.

The Unity people went often by sailboat to Fort Myers or to cottages on land they owned at Estero Beach and Mound Key. Their voices were quiet in all that peace and mutual helpfulness, released as they were from the common economic worries. Dr. Teed traveled and lectured everywhere, making new converts.

Florida was to be the place where Dr. Teed decided to prove the physical aspect of his revelation that the earth was a huge hollow sphere with the sun and the stars within. An accurate account of this has been written by Mr. A. H. Andrews, whose father was Dr. Teed's first convert and who, as a boy, was among the first party to arrive to work at Estero.

> In December, 1896, a geodetic surveying expedition arrived from Chicago, organized and equipped by Dr. Teed for the purpose of ascertaining the direction of the earth's curvature, whether convexly as held by modern physicists or concavely, in accordance with the discovery by Dr. Teed in 1870.

In this survey, conducted on the Gulf Coast at Naples, a simple device known as a rectilineator was employed, consisting of a number of sections of large double T-squares. When mounted on standards that were affixed to the ground, the double T-squares, adjusted end to end, automatically extended a straight line, independently of any visual survey. All measurements were taken from the near-by water's surface which conforms to the general contour of the earth's surface, whatever it may be.

Starting at a height of 10 feet and 8 inches from the water's surface at the end of the first mile, the survey line was eight inches nearer the water than at the starting point, proving that the water's surface had curved upward, and not down as generally believed.

At the end of four miles the surveyed line ran into the water. Optical experiments were also conducted, such as bringing into view with a telescope ships' hulls, right down to the water line, that have passed the horizon.

A section of the rectilineator was set up on the platform of the Art Hall and with the gold-covered model of the hollow world, which opening reveals the painted continents and the sun and stars emplaced within, became a feature of interest to guests and wondering tourists.

The Koreshan Unity maintained its tranquil existence through years to come, although fewer converts were made. The children brought up in its careful way of life might go out into the world and marry if they chose. Many of them did. Dr. Teed died and was buried on Estero Beach. His tomb was washed away in a hurricane.

Those who remained, growing older, as their trees grew taller, taking their religion calmly, reading widely and working hard, never lost their faith in co-operation and celibacy. Many lived to be very old. Later, some of the men and women who had been brought up there came back from the world to build

305

up the place again under courageous and determined leadership. Mr. Allen H. Andrews, who from young manhood had edited their weekly paper, the *American Eagle*, made it the leading horticultural paper in South Florida, a forum and force for liberal and sensible ideas.

With the development along modern lines of their excellent store and a fine trailer camp, the colony would emerge after World War II firmly established financially. But in those early days the fishermen of Estero looked a little askance at the well-dressed Chicago people who had such queer ideas. They were often suspected of strange things, who in their busy years of building were hardly aware of what was going on in the world of Florida about them.

Neither they nor anyone else here knew about an even less conspicuous man who in 1896 slipped in and out the bays and islands in a boat, staring at Indian mounds. On this coast, where every old-timer tells stories of a vanished giant race and where men claim still to have seen dug up enormous thigh bones and jawbones twice as big as their own, there had been a few archaeologists already: Andrew E. Douglass, collecting Indian artifacts in his yacht *Seminole*, and Clarence Moore, a retired businessman who had brought a keen intelligence to the work of studying traces of prehistoric Indians.

This man was Frank Hamilton Cushing, one of the most brilliant and original ethnologists of his day. They say he looked a little like an Indian, lank hair and dark skin and sharp nose. He had lived among the Zuñi Indians of the Southwest and had written brilliantly about them.

It seems that Captain Bill Collier, that "hardheaded old infidel," had been digging muck in a mangrove-filled cove by the high mound at Marco. Out of that muck Captain Bill's shovel brought up some queer things: a highly polished cup made from a conch shell, a curiously carved block of wood. A day or two later, an Englishman, Lieutenant Colonel Durnford, staying at General Haldeman's new resort on that beautiful beach at Naples, came to Marco and dug also. On his way north he stopped in at the University of Pennsylvania Museum and saw the director, Mr. Stewart Culin. There at the same time, with his dark eyes fixed instantly on those objects from Marco, was Mr. Frank Hamilton Cushing.

Mr. Cushing went at once to Marco, with the assistance of his own director of the Bureau of Ethnology and Dr. Pepper of the University of Pennsylvania Museum. He went by rail to Punta Gorda and on south by fishing sloop, vastly astonished and exhilarated, as he wrote in his report, "by the bright waters of those connected bays and sounds which formed a far-reaching and anon wide-spreading shallow inland sea," Charlotte Harbor, Pine Islands Sound, Caloosa Bay, and the open water to Marco.

He worked his way through heat and stinging insects into dense mangrove islands and found in the green gloom platforms, landing places, terraces, level-topped mounds, and connecting channels which he saw at once were the work of prehistoric man. He found and explored more than seventy-five sites on his way to Marco.

Marco Key, as they called it then, was to be the greatest single discovery made in Florida by any archaeologist. Many years later Mr. M. W. Stirling of the Smithsonian was to find a most valuable site at Mound City near the present Canal Point, which proved that the lake people had the same culture as the Calusas. But in point of actual material Cushing's was the first, the greatest discovery.

On this, and a later trip, with more men and equipment, he found that the whole key had been built from the sea level upward in high terraces to a central elevation, a temple summit. Below it, a series of long canals ending in courts reached from the west. And below all that, in the mangrove-covered muck enclosure that he called "the Court of the Pile Dwellers," he went to work.

He found timbers, charcoal, the plaster of hearths, decayed thatch, and carved shell ornaments and tools.

Groping through the muck he found and washed off pottery bowls and cooking pots, fishhooks pointed with bone, barbed "grains," mortars, nets, net sinkers, dozens of those fine shark-tooth knives with handles carved with gnawing rats, snakes, a horned deer's head; war clubs of wood and split wolf jaws, throwing sticks for spears, and all that quantity of personal ornament, pendants, and ear plugs which the Calusas loved.

All the carved wooden objects showed, in the light, the orig-inal paint, black, white, gray-blue, and red. The muck had preserved them exactly as they had been, blown down, he began to think, in some hurricane that must have destroyed the whole village.

But as he lifted them and washed them off, in the brilliant sun he saw to his horror that as they dried they began to dis-integrate. In finding them he was destroying them.

They set frantically to work wrapping them in damp cloths and preserved what they could. They saved some plaques and masks and animal figures, since judged to be the finest carved work of any eastern Indians. They are the basis of present-day knowledge of those prehistoric Glades people. The collection is now divided between the Smithsonian and the University of Pennsylvania.

Mr. Cushing published a brilliantly written preliminary re-port, but died before he completed a final one. On the west coast, almost nobody knows of his discovery except an elderly man or two, like Captain Albert Addison of Marco, who sits on his front porch and looks at the mounds and the half-oblit-erated canals that Mr. Cushing made real to him.

In the next few years Mr. Clarence Moore tried to duplicate Mr. Cushing's find on the lower rivers, with no success. He barely escaped getting shot by a spring gun set for a panther.

These quiet goings on, however, occurred only on the periphery of the central problem of the Everglades. The Internal Improvement Fund was out of bankruptcy but it had no money. Everglades lands were not selling.

The new governor, William S. Jennings, a keen-minded lawyer of Jacksonville, broke the deadlock. His message to the legislature in 1903, after two years' intensive study, made the legal situation clear. The trustees of successive Internal Improvement Funds, in encouraging railroads and canals, had authorized legislatures to give deeds for swamplands in amounts from 3,840 to 10,000 acres for every mile of railroad and canal constructed. Little of the work had been done. The railroads had received deeds to lands to which they were not entitled. Now they actually laid claim to as much, if not more land than the Internal Improvement Fund controlled, or the Everglades contained.

The Internal Improvement Fund trustees, with Governor Jennings in the chair, now stated that former trustees had had no right to bind their successors by obligations that could not be fulfilled. They therefore declared that issues of such lands were invalid. The United States government, which had never given the state of Florida a patent for the swamplands, on April 23, 1903, issued a patent to the Internal Improvement Fund trustees for Everglades lands far in excess of two million acres.

Promptly the leading railroads filed suit, claiming their rights to the lands were superior to that of the present fund's. This suit was settled five years later by a decision of the Supreme Court which stated that the title vested in the trustees was superior to that of the railroads.

The Everglades themselves, then, for all the talk, were the same untouched and remote wilderness of the saw-grass river and its coasts.

John Kunkel Small, the botanist of the New York Botanical

Garden, irascible, keenly intelligent, great plantsman, brilliantly described the ferns and rare jungle plants he studied poking about Lake Okeechobee in his small boat. It was still all fresh and wild and untouched, but in every yearly trip thereafter he would mark with bitterness the spreading of destruction.

The killing of plume birds had continued to scandalous proportions. In New York, one millinery wholesaler alone bought two hundred thousand dollars' worth of plumes. It was not only the egrets. Bright-colored birds of every kind were trapped and sent in cages to Havana or New York. Women even wore dead mockingbirds on their overloaded hats.

Augustus, the Portuguese fisherman at Big Carlos Pass, said to some visiting ornithologist, "Them Frenchman's payin' two bits apiece for bird plumes, and I think you could make more a-plumin' than a-studyin' 'em."

T. Gilbert Pearson, a bird lover born in Florida, had already begun to organize state Audubon societies. It was he who would carry to the New York legislature in 1910 the fight, against the organized opposition of the $17,000,000 milliner business, for laws which would prohibit the sale of plumage, skins or bodies of birds from out of the state.

In 1905 one of the young Audubon Society's first attempts at direct protection was to hire a warden to guard the rookeries of American and snowy egret about Cuthbert Lake, in that mangrove-and-brackish-water wilderness at the southeast edge of the saw grass.

The warden was Guy Bradley, son and brother of the two Bradleys who had once walked the mails down the beaches from Lake Worth to Miami. His parents were people of education. When Mr. Flagler's Model Land Company was organized for the care and sale of the lands granted the Florida East Coast along its projected right-of-way from Cape Sable to the keys, Guy Bradley's father was made the land agent. They lived for nine or ten years at the little settlement of Flamingo, already astir with great expectations. The Bradley family's hopes for a fortune were ruined by Mr. Flagler's decision to begin the Key West extension from Homestead to Key Largo.

Guy Bradley was glad to get the job of bird warden for the Cuthbert rookeries. He was a pleasant, quiet young man, not tall, fair, with blue eyes, always whistling and a pretty good violinist. He wasn't wild like a lot of these other boys he had grown up with, fishermen and plume hunters. But he had an easy courage.

Guy Bradley had a neighbor at Flamingo whose son was a plume hunter. Guy overhauled their schooner a few miles off Flamingo in his light sailing skiff.

Later that day the schooner came up to the Flamingo dock. The man's wife and family went hurriedly on board and sailed away. By late afternoon, when Guy had not come back, his brother Louis and another man went out to look for him. They found his boat with the sail caught in the mangroves. Guy lay in the bottom in a pool of blood, dead.

The bullet had gone into his shoulder by the neck and down his back. He must have died slowly and in agony. It was clear that he had been shot from above downward, as from a higher deck. They buried him behind the coconut grove someone had planted on East Cape, and the National Association of Audubon Societies put a bronze tablet there.

The man who killed him got down to Key West and gave himself up, pleading Bradley had shot first and showed a bullet in the mast. All six bullets were found in Guy's revolver. The Bradley family did not want trouble, so they asked that prosecution be dropped. It was said afterward that that man went around telling everybody, "I'm the man that killed Guy Bradley."

Drainage, and the problems of drainage, seemed very far from that frontier.

Governor Jennings announced that he thought the Everglades

could be drained by cutting the natural rock dam in all those rivers and letting the water run out. On the other hand, his engineer, Mr. Fred C. Elliott, advised diking and pumping small areas.

So, Napoleon Bonaparte Broward took the stump for the governorship, since under the Florida law Governor Jennings could not succeed himself. Broward's big body, the forthright stare of his black eyes, his river pilot's black handle-bar mustache, his air of power and resourcefulness, had lost nothing in picturesqueness as sheriff of Duval County since he had gone gunrunning with the *Three Friends* in the Spanish-American War.

He did not base his campaign entirely on drainage of the Everglades, but it became, especially in the southern counties, the most dramatic factor. He unfurled big maps of the Glades area, showing how the canals should run and how they would serve not only for drainage, but for transportation by boats, to build up the country.

Then was born the phrase that would echo all over the country: "The Empire of the Everglades." It was enough to get anybody excited about it, the way Napoleon B. Broward would rear up that great frame of his, and in a voice that spoke intimately to every man roll out the long sentences so that the spines of all the little boys listening on the edge of the crowd would fairly prickle. "Look at Egypt and the Nile," he would say. "Look at Holland."

"It would indeed be a commentary on the intelligence and energy of the State of Florida," he wrote in an open letter to the people of Florida in sonorous and rolling sentences in which one can still hear the wind of his oratory, "to confess that so simple an engineering feat as the drainage of a body of land 21 feet above the sea was above their power." Like the people to whom he spoke, his words drawled and slurred. He must have said "inergy" and "Flo-ida" and "pow-ah." He continued:

Today for hundreds of miles the mighty Mississippi River is confined by levees and so controlled that millions of acres of swamps have been turned into arable lands and are in yearly cultivation, yet the water in the river is often twenty feet above the level of the farms. How much simpler it would be to drain the Florida Glades where no danger from overflow would exist once canals of sufficient capacity were cut and the canals themselves would serve as effective channels of communications between the different parts of the State.

Centuries ago the people of Holland found themselves cramped for room because of the rapid increase of population. They looked out over the adjacent salt and shallow reaches of the sea and said, "Here is land in plenty which the sea does not need, we will take it." They built dikes, shut out the sea, pumped out the water and today the bottom of the sea has become the garden spot of Europe, the home of millions of happy and prosperous people, and the very sea whose land was taken has been harnessed between canal banks and made the contented carrier of a nation's commerce.

In Egypt the turbulent Nile, fed by the torrential floods of equatorial Africa, for ages overflowed the land, and as the price of a fertile soil, exacted an annual tribute of sickness and suffering but the British Government undeterred by the item of expense or the fear of failure built the great Assouan Dam which harnessed the Nile floods and made them obedient to the finger touch so that the healing waters could be parcelled out at will as the seasons required.

With such an example before them shall the sovereign people of Florida supinely surrender to a few land pirates and purchased newspapers and supinely confess that they cannot knock a hole in a wall of coral and let a body of water obey a natural law and seek the level of the sea? To answer "yes" to

313

such a question is to prove ourselves unworthy of freedom, happiness or prosperity.

He swore that one dollar an acre would be a large allowance for the expense of draining all the Glades.

It was true that the railroads were bringing suit for the lands they claimed. But many newspapers and more private individuals were arguing against the too-hasty drainage. No one knew enough about it. It should be given years of careful study. But the land companies and real estate agents insisted that everyone who was not for Broward and drainage was in the pay of the railroads.

The campaign was too dramatic for calmer voices to be heard. Napoleon B. Broward, by everyone conceded to be a completely honest man, was elected governor and therefore became the president of the trustees of the Internal Improvement Fund.

At his request, the legislature passed an act to create a Board of Drainage Commissioners which would consist of the same officers, empowered to drain and reclaim swamp and overflowed lands by canals, dikes, or anything else they could think of, to levy drainage taxes up to five cents an acre and create a drainage district to include only the Everglades. They were to enjoy all powers of a corporate body and the right of eminent domain.

In November, 1905, two dredges, the *Everglades* and the *Caloosahatchee*, were put to work up both branches of the New River. Governor Broward himself lifted the first shovelful. The rock ledges of the north and south branches were dynamited as the dredges worked their way through rock to muck, westward. The first humus-laden dark water began to creep unnoticed down the clear current of the lovely river, staining the bright white bottom sands.

That same year the "Government Cut" was dredged across

the beach from Miami and a channel of sorts to the Florida East Coast docks on the mainland. Then also Mr. Flagler's construction crews worked down the pinelands south of Miami and began the long project of the Overseas Highway by which the bridges and viaducts would creep slowly southward through the lime and milk-green and sapphire waters.

Miami was a small town still. Miss Hattie Carpenter, who taught the few high school students in the single grammar

school, bicycling home to Brickell Hammock with a beefsteak in her basket, was chased by a panther. The streets were blinding white sand. The antisaloon ladies had made it a prohibition town, so that when the railroad crew came roaring in off the extension on a Saturday night they had to get drunk across the line in North Miami saloons. By morning, dead drunk, they would have been rolled across the line into Miami, with their pockets all pulled out. They would be arrested and jailed. In Monday morning's court, all Judge Frank B. Stoneman could do would be to sentence them back to work again.

The Supreme Court handed down its decision about the rights of the trustees over those of the railroads and drainage seemed assured. Governor Broward announced the building of four more dredges, two for the Miami River, one to join the north New River Canal from the lake, one for the Kissimmee River.

Everglades land was now selling at five dollars an acre.

In 1909 the rocky ledges where the rapids of the Miami River held back the salt sea's tides from the fresh-water Glades were dynamited. The dark muck-stained water worked its way over the clear sands, staining the bay bottom. There was nothing to keep the tons of Everglades muck from silting the shallows at the mouth of the river, silting up the bay, creeping out to the sea gardens. In dry times the salt tides worked their way upriver.

But the farmers along the river and the canal which the dredge was slowly pushing west could get to town now with their vegetables.

The dredge stuck at Hialeah, where they meant to put a lock. It sank and the lock sank. The man who contracted to finish that canal to the lake was to be paid by the cubic foot of spoil bank. But as he went west, no matter how he piled it up the muck slithered back. He went bankrupt. The canal from there to the lake was never more than a surface ditch.

The North New River Canal had gone nine miles.

R. P. Davie bought 25,000 acres of black muck on the edge of the Glades by the South New River Canal north of Miami where there was a settlement called Zonia. He renamed it Davie and advertised "Davie Farms" and the amazing quality of Everglades lands all over the west. He paid $2 an acre and sold it at $30.

But the spectacular sale, Governor Broward's chief triumph, was to the big western land promoter of Colorado Springs, Richard J. Bolles, called Dicky Bolles. The day of speculation in western lands was about over, but the nation-wide fever for "getting in on the ground floor," having been whetted again on the gold fields of the Klondike, needed only some other place to go. The Everglades—the "Empire of the Sun"—were the latest hope.

Mr. Bolles fell under Governor Broward's powerful spell.

Mr. Bolles agreed to take 500,000 acres of rich lake-bottom land in Dade and Lee counties, for $1 an acre. Lee County was now separated from Monroe and reached across to the Dade line, south of Okeechobee. With the drainage commissioners he signed an agreement that his land should be drained by five canals, the Miami, the North and South New River, the Hillsboro, the Caloosahatchee, and two smaller ones. Of these only the North New River and the Hillsboro were being completed to the lake. Another canal, named for Bolles, would be dredged five miles south of the lake between the North New River and the Hillsboro canals. If Bolles completed his payments the trustees were pledged to dig all the other canals.

Governor Broward left office feeling that his work was well begun. There was a long dry spell. People everywhere said, "Broward has drained the Everglades." He recalled in triumph how people had said there must be years of study first. He had said, "I will be dead by that time. Let's get a few dredges and begin."

All over the West high-pressure land agents were selling Everglades lands to retired schoolteachers, men back from the Klondike, lecturers, retired but still hopeful farmers, and people who cared for nothing but quick returns on an investment. Excursion boats loaded with land seekers came up the Caloosahatchee, roping around the curves, stopping for barbecues at some of the quiet settlements, into the lake where the lone cypress stood on a bit of high land by the canal entrance, and across it to the big board hotel Bolles had had built on Ritta Island.

317

Along some of the canals, where the saw grass stood on dry-ing banks, here and there small wooden houses were being built by hopeful new owners. They had been told that all they needed was a tent, a hoe to clear the land, and some beans, to begin their fortunes. They found the saw grass difficult to clear with even a month or two of work. They found mosquitoes and loneliness and alligators. The smoke of their fires rose here and there out of the vast saw-grass wilderness. Everything had to come up from Fort Lauderdale on the New River Canal by the regular run-boats, which in the nights went back and forth past the acres and acres of white-blossoming moonvines.

They saw an amazing first growth. Vines started up over-night to cover the small plain houses. Cane sprang high. Cab-bages grew over four or five feet across. Tomatoes as big as green small melons ripened overnight to brilliant red. It was what the land agents had promised.

But here and there, overnight again, those vigorous green things began suddenly to wilt and die back. Crops were lost in a week. Nobody could understand it. It occurred to only a few people that perhaps there were not in that rich-looking muck all the minerals essential to plant growth. People left their lands, impoverished. A few stayed and experimented, trying another crop. A few vegetables were shipped.

Beyond that, beyond the empty sweep of saw grass south-east, south, and southwest, there was still the frontier.

The Dimocks, A. W., the writer father, and Julian, the photographer son, found it so, discovering the brilliant waters, the emptiness of the mangrove, the teeming fish, the disappear-ing alligators, and published in American and English news-papers the first articles describing the sports life of the Ten Thousand Islands. They saw men making moonshine in hidden stills. They caught and studied and photographed the manatee, and especially the fighting tarpon. Their photographs and rec-

ords increased hunting and fishing by wealthy winter sportsmen who spent money lavishly on houseboats and guides and
shot or caught everything they could see.

By 1910, against the new life of tourist money and respecta-
bility flooding the small coastal cities, against the portents of
change in the dredges thrusting their way across the retaining
rock into the saw grass, it seemed as though the frontier boiled
up in a long, slow climax of violence.

Halfway up the empty Chatham River a circumspect man
named Watson had built a respectable two-story frame house
high on an old sand-and-shell Indian mound that commands a
great sweep of river east and west. There was nothing to be
seen but the fish jumping and the birds flying. It had a porch
and high bare rooms, a rainwater cistern, a plank dock for his
boats. He set out a cane patch, horse bananas, and the usual
vegetables. He planted palm trees along the river, and two
royal poinciana trees flamed against gray house and dazzling
blue sky.

In the nights, in all those thousands and thousands of acres
of dark mangroves and the starry-glinting dark river, where the
night herons flew over with their loud sudden "quawk," there
was no light anywhere but the small spark of his lamp.

Nobody seems to know when Watson first came to Chatham
River. Nobody over there even now seems to want to say much
about him. But of all the men who lived silently along those
coasts with the air of strange deeds behind them, Watson's is
the figure about which multiplying legends seem most to cluster.

He was a Scotsman with red hair and fair skin and mild blue
eyes. He was quiet spoken and pleasant to people. But people
noticed one thing. When he stopped to talk on a Fort Myers
street, he never turned his back on anybody.

It was said freely that he had killed people before he came
to Florida, that he killed Belle Star and two people in north-

319

west Florida. That was nobody's business here, from Fort Myers to Shark River. From time to time he went up to Fort Myers or Marco in his boat and took down to work at that lonely place of his on Chatham River people variously described as a boy, a rawboned woman, two white men, a Negro, a Russian, a Negro woman, an old woman. No one seems to know how many. No one seemed to notice for a while that none of these people came back.

He was, of course, a plume hunter and alligator skinner, and he shared many feuds with the quick-shooting men of that wilderness. He acquired the name of "the Barber" when three men tried to "get" him with a false warrant for his arrest. The ringleader was none other than Lieutenant Willoughby's ex-guide, Ed Brewer. Watson shot his mustache off. A sheriff is said to have come up the Chatham River looking for someone who had disappeared from Key West. Watson took him in and treated him well and the sheriff went back to Key West swearing he was one of the nicest men he'd ever known.

In 1910 a man and his son sailing up the Chatham River saw something queer floating by the bank. It was the body of an old woman, gutted, but not gutted enough to sink. The man said, "Let's get along to Watson's and tell him about it."

The son said, "Let's get back to Chokoloskee and talk to Old Man McKinney." At Chokoloskee they found several men talking to a Negro in McKinney's store. The story the Negro told was that he'd worked for Watson a long time and seen him shoot a couple of men. The Negro said he'd buried a lot of people on his place, or knocked them overboard when they asked him for their money.

Watson was away, the Negro said. His overseer, named Cox, killed another man and the old woman and forced the Negro to help him cut them open and throw them in the river. He said he would kill him last, but when the Negro got down on his knees and begged to be spared Cox said he would if he'd promise to go down to Key West and get out of the country. The Negro came up to Chokoloskee instead and told everything.

A posse went down to Watson's place and found plenty of bones and skulls. The overseer got away and has never been seen there since.

The next day Watson came back in his boat from Marco and stopped at McKinney's store in Chokoloskee. He came walking along the plank, quiet and pleasant, carrying his gun. And here were all the men of Chokoloskee standing quietly around with their guns.

Mr. McKinney walked up to Watson slowly and said, "Watson, give me your gun."

Watson said, "I give my gun to no man," and fired pointblank at McKinney, wounding him slightly. As if it was the same shot, every man standing there in that posse fired. Watson fell dead. Every man claimed he killed him, and nobody ever knew because there were so many bullets in him.

They dragged his body into the water and towed it behind a boat down to Rabbit Key and buried him on that long oyster and mud bank which at low tide stretches out from the mangroves to a lone twisted mangrove tree at the very end. Later his body was reburied on the mainland. His house was left alone up Chatham River. One woman who lived there went crazy and kept trying to burn down all the trees except one of the big poincianas, with its snaky roots and flaming blossoms that still stands there.

Nineteen-ten. The east coast had its Ashley gang.

Mrs. Joe Ashley of Gomez, just north of Hobe Sound, had five dark, tall sons, John, Bob, Tom, Ed, and Frank, like Old Joe himself, familiar with the Everglades and with Indians, hunting and shooting plume birds and drinking; fine, easy-spoken, drawling boys, dead shots, wild as hawks.

John Ashley worked on the dredge boat up the New River Canal and with Bob ranged as far south as Miami, selling plumes and skins. They shingled a house for Dr. John Gifford in Coconut Grove once, a job good for thirty years, nails driven only two-thirds in and the shingles set a little apart, so that they'd swell in the rains.

At Christmastime John Ashley came in from the Everglades behind Fort Lauderale to the Indian camp of De Soto Tiger. He had liquor with him and he and De Soto Tiger sat in John's canoe and drank and quarreled. Jim Gopher, another Indian, heard two shots and saw somebody fall overboard. In Miami, J. D. Girtman paid John Ashley $584 for eighty-four otter skins. Tiger's body was picked up by the dredge men and Jim Gopher told the sheriff what he'd seen.

It was remembered then that John Ashley had often said he would not mind killing an Indian any more than he would mind shooting a buzzard. The law did not get its hands on Ashley for two years until they got word from his father, Joe Ashley, that he'd sent word to John to come in and surrender. They arrested him in a disorderly house. But he jumped his bond of $25 and got away. For a while there were a lot of small robberies, grocery stores and general stores, and people began to talk about "the Ashley gang."

In the settlements beginning on the East Ridge of Lake Okeechobee, everybody said that smooth-talking John Ashley, romantic with his crimes and escapes, was the lover of a dark-eyed, tough and handsome lake girl, Laura Upthegrove.

In the Everglades, the trustees of the new Gilchrist adminis-tration boasted that where there had been only twelve land-owners there were now fifteen thousand.

The boom in Everglades land continued all over the country. The Internal Improvement Fund trustees were forced to issue a statement that they had nothing to do with the extravagant plans and promises of the land companies. The Bolles Company had sold ten thousand farms in 10-acre tracts for from $20 to $24 an acre; the Everglades Plantation Company, a thousand farms at $30 to $50 an acre. People came in and began to clear land, some still underwater, but the greatest number had bought solely for the purpose of speculation. The companies that had refused to pay the drainage tax made an agreement with the trustees which resulted in contracts for two hundred miles of canals to be dredged in three years.

Still, no one had made any kind of study of the land itself, the varieties of soil, its nature and possibilities, and the possible results of all these reckless ideas of drainage.

Favorable reports had been written and widely circulated, beginning with the Senate Document No. 89 in 1911, written by Dr. Thomas E. Wills of Fort Lauderdale, a big purchaser of land and keenly interested, as few were, in right development.

Dr. Wills had been a Populist in the days in the Middle West when that was a wildly radical thing to be, an able thinker, a scholar of unquestioned ability. He had been ousted, because of his Populism, as president of Kansas State Agricultural College. Now in Florida he drew heavily on the Buckingham Smith report on the Everglades in 1856. But, like the first Smith report, it all went to show with what great success the problem of the Everglades could be met.

Dr. Wills was planning the development of a new town on the Bolles Canal to be called Okeelanta, a combination of "Okeechobee" and "Atlantic." He was not interested in speculation. He wanted to build a good place to live. He wanted to sell only to settlers and people who would work with him, farming and developing. Alone of all the towns or cities planned in the entire area, except possibly the little town of Alva on the Caloosahatchee, Dr. Wills had a real town plan. The residential streets would be set about a big central park. Each lot would have ten or fifteen acres of farm land on radiating roads beyond, so that people could come in to share the "people's house" and school and church and a chance to learn about all sorts of things besides Glades farming.

He cleared the saw grass and laid out the townsite and planted many farms intelligently, and saw the first harvests and new houses going up.

The legislature passed an act enabling the drainage commissioners to bond local districts for drainage. They had already spent over two million dollars on 142 miles of canals and two locks. The much-praised Wright report of 1909 was found not to have taken into consideration any rainfall or weather statistics.

That was evident now, because over the Glades that Broward had drained it began to rain. It rained up the Kissimmee and the marshes of Fisheating Creek and all that water flowed down into the lake and out over the southern rim, partially denuded of the restraining jungle, and down into the great saw-grass river. People saw the water rising in the new canals, over the gardens and up into the new board houses. Boats went up and down rescuing people.

Davie was flooded out. Miami was full of men raging and holding meetings of protest. Many borrowed money and went back home. Many got jobs in grocery stores, print shops, newspaper offices, and increased the permanent population. Scandals in land sales were made public. The phrase was "land sold by the quart." Several heads of land companies were arrested in other states and indicted for using the mails to defraud. One man was sent to jail.

The rain stopped. The sun began to dry everything. Lake Okeechobee shrank back to its shallow normal misted expanse. Richard J. Bolles, having asked for more time to make payments on his holdings, sold more land and satisfied his mortgage. A few people went back to their Glades lands and began over again trying to grow vegetables in the muck.

There was a war in Europe, which only Germans and a few excitable Frenchmen talked about.

A United States Department of Agriculture Soil Survey was made of land along the North New River Canal in 1915. It stated that this land, if drained, irrigated and fertilized, was still too costly to be worth the effort. Land companies and sales agents in Fort Lauderdale were so infuriated that overnight they collected every copy and burned them all.

Richard J. Bolles was charged with the use of the mails to defraud. It was said that his companies, "The Florida Fruit Lands Company" and the "Okeechobee Fruit Lands Company," sold lands which they claimed the state would drain, not using the necessary phrase: "In so far as the state was able." He was acquitted because no jury could decide whose fault it was.

But the general public, enjoying the sun, was much more excited by the first robbery of a Florida East Coast train. Then the Bank of Dania was robbed and a group of hunters near Boynton were attacked. Everybody said it was the Ashley gang.

Before anything more could be learned about that the Bank of Stuart was robbed of $4,500 and there was no doubt at all who did it, because John Ashley, with a bullet lodged behind an eye from an accidental shot through his jaw, gave up to the posse. He was turned over to Sheriff George B. Baker and lodged in the West Palm Beach jail.

John Gramling of Miami, the prosecutor, insisted on a change of venue from West Palm Beach to Miami, because he said he could not get a jury up there who wouldn't be afraid of the Ashley gang, or friendly to them. John Ashley, lodged in the Miami jail, with his still-bandaged face, was bitter against the doctor who had removed the bullet, and the eye too.

His brother Bob suddenly walked in the jail door with his gun in his hand. When jailer Wilbur J. Hendrickson reached for his gun, Bob shot him cold. He ran out and down the street with a policeman, Bob Riblett, running and firing behind him. Ashley turned and fired, wounding Riblett, who kept on firing. Ashley dropped dead.

Joe Ashley, his father, came down from Gomez for Bob's body and John Ashley still sat in jail, awaiting his trial for the murder of De Soto Tiger and a bank robbery.

The contract for the St. Lucie Canal, which would drain the lake directly east to Stuart, was let.

There was trouble on the Mexican border. It was announced that a railroad would be built across the state to be called the "Fort Myers, Marco Bay and Miami Railroad." But Captain J. F. Jaudon, who was deeply interested in the far mangrove country about Chevalier Bay and Chatham River where the Watson house still stood, said that what the country really needed was a road across the state from Miami to Fort Myers and Tampa. There was no way of getting across there yet. William S. Hill, a reporter on the Miami *Herald*, thought a good name would be the "Tamiami Trail." The name caught. It was always good for an editorial in the *Herald*. Slowly Dade County pushed out a rough road west of town to the edge of the Everglades. That would be all there was of it, for years.

John Ashley came to his trial in the Miami courthouse, where the smoke from the trains blew in and the bells and whistles drowned out the voices of witnesses. He wore a good suit and a pair of yellow shoes. The old charge of murder was dismissed. He was sentenced to Raiford for seventeen years, where he would be fitted with a glass eye and from which he presently escaped. Laura Upthegrove on the lake, where there were more settlements and the hopes of two railroads, presumably saw him again.

It was the last gesture of the old frontier. Both it and the talk about drainage would be forgotten in the great days of change already impending.

14

Boom, Blow, Bust, and Recovery

THE tempo quickened. At the end of World War I new men and events began to crowd and hurry about the coasts and the lake and the Everglades, with a new recklessness, a greater violence.

The southern lake shore was bare, where the last moonvine-covered jungles were being cleared away. Careless weeds and castor-oil plants grew rank in the drying muck. Where the lone cypress stood by the Moorehaven Canal, men began to talk about sugar cane again.

John C. Gramling, who had sent John Ashley to Raiford but had not been able to keep him there, had cleared one hundred twenty-five acres of weeds and saw grass and saw his first cane shoot up. F. E. Bryant and then V. G. Dahlberg, near Canal Point, watched the huge rectangles of their cane plantings grow brilliant green against the immensity of brown saw grass all beyond. The first sugar mills were brought up on barges along the canal and the smoke of first grinding was a tall pillar in that enormous flatness.

Nowhere else in the world, men said, forgetting what had happened to Hamilton Disston's St. Cloud, was the land so rich for sugar. The state of Florida built an Experiment Station at Belle Glade for the first study of the muck. They discovered why the early crops had died back. The soil lacked copper, manganese, zinc, and other trace elements. But cane would grow here all year round, and when the missing chemicals were replaced, the cane planters began to get lusty crops.

They had begun planting in a dry cycle, the mucklands drying and shrinking and oxidizing under the hot sun. When they burned the rattling saw grass to clear new acres, no one cared how far the fires swept. Water from the lake flowed sluggishly to the sea by the few canals.

Then the rains came back, brimming the marshy plains and the inflowing rivers to the north. The water rose hissing as it always had and seeped down over the mucklands and the cane fields and brimmed the streets of the little towns and ran and glittered again far away along the course of the river of grass. A shallow lake spread miles beyond Moorehaven. Men went in boats about the swirling streets of Clewiston, which had been Sands Point. The vegetable fields of Ritta Island were deep with water. The few houses left at Dr. Wills's Okeelanta and the new railway lines were overwhelmed with flood.

Many men quit in disgust. Others, who loved the flat brilliant lake country and believed passionately in its black soil, went fishing. It was by their insistence that a muck dike was thrown up along the lake rim eastward from Moorehaven. When the weeds were green on it and the black roads only a little moist with the constant gentle seepage, the southern towns felt safe again. Vegetables were set out. Cane fields were replanted.

In Miami, in the winter of 1920-21, there was a small boom. Streets were pushed out among farther palmettos and around the new houses the Caribbean pines, injured by the builders' carelessness, were dying. New stores were opened, new hotels finished. Crowded steamers came into the city docks. Cars drove from the north along the Dixie Highway. Yachts came down the inland waterways to Palm Beach and Miami, and along the Gulf Coast to Fort Myers. Sportsmen fished about the keys and the Ten Thousand Islands. There was good money for fish guides and for the Indians of the Big Cypress from northern sports hunters going out for deer and turkey. Sawmills whined on the edge of pinelands all about the Glades. Everybody had money in the rising stock market, the expansive Republican promise of the Harding administration.

Across Biscayne Bay in 1915 Carl Fisher had cleared the mangroves and pumped the white bay bottom to fill the outlines of Miami Beach, set with new streets and small bristles of Australian pines and palm trees. Now people were buying lots around his hotels and polo fields. On the long beaches the casinos and pools were gay with bathers. Over the new County Causeway or the old wooden two-mile Collins Bridge, named for the man who first cleared a plantation there, people could drive up the beach road all the way beyond Baker's Haulover and the old House of Refuge, with only the sea lavender and the palm trees between them and the superb color of the sea. It was said then and rewritten many times that, if that road was not secured for public use, someday there would be no sea boulevard at all. But people were too busy boasting about the future. They could not work for it.

329

There was a quick depression. But to the people about the Everglades and the sea frontier it was hardly noticeable, because of Prohibition. All the plume hunters whose market had been ruined by bird protection, the alligator hunters who had killed off the alligators, turned, like slave smugglers and gun and blockade runners and petty pirates before them, to rum-running. Their fast motorboats roared in out of the dark seas from Cuba and the Bahamas. Trucks waited for their cargoes on remote wharves. Profits were enormous.

Hidden stills among the mangroves or in Everglades hammocks increased the amount of liquor. Hijacking began. There were gang wars.

Chinese from Cuba were smuggled in at exorbitant prices. They could be set ashore anywhere or left on islands, or shot, or dropped overboard if capture seemed likely. Murders were committed boldly. There were never enough officers to patrol the endless coast or the Everglades' depths.

Corruption spread into local politics and left its mark. There would be honest officials yet. But in a city like Miami, growing incredibly by the periodical influx of migrant people, rich and poor, with no civic responsibility, thoughtful citizens were unable to prevent it.

The Ashley gang ranged again, not as a unique Everglades institution but as part of that nation-wide crime wave. Ed and Frank Ashley ran liquor from Bimini until they were killed by hijackers. Joe Ashley, the father, was shot by Prohibition enforcement officers in a battle over a still. They were all rum-runners, hijackers, bootleggers.

But John Ashley, glass eye and all, smooth spoken, well dressed, with his wild shrewd energy, always remembered that he was a bank robber. He and his nephew, Hanford Mobley, Ray Lynn, and a Chicago gunman named John Clarence Middleton, robbed the Bank of Pompano. Two days later John sent

Mobley into the Bank of Stuart veiled and dressed like a woman. While Mobley held up the cashier, the gang took everything they could lay their hands on. They got away northward.

Sheriff Bob Baker, son of the man who first had arrested John Ashley, had already surrounded the old Ashley place at Gomez, hiding his men in the bushes. But old Mrs. Joe Ashley was too smart for them. When she heard the far roar of John's heavy car on the highway, she walked out the door and fired her gun in the air. The officers could only listen to the squeal of brakes as the car stopped and turned and roared diminishingly away.

From a hideout near Canal Point he sent Bob Baker a bullet and the message "Come on out in the Glades and get me." But the Glades that had given him security were not enough for him now.

Baker got a straight tip that Ashley and his gang were heading for Jacksonville. He got to Sebastian Bridge before they did and hung across it a heavy chain and a red lantern. When the roaring car stopped and John Ashley stuck his head out, Baker started shooting. All four men were brought back to West Palm Beach in handcuffs, full of bullet holes, and dead. There was some question about when the handcuffs had been put on them. Nobody followed that line of thought very far.

In his wild head John Ashley's glass eye still glared its defiance. Sheriff Bob Baker had always admired the look of that glass eye. He had often threatened that he would wear it on his watch chain. Now he reached over and took it out.

It was extraordinary how fast that word traveled and how fast the message came back to Sheriff Baker from Canal Point from Laura Upthegrove, the "Queen of the Everglades" who had loved John Ashley. Her message to Bob Baker was: "If you don't put that eye back again, I'll crawl through hell on my hands and knees to kill you." The sheriff put it back. Or so the legend goes.

John Ashley was buried with it, alongside the others, in the family plot at Gomez, with only old Mrs. Joe Ashley to mourn him. "It was all Bob Baker's fault," she said.

Before that in Miami a white Episcopal minister, a crippled Englishman who preached in a mission for Negroes, was tarred and feathered and dumped out on Flagler Street by a gang of masked men. They were never arrested or looked for. They may or may not have been members of the newly organized Ku Klux Klan but the local newspapers never printed a word of it.

There were gun battles in Biscayne Bay and off Fort Lauderdale between rumrunners and the Coast Guard. John Alderman was hanged for murdering a Coast Guardman. Red Shannon, the romantic hero of Miami Beach night clubs, was shot by another guardman after he had run around the bay in that high-powered boat of his, tossing out cases of champagne across the bows of the revenue boats. When Prohibition was repealed, west coast men would mourn its going. Its influence would remain.

But around the southern edge of Okeechobee there were more sober and hard-working men who clung to other dreams of riches. They knew more about vegetables now. In one year of dry weather they shipped four million dollars' worth of tomatoes and beans and peas and cabbage. Hope kept their hearts stout through rains and frosts.

In the cities the excitement of greater winter crowds and easier money began to lift again. The new hotels overflowed with tea dances in their palm gardens. The pounding jazz of night clubs and gambling joints, the streets crowded with new cars, in one season began to change the shape and color and feeling of Miami growing out of narrow streets and wooden houses under oak trees. The stimulus of big money quickened the minds of citizens with real estate to sell.

It was the concern only of a minority that the city was still without adequate sewers, schools, hospitals, libraries, parks and playgrounds where so recently there had been nothing but land and hope. Colored-town slums spread unnoticed. The river and the bay were slowly darkened and fouled. The glitter, the whiteness, the play of light, the stimulus of the sun, the sense that a great city was building here made it impossible now for people to check ills daily growing greater.

Times and events quickened and rushed forward, as a river gathered to the drag of a cataract.

For some years now George Merrick, who as a boy had stayed in the old Peacock Hotel in Coconut Grove while his father bought and planted his first grove in the pinelands west of Miami, had been drawing up plans for a city that he meant to call Coral Gables. He saw it clearly from the beginning, with wide streets and green parkways and trees and gardens, ornamental gateways and houses of Spanish architecture, churches and stores in one section, a few selected industries in another. He began to advertise and sold his first lots. Miami Beach lots were already selling and reselling.

On the west coast, Barron G. Collier, the New York advertising man, bought acres of mangrove swamps around the Allen River toward Chokoloskee Bay and more dry land up the coast. Much later he would get the legislature to set aside land from Monroe and Lee counties and call his "Collier County," just as already, in 1920, Palm Beach County and Broward had been set apart from northern Dade. Mr. Collier bought land on the old island of Marco, where Captain Bill Collier, who was no relation, had homesteaded and where Cushing had made his great forgotten discovery. There was a central ridge on which squatters had lived for so many generations that it was forgotten that they never had taken title. There is a tale of a drawn battle between the titleless people and men of the Collier interests. The people were ejected. He went on building good roads through the salt marsh and mangrove, laid out the new clean company town of Everglades.

Calvin Coolidge's Republican prosperity followed Harding's Republican "normalcy." The stock market was rising, but Miami real estate rose faster and more people talked about it and hurried to profit by it. Trains, boats, automobiles arrived jammed with people. Hotels and rooming houses were packed. Tourists slept on porches, in tents, on park benches.

The air was electric with talk of money. "Hundreds" became "thousands." "Millions" became a common word. Business lots, house lots, buildings, houses, tracts at the edge of the city, and tracts beyond tracts began to sell and resell as fast as the papers could be made out. Sales were made with small down payments of cash and any number of mortgages. Paper profits were dizzy.

George Merrick's Coral Gables was sold and resold and sold again. In that first year of the boom his sales added up to $150,000,000. He planned to put $100,000,000 back into city development, for more parks and gateways and golf courses. He bought more land on all sides of his original tracts and sold lots as soon as they were platted. He gave mortgages and took mortgages. His sales organization and his advertising mushroomed. He announced a million-dollar hotel, among other hotels. He planned a million-dollar university. Few felt that there could be limits to the expansion.

Seven million dollars in construction was announced for Miami Beach, where beach estates and building lots were valued at fantastic figures. The Deering Estate north of Miami was sold for $30,600 an acre. It was all cloudy, all visionary, all on paper, but everybody making these heady millions clung fiercely to the belief that it was real and that it would go on indefinitely.

Outside Miami subdivision after subdivision, to the very edge of the watery Glades, had their barbecues and advertisements and auctioneers bellowing to waiting crowds. Vast gateways were erected, through which sidewalks and street lights led to nothing at all but more land. Streets were laid out in the usual gridirons, with no other planning, no parkways, no parks, no provisions for anything but a quick turnover of money.

The excitement of Miami's boom went roaring up the coasts.

Joseph W. Young spent twenty million dollars filling a swamp and pineland approach to a beach south of Fort Lauderdale. He ran buses from Miami filled with would-be buyers. His first section sold before it was finished. He gave free trips to more people from New York and Chicago. He built a big beach hotel and planned a harbor at Lake Mabel, to be called Port Everglades.

Fort Lauderdale boomed. Canals and islands were cut in the harbor mangroves. River-front subdivisions were laid out and sold and resold. Big new cities were planned in all the pinelands between the ridge and the Everglades. Each had its promoter who was hailed as one more "man of vision."

West around the palm-shadowed city of Fort Myers the boom spread its subdivisions and its talk of money, and south to Collier's planned cities and north like a hurricane along the coast to Tampa and beyond to the Carolinas in a flowing avalanche of excitement about real estate. It moved up the quiet towns of the Caloosahatchee.

Palm Beach, in spite of its aloofness to the rest of Florida, felt the surge. Addison Mizner was reshaping Mr. Flagler's yellow-and-white American Victorianism to a Spanish harmony of pink walls and tiled roofs, patios behind iron gates, swimming pools and loggias more secluded than ever behind high masonry walls planted with sea grape and palms and oleanders and Spanish bayonet. The blue Gulf Stream, which here moved nearer to the white raked beaches in an amazing purple-blueness, the fine light, the air, were the only things unchanged as the brief Palm Beach season heightened its unreal luxury.

The fine Spanish buildings would find their echo all over the region, in new subdivisions or in flimsy and dubiously colored stucco under the old live oaks in such remote towns as La Belle. Palm Beach emeralds and diamonds would be duplicated on the fingers of wives of real estate plungers and bootleggers, driving equally exotic cars to louder night clubs. Fishermen wore silk shirts. Paper millionaires bought yachts. They shared alike the belief symbolized by Palm Beach, that success meant expensive waste. It was a recurrence of the great human mass hysterias.

It is hard to make anyone believe that there were people in those cities whose quiet lives were never interrupted by all that uproar. There were a few like Charles Torrey Simpson, fellow of the Smithsonian, in his fine garden in Little River, who more than any other man knew the plants of this region and wrote beautiful books about the lake and the keys and the Everglades; Edward Simmonds in the Plant Introduction Garden, whose hope was that there would be mangoes and avocados growing here in plenty for everybody. There were other plantsmen, like Dr. David Fairchild, foresters like Dr. John C. Gifford, teachers, and editors and workers; thousands of thoughtful people who had nothing whatever to do with the boom, who saw with dismay the improvidence, the recklessness, the mounting public indebtedness. When it was over, they were the ones who would carry on.

Bearing grapefruit trees, gardens planted to tropical trees and avocados and the fine Haden mango that had been developed in Coconut Grove, the jungles of native hardwoods, were cleared ruthlessly and cut into building lots and sold, and sold again.

It was all paper, a juggling of paper checks and paper mortgages. And then came the binders. The streets of Miami in the second spring of the boom were crowded with suddenly arrived people from all over the country soon known as "binder boys." They gambled with small cash payments called binders, good only for a short time, on lots doubling in value from one day to the next. They began to raise a structure of credit so flimsy that the first wind would flatten it.

The wind would rise.

Building in Miami, like the prices of lots, had its own boom. Railroads could not begin to handle the southbound freight in lumber, plumbing fixtures, wallboard, nails, roofing, window frames, everything. Railroad yards all the way north were congested. Carefully iced vegetable cars moved south full of brick. Tracks were too crowded for passenger trains. The Florida Coast and the newly extended Seaboard declared a freight embargo. Fleets of trucks then moved south with building supplies. Sailing vessels from as far away as Portland, Oregon, barks, barkentines, even one full-rigged ship were chartered, crammed full of building materials and pushed down to Biscayne Bay. A forest of masts lay along the bayfront. The narrow channel to the cut was filled with old windjammers, coming and going with their tugs.

The long four-masted *Prinz Valdemar* broke her towlines

and slued across the channel and sank. The ship channel was locked shut. More windjammers let go their anchors on the reef outside the beach where in the nights they looked like a long lighted town. For two months, while salvage men dredged and pushed and dug, the *Prinz Valdemar* lay where she was. The rigged ships along the bayfront grew barnacles. Building in Miami stopped for the summer.

Lots were still selling. People said the embargo gave everybody a chance to get caught up so that the boom could begin again in the fall. Full-page announcements of new subdivisions, Opa-Locka with its lovely minarets, and new towns with nothing but gateways weighted the newspapers. Forty miles of waterfront were advertised for Coral Gables as the dredges cut canals in the rock south of Coconut Grove and moved a deep trail of salt water inland.

The physical appearance of Miami was already much changed, although a dozen elaborate new buildings still bristled with scaffolding. The Venetian Causeway to Miami Beach took the place of the old Collins Bridge. The Miami Woman's Club and many downtown churches on land Mr. Flagler had given them sold and built elsewhere. The old trees were torn down and tall buildings that might have stood anywhere were raised flush with the sidewalks, dwarfing the already narrow streets.

The yellow-and-white Royal Palm Hotel, among its fine gardens by the river, held its old charm and dignity. The crowded streets were overhung with signs. Only over the downtown roofs thrusting higher, in that late summer of 1926, against the remoter loveliness of the skies, pearly and violet and white frothed with the mountains of dazzling summer clouds, the night hawks in their unbelievable flight still slid and dived and tumbled and skated. Their fine twitterings, the deep thrum of wings, as they dived and sharply recovered, were never heard over the city's traffic. But they had their freedom of it still.

338

The sickle wings of the night hawks began the long beat southward in their fall migration. In their skyey courses they may have been the first to feel that vast shape of air spinning up from the equator along the line of the Bahamas. The word reached Miami on the morning of Friday, September 17, that a hurricane moved there somewhere. A fine gray rain began and blew and stopped and blew again. The sky darkened with a greenish light southeastward. The fine rain blew white against it and stopped. A dark sudden gale gathered. There was more rain. Then none, and for a while no wind. Old-timers, remembering hurricanes, felt their skins prickle and began to board up.

Most people knew nothing of hurricanes at all. It was reported from Nassau that hurricane winds higher than a hundred miles an hour had hit them. The center had curved before that, turning across the Gulf Stream. It moved directly on Miami.

Late that night, in absolute darkness, it hit, with the far shrieking scream, the queer rumbling of a vast and irresistible freight train.

The wind instruments blew away at a hundred twenty-five miles. The leaves went, branches, the bark off the trees. In the slashing assault people found their roofs had blown off, unheard in the tumult. The water of the bay was lifted and blown inland, in streaming sheets of salt, with boats, scows, ships, the *Rose Mahoney*, coconuts, debris of all sorts, up on the highest ridge of the mainland. Miami Beach was isolated in a sea of raving white water. Far out to the Everglades shacks, garages, sheds, barns, were smashed flat by the wind and trampled into mud by the machine-gunning of the steely rain.

At eight o'clock next morning the gray light lifted. The roaring stopped. There was no wind. Blue sky stood overhead. People opened their doors and ran, still a little dazed, into the ruined streets. They shouted and climbed up on collapsed walls, and walked and stared. A few people complained that their ears clicked or hummed, as if they were going down in an elevator. Only a few remembered or had ever heard that in the center of a spinning hurricane there is that bright deathly stillness.

It passed. The light darkened. The high shrieking came from the other direction as the opposite whirling thickness of the cyclonic cone moved on over the darkened city.

People died then in the streets, drowned, blown against walls, injured by bricks, planks, corrugated iron, blown and smashed down on them. For hours the screaming blowing terror of the storm went by. The center passed through the Everglades in a great swath, crushing the stiff saw grass, dwarfing the lake. The water was blown across the southwest rim, smashing the muck dikes that had been built to keep Moorehaven dry. The white foaming water poured out for miles back into the saw grass. Three hundred twenty Moorehaven people and people on remote farms along the canals, people huddled in boats, and on the roofs of floating houses were killed or drowned.

By sunset that same night in Miami the wind was gone. Two thousand houses were down, three thousand badly damaged. In Fort Lauderdale twelve hundred houses were smashed. Streets, bayfronts, rivers were obliterated with debris. Relief workers made their way to Hialeah rescuing people trapped under houses, women giving birth to babies among ruins, picking up people bleeding to death or dead. There were no lights, hardly any food or water. The relief trains began to come in.

Yet in the ruined city the cheapness, the flimsiness, the real estate shacks, the billboards, the garish swinging signs, the houses badly built, the dizzy ideas, the boom itself, was blown away. What was left were such foundations of buildings or ideas as had been well and truly laid. There was the sea and the bay, tranquil and innocent already as blue flowers. There was the rock below, the sun, the fine exuberant air. And the courage, the fundamental character, of a sobered people. Hundreds left. Those who stayed, newcomers or old-timers, worked together at last. When relief was no longer necessary and the city cleaned and patched, the days of mourning over, they saw that the place was real again.

Men, doubly ruined by boom and blow, went to work at anything they could get. Many who had been paper millionaires remembered that they had been bakers. "Men of vision" saw that they were still lawyers or printers. Those who had come here because they were promoters and had not yet learned to care for any place they could not exploit had left long before. Men stayed, operating elevators, working in grocery stores, going back to reporting or selling hurricane insurance or searching for clear titles through the vast layers of worthless paper mortgages. They learned that they had come because they loved the unique country, and they were not changed. There was still fish in the unharmed sea. A man could plant a sapling and watch its quick tropical growth and eat its fruit.

For years to come Florida real estate would be a laughing matter. But what had been the Florida boom, the hot released passion for easy money from land, which had gripped the country recurrently since the Civil War, was certainly the same kind of hysteria which had helped discover and populate the New World. Now, throughout the United States, speculation in land was at a standstill. The fever translated itself into speculation in stocks in one of the greatest quick-money epidemics the world has seen.

Miami and South Florida lived through a series of after-the-boom bank failures. It worked on slowly at its own recovery, looking askance now at the rest of the country going mad.

The year after the hurricane people in Florida had also wakened to the idea that all the talk about draining the Everglades was equally unreal. They had a few canals which had cost fourteen million dollars, built for transportation as much as for

341

drainage, which were good for neither. In high water the canals could not carry off the surplus. In low water and dry times, with no water control, they merely took away water increasingly essential.

Moorehaven streets were still subsiding. There was a hit-or-miss patchwork of lesser canals wherever a drainage district had been able to put one in, and mounting indebtedness. No one had yet made an accurate study of the Everglades themselves.

Governor Martin, elected on a campaign of good roads, went also into the drainage question. He dug up the Randolph report of 1913, which had called for twenty more canals to carry off water that was not always there. Governor Martin asked specifically for an Engineering Board of Control to build canals east and west and a great levee along the whole southern rim of the lake. He asked for a Bond Plan that would raise twenty million dollars for that project.

There was a storm of opposition chiefly from Dade County, suffering from poverty and its own overbonding. The Dayton Morgan Engineering Company reported that nothing practical could be accomplished in the Glades without a liquidation of past mismanagement and the elimination of politics, a sound study of facts and over-all administration.

Governor Martin and the Internal Improvement Fund trustees had to see all the drainage work slow down and stop. They had no more money. But one great project was finished after more than fourteen years of stopping and starting and leaving alone—the Tamiami Trail.

It leaps like a flung lance, blue-black in the blazing distance, shimmering with a mirage, clear and clean across the whole of South Florida. Along it the buses thunder between Miami and Fort Myers and Tampa, and automobiles and huge trucks. The road roars with their passing, but after that the silence flows back again, the ancient inviolable silence of the Everglades.

The winds from the far sea make the silence, rustle the grasses, sing in the wires. Part of it is the thin-edged cry of a ranging sparrow hawk and the little splashing of coot and pied-billed grebe and gallinule, tacking among their own ripples in the canal alongside. The buzzards drop back to clean up a snake killed by a car. At night the eyes of raccoons glitter in the headlights.

It reaches and vanishes from sky into sky; from dawns of pale silver and tangerine over the grape-colored ramparts of Gulf Stream clouds to sunsets in blue winters like explosions of orange and bronze and brass. The eye goes far away from it and is widened and cooled with distance, monotonous among the green-humped hammocks, austere with saw grass. The few white people who live along it have quiet eyes. The Indians use it.

People rushing across it look and see nothing. "But there's nothing," they say. They see neither the Everglades nor the Trail's drama.

In 1916, when Dade County voted $125,000 to begin it, a rough road was carried west some sixty miles and stopped. Captain J. F. Jaudon, more than ever absorbed in the development of his holdings from mid-Everglades to Chevalier Bay in Monroe County, expected the trail to grow through his projected townsite at Pinecrest, the pine ridge in the center that is the only evidence south of Okeechobee of that upthrust of Pleistocene rock. Lee County voted $355,000 and sent a couple of dredges to gnaw out a beginning from the west. Then the war came and nothing more was done.

But under Governor Martin's good roads program and the prodding of energetic Barron G. Collier, from what would be Collier County, the Dade and Lee County stretches were extended. Collier advanced some money. The Monroe County route was abandoned for one going straight to Carnestown, where Collier's road went down to the town of Everglades.

Both ends would meet in 1928, but only after unbelievably hard work had gone on for all those years.

The very last expedition of the Fort Myers "Trail Blazers" in 1923, like every effort of white men to get across it in some way other than the Indian's, met every sort of hardship in the thick saw-grass muck.

The highest point of land anywhere along this line is only twelve feet above sea level, and in seasons of heavy rain was almost entirely underwater. Under the layer of muck and water, not so deep here as in the Upper Glades, the limestone rock reaches, pitted and pocked and worn jagged. They had no idea at first how to build a road through this. First they tried putting rock over the muck. In wet weather it sank out of sight. In dry weather, in the fires devastating the Everglades, the muck burned out below it.

They found that they must blast down to the basic limestone, scoop out the soft muck and fill with rock to the surface, making a great limestone causeway all the way across the state.

Every foot of the way had to be dynamited. During the years when the trail was under construction, Collier County alone used 2,598,000 sticks of 60 per cent dynamite.

The job was a man-killer. First a crew went forward through saw grass and water and rocky hammocks with axes and machetes, cutting a trail. They worked up to the armpits in water, tormented with mosquitoes in the season, always watchful for rattlesnakes and the uncounted dark heads of moccasins. They lived, ate and slept in muck and water.

Behind them a gang constructed a crude sort of railway of cypress logs, across which the heavy drilling machines were dragged, to make holes in the rock for the dynamite. Sometimes the drills stuck in the mud and there would be days of back-breaking man-labor, with heavy hand jacks, to set them up again.

After the drillers, in that slow heavy pace, crept the ox teams of dynamite, floundering in the muck, the wheels slipping off the logs, getting stuck, getting hauled out. After the dynamiting, mile by mile, the dredges that were to dig limestone for the roadbed moved ponderously up in the canal of their own making. The dredge men had their own particular hell of mired beams, and dredges sinking. Men were scarred, were drowned, battered, snakebitten, and blown up.

The work crept forward. At best, as much as two miles might be built in a month.

The final cost was something like six million dollars. But the trail crossed the Everglades.

The year the Tamiami Trail was opened, the total cost of drainage in the Everglades was $18,000,000. Land was up from $68 to $92 per acre. J. J. Connors had extended his first rough Connors Highway to the lake and northeastward, through the saw grass and cypress where Zachary Taylor had fought the Indians. Two railroads reached it. In all the small settlements and farms there was a population of 48,000, not counting the Indians. The value of the Everglades was proudly stated to be $106,000,000. In that same year it would have been almost impossible to prove.

Because in that fall another hurricane swept up from the West Indies, roared inland from West Palm Beach, and in a day of terrible gray wind and whipped white water spread darkness and horror over all those little towns in the muck. The lake with a long howling swept over everything, over the cleared lands, over the canals, the cane fields, the scattered houses, the far roads.

Men and women were caught and drowned out of overturned boats, in unroofed houses, among uprooted trees. Lives were smashed out under tons of water in the night, choked with mud, crushed under the weight of blown debris. When the light came back to the lake there was one wilderness of water everywhere, in which the dead lay like logs.

The ultimate damage of that hurricane was not known for weeks. Battered schoolhouses were full of refugees. Boats went up and down to gather in the living. As the waters crept back under the renewed sun, the steaming mud stank of rotting flesh. Bodies were piled up like cordwood along railroad landing platforms. Trains crept in slowly with supplies and coffins. Eighteen hundred people had been killed. The living had gray, vacant faces.

Something had to be done about the control of Okeechobee waters in storms or all that southern rim would be depopulated. Under the Carlton administration the state co-operated with the federal government in a new development of the Okeechobee-Caloosahatchee-St. Lucie-district. A vast dike was constructed from east to south to west of the lake, within its average rim. Canal gates were opened in it. It rises now between the lake itself and all those busy towns, Moorehaven, Clewiston, Lake Harbor, Belle Glade, Pahokee, Canal Point, and the rest.

To see the vast pale water you climb the levee and look out upon its emptiness, hear the limpkins crying among the islands of reeds in the foreground, and watch the wheeling creaking sea gulls flying about a man cutting bait in a boat, by a shack on a bushy ridge of mud. They are hidden in a world of their own far from the busy black roads to the south of the levee, the packing houses, towns, cars, roadside stands, brilliant green lawns and trees, and juke joints.

From the lake the control project extended west, cutting a long ugly canal straight through the green curving jungle and the grove-covered banks of Caloosahatchee. The dredge tore through the water oaks, the cypress, the trailing vines, the strata of ancient fossils. The spoil banks were run far back beyond the groves, or in some places heaped in raw piles to the very roofs of nearby houses. It ran through all those old meanders as the parallel lines cut the curves of the dollar sign. They left standing innumerable half-moon-shaped islands covered with old trees, behind which the old loops and half-cutoff lagoons live still their watery green and reedy lives, with the fish jumping and kingfishers clucking across, and the small green herons feeding.

When the glossy brown water of the river is undisturbed it still reflects like a dark mirror the vines re-covering the raw banks and the leaning trees where the slow cows come down to drink. But when the launches of the engineers roar through, or yachts or oil boats from one coast to another, their wash cuts under the old banks and stirs up the dark mirror to foam brown and yellow with sediment. The Caloosahatchee is changed utterly. It will never flood again the orange groves or leave its silt under the live oaks.

"A good thing," the cattlemen say, whose fires south of the river in the drying flat country crackle along the pinelands and invade the edges of the drying orange groves. Locks at Ortona and St. Lucie control the flow. The lake level was at once lowered five feet. The surrounding fields dried to powder. The water table, even in the groves along the banks, was down seven feet. People were not sure that everything was turning out exactly for the best.

But worse than that, up from the Gulf of Mexico the salt water, which the slow push of the fresh water down those multitudinous loopings had kept back, now crept far up the canal with every high tide. Cypress trees began to die along the banks. Wells near the river turned salt. The old bridge tenders from their shacks under the old oaks, standing with their elbows on the rail over the empty river, began to think they needed more locks, downriver, against the salt. There was no sale for grove land. As the traffic from army fields roared along the main highway to Fort Myers, the river, with its quiet emptying towns, was more and more forgotten.

347

Five feet of water let out of the lake brought bottomlands of lake islands into cultivation again, fields unbelievably green with their roots in the sweet water. Grass grew rank, trees tall. All along the roadways, where the towns clustered more and more thickly, great shaggy masses of bamboos and casuarinas marched in their humped exact lines, walling the roadways across the flat glittering levels between cane fields and vegetable fields where the saw grass had been.

The land was dry enough now for beans and peppers and cabbage and eggplant and celery. But the Experiment Station had proved that to replace the elements that the soil needed in greater quantities every year, irrigation to keep the porous muck from drying out and blowing away, dusting against insects, the increasing labor costs, was an expensive business. The black muck, from which its old cover had been removed, and with the water table lowered, gave up its heat more quickly after the sun was down. The quick biting frosts the northers brought struck more deeply into tender crops. Frost damage was as great a gamble as flood damage had been.

With all these expenses and added risks, development in the mucklands came more and more into the hands of larger corporations. The day of the small farmer around the lake was about over.

The lake water, which for so many centuries had flowed southward in the great arc of the saw-grass river, was now empounded. Only the rains could flood the Everglades now. But drainage, some people said around the lake, seeing the great sugar developments, the trainloads of winter vegetables, was a success at last.

Anybody could see, in this time between two wars, that the Everglades had been changed. There were more changes coming.

15

The Eleventh Hour

T HE Everglades were dying.

The endless acres of saw grass, brown as an enormous shadow where rain and lake water had once flowed, rustled dry. The birds flew high above them, the ibis, the egret, the heron beating steadily southward along drying watercourses to the last brackish pools. Fires that one night glittered along a narrow horizon the next day, before a racing wind, flashed crackling and roaring across the grassy world and flamed up in rolling columns of yellow smoke like pillars of dirty clouds.

Perhaps the wind dropped and a quick rain came and put

349

out the fire that had moved too fast to burn deep. Where it had spread its blackness the saw grass had thrust up its green again, thinly, in drier muck. The insects shrilled. The sun blazed. But in all the creatures of those solitudes where the Tamiami Trail and the long canals stretched their thin lines, and in the hearts of the Indians, there was a sense of evil abroad, a restlessness, an anxiety that one passing rainfall could not change.

The cities did not feel it.

Miami rejoiced, after the depression, in its increasing growth. It grew as great cities seem to grow, as if there were places and times in which human activity becomes a whirlpool which gathers force, not only from man's courage and ambitions but from the very tides of disaster and human foolishness that otherwise disperse them. It grew almost in spite of the mistakes of its people, by some power which puts to work good and bad, fineness and cheapness, everything, so long as it has fiber and force and the aliveness that makes more life. Miami grew with the tough thrust and vigor of a tropical organism. Its strength was that nothing human was foreign to it.

It had a hundred thousand regular inhabitants and more, twice that in the area, double that again as the winter crowds filled stores and narrow streets and the elaborate race tracks and the night clubs; all year round, a steady growth of working residents, children crowding the schools, houses and trailer camps and apartments going far beyond the city limits. High buildings crowded downtown streets. Traffic conditions were impossible. The old Royal Palm Hotel was torn down, its gardens gone, in anticipation of some enormous citified structures. Where there had been trees were bare ugly parking lots. But in the outlying districts gardens grew deep and green and life went on quietly under the same sun.

The men of the boom days were almost forgotten. Many of them were dead. New expansions covered old subdivisions.

Coral Gables was sound again after its involved financial troubles, zealous for its parkways and fine trees, and aware that George Merrick's underlying city plan, after the fantasies were swept away, had been good. Miami Beach, first to recover after the depression, was a forest of new hotels that shut out the sea. The opportunity for a spectacular beach boulevard was lost forever. The openness of Biscayne Bay between beach and mainland was filled with islands and houses and trees and causeways where the clear shallows had once glittered with fresh color. The water was darkened and there were smells at low tide.

Miami had even learned to be proud of the most important thing the boom had begun and the bust had not killed, the University of Miami. It lived and grew because of the dogged courage of one man, Bowman F. Ashe. George Merrick in his expanding vision had touched on the idea of a university, endowed it with a million dollars of boom money and some land. There were paper promises of millions more. Ashe, a man with unlimited experience in practical education, had been employed as executive secretary to get the university going. When the boom and the hurricane were over there was the land and the cement beginning of a vast Spanish building, no money at all, and Bowman F. Ashe. He had said emphatically when he came that he wanted never to work for an institution for which he would have to raise money. Everybody else gave up, not he. He had had an idea about how much a university was needed here, on this frontier between two continents. He thought he saw what could be done. So he was made president.

Dr. Ashe and the university went on somehow through years of almost complete destitution. He leased a big unfinished hotel building in Coral Gables, and scraped together a faculty willing to live on small pay and great hopes. A first class of a hundred twenty-five was graduated from that hotel, with its celotex walls and cement stairs and temporary partitions. Dr. Ashe believed that a university could live on its tuition fees. Several years the faculty members who saw it as he did followed his example and voluntarily cut salaries and lived as they could on next to nothing. The others quit.

They got small help from the people. The city of Coral Gables began to give money from the publicity fund. There were a few donations. The school lived through days when the faculty itself was torn with dissension, when the president was lied about and his aims belittled.

He held on through that, sweating out the summers when it looked as if they might not be able to open in the fall. His face, with its jutting nose, the flexible big mouth that can shut so tight, the eyes, deep set in the big skull and alive with the constant progress of his thought, showed the strain that carved deep the granite of his patience and his tenacity. The university went on. Trustees who could not stand the strain resigned and other men took their places. Men and women of his own caliber stood by the president, growing gray with him: Franklin Harris, Bertha Foster, Mary B. Merritt, and many others.

Arnold Volpe began a student symphony orchestra. They did not play very well at first and their public concerts were not crowded. Little by little the students improved. The orchestra added better musicians, attracted great guest artists. People began to attend the concerts in crowds. He died having devoted his life to it, as did Orton Lowe who had begun the English department and the Winter Institute of Literature. A School of Law was added to the School of Liberal Arts and the School of Music. A School of Education went directly out into the Dade County school system with experimental schools and classes for teachers. The Department of Adult Education opened classes to everyone.

The student body and the alumni grew proud of being part

352

of a university in the making. They had a better football team, a distinguished tennis team. Miami began to be proud of it and refer civic problems to its faculty. The university went on, held together and improved by the man who had planned it as a university in which politics had no place and where teaching and thought might be sound and free.

Dr. Ashe saw hundreds of boys trained in his classrooms during the war, navy men, hundreds of young navigators for the Royal Air Force of Great Britain. Winston Churchill, in one of his two public speeches in the United States, expressed his recognition of that aid before a great university convocation at which he was awarded an honorary degree. Dr. Ashe would see a great new campus for a student body of more than five thousand young men and women.

In Dade County an unusually able group of county commissioners began a system of parks, cleaning and landscaping rock pits, making playgrounds, planting avenues of trees along bare highways and developing palm-set public beaches along the mainland, looking out to open sea. It included Matheson Hammock Park, named for the donor whose wisdom may some day be proved to have conserved the last bit of the ancient Miami hammock, the Fairchild Tropical Garden, privately begun and directed as the nucleus of the only tropical botanical garden on the mainland of the United States, and plans for a great series of parks on the undeveloped keys. Parks and playgrounds grew down the county.

In Broward County the boom-planned Port Everglades, ably managed, proved to be the best port on the southern coast. Fort Lauderdale's beautiful bay and islands were improved, although the ancient jungles of the New River were being destroyed. Fort Lauderdale people began to think of better city planning as permanent residents were attracted to its real charm. Fort Myers, on the west coast, beautiful with its cher-

353

ished palm trees, planned and carried out an excellent river-front development.

If all these cities were growing too fast for any but sporadic improvements, their streets still too narrow, their utilities inadequate, the problem of their colored slums still unsolved, with no adequate future planning, they were hardly aware of it yet. Nobody then thought much about the Everglades.

From Homestead north along the railroads the increasing vegetable fields stretched out to the drying Glades. Packing houses hummed in the season as the trucks came in from the fields with loads of potatoes and beans and tomatoes. Dark-green groves of avocados and mangos reached out around the Redlands. Everybody made money again in the years between light frosts. Broward County extended its vegetable fields enormously along the South New River Canal. Palm Beach County, west of Lake Worth, sent out thousands of trainloads of winter vegetables.

Because of the great lake levee and the two main canals, no more water seeped over the lake edges to the Everglades. Locks let the water out into the North New River, the West Palm Beach Canal, the St. Lucie. The Miami, the South New River, the Hillsborough that never had been completed, were half filled with muck and water hyacinths and served neither to drain nor to irrigate. But land could be cultivated along their northern reaches and along the maze of laterals where local drainage boards had installed dikes and pumps that kept their own water constant, whatever it did to the virgin surrounding territory.

Business boomed in the lake towns that reached almost continuously along the great south roadway roaring with traffic. From Port Mayaca on the east by the entrance to the St. Lucie Canal, set with groves and irrigation ditches roofed with Australian pines, the highway went along the ridge where Zachary Taylor's men had fought the Indians; Pahokee, with the green lawns of its residential streets and its migratory workers' camps; Canal Point, jammed with shacks and stores and filling stations and bars; the sprawling city of Belle Glade, packing houses, seed companies, neat small residences, the valiant Woman's Club Library, the Experiment Station; South Bay where Highway 26 comes up from the east coast through the heart of the saw-grass country; Lake Harbor's two railroads and the U.S. Army Engineers' Headquarters and lake locks, and the United States Sugar Company's superior town of Clewiston, laboratories, offices, hotel, school, residences all white, planned, green with trees and parkways, cultivated and precise; and far beyond Moorehaven, in the utter flatness of the drained lake bottoms.

Between the canals glinting in the sun, where the fish jumped and the coot fed, and along the lines of huge dark bamboos and Australian pines marking the straight highways, the vast fields of celery, beans, cabbage, carrots, and the rest grow brilliant emerald in the black velvet, the brown velvet of the muck, and the peaty muck soils. Brown dust blows up in clouds behind the wheels of tractors and cultivators. The cane fields also are endless dark green, light-green jungles round the chimneys of the sugar mill.

Everything was worked out with scientific exactitude, as directed by the Experiment Station or the laboratories of the sugar company, where soils are tested by light rays that cast a spectrum on a screen. The huge fields are set with dikes and irrigation ditches from which pumps bring up the water level to a required height every twenty-four hours. A tractor drags a cylinder six inches under the surface to make a covered drain like a long mole hole. Fertilizers and chemicals are added, plants dusted against insects. Wise growers are bringing in cattle to be fattened through the winter on half of their fields planted to grass, and with which the crops are rotated.

The result is that more and more saw grass is burned and

cleared for greater holdings, more ditches are dug, more water pumped from the lowered main canals. More vegetables are shipped. Cane is raised to the capacity of the mill and the government allotments.

The landscape everywhere about this country, which never sees the far levee-hidden surface of the great Lake Okeechobee, is crammed with the bustle and energy of people making money in a hurry: trucks on the roads, the far glitter of green things growing under the sun. At night, in the first vegetable boom days, the lights of juke joints blazed across the dark, crammed with excited white men and women. Men worked hard. Crops came fast. Money was big.

There is still the curious fever of a mining town that has struck pay dirt. It is like mining vegetables. The quick, fierce crops take from the soil, as miners do, what the work of centuries put there. When the season here is over, many of the carrot men go north to plant more carrots, the celery men plant more celery. Next year they will be back, many living in hotel rooms, without their families, detached from any interest in local problems, thinking only of profits. They have little or no feeling for the strange flat brilliant country.

The hordes of migratory laborers, on whose stooping backs under this sun the ultimate work of this lake country is laid, hate it.

The migrant whites, before World War II, families in frowsy cars or trucks or homemade trailers, filled every possible shack and lot on the edges of the white towns or the white migratory camps. They worked in the packing houses, the men loading the heavy crates, the women packing or sorting, the children carrying the empties. They followed the crops north and back again, year after year, alien and set apart. They brought little to the towns except their labor, and received little in human services until the federal government put in housing and hospitals and schools for them. With the beginning of the war the white migrant labor almost vanished.

The Negroes, more than fifty thousand yearly, brought in by the labor contractors, took the white men's places in the packing houses as well as in the burning endless labor of the fields. They come in, with the beginning of the winter, in battered overloaded cars or even walking. They stand up jammed in trucks jolting down the long roads from the Carolinas and Georgia, riding all night long, or days and nights, half of them sleeping, half standing up. Their eyes, turned on the world streaming by them in dust or in darkness, do not look ahead.

From Christmas to April, from Homestead in Dade County to the lake towns, they pour into the tumble-down shacks, the narrow monstrous row houses, abandoned buildings, government migratory workers' camps and housing units, and crowd every inch of the colored towns that sometimes dwarf the white towns they edge. Thousands sleep packed together in sordid rooms, hallways, tar-paper shacks, filthy barracks with one central faucet and toilet, sheds, lean-tos, old garages, condemned and shaky buildings. The patched and peeling walls seem saturated with their heavy smell of dirt and fatigue and disease and misery.

The long muddy main street of the colored town of Belle Glade by the lake seems the very heart and pulse of these extraordinary Everglades slums, a human jungle that has sprung up from the soil where once the water crept and the clean trees grew. Balconies and broken roofs and signs hang out over the littered irregular sidewalks before the shabby stores, barbershops, frowsy small lunchrooms, pool halls, bars, fortunetellers' hovels, the office of the white man who sells a marriage license and the ceremony for two dollars, the lavish decorated building of the quack who advertises cures for venereal disease.

At night the lighted cavernous blue pool halls and juke joints are crammed with moving dark people. The lights fall across the wide mud streets where the crowds move slowly, laughing or screaming or quarreling, or walking silent and heavy with fatigue and dirt. In nights of penetrating damp cold they try to keep warm around fires built at street corners. Except for Saturday night they sleep early here, windows locked against the sweet lake air.

The lights go on early in the dark chill mornings of winter all over the level country, in hotel bedrooms or in the neat houses of planters scattered about the roads. Colored town shudders and rouses. White men in mucky clothes and knee boots clump noisily down hotel stairways and along sidewalks to lighted lunch counters. Car starters whine and trucks endlessly rattle out to the long field roads. By the time the sidewalks are empty again the sun is almost up.

In colored town the lights fall across a solid mass of dark men and women moving up and down before a long line of high waiting trucks. The men wear muck-stained work clothes and rubber boots, the women red and green and blue flowered dresses or stained and faded blouses and skirts above muck-stained trousers. Some of them wear rubber boots also, and big hats tied under their chins. If it is cold they shiver under an accumulation of rags or burlap bags. They gnaw at bread or eat peanuts and carry greasy paper parcels of lunch.

Over the louder and freer uproar of their voices the hoarse shouts of the barkers on the trucks bargain for them. They listen to the prices for the day's hampers, the quality of the fields, the extra inducements if the crop must be moved fast, like ice cream at the end of so many rows. They wait as long as they can as prices rise. Perhaps a truck is filled, the men, the lithe young trousered women swarming up the sides, the older women hauled up. At a higher price up the street the whole truck will empty at once, as the watchers shout with laughter. Everybody knows which are the good companies, the

358

good fields, the mean foremen. Sometimes several trucks must go away empty and come back later to see what they can do among the men standing on street corners. They move out to the fields as soon as they are crowded and the workers wait at the edge of bean fields for the sun to rise and the dew to dry up.

Families of pickers, kneeling in the yielding, grainy muck soil, work down the rows between the high standing sunflower plants that at first cut off the sun and then cut off the air. Mothers stop picking long enough to nurse their babies. The men and boys, the younger women, work fast. The least children carry empty hampers. At the end of the rows they get their tickets.

Down some celery field, carefully prepared for planting, a group of workers follows a planter-tractor, their faded pink or red or khaki sleeves and trousers tied at ankles and wrists. They string the limp young plants on the grooves on the planter wheel in exact rhythm, treading them under. If something is wrong the white field boss shouts at them, his face darkened with the muck soil almost to the color of theirs. They look at him as if there was a wall between them.

The sun lifts high as the day grows. The heat in the shadeless fields beats down on the steaming black earth that gives it back again. Feet sink in the loose earth and from it, with every stir of wind and wheel, the dust blows in choking brown clouds. It covers the sweating, stinging skin, sifts into eyes and ears, is breathed into the lungs, works through the layers of clothing, up the sleeves, down the neck. It burns with the myriad unrotted points of saw grass, glittering silica as sharp as powdered glass.

The day is long, bearing down in heat on the stooping backs. Day after day, day after day, there is nothing but that. It is better in the packing houses, in the clean smell of washed celery, the acrid smell of beans.

Nights are short on the beds of hay or rags or thin dirty mattresses, short with fatigue and drunkenness and passion. Love, which is here too, man-and-woman love, mother love, family love, is degraded with the constant crowding, dirt, weariness, the struggle for life that is little more than living.

They receive high wages that go at once for lodging and the food they eat, crackers and soft drinks and mushy bread, fish from the canals and a little greasy meat. Gambling, the numbers, lotteries, hardly help the monotony, the tragic weight of labor that the genius of their laughter cannot lighten, or their dulled unconscious despair.

The nonmigrant sugar-cane workers for the great companies fare better. They have better houses and hospitals and ball games and schools. For all these migrant people the federal government provides some housing, excellent but not enough, and a good hospital. The small towns themselves seem overwhelmed by this horde of migrants whose problems they cannot solve and on whose labor they depend. A curious wall of contempt and coldness, in consequence, lies between many of the white people and the black ones. The hard-working and ambitious white men resent the prices they pay for labor which they feel is indifferent. The sullen black men know too well what little they get from this work they hate.

When the vegetable season is over, the migrants move on, white growers and black labor. The Negroes stand crowded in the space for which they must pay in the labor contractor's trucks, traveling by night to fields farther north, the same crowded and inadequate and feverish living, the same dirt and disease. Their eyes turn to the place where they have been, without regret and without hope. It is not the Everglades alone that has done this to them.

Behind them, in the summer-emptied towns around the lake, the fields lie baking under the enormous heat and light of the sun, open entirely to the blowing winds. The empty roads glisten with heat mirage. The vast white clouds pile up to dazzling heights and are still. At night winds from the unseen lake cool the hot roofs. The men who live here because it is their home, and because they like it, sit on the backs of benches in front of the drugstore in the twilight, talking slowly. Voices of playing children pipe far away over the flatlands, like the meadow lark's.

These are the men who remember what the lake was like before the levee was built and all the jungles cleared. They remember the first three tents at Dr. Wills's Okeelanta and the first house at Belle Glade, which was heated in the chill winter by an airtight stove burning chunks of Everglades peat. They remember the names of the settlements that sprang up like the first Everglades crops, and as quickly disappeared: Gladeview and Geerworth and Glade Crest and Gardenia and Tantie and Fruit Crest. They remember Chosen, where the homesteaders on the lake bottom said of their bean rows, "they wasn't very long, water on one end, rabbits on the other, and frosts in the middle." They remember the despair and bitterness after the Big Blow, when some of them had to go back to seining for catfish, "shirt-tailing" the seines in, up to their armpits in cold water all day, and cleaning fish in the cold winds at night.

These are the men who never want to look at the lake at all, proud of the great development and yet a little uneasy, as though they were lost in it.

The thoughtful ones among them, often successful growers working hard and intelligently, know, better than any, what is happening here in what has been called one of the greatest areas of organic soils in the world.

They have seen the cushiony layer of dark muck and peaty muck shrink and oxidize under the burning sun as if it was consumed in thin, airy flames. As the canals and laterals and ditches were extended by local drainage boards, and the peaty muck was dried out and cultivated, it shrank over a foot a year for the first five years. It is still shrinking. Every canal and ditch that drained it made a long deepening valley in the surrounding area. On the east and south the subsidence was so great that half that land does not drain eastward into the sea at all, but back into the lowered lake. It needs constant irrigation.

Many migrant planters, thinking of quick money, do not care what is happening. The intelligent and the responsible, doing everything they can to replace lost elements from the soil, mole draining, rotating their crops with grassed cattle lands, say, "It will not last a hundred years."

West of Clewiston lies now a great cattle country.

Here the United States Sugar Company has fenced in wide tracts of land on which to fatten cattle on lemon grass and black strap. West still, where the whitish sandy soil is thinly covered with grasses and clumps of palmettos, which every year the cattle men burn off for greener grass, more and more cattle move and graze. Some few who heed the warning of the soil scientists, that burning destroys the valuable elements in the soil, experiment with forage grasses. The others burn and graze far south into the Devil's Garden and the Big Cypress.

These cattle are no longer the scrawny creatures such as the first crackers herded to the Cuban boats. These are big animals with wide Brahman horns or the solidity of the best American beef stock.

La Belle, the county seat of Hendry County, was the center of a small cattle boom. Cowboys crowded the main street on Saturday nights, and the lighted stores closed during the week: barbershops, clothing stores, payroll offices. Men in clean overalls and women and children in cotton dresses came in to see the cowboy movies at the motion-picture show and eat ice cream afterward in the drugstore.

But what had most improved the cattle business in Florida, and the quality and prices for Florida beef, was the campaign the State Livestock Sanitary Board, with the Federal Bureau of Animal Industry, carried on to eliminate the "fever tick," which had kept Florida cattle thin and poor. When the surrounding southern states had eradicated their ticks by dipping, they quarantined against ticky Florida cattle. All out-of-the-state shipments stopped. Cattlemen united for the elimination of the tick in a fervor that was almost hysterical.

Dipping, people began to say, did not do the work fast enough. Animals other than cattle must harbor the ticks and spread them. In Osceola County one hundred and twenty-six animals were tested for ticks—squirrels, rabbits, rats, and seventeen of the small brown Florida deer. The seventeen deer had a higher proportion of ticks than the other animals. Then cattle experts said that if even two ticky deer were left in an area the cattle could never be tick free. The deer must be slaughtered.

The cattlemen never did like the deer anyway. They ate where the cattle grazed and jumped fences around the good grass. Deer hunters were likely to be cattle rustlers. The cattlemen, representing the overwhelming political power of the thirty million dollar cattle industry, brought pressure to bear on the Florida legislature. The Board of Livestock Sanitary Control was authorized to spend $50,000 to exterminate all deer in the central and southern counties of Florida.

Gangs of deer-killers moved into the central counties, where there were not more than a few hundred deer. When the deer were killed and the cattle dipped, those counties were declared tick free.

The La Belle cattle market was closed because there was no sale for the more than thirty thousand head of tick-infested cattle that grazed in that area and down to the Big Cypress, where the greatest number of deer were concentrated.

Everybody killed deer, along with the well-paid gangs of deer killers. The deer were "shined," shot at night, dazzled with lights in their eyes. They were killed in the daytime with shot-guns, with slow trail dogs and with fast trail dogs.

No one objected but Wild Life Associations, sportsmen's groups, and some newspapers which had no influence against the cattlemen. They insisted that all sorts of wild animals had ticks besides the deer, panthers and wildcats, rabbits, rats, raccoons and otters, even the moccasin and other snakes. The slaughtered bodies of the killed deer were never examined. The men who killed them, and enjoyed their work and their pay, were required to turn in only the ears.

The protests of taxpayers, at whose expense the deer killing was carried on for the benefit of the cattle industry, were dis-regarded. It was promised that at some future time when the deer were all dead, the game-refuge areas would be restocked with northern tick-free deer at thirty dollars a head.

The deer killers moved slaughtering toward the small Indian reservation in the Big Cypress, a matter of twenty thousand acres, six miles by eight miles along the edge of the saw-grass Glades.

The killers were stopped by a group of Indians. The white men said they had come to kill the deer by order of the state of Florida. The Indians said, "No."

It had occurred to no one that the Indians had any say about it.

The white men learned with astonishment that the state of Florida had no jurisdiction over the reservation. It was de-cided that $5,000 should be appropriated to buy beef for the Indians. The Indians refused it.

The state of Florida appealed to the Bureau of Animal In-dustry in Washington to ask the secretary of agriculture to write a letter to Secretary Harold L. Ickes of the Department of the Interior to request him to tell Mr. John Collier, the commis-sioner of the Office of Indian Affairs, to tell the Big Cypress Indians that their deer must be killed.

364

Mr. Ickes wrote: "If it is proved beyond a reasonable doubt that the slaughter of the deer is necessary, this department will do everything in its power to facilitate such action as is decided upon by the duly constituted authorities of the state of Florida and of the United States government." But it had to be proved. Mr. Ickes sent Mr. Collier back down that long rough road into the Indian reservation to confer with the Indian council. It was a question of the pledged word of the United States government to the free people of the Big Cypress.

These were the undefeated Mikasukis, descendants of the Calusas and of those fiery and independent Florida Indians whose chief Arpeika had refused to stop fighting until they were let alone. They had nothing to do with the agreement between the United States and the Seminole Billy Bowlegs.

It was only in 1935 that they had their first formal conference with any representative of the United States government, when Secretary Ickes himself, and Mr. John Collier, had made the trip to the Big Cypress to tell the Indians about the Indian Re-Organization Act. It was fully recognized by the Office of Indian Affairs that these people had never signed a peace treaty. The Indian Re-Organization Act, which had given self-government to the western Indians, offered protection to the Glades people and assurance of their access to game.

Beyond the Council Ground where the elders conferred with Mr. Ickes, stood in watchful silence the old powerful women, the grandmothers of the tribe. They had known the Glades were drying up. Now at last the help of the government was seen as a good thing. The Mikasukis and the Seminoles, who preferred now to call themselves Cow Creeks, both signed, bringing themselves under the protection of the act.

Now, if the deer were killed over their protest, they would know once and for all that the word of the United States meant nothing.

Mr. Ickes persuaded the Department of Agriculture to leave

the decision about the deer killing to a private institution, the Audubon Society. A trained investigator went to the Big Cypress and reported, after considerable study, that all the animals carried ticks as well as the deer. Killing the deer would do no good at all. Mr. Ickes's stanch common sense had therefore helped save the Indians' four hundred deer to be preserved for the state under their own ancient methods of conservation.

It was like the small beginning of new hope, in the century-long history of man's destructiveness here, by which long ago the parakeets and the ivory-billed woodpecker had been exterminated, the egret and the white ibis only just saved by the Audubon Society that was still trying to protect the last of the roseate spoonbill, the Everglades kite and the almost vanished crocodile.

These Indians still live in their own way. They are, in consequence, the healthiest Indians in the entire United States. From the probably incorrect estimate of their numbers at the end of the Indian wars, they had increased, by a count made by the Indian Office in 1945, to 684.

The two groups, the Hitchiti-speakers and the Muskogee-speakers, had kept themselves apart and faintly hostile, until very recent years. Little by little, as the white men increased about their region and crowded them back from the coasts, they had changed their surface habits with quick Indian adaptiveness, when the need was logical and important. But not their fundamental Indianness.

The Cow Creek Seminoles of the east coast, with their old blend of Negro blood, were always more ready to respond to white friendliness. It was with them that the first special Commissioner, sent by the government in 1913 to negotiate, had begun his work. He was Captain Lucian A. Spencer, an experienced Indian worker, who reported that nothing could be done with any of these people without years devoted to gaining their confidence. He was a bluff, hearty, understanding man, an Episcopal minister, although he did not believe missionary work accomplished anything for them. He learned to speak a little of both languages, hunted and joked with the men about their campfires, and gained their respect. He was able to establish a reservation at Dania, with a hospital and a school and land for gardens in five-acre tracts and houses that were immediately filled. It was a long time, however, before they allowed their children tc come to school.

These Cow Creeks range between Dania and Fort Pierce and a new reservation at Brighton, north of Fisheating Creek, where some of them raise cattle under a government arrangement. Later, the work at Dania was turned over to Baptist missionaries who encouraged several young people to go to school and to college. Ada Mae Tiger was the first girl to study to be a visiting nurse among her own people, the granddaughter of the first Mikasuki woman to be allowed by that council to marry a Cow Creek man.

But Captain Spencer could do little with the more independent Mikasukis of the Big Cypress. In 1907 Episcopal Bishop Grey and a committee of gentlemen had obtained the reservation from the state, when the Supreme Court had upheld the title of the Internal Improvement Fund to Everglades land over the claims of the railroads. But it was a long time before the suspicious Mikasukis did more than hunt in it. Captain Spencer had been allotted $6,000 to spend for them by the Indian Office. They would not accept a penny of it.

They had seen the heart of their Everglades invaded by the Tamiami Trail. When Mr. Ickes, at their insistence, protected the deer of their reservation, they began to value it more highly.

They had adapted ingeniously to the trail itself. Poling their shallow canoes along the canal and its laterals into the Glades, they built temporary camps along it, generally opposite those trail stations that sell gasoline and canned goods and sandwiches and soft drinks to passing cars. Mikasuki children in dirty striped gowns, their black bangs straight over their gleaming Asiatic eyes, buy candy bars before they can speak any English word but "candy." The tourists pay quarters to stare in faint disgust at the camp behind the high palmetto fence, at the circle of open chi-kees, around the bare ground centered by the roofed fire, at the air of primitive untidiness, the flies about the pots and pans that would be washed only as they were needed, the barefoot people in their gaudy dresses. They do not understand the backs turned or the blank faces, nor why some old woman hunched on a shadowy platform spits violently over her shoulder at their loud voices and the staring rudeness of their bad manners.

The surface of Indian living is changing. The young men wear white men's trousers over bare feet, and big black cowboy hats. Only the old men keep to the intricately patterned striped skirted blouses. The fine cotton shirts are kept chiefly now for ceremonial garments. The women's skirts are made fuller, the elaborate stripes sewed in basket patterns. The stylish young girls wear, over tight bodices or pink brassières they buy in the dime store, long thin capes of brilliant red or blue silky stuff to their finger tips.

The older women's, the matriarchs', beads, all thirty pounds of them, are still heavy blue and green to their high chins. But the young girls' beads hang loose around their young throats. Their lank black hair flows long on their shoulders, in imitation of white girls. The mature women, who used to wear small stiff pompadours and bangs, have for some years put their long black hair up over great black cloth-covered brims, like wide hats, over which they pin their hair under hair nets and dimestore bright hairpins.

When a group of Indian women, small and comely for the most part, as the Calusa women were, walk along the edge of the trail at evening, their thin capes blowing in pure color, fat children clutching their skirts flowing over their bare feet, they walk in poise and grace, as their own Indian phrase puts it, "like the wind in the grass."

They like some of the white man's food, store crackers and canned peaches and candy bars and soft drinks, as well as their own fish and constant turtle, some deer and a little turkey. They use store-bought grits for the immemorial sofkee. Some men and a few women drink heavily on trips to town, but in the home camps by far the greater number of them are sober and responsible people, happy among themselves, though oppressed more and more with foreboding about the Everglades.

They have a number of ways of making money. In Miami commercial camps they accept the stare of tourists for money. Boys with an effortless grace stir up the hissing alligators in the pens. One will pry open a long toothy jaw to stick his head in and out and let the jaw shut with the slam of a closing trunk lid and pick up the tossed nickels and dimes, without once looking at his audience. Some medicine man will be paid twenty-five dollars to put on a fake wedding ceremony, dancing the crazy dance and making up crazy words to chant over some long-married Indian couple, grinning at their prospective ten dollars apiece. It is part of the Indian's contempt for the white man that they take money coolly for such nonsense.

Both groups of Indians make money picking vegetables in the Glades season. They live gaily in their temporary camps near the fields. They have proved hard working and reliable. Malaria, which the Negro brings down from the Old South to this hitherto malaria-free world, is spreading among them. It is the most dangerous health problem of the Glades today.

During the war, Indians drove trucks and boys worked in

Miami parking lots. A Cow Creek boy volunteered for the
Marine Corps, but the Mikasukis ignored everything but the
difficulty of getting gasoline, subjected, like the white man,
to the requirements of ration tickets. They are learning to
respect the superintendent of the Indian Agency, which has
been moved to Fort Myers from Dania, although they have
not incorporated for tribal business, as they are free to do
under the Indian Re-Organization Act.

In the guarded privacy of their camps all these Indians are
free. The men hunt and fish and help the women scratch a few

gardens. They make good money selling frogs' legs, now that
they have gasoline again for the "pile-putki," the "air boats,"
a Ford engine with an airplane propeller mounted on a flat-
boat, with which they roar up the laterals, if there is any water
in them, to the frogging grounds. They use "Glades buggies,"
old automobile bodies mounted on huge double wheels, with
which they cross the drying Glades to the Big Cypress, where
the canoes used to go.

The women cook and do the camp work and take care of
their children in that easy Indian way which gives a child what

it wants when it wants it, so long as its need for food or sleep or play is natural. The children are good and healthy, educated from babyhood in all the ways of Indian life, learning with their first speech the proper and respectful forms of address for all the elders of this extended family. No Mikasuki child has ever been allowed to attend a white school, and an Indian school at the reservation has been found almost impossible to maintain for any length of time. The elders say they do not want the children to learn how to lie and cheat, in the way of the white man. What they need to know they are taught by family and clan and tribe, in the formally regulated, traditional Indian world.

The women are busy in their leisurely fashion, sewing the intricately made beautiful garments for themselves or the men, making Seminole dolls and baskets and handbags for the profitable tourist trade. Their work centers about the chi-kee of the ruling matriarch of their family. The young girls and the young married women are diligent and quiet about her. Some young Indian mother sits on the shadowy platform, one graceful knee up under her flowing bright skirt, with her baby's square black head at her breast under the thin red silk of her cape, against the brilliant light beyond the thatch. Children and chickens run in the dust. An old man, in the long striped skirted blouse wanders about, petting a favorite great-grand-child. Under the shade of a great cypress tree, surrounded by bananas and guavas and grapefruit, life is quiet and serene.

At night the young men listen respectfully to the talk of the old men about the fire. Young cousins laugh beyond. Some father in his own house tells old stories to the children as they go to sleep, or a mother hums to the baby high in his little hammock under the thatch. It is a life in which respect and affection, laughter and good manners are balanced in the old Indian fashion.

371

Their green corn dances are held in secret places, and few white men have been invited to them. Perhaps there is a good deal of drunkenness in the days of feasting. But they still use the purge of the black drink. The medicine man still lights the new fire in the cleared ground, with the old chants and the old solemnity. Men and women in the long ancient dances stamp and pass and repass in the firelight. The young men pray and fast before initiation, and the girls too, to bear stoically the sting of splinters burned in their round young arms. The council sits with its old dignity and power. Women who bear illegitimate babies receive the old punishment. Men who commit murder are shot by a designated elder or by their own hands, as the council decrees. Drunkenness and traffic accidents and shooting game out of season are handled by white courts.

The medicine man still studies the ancient ways of his calling, searching for herbs along the trail itself, as well as in the deep Glades, making his medicine with the old magic. But he respects the white man's medicine also, and calls the visiting nurse, and sends people to white hospitals.

Along the trail, firmly driving her small car which is often full of Indians, goes Deaconess Harriet M. Bedell, in her blue uniform, the collar neat and white under her firm chin, the blue veil switching determinedly from her deaconess cap. Once she worked with the Indians in Alaska near the Arctic Circle. When she retired she came to Florida to build up the old Episcopal Glades Cross Mission, which she moved to a small house in the town of Everglades.

The deaconess, like a small steam engine in dark-blue petticoats, walks fast in and out the trail camps, speaking to everybody by name, asking about the sick babies, bringing some old man a mattress pad for his aching bones, trying to get them to use and scald individual drinking cups, scolding a man after a long drunk, taking somebody to the hospital, or getting work for the boys. But her most valuable work has been the improvement of their handicrafts. She has built up for them a profitable trade in Indian dolls and baskets and Indian shirts and skirts.

The deaconess has been asked sometimes by the trail Indians to take part in some funeral of theirs in the deep Glades. With them in the dusk before dawn she has seen the medicine man stand, arms uplifted, waiting for the sun. Silence holds as the great light lifts. The people hear the old chants they have always heard, the prayers that recognize the two souls of man, the weak one remaining with the body, the other wandering east and north, and then, beyond any power of recall, westward, where the two are joined in strength as the upright man walks firmly the log over the chasm dangerous to the unrighteous. Or as he sees beyond the long course of the Milky Way the gleam of the Fortunate Fires and hears the happy voices of the Old Beloved Ones calling him and strides boldly forward, up to his knees in the blowing mist of stars.

When that is over someone nudges the deaconess and says, "Now you begin," knowing well that the sincere prayer of a friend does no harm.

All the bustling hurrying people of the trail know the deaconess: the bus drivers, the oilmen who congregated at Szady's Forty Mile Station when the test wells were being drilled, Mr. Szady himself and his daughters, tractor plowing that three-mile long narrow garden of his, the white people living down the Old Loop Road just as they used to live in North Florida, butchering their own hogs and raising a fine garden; they are all her friends.

The Indians, before anyone else, knew that the Everglades were being destroyed. During the war there was less and less rain, in one of those long, unpredictable, unpreventable dry spells, in which year after year the fresh water, like the soil, shrank away.

The surface of the great lake that had been so arbitrarily

lowered still discharged quantities of the good water out the main canals, the Caloosahatchee and the St. Lucie. The lower Glades suffered. The land along the laterals dried and sank in deeper and wider valleys. Where there had been the flow of the river of grass, there were only drying pools, and mosquitoes.

The saw grass dried, rustling like paper. Garfish, thick in the pools where there had been watercourses, ate all the other fish, and died and stank in their thousands. The birds flew over and far south, searching for fresh water. The lower pools shrank and were brackish. Deer and raccoons traveled far, losing their fear of houses and people in their increasing thirst.

The fires began.

Cattlemen's grass fires roared uncontrolled. Cane-field fires spread crackling and hissing in the saw grass in vast waves and pillars and blowing mountains of heavy, cream-colored, purple-shadowed smoke. Training planes flying over the Glades dropped bombs or cigarette butts, and the fires exploded in the hearts of the drying hammocks and raced on before every wind leaving only blackness. Palmetto burst in the fiery heat that spread from pine tree to pine tree in flaming brands. The flames ate down into the drying ancient saw-grass muck and smoldered and burned and glowed there for weeks, slow orange glares in the night or constant rolling smoke by day, eating down to the ultimate rock.

The acrid smoke drifted over the cities, and people choked and suffocated in it. Many left.

Men watching from fire towers got tired of counting smokes against which they could do nothing. There was no water in the canals with which to fight them. Houses, trees, groves, were burned. The fires swept along the Tamiami Trail and burned the camps as the Indians fled from them. There were weeks when the trail and the other roads were closed to traffic, blinded by the dense covering choking smoke.

All night long the fires stood about the sky, their glare as high as the sky, the flames reflected on the churning orange pillars of their smoke. And when in the daytime they had passed slowly, burning and glowing down to the rock, behind them was only the blackness of desolation.

The whole Everglades were burning. What had been a river of grass and sweet water that had given meaning and life and uniqueness to this whole enormous geography through centuries in which man had no place here was made, in one chaotic gesture of greed and ignorance and folly, a river of fire.

Then, all the people of the cities who had not paid much attention to the Everglades were startled by another thing. The sweet water the rock had held was gone or had shrunk down far into its strange holes and cleavages. The rim of the rock, which in perfect balance had established the life of the Glades, had also held back the salty unending power of the sea. Now the tides moved easily up through the cuts and breaks men had dynamited in the rocky eastern retaining walls. The heavy salt water crept up the rivers and to their headwaters and beyond, up the canals and the least drying watercourses.

The salt water invaded the land, 230 feet a year in the first years, and then faster, spreading through banks and soil 890 feet, nearly 1,000 feet a year. It invaded the wells in all the porous rock rim eastward and invaded the rock itself where the old sweet springs had dried long since. The salt penetrated the soil of the tomato prairies, and the strawberry lands up the Miami River. Wells in southeastern groves turned brackish and the salt stayed in the soil as the groves died. With no rain, the salt was not leached out. The Homestead well field, where the new pipeline went to the keys and Key West, was endangered. The salt water moved into the well field of the city of Miami, far above where the rapids had once guarded the Glades from the sea.

In the Glades the fires raged. Up the rivers and the canals, through the rock and the soil, across the lowlands not much higher than high tide, the salt worked.

Where the herds browsed along the old lake bottoms above the Caloosahatchee, the cattle on the burned-over fields bawled for water and there was none. There was no greenness in the dried canal beds, and little shade under the few trees. The herds began to die.

Far south, where Royal Palm State Park had kept the beauties of Paradise Key as they had been, a dark tropical jungle dominated by majestic native royal palm trees, the fires raged across the saw grass. There was no water in the old sloughs around the park. There was no one to watch the flames. In a week in which the fires spread into the drying jungles, flashed across the firebreaks, the flames worked and smoldered deep in the roots and hearts of the beautiful old live oaks. All the fine tropical trees of the jungle were eaten out. Birds, snakes, deer, small animals were caught in the flames. The delicate tree snails were burned, the orchids, the air plants, the ancient leather ferns, the butterflies. What had been unique and lovely and strange was a black monotony of destruction.

The Indians stared at the smoke, the creeping fires, with the stoic faces of fatalism. This was the end of their world.

But the white man, in all his teeming variety, men of the farms and the Glades, men of the cities and of the sea, whose inertia and pigheadedness, greed and willfulness had caused all this, as if for the first time seeing what he had done, now, when it was almost too late, the white man was aroused. For the first time in South Florida since the earliest floods, there were mass meetings and protests, editorials, petitions, letters, and excited talk. Thousands, choking in acrid smoke, saw for the first time what the drainage of the Glades had brought to pass.

Governor Millard Caldwell's plan for over-all water control

was defeated in the legislature. Only in Dade County, where the fires and the salt intrusion were of the gravest consequence, was anything done.

In that late spring of 1945 Dade County pushed through the legislature a bill to take control of the water situation from the local Drainage Board and vest it in the county commissioners, with every possible power.

In Broward County public opinion was aroused to oppose their County Water Control Bill because the large growers did not want to lose the right of draining as they pleased. The bill was defeated. In Palm Beach County, completely dominated by the big growers, and vegetable corporations, who wanted no interference from anyone, no bill was even introduced.

In the west, in Hendry County, although the cattle died all that summer, the cattlemen could not yet bring themselves to see that the excessive drainage had damaged the land and their cattle at the same time.

It was a long hot fiery summer, the smoke from the Glades blowing, mosquitoes from the mud and the stagnant last of the pools, and by night the far-off flames. The fires stopped only where there was nothing left to burn, or were checked by the fall rains. Thousands of acres of organic soils were utterly destroyed.

In Dade County people who had really become aroused, thoughtful people, residents and public officials worried at last about the water supply, began to see that it was never just a local problem, to be settled in makeshift bits and pieces. The Everglades were one thing, one vast unified harmonious whole, in which the old subtle balance, which had been destroyed, must somehow be replaced, if the nature of this whole region and the life of the coastal cities were to be saved.

There were two things, and two things only, that gave any hope at all in this eleventh hour of fire and of salt. The first

377

was the large number of aroused citizens all over this area, east coast and west, who were now angrily insisting that something constructive must be done, and fast.

An aroused public opinion would have been ineffective if for the first time in the history of the Glades an exact, scientific and complete study had not already been in the making. The University of Florida Experiment Station at Belle Glade, in 1933, had begun its analysis of the varying soils. During the war a federal program of study of national resources brought about a co-operation of the state work with the Soil Conservation Service of the United States Department of Agriculture and the United States Geological Survey, in an over-all "Everglades Project of Soil and Water Conservation." Implemented with a Congressional appropriation, this was completely divorced from state politics and local influences. Even as the fires began, therefore, the engineers worked their way throughout the Glades, in air boats and Glades buggies and tractors and navy "weasels," putting down test wells, studying the rock, the water, the soil, the effects of drainage, and the hope of water control and of conservation.

So that at last, with the lands drying and the smoke still drifting from the fires eating at the valuable muck, the problem of the Everglades was seen whole.

Now all the years of tall talk and resounding claims for these four and a half million acres of Everglades were reduced to available facts.

It was shown that the productivity of the Everglades soil varied with the distance south from the lake. Its usefulness depended on the depth over the rock of the black saw-grass muck and the dark-brown peaty mucks; 150,000 acres of these were already under cultivation, south around the lake, and to a lesser degree along the Atlantic coast. If the muck was deeper than five feet they were capable of a high productivity, but only

378

with expensive and continuous operations of drainage and water control and fertilization and pest control. This soil had subsided in great valleys along the canals, five feet in thirty years of indiscriminate drainage. The muck lost two-thirds of its volume and three-fourths of its weight as it dried in the sun and was destroyed by overuse, and oxidation and fires.

South of all that, where the muck is less than five feet deep, crops can be grown only under extreme, and therefore dangerous, drainage. Their margins can be used for grazing, as in the old lake bottoms between the lake and the Caloosahatchee. But many of these useless lands, it was strongly recommended, should be reconverted into wide natural reservoirs of fresh water, which would help combat salt intrusion and raise the surrounding water tables and no doubt help equalize the temperature. In such marshy, reedy, flowery areas, with a little drift of water, the duck and the waterfowl would increase by the thousands, a most valuable asset to all this territory. The Loxahatchee Slough, the tidal marshes, and the lower swamps should be also great natural wildlife refuges, immensely valuable for the great winter influx of sportsmen.

South still, the scientists recommended that the Glades islands and hammocks and ridges should be left to the tropical hardwoods that clothed them, or set with valuable new introduced varieties.

The whole lower area of the Everglades, from some distance north of the Tamiami Trail to the warm shallows of Florida Bay and the white beaches of Cape Sable and the vast mangrove country, is totally unfit for cultivation. It is the last refuge for the roseate spoonbill and the vast flocks of other Everglades birds, of the manatees, the crocodiles and the alligators, of the deer, the raccoon and the otter. It is known only to hunters and fishermen, to bird-killers and ruthless collectors of tree-snails and of the native orchids of the hammocks.

379

No drainage of any kind is possible for it. Even diked in units of fifty thousand acres, as was attempted with pumps working every day to draw off the fresh water, it was found that through widening craters in the porous and spongy rock the pumps drew up the sea itself.

In 1928 Mr. Ernest F. Coe, a landscape architect who was fascinated by the strange beauty of this wilderness, conceived the idea that it should be made a national park. He fought almost single-handed, through years of depression and of disinterest, to gain public backing. His tall, spare figure, his suave voice, the absent gaze of his blue eyes as he talked and wrote and argued and lectured and, as he said, "made a nuisance of himself," was the very figure of a man obsessed. He was laughed at and he laughed at himself. He sacrificed his career to keep the hope of the park going.

The National Park Service approved the idea. The problem was that the land must be given outright by the state of Florida to the Park Service before it could become a National Park. The state passed an enabling act by which the land, as acquired or owned already, could be conveyed to the nation. Year by year the state-owned area increased. But too slowly.

It was not until April, 1946, that Governor Millard Caldwell set up an Everglades National Park Commission, an official state agency, with the right to acquire land for the park. There was at once a wave of land piracy. There had been 157 private owners of 600,000 nearly worthless acres. By all sorts of fraudulent schemes the number was increased to 217. One elderly couple was induced to buy nine lots for which they paid $3,440. The actual value of what they bought was 90 cents an acre.

By consulting the fine Everglades studies of the United States Soil Conservation Service, the Commission found that in all that area there were only 180,000 acres that offered any promise for agriculture. Not one acre of the other 212,000 could be considered of any value at all.

The Commission determined to freeze the area against speculation with a blanket condemnation action. It learned that if it could proceed under a Federal Law called "A Declaration of Taking," the Department of the Interior could take over at once, leaving the haggling about prices to later court processes.

An unusual contract was drawn up between the state of Florida and the Federal government, by which the government agreed that if the state deposited two million dollars to Federal credit, it would go on with the "Declaration of Taking" condemnations and complete the land acquisition program. The state's one million acres previously had been deeded. On June 20, 1947, in Washington, Governor Caldwell transferred the check to Secretary of the Interior Julius A. Krug. The Secretary thereupon declared the park to have been established.

The Everglades National Park is at last a reality. It will save the lower Glades and the Cape Sable beaches. It will be the largest national park in the United States as soon as the Federal government can control additional acres north of the Tamiami Trail in which it can impound the surface freshwater on which the whole life of the lower Glades depends. It will be the only national park in which the wild-life, the crocodiles, the trees, the orchids, will be more important than the sheer geology of the country. Much of it will be a marine park, with water-trails that will follow the canals of the ancient Indians and reveal mounds and forgotten village sites and provide observation places for the flights and rookeries of the amazing birds.

Along the edges of the Everglades, according to the project reports, there are areas of fine mineral soils easily drained and cultivated, of a high degree of productivity; among these are the marls of Perrine, Hialeah, Hollywood and Hallandale; the loam of Palmdale in the west; the mucky sands of Pompano, Clewiston and Davie; the useful sands of Broward and Palm Beach counties; the sandy marls of Ochopee on the Tamiami Trail and of Flamingo at Cape Sable and the excellent rock lands south of Miami. Their problem is water control and salt intrusion.

Water control is the problem of the entire area. The Water Report of the Geological Survey, like the Land Use Report, was clear and definite. The water in the soil and of the rock, throughout the Everglades, is one body. Rain is its only source of supply. In southeast Florida a great reservoir of porous rock reaches eighty miles from Homestead to Delray Beach, fifteen to eighteen miles wide. The porous rock holds all that rain water and absorbs it, over the layer of hard rock below. But it is open to water above and to each side, and to salt intrusion.

Before the Everglades were drained by the reckless and still ineffective canals, the fresh water in this reservoir and the salt outside were held in balance. After 1942 the salt water began to work inland at the rate of 235 feet a year, increasing to over 800 feet a year in the dry weather of 1944.

The domestic water supply for the east coast cities is dependent upon the store of water in the permeable rock. There is no ground source of water for Broward and Dade counties. Their supply comes from the rainfall.

Drainage and control, as presently handled, is inadequate and confusing. The army engineers maintain the lake at a level adapted for navigation, and at least five feet lower than the old average. The water pours out constantly through the Caloosahatchee and the St. Lucie and the North New River Canals to the sea. Locks do not regulate the flow in dry weather or prevent overflow in wet. The subtle ratio of evaporation and runoff is not recognized. Water tables are kept too low. Local Drainage Boards have tried only to affect local situations, and the result is the visible drying and shrinking and destruction of their soils, and the fires.

The most important single recommendation of the Everglades Project Reports was for a single plan of development and water control for the whole area, under the direction of a single engineer and his board. Only in that way could the conflicting demands of local areas be equalized, so that the soils fit for high cultivation could be used and maintained without detriment to the water supply of the lower areas. It would maintain areas for water conservation. It would control salt intrusion. A well-planned system of canals that would discharge excess lake water into the open Glades would permit the river of grass to flow again with sweet water.

The report was made available to the public. It was studied by the thoughtful men in the growing cities. Its recommendations received wide attention and support, although there was opposition by local interests with political power. The growers about the lake were still afraid of floods, and they felt that water control would endanger the lands already under production. The cattlemen of the west were still resentful of an over-all control. Many owners of great areas of mucklands, draining and diking and pumping their irrigation ditches full from the seaward-flowing canals, refused to consider anything more important than their own immediate profits and would fight more fiercely than any others a co-ordinated control.

It was too soon to expect that all these people would see that the destruction of the Everglades was the destruction of all. They had all cried for help in times of extreme wetness and of extreme dryness, as if they could not realize that they lived under a regular alternation of extremes. They received the help always given in emergencies. But they could not get it through their heads that they had produced some of the worst conditions themselves, by their lack of co-operation, their selfishness, their mutual distrust and their wilful refusal to consider the truth of the whole situation.

Time and the destruction of the soil, the ruin of the Glades, went on surely and inevitably. It was later than they thought.

The fall rains in the year 1945 put out the fires. The people, all those diversified masses of people who lived in this still sunny and beautiful country, by the great sea, under the silken and moving airs, in a land which was still green with trees and gardens and growing groves, forgot. The old wastefulness went on. The bulldozers of new lot owners destroyed the hardwood trees of the cut-up ancient hammocks. In the Big Cypress the lumber companies were cutting out the tallest of the ancient gray trees. A new wave of hungry life, after the war, moved down into the sun and the expanding coastal cities. Again the life and death of the Everglades went unrecognized.

But in Dade County, where the County Commission had been given complete control over the water situation, one small thing happened, a hopeful thing, like the saving of the deer.

The commission's work had been to restore, as far as possible, the old natural rock rim which had been the thousand-year barrier to the eating salt. Engineers built the first temporary dam in Snapper Creek, one of the lower and smaller canals. They had a fight on their hands to put in a temporary dam in the wide Coral Gables Canal, against the opposition of some of the residents. They won that fight.

They began the long battle to put a dam in the Miami River about where the rapids had once foamed, where the annual height of the fresh-water table is two and one half feet above mean sea level. The people who had defaced that once-charming river, with the permission of the Zoning Board, with scrap heaps and junkyards and factories, fought harder than the boatmen, who made the river picturesque still, even as the salt water went by them upstream. There was strong political opposition from people who lived in the overdrained lands farther up the canal.

There was a sign. Above the first dam at Snapper Creek, in the old potholes in the rock where the ferns had once been green, the old, old sparkling springs of fresh water began to flow again.

The rain came again over the Glades in the summer of 1946. There were no fires. In the blackened and burned-down soil, thin spears of the indomitable saw grass thrust up again, faintly green. There were tender leaves here and there in the burned-out hammocks. Over the ancient course of the saw-grass river the rain drummed and blew. Water in widening pools lay over the destruction like the mercy of God.

The work of the Soil Conservation Service and of the Geological Survey has pointed the way to what should be done. The Army Engineers have now taken the initiative in putting all that research to practical use. How far they will go with the great plan for the whole Everglades will depend entirely on the co-operation of the people of the Everglades and their willingness, at last, to do something intelligent for themselves.

Unless the people act the fires will come again. Overdrainage will go on. The soil will shrink and burn and be wasted and destroyed, in a continuing ruin. The salt will lie in wait.

Yet the springs of fine water had flowed again. The balance still existed between the forces of life and of death. There is a balance in man also, one which has set against his greed and his inertia and his foolishness; his courage, his will, his ability slowly and painfully to learn, and to work together.

Perhaps even in this last hour, in a new relation of usefulness and beauty, the vast, magnificent, subtle and unique region of the Everglades may not be utterly lost.

385

Acknowledgments

THE problem of research in a comparatively unknown area like the Everglades is a curious one. No comprehensive book on the subject has ever been written before this attempt. There is little actual source material, in spite of much descriptive writing. One has to depend on the memories of people. But, most fortunately for me, a few sound studies of various phases of the Everglades have just been completed. So my heartfelt thanks go out to people everywhere, scientists or old-timers, who have given me so generously of their knowledge or their own exhaustive studies.

When Hervey Allen asked me to do this book, I was overwhelmed with the realization that although I had lived in South Florida for many years and had known some parts of the Everglades, I had no idea at all what they were or where I could begin to write about them. So I began, as I so often have done, by asking John Pennekamp, editor of the Miami *Herald* and now a member of the Everglades National Park Commission. He sent me directly to Garald G. Parker, head of the U.S. Geological Survey, whose remarkable studies of the geology and ground water of the Everglades are the first thorough studies ever made. Mr. Parker gave me my first clear idea of the single nature of the Glades area, with its characteristic, the saw grass. From him I was sent to C. Kay Davis, Project Engineer for the U.S. Soil Conservation Service, on whose work for Everglades conservation the whole future of the Everglades is based. Mr.

Davis turned over to me all the resources of his department, and John Stevens, associated with Mr. Davis, carried on my education. Generous assistance was also given by Mr. R. V. Allison, head of the Florida Everglades Experiment Station.

To Ernest F. Coe, without whose vision and single-minded devotion there never would have been even the beginning of an Everglades National Park, I have been indebted for many years for information, field trips and constant encouragement.

In the hitherto almost untouched and certainly unco-ordinated study of archaeology, I was incredibly fortunate that Mr. John M. Goggin, after years of special research, had just completed the first chronology and over-all study of the prehistoric Glades Indians, in connection with his work with the Graduate School of Anthropology at Yale University. From the very beginning, Mr. Goggin gave me whole-heartedly from the store of his own scholarship, and patiently checked and rechecked my presentation of his intricate and fascinating subject.

Mr. Mathew Stirling, chief of the Bureau of Ethnology of the Smithsonian Institution, who made the great diggings at Belle Glade, and Mr. Gordon Willey of the same department, were most generous and helpful.

For the early history of African slaves I wish to thank Dr. Melville J. Herskovitz of Northwestern University for aid even beyond his books, and Mrs. Maxfield Parrish and, again, John M. Goggin, on the subject of Negroes and Seminoles in the Bahamas.

In all matters relating to the vast subject of Glades horticulture I received great help from Dr. John C. Gifford, Dr. David Fairchild, Dr. Eleanor Scull, Dr. Walter Buswell, Mr. B. S. Clayton of the Everglades Experiment Station and Mr. A. H. Andrews of Estero. The late Dr. Frank M. Chapman was my great preceptor on the subject of the birds, as well as the late

387

Dr. Gilbert Pearson, Mr. John H. Baker, Jr., of the National Audubon Society, Mr. Daniel B. Beard of the Fish and Wildlife Service, and Mr. Irvin Winte and Mr. Homer Rhode, Jr., state game wardens. Mr. Maxwell Reed kept me from too great confusion concerning pre-historic mammals, and the late Dr. Thomas Barbour, Mr. Marshall Bishop and Mr. George Coffin were sources of information about living creatures here today.

In the field of history, Mr. David O. True, secretary of the Historical Association of Southern Florida, gave me most valuable assistance, from beginning to end, with special reference to the interesting controversy on the landing of Ponce de Leon. I was completely overwhelmed by the eager generosity which historians everywhere displayed toward me in regard to original ideas and manuscripts; the late Mr. A. J. Wall, then president of the New York Historical Society, Dr. Mark F. Boyd, Mr. Julian C. Yonge and Mrs. Alberta Johnston for the Florida Historical Society; Mr. W. T. Cash, State Librarian; Miss Dorothy Darrow of the Ft. Lauderdale Library, Mrs. Frances Parsons and Mrs. Allen Cross of the Miami Public Library, Miss Peggy Beaton of the Coral Gables Library and Miss Josephine Wirth of the Coconut Grove Library, were constantly helpful.

Mrs. Lucian G. Spencer sent me Captain Spencer's fine manuscript on the Indians which few have ever seen, and no one was more generous with original material than the late Mr. Howard Sharp of Canal Point whose excellent history of the Okeechobee region was never completed.

For more light on the difficult subject of the Indians in the Everglades today, I have to thank Deaconess Harriet M. Bedell of the Glades Cross Mission, Everglades, Florida, Mrs. Frank Stranahan of Ft. Lauderdale and Mr. Kenneth O. Marmon of Ft. Myers, Special Commissioner to the Indians. Mr. Robert F. Greenlee of Ormond, Miss Marianne Sweitzer of Yale University and Mrs. Ethel Cutler Freeman of the Natural History Museum of New York were all most generous. Here again John M. Goggin's knowledge was inexhaustible, and I believe we will in future be able to look to the work of Miss Ada Mae Tiger among her own people for information even more valuable than that she was good enough to give me.

The most important contributions to this book came not from books but from the minds and memories of innumerable people who have lived in and about the Everglades for many years. I could never list them all. I don't know the names of half the people with whom I leaned on bridges or drank cokes in Trail stations or hailed from fishing docks or gossiped with in lonely houses, on hidden roads, on beaches or by solitary rivers or on the corners of crowded streets. But my grateful recognition goes to those good friends everywhere whose knowledge has become part of my own thinking: Mrs. Ada Price, Mr. A. H. Andrews, Mr. Lou Staton and Mr. Laurence Dubbitt of Estero; Mr. Graham Copeland and Mr. and Mrs. Senghaas of Everglades; Mr. Smallwood of Chokoloskee; Mr. and Mrs. Tooke of Lostman's River; Mrs. Tommie Barfield and Captain Albert Addison of Marco; Mr. Carl Hanton and Judge Nathan G. Stout of Fort Myers; Mrs. Jane Walker and the girls in the drugstore at La Belle; Mr. R. Y. Patterson of Clewiston; Mr. Thomas E. Wills, Jr., and Mrs. S. P. Parsons of Belle Glade; Mrs. W. J. Krome of Homestead; Mr. Wirth Munroe, Mrs. Florence P. Haden, and Mr. Charles Frow among many others in Coconut Grove; and in Miami so many friends and old-timers that it would be like reprinting the directory. However, I must thank especially Mr. Isidor Cohen, Mr. John C. Gramling, Ruby Leach Carson, Senator F. M. Hudson, Karl Squires and John M. Baxter. And before anyone else, my thanks go to the first friend I had in Florida, from whom I learned most of all about old Florida, Mrs. Frank B. Stoneman.

Finally, since transportation in and around and over the Glades is an adventure in itself, I am more than usually grateful for friends and companions who provided and shared automobiles, canoes, motor boats, houseboats, row boats, airplanes and dirigibles, or were good at clearing paths with machetes: Miss Marion I. Manley, Mrs. Frank C. Cox, Captain C. C. von Paulsen, Mr. C. Kay Davis, Mr. and Mrs. Peter Van Dresser and Mr. John de Groot, Mrs. Barfield, Deaconess Bedell, Mr. William S. Hard, Miss Elinor Smith, Mr. Gardner Royce, Mr. John M. Goggin, and the indefatigable illustrator, Mr. Robert Fink.

Afterword
by Michael Grunwald

Marjory Stoneman Douglas was never one to mince words, and at the end of *The Everglades: River of Grass,* she was typically blunt about the condition of the ecosystem. She titled her final chapter "The Eleventh Hour," and crammed it with images of drought and devastation, soil subsidence and saltwater intrusion. "The Everglades," she wrote, "were dying." The river of grass had become a river of fire: "Unless the people act the fires will come again. Overdrainage will go on. The soil will shrink and burn and be wasted and destroyed, in a continuing ruin. The salt will lie in wait."

But Marjory remained optimistic about the long-run future of the Glades, because she remained optimistic about humanity. She had written a chronicle of greed and folly, but she still had faith in man's ability to learn from his mistakes. So she finished on an up note: "Perhaps, even in this last hour, in a new relation of usefulness and beauty, the vast, magnificent, subtle and unique region of the Everglades may not be utterly lost."

In 1947, Marjory could already see evidence that mankind was beginning to recognize the usefulness as well as the beauty of the Everglades. President Harry S Truman's administration was establishing Everglades National Park, a million-acre refuge where gators, otters, and panthers would be safe from homebuilders, road-builders, and farmers. "It will save the lower Glades," she exulted. And the Army Corps of Engineers was devising a massive plan to solve all the problems of the Everglades at once—floods and fires, soil subsidence and saltwater intrusion, overdrainage and underdrainage. In an effusive unpublished essay, Marjory called it "the first scientific, well-thought-out plan the Everglades has ever known." She said it would "keep the waters of the Everglades in balance, just as nature had once maintained it."

Sixty years later, it's clear that Marjory was absolutely wrong.

And absolutely right.

In 1947, the story of the Everglades was nowhere near its final chapter; it was just entering a new chapter. The rampant development that Marjory found so shocking at the time was almost laughably insignificant compared to the boom on the way. The national park turned out to be a huge success, but it couldn't save the Glades; even its protected wilderness remained vulnerable to human activities outside its borders.

392

And while the Army Corps project did a great job controlling floods, making south Florida safe for one of the most spectacular development frenzies in human history, it had little to do with balance, and even less to do with nature. "What a liar I turned out to be!" Marjory later declared.

In fact, there has been more action and more change in the Everglades ecosystem in the 60 years since Marjory's book than in the 5,000 years before Marjory's book. It now contains seven million residents, 50 million annual tourists, 400,000 acres of sugar fields, and the world's largest concentration of golf courses; it is also home to 69 species on America's endangered list, including Florida panthers, Cape Sable seaside sparrows and Everglades snail kites that are found nowhere else on earth. Disney World was built near the headwaters of the Everglades; the Sawgrass and Palmetto Expressways replaced sawgrass and palmettos; the historic Everglades now contains the Sawgrass Mills mall, the Miccosukee casino, and boomtowns like Weston, West Kendall, West Miami, Wellington, Margate, Miramar, Miami Lakes, and Miami Springs. As I write these words in May 2007, the haze is so bad in downtown Miami that I can barely see out my window, because 40 miles away, the Everglades is burning again. Lake Okeechobee is running dry again. South Florida is facing the worst drought in its history—again.

Funny: just a few months ago, the lake level was dangerously high, so the Army Corps blasted billions of gallons out to tide, ravaging the estuaries at the fringes of the Everglades, massacring manatees and dolphins and oysters. There was water, water, everywhere—but now the lake is at its lowest level ever, the gator holes that serve as the Everglades equivalent of African watering holes have dried up, and south Florida has the strictest lawn-watering restrictions in its history. Meanwhile, developers are still pushing to bulldoze wetlands in the Everglades and suck water out of the Everglades.

393

Clearly, some things have not changed. The south Florida ecosystem still provides outstanding habitat for greed and folly. Still, the debate has been transformed.

Before Marjory, most Americans saw the Everglades as a pestilential swamp that ought to be drained and developed in the name of progress. They would have been thrilled to see mankind "reclaim" and "improve" its impenetrable morasses for strip malls and subdivisions, Comfort Inns and Jiffy Lubes, highways and driveways and fairways. But today, Americans all the way across the political spectrum see the Everglades as a beautiful and useful national treasure, and the U.S. government has launched the largest environmental restoration project in the history of the planet to try to revive it.

Marjory was one of the people most responsible for that new consensus. After helping to popularize the Everglades as an author, she helped to save it as an activist. She was in many ways an unlikely savior of the Glades, a Massachusetts native who had never thought much about the environment and had confidently proclaimed as a young *Miami Herald* reporter that "the wealth of south Florida . . . lies in the black muck of the Everglades, and the inevitable development of this country." (She also wrote two poems celebrating the "greatness" of the Tamiami Trail, the ecologically destructive highway that slices across the Everglades like a dam.) When the editor of the popular Rivers of America series asked her to write a book about the Miami River, she replied that there wasn't much to say about it, but she thought it was somehow connected to the Everglades. She then asked a brilliant Florida hydrologist named Garald Parker if he thought she could get away with calling the Everglades a "river of grass," so it could qualify for Rivers of America. He said he did think so, and as she wrote in her memoirs, "I was hooked with the idea that would consume me the rest of my life."

394

It was a remarkable life that was barely half finished when her masterpiece was first published. Nearly 50 years later, at the tender age of 103, Marjory was still fighting to save her beloved river of grass; even though Clinton had just awarded her the Presidential Medal of Freedom, describing her as Mother Nature in the flesh, she attacked his administration's plan to clean up the Everglades as insufficiently tough on the sugar industry, and forced the Florida Legislature to take her name off the cleanup bill.

It's no insult to Marjory or her memorable book to say that the story of the Everglades has gotten a lot more interesting since *River of Grass* was published, and even more interesting since she died in 1998. As Marjory always understood, greed and folly are persistent themes in Florida and in America. It's a tribute to her tremendous influence and her educated optimism that the Everglades is not yet utterly lost.

On December 6, 1947, a month after her book's publication, Marjory attended the dedication ceremony for Everglades National Park. Along with Ernest Coe, the grating activist who led the fight for the park, and Senator Spessard Holland, the genial power broker who finally made it happen, she watched President Truman eloquently explain why the government was protecting the forbidding wilderness she loved so much:

> Here are no lofty peaks seeking the sky, no mighty glaciers or rushing streams wearing away the uplifted land. Here is land, tranquil in its quiet beauty, serving not as the source of water but as the last receiver of it . . . For conservation of the human spirit, we need places such as Everglades National Park, where we may be more keenly aware of our Creator's infinitely varied, infinitely beautiful and infinitely bountiful handiwork.

It was a stirring speech, but it masked the divisions on the dais. Coe had insisted on a two-million-acre park, alienating just about everyone he met with his uncompromising crusade. Holland had cut the deals that cut the park in half, eliminating Key Largo, Big Cypress Swamp, and other huge swaths of real estate to appease developers, farmers, and sportsmen. Coe was enraged by the shriveled boundaries, and Florida conservationists would spend the next several decades fighting to save areas he had wanted for the park—including Big Cypress National Preserve, Ten Thousand Island National Wildlife Refuge, Biscayne National Park, and John Pennekamp Coral Reef State Park, as well as the Hole in the Donut and northeast Shark Slough, which were eventually added to the park. But if Holland hadn't cut his deals, there wouldn't have been a park in the first place.

In Florida, people-first conservationists like Holland, who wanted to preserve the Everglades for utilitarian reasons, had always trumped nature-first conservationists like Coe, who wanted to preserve the Everglades for its own sake. In fact, people-first conservationists had pushed to drain the Everglades, because they had seen wetlands as wastelands, and conservation as the opposite of waste, the "wise use" of natural resources. After all, God had instructed mankind to "be fruitful, and multiply, and replenish the earth, and subdue it: and have dominion over the fish of the sea, and over the fowl of the air, and over every living thing that moveth upon the earth." Nature had been created for our benefit, and that included the morasses of south Florida. So Holland only supported the park once soil studies had proved that draining the entire Everglades wouldn't work, and he made it clear he would abandon that support if Everglades oil fields turned out to be economical. They weren't, so Holland embraced the park as the next best way to turn swampland into prosperity—by attracting visitors to Florida.

For all his lyricism, Truman felt the same way. He hailed the preservation of the southern Everglades as a sterling example of "the wise use of natural resources," providing enjoyment and enlightenment to future generations of Americans. At the same time, he also called on Americans to "make full use of our resources" in the rest of the Everglades. And Holland was already orchestrating a plan for the Army Corps to do just that. The Corps called the plan "CONSERVATION IN ACTION."

That plan would guide the Everglades into the 21st century.

Before World War II, Florida was still a poor, rural state with fewer people than Mississippi. And in 1947, Mother Nature reminded the world why, when two autumn hurricanes dropped 100 inches of rain on Florida's southern thumb, drowning five million acres and keeping them underwater for months. "Everglades Is Unconquered Despite Man's Great Fight," wrote the *Herald.* The Everglades Drainage District issued a report featuring a cover portrait of a crying cow up to its belly in water, along with bleak photos of underwater tomato farms, orange groves, suburban cul-de-sacs, and military bases. "Only when the Everglades has an adequate water control and protective system will the agricultural interests and coastal communities feel secure," the report concluded.

Holland and the Corps (along with Holland's friends in the farming, ranching, and development industries) designed that system, the Central and Southern Florida Project for Flood Control and Other Purposes. It created a bewildering maze of 2,000 miles of levees and canals, along with spillways and floodgates and pumps so powerful their engines had to be cannibalized from nuclear submarines. It was the largest earthmoving effort since the Panama Canal, designed to control nearly every drop of rain that landed on the region, to end the cycle of not-enough-water and too-much-water that had destabilized the frontier and stunted its growth. An over-the-top Army Corps propaganda film called *Waters of Destiny* summed up its mission: "We had to control the water—make it do our bidding . . . Central and Southern Florida just lay there, waiting hopelessly to be soaked and dried and burned out again . . . Something had to be done, and something was."

The sinuous Kissimmee River, just below the headwaters of the ecosystem, was manhandled into an arrow-straight ditch, a deep and reliable sewer pipe for Orlando and the cattle empire that colonized its floodplain. Lake Okeechobee, the heart and lungs of the ecosystem, was converted into a gigantic reservoir, the northern Everglades into a vast Everglades Agricultural Area, the central Everglades into even more gigantic reservoirs euphemistically known as "water conservation areas." The eastern Everglades was walled off with a 100-mile-long "perimeter levee," then drained into farms and suburbs that offered the postwar version of the American Dream. And none of this was controversial; more than 90 percent of the voters in Dade, Broward, and Palm Beach Counties supported the plan, along with every major Florida industry and politician.

So did Marjory, who crowed that "the ancient southwest course of the grassy river is fully preserved. The water will flow again, as it always did." So did the National Park Service, the U.S. Fish and Wildlife Service, and of course the Corps, which said the plan was "necessary to preserve and restore the unique Everglades region." One Audubon Society official warned that it might not be so smart to leave the park's water supply in the hands of the Corps, but even he called the overall plan "cause for cheering."

It certainly was for Everglades landowners like U.S. Sugar, which held 130,000 acres in the new flood-control district, and Alcoa chairman Arthur Vining Davis, who owned another 100,000 acres. And it must be said that the flood-control project—even more than air conditioning, bug spray, or Social Security—helped transform a watery backwater into a concrete megalopolis. Overall, Florida's population grew at four times the national rate during the postwar boom, catapulting from 27th to 9th in the nation in two decades. Over the same period, Florida's bank deposits increased 1,250 percent, and tourism increased 500 percent even before Walt Disney converted a large swath of central Florida marshland into the mother of all theme parks. The assessed value of land within the flood-control district skyrocketed from $1.2 billion to $15.8 billion, while satellite photos showed that man's footprint on the region had quadrupled.

Thanks to water control, Mother Nature was in retreat. The Everglades had been America's final frontier, a watery wilderness long after the West was won, but engineers were finally taming it, remodeling it, subduing its wild water, harnessing its resources for man's needs and desires. "Now it just waits there—calm, peaceful, ready to do the bidding of man and his machines," declared *Waters of Destiny*'s stentorian narrator. "Central and Southern Florida is no longer nature's fool."

But by the late sixties, it was clear that central and southern Florida was still nature's fool, still yo-yoing between severe floods and even more severe droughts.

Salt had invaded the overtapped wells of every Gold Coast city. Scientists had concluded the Everglades Agricultural Area would be out of soil by 2000. The Kissimmee basin's wetlands were sterile pastures; Lake Okeechobee's catfish were contaminated with DDT; the St. Lucie and Caloosahatchee estuaries were shrouded in chocolate-colored scum. The last few dozen panthers were hanging on in southwest Florida, but sprawl was crushing their habitat and cars were crushing the cats.

399

Everglades National Park was already the National Park Service's most endangered property. Water managers pumped rain out to sea during wet seasons, skewing the balance of fresh and salt water in the estuaries that ringed the Everglades, while leaving the watershed parched in dry seasons. Brushy vegetation began to invade sawgrass marshes, and one old-timer noticed that "Marjory Stoneman Douglas' River of Grass is rapidly becoming, in the vernacular of a native frogger, a 'hell's nest.' The invasion has become so general that unless it's controlled the Everglades could become a solid jungle" In drought years, fires again raged in desiccated wetlands, producing pillars of smoke so huge they grounded the new traffic helicopters that monitored the region's snarls. In flood years, thousands of white-tailed deer were stranded in the Everglades to drown or starve. "This beautiful part of the world has been pushed to the brink of ecological death by men who believe that nature has an infinite capacity to give and forgive," *National Geographic* reported.

Swampland politics was part of the problem. Florida was the only state that still outlawed zoning, which many of its politicians still considered a form of communism. It still used its water bodies as sewers, and still gave away its bay bottoms and lake bottoms to well-connected developers. But the heart of the problem was the flood-control project. Its expanded canals whisked more water out of the Everglades at a time when expanded cities and farms were increasingly dependent on water in the Everglades. Its flood protection prompted more development in the floodplain, which prompted demands for more flood protection. And its water managers refused to let valuable water flow to the park, except during floods, when they dumped billions of gallons of dirty runoff into it. They routinely manipulated water levels to accommodate irrigation schedules and development schemes, disrupting the ecosystem's natural rhythms and flows. They weren't a Corps of Biologists, after all. "To anyone who has ever so much as heard the word 'ecology,' the project is a horror," the author Gene Marine wrote in 1969. "It is an uncaring and terrifying symbol of the triumph of the Engineers and the rape of America."

Throughout America, the postwar economic expansion had proceeded with almost no environmental safeguards, and progress was revealing its price: a river on fire in Cleveland, the near extinction of the bald eagle, communities buried in raw sewage and pesticides, a new phenomenon called "smog." But the country was experiencing an extraordinary awakening in this Earth Day era, a national embrace of the notion that human beings should stop fouling their own nests, a notion symbolized by the iconic antipollution ad starring a weeping Indian. Hippies weren't the only Americans who wanted to save the whales and the redwoods—not to mention the air they breathed, the water they drank, the landscapes they liked, and the fisheries that fed them. In 1969, a secret poll conducted for President Nixon found that Americans were more concerned about the environment than any other issue except Vietnam. Nixon often demonized environmentalists as radical leftists, but he also created the Environmental Protection Agency and signed an array of sweeping environmental laws, including the National Environmental Policy Act, the Clean Air Act, and the Endangered Species Act.

Florida was at the forefront of this backlash against man's abuse of nature. A coalition of scientists, activists, and politicians called Conservation 70s began lobbying the Florida legislature, and helped pass 41 eco-friendly bills its first year. Biscayne Bay activists stopped plans for an oil refinery and a new Miami Beach-style city, prevented a nuclear plant from dumping hot water into the bay, and led a campaign to create Biscayne National Park to preserve the bay forever. When it

401

became clear that a huge canal the Corps had dug for a fly-by-night aerospace company was creating a saline superhighway into Everglades National Park, environmentalists filed a lawsuit that forced the Corps to plug it. They also secured a congressional water guarantee for the park—a toothless guarantee, as it turned out, but an important symbolic gesture nonetheless.

The new movement was led by a new breed of Florida visionaries. Art Marshall, an intense marine biologist who had liberated concentration camps as an Army captain during World War II, became the moody apostle of the Everglades, preaching the gospel of nature-first ecology in his rich baritone, thundering that south Florida was on the road to hell while pointing out the road to redemption. "Do not take Art Marshall lightly," Marjory once chastised a panel of Florida bureaucrats. "He is your Paul Revere!" Nathaniel Reed, a blue-blooded Republican outdoorsman whose family developed posh Jupiter Island, became Florida's first environmentalist government official, a traitor to his class. As a one-dollar-a-year aide to flamboyant Republican Governor Claude Kirk and then sober Democratic Governor Reubin Askew, he launched a statewide crusade against pollution and degradation, taking on chambers of commerce and local politicians who had never been held accountable before. And then there was Joe Browder, a dogged young TV news reporter who became the Audubon Society's southeastern representative after he decided he could no longer pretend to be objective about the ongoing rape of south Florida. He represented the new breed of green activist, an abrasive but effective strategist, using his media savvy to stir up publicity that stirred up the public.

These green warriors helped block a lot of crazy schemes in south Florida. But when the Everglades faced its most dire threat—a proposed airport four times the size of Miami International in Big Cypress Swamp, just six miles upstream from the national park—they could not save it by themselves. They needed Marjory.

The Dade County Port Authority's leaders never got the memo about Earth Day. They bragged that their 39-square-mile "Everglades jetport" would attract 50 million passengers a year, and that a city of half a million residents would sprout in the swampy morasses of Big Cypress. There would be a takeoff every minute, and a "super-train" linking it to the Gold Coast through the Everglades. It would cut off the flow of fresh water into the park, but the Port Authority's analysis only mentioned the park once, to note that its existence ensured the absence of neighbors who might oppose it.

The jetport's backers had already built one runway, and another was under construction; they thought the project was a done deal. So they didn't bother to disguise their hostility to the Everglades, dismissing its endangered species as "yellow-bellied sapsuckers" and its defenders as "butterfly-chasers," quipping that "alligators make nice shoes and pocketbooks," describing Big Cypress as "typical south Florida real estate." Florida's transportation secretary said he'd miss the gators no more than he missed the dinosaurs. One port official adopted the pious rhetoric of Florida's pioneers, proclaiming that "we will do our best to meet our responsibilities, and the responsibilities of all men, to exercise dominion over the land, sea, and air above us." At one contentious meeting, Dade County's mayor denounced Browder, Reed, and Marshall as "white militants."

Browder loved Big Cypress. Its dark and mysterious bogs evoked the coal swamps of the Carboniferous Era, dominated by 500-year-old bald cypress trees with massive trunks flared out like bell bottoms on steroids. It sheltered some of the last Florida panthers and a spectacular collection of orchids, and he was determined to prevent supersonic jets and a new mega-lopolis from drowning out the *kuk-kuk-kuk* of its pileated woodpeckers. Browder frantically mobilized opposition, exhausting his annual phone budget in three months, bringing together interests as diverse as the Miccosukee Tribe, hunting groups, airline unions, and Everglades National Park's most notorious gator poacher as well as Reed and Marshall. He ginned up a flurry of local and national publicity, while coordinating a new group called the Everglades Coalition, a partnership of 21 local and national green groups that came together to oppose the jetport.

One day, one of Browder's employees ran into Marjory at a grocery store, and told her about the battle. Marjory breezily said she'd do whatever she could to help. The next day, Browder showed up at her door in Coconut Grove, and asked her to issue a ringing denunciation of the jetport. "I suggested that nobody would care particularly about my ringing denunciations of anything, and that such things are more effective if they come from organizations," she recalled in her autobiography, *Voice of the River.*

"Well, why don't you start an organization?" Browder replied.

So at 78 years old, Marjory founded Friends of the Everglades, and began a new career as a tart-tongued activist, the living symbol of her beloved river of grass. She issued hundreds of ringing denunciations, delivering speeches around Florida in floral dresses, dark glasses, and floppy hats that one writer said "made her look like Scarlett O'Hara as played by Igor Stravinsky." She spoke with precise Victorian diction—e-lo-cu-tion, she called it—and she knew how to exploit her moral authority as the grandmother of the Glades. "Nobody can be rude to me, this poor little old woman," she once confided. "I can be rude to them, poor darlings, but they can't be rude to me." She informed her audiences that America had a choice to make: it could have a fancy Big Cypress jetport, or it could have a river of grass, but not both.

Ultimately, America chose the Everglades. While Marjory and Browder led the outside war, Reed led the inside war, ultimately persuading Kirk and President Nixon to abandon their support for the jetport. There is still a runway in Big Cypress, but the rest of the swamp is off-limits to development forever.

The jetport battle marked a turning point: open season on the Everglades was over. From then on, environmental politics would be smart politics in Florida, and all politicians would at least pretend they cared about saving the River of Grass.

Governor Askew didn't have to pretend. In 1971, he convened an unprecedented conference on south Florida's water crisis, warning that unless the region could repair its relationship with nature, it would become "the world's first and only desert which gets 60 inches of annual rainfall," a genuine paradise lost. It was the first time a Florida governor had publicly questioned the goodness of growth. "I'm eighty-one. I won't live to see this through," Marjory snapped during one panel discussion. "But get on with it!"

Askew did. He converted the conference's recommendations into sweeping growth management laws, along with a $240 million bond for buying environmentally sensitive lands. "It is not offbeat or alarmist to say that continued failure to control growth and development in this state will lead to economic as well as environmental disaster," he warned. Ever since Askew's "Lands for You" bond, Florida has led the nation in land acquisition, buying more than one million acres of environmentally sensitive real estate under governors of both parties. And Askew's growth management laws sent a vital symbolic message that runaway development was no longer officially condoned, that it was overwhelming roads, schools, hospitals, sewers, dumps, and aquifers.

But money still talked in south Florida, and growth still trumped management, with 100,000 new residents still moving to region every year, and developers still free to build just about anywhere they wanted. Half the Everglades was gone. The other half was an ecological mess—sometimes too wet, sometimes too dry, obstructed and convoluted by highways, levees, and canals. More than 90 percent of its wading birds vanished. Most of its canary-in-the-coal-mine "indicator species" were at risk of extinction, including the panther, Everglades snail kite, Cape Sable seaside sparrow, and American crocodile—the barometers of the ecosystem's uplands, wetter marshes, drier marshes, and Florida Bay, respectively. Exotic vegetation like melaleuca trees and Brazilian pepper bushes—so pervasive they became known as "Florida holly"—were invading distressed wetlands and crowding out native species.

To Marjory's friend Art Marshall, the root cause of all the problems was clear. "The Everglades is not just stressed," he said. "It is distressed—a condition brought about to a major degree by past works of the flood-control project." The natural ecosystem had been a unified organism, connected from head to toe by clean, fresh, slowly flowing water. But the project sliced up the organism into a disjointed marionette. The Kissimmee River was wrestled into a ditch that no longer meandered or flooded its floodplain; it was now known as the C-38 Canal. Lake Okeechobee, imprisoned by its dike, no longer flowed into the upper Glades, except when sugar growers demanded water for irrigation. The upper Glades, a sugarcane monoculture, no longer flowed into the central Glades, except when growers needed to dump water during storms. The central Glades, divided into five impoundments, only flowed into the southern Glades when water managers decided to flood the park. Shark Slough and Taylor Slough no longer carried much fresh water to the Ten Thousand Islands and Florida Bay, which began mutating from brackish estuaries into saltwater lagoons.

The system did a nice job of protecting suburban lawns and sugar harvests, but a horrible job of protecting nature. Wetlands that had filtered and stored water were gone. The aquifers they once recharged were parched. The natural rise and retreat of the river of grass was overwhelmed by artificial pulses and drawdowns that discombobulated the natural spawning and nesting and mating cues of fish and wildlife. "The Everglades ecosystem as we know it is literally going down the drain," Marshall wrote. "Man has played Russian roulette with the Glades for a very long time. One day soon he may pull the trigger on a loaded chamber." And the worse the situation got, the harder the concrete-pourers of the Army Corps pushed to tighten their control of nature. "Their mommies obviously never let them play with mud pies," Marjory complained. "So now they take it out on us by playing with cement!"

Marshall had a better idea. His Marshall Plan was an eighteen-point program to reconnect the ecosystem and recreate its gentle sheet flow by removing levees, refilling canals, buying sensitive land and revamping water management. He saw summer rains as paychecks for the Everglades; instead of whisking the water out to tide, his goal was to keep water on the land as long as possible, until the next summer's rains could replenish the account. His first priority was to restore the Kissimmee, by backfilling the ditch and blowing up its dams. "The river is still there," he wrote to Marjory. "It's the water that's been taken away." He then hoped to restore the southern end of the agricultural area, remove some of the levees that fragmented the conservation areas, and eventually revive Shark and Taylor Sloughs. Marjory printed up the Marshall Plan as a four-page pamphlet, and the usually gloomy Marshall began to believe that man could undo his mistakes in southern Florida. After years of playing defense, he loved the idea of winning back ground for Mother Nature. "We shall see the Kissimmee River flowing sweet and beautifully again," he wrote. "We are on the road, Marjory. Not only for the Kissimmee, but for Lake Okeechobee and restoring the River of Grass."

In the 1970s, Florida's population continued to grow at four times the national rate. But in 1981, after an article in the *Sports Illustrated* swimsuit issue declared that Florida was "going down the tube," Marshall got to present his plan to Governor Bob Graham. Graham's family had made millions from growing sugar, raising cattle, and building houses in the Everglades, but Graham was an environmentalist, and he knew Florida was killing its golden goose by destroying its beautiful places. "Okay," he told Marshall. "I'll do it." Graham turned the Marshall Plan into his "Save Our Everglades" program, an effort to turn back the clock so that "the Everglades of 2000 looks and functions more like it did in 1900 than it does today." Graham publicly renounced a century of drainage, declaring that people were as dependent on the natural flow of the Everglades as swamp lilies or blue herons: "We face an awesome truth. Our presence here is as tenuous as that of the fragile Everglades." He knew "restoring" the Everglades to its pre-drainage condition would be as impossible as restoring a half-eaten omelet to its egg, but just because it couldn't be perfectly natural didn't mean it couldn't become more natural. "Whatever the price," he said, "the price of inaction is higher still." Joe Podgor, the director of Friends of the Everglades, put it differently in a line that Marjory often used in speeches: "The Everglades is a test. If we pass, we may get to keep the planet."

By the time Marshall died in 1985, his vision of a free-flowing ecosystem was already supplanting the dredge-and-destroy

Waters of Destiny mentality. Projects were under way to restore Lake Tohopekaliga, Turner River, and Taylor Slough; to expand Big Cypress Preserve; and to protect reefs in a Florida Keys National Marine Sanctuary. "There is in all of this," Marshall told Marjory, "an opportunity to regain some of that most needed natural resource—HOPE." After moving to the U.S. Senate, Graham pushed through an $89 million plan to restore Shark Slough and a $500 million plan to restore the Kissimmee River, the first environmental projects ever assigned to the Army Corps.

But these early restoration efforts were still just a start, an initial pushback against a continuing tsunami of development. "Not enough, Bob," Marjory chastised Graham at the groundbreaking for one modest project. "Not nearly enough." And newcomers were still pouring into Everglades suburbs; Pembroke Pines grew 83 percent in the 1980s, Davie 130 percent, and Hialeah Gardens 186 percent. The new suburb of Weston—built by Arvida, the company formed from the vast land holdings of ARthur VIning DAvis—actually jutted into Shark Slough, but Graham attended the groundbreaking anyway, and 50,000 people moved there within a decade. "Despite the free advice of the birds," Marjory wrote, "we do not pay attention." When Marjory—now in her nineties, and legally blind—called for development restrictions in the eastern Everglades at a public hearing, landowners booed and yelled at her to go back to Russia. And the long-dormant southwest coast was sprawling into the western Everglades, ripping up panther habitat for subdivisions with names like Wildcat Run and The Habitat. Soon there were only about thirty panthers left, and they were so inbred that males were being born without testicles. Wildlife officials had to import Texas cougars to try to diversity the gene pool, raising questions about whether the next generation of panthers would really be panthers at all.

Now the ecosystem really was in its eleventh hour. Floods

and fires had erased nearly half the tree islands in the Everglades. Along the Gulf coast, red tides the size of small states were killing dolphins and manatees. Florida Bay, the magical estuary at the bottom of the ecosystem, simply collapsed; vast swaths of its sea grasses, sponges, and mangroves died, its gin-clear waters turned a slimy pea green, and its pink shrimp, spiny lobster, and stone crab catches crashed. "Mother Nature is having a nightmare," lamented *Outside* magazine, "and the nightmare is the Everglades."

The basic problem was that fast-growing communities, influential agribusinesses, and the Everglades all competed for the same water, and the competition was intensifying every day. Invariably, the winners were the suburbanites who wanted to wash their Jeeps and the sugar barons who wanted to irrigate their cane; the losers were otters and wood storks. A few environmentalists began to think about a megaproject that would store the region's water for nature as well as people instead of dumping it out to tide and ravaging some of the world's most productive estuaries. They began dreaming about converting Marshall's vision into a multi-billion-dollar mission, replumbing the region's original replumbing to sustain the Everglades in the 21st century, transforming the flood-control project into a multi-purpose project that supplied water for sawgrass as well as suburbs.

But first, the Everglades had a more immediate problem.

That water was dirty.

Save Our Everglades was mostly pain-free environmental restoration; nobody's ox was really gored. But in the 1980s, it became clear that runoff from sugar fields in the Everglades Agricultural Area was polluting the River of Grass, and transforming it into a sea of cattails. And no one had ever gored the sugar industry's ox.

Thanks to lavish campaign donations and A-list lobbyists, Big Sugar was one the most powerful industries in Washington, and was rivaled only by real estate as the most powerful industry in Tallahassee. Its profits were a direct result of its clout—especially in the Everglades, where the industry owed its existence to billions of dollars worth of government largesse: import quotas, tariffs, price supports, and the flood-control project, which provided irrigation in the dry season and drainage in the rainy season. Big Sugar received half the project's water releases, while paying less than one percent of its taxes. Meanwhile, state and federal research scientists helped the industry conserve soil, eradicate pests, and breed more profitable cane at taxpayer expense.

It was clear that Big Sugar was also damaging the Everglades; Marjory once wrote Graham to express her "violent conviction" that the entire Everglades Agricultural Area should be returned to nature. It was, after all, in the middle of the Everglades, blocking the original River of Grass like a giant clot. Big Sugar's voracious demand for water (for which it paid virtually nothing) also exacerbated droughts. And in the eighties, it became clear that phosphorus from its fields was polluting the Everglades. Phosphorus is a natural nutrient found in most fertilizers; sugar growers argued that it was good for the environment, because it made things grow. But the things that extra phosphorus made grow didn't belong in the Everglades; it was a phosphorus-limited ecosystem, with even fewer nutrients than Evian in its natural state. Scientists soon demonstrated that phosphorus from the sugar fields was turning sawgrass marshes into swaths of cattails so thick that fish and birds couldn't swim or land in them, destroying about five acres of Everglades per day. Marjory spent her twilight years passionately fighting Big Sugar.

In October 1988, Dexter Lehtinen, the U.S. Attorney in

Miami, sued Florida for failing to enforce its own water quality laws—and damaging Everglades National Park and the Loxahatchee National Wildlife Refuge—by allowing Big Sugar to pollute the Everglades. (He knew his bosses in the Reagan administration would never approve the lawsuit, so he filed it without telling them.) And in May 1991, Governor Lawton Chiles appeared in a Miami courtroom and shocked his own legal team by announcing he wanted to surrender his sword. The resulting settlement established strict phosphorus limits and mandated the largest nutrient-removal project in world history, calling for tens of thousands of acres of sugar fields to be converted into artificial filter marshes. By 2002, the Everglades would have to be pristine.

But Big Sugar hadn't surrendered its sword. And its lawyers began hacking away at the settlement like cane-cutters at harvest time, tying up the cleanup in court. In 1993, Bruce Babbitt, the former head of the League of Conservation Voters who was now President Clinton's interior secretary, decided the quagmire had to end. He truly believed the Everglades was a test, not just for America but for the world, and his top priority was a hydrological restoration project that could show the planet how to balance a growing population with an imperiled ecosystem. He saw phosphorus as a distraction from the bigger challenge of replumbing. So did Chiles, whose Governor's Commission for a Sustainable South Florida featuring developers, farmers, business leaders, tribal leaders, government officials, and environmentalists was already seeking consensus solutions for the region. Senator Holland had insisted on unity for the original flood-control project; Babbitt and Chiles believed unity would be just as necessary to reconfigure it, and they didn't want to drive the various interests apart by litigating endlessly over a few parts per billion. "We had our eyes on the bigger prize," Babbitt recalls.

So Babbitt and Chiles cut a deal with Big Sugar. The result was the cleverly named Marjory Stoneman Douglas Act, much of which was written by sugar lobbyists. It delayed final phosphorus standards until 2006, and included loopholes that left it unclear if the Everglades would end up pristine. Lehtinen, now representing the Miccosukee Tribe, warned that the bill would substitute fuzzy promises for legal guarantees. Browder publicly accused Babbitt of selling out the Everglades, and the Everglades Coalition unanimously denounced the bill as a sweetheart deal. Marjory demanded her name off it. "I disapprove of it wholeheartedly," she wrote Chiles. But it was renamed the Everglades Forever Act, and the Florida legislature overwhelmingly passed it.

In fact, despite the warnings of Marjory and other environmentalists, Everglades Forever has not turned out to be a death sentence for the Everglades; it has made the Everglades cleaner. Thanks to more than 40,000 acres of filter marshes, phosphorus levels have declined from 200 parts per billion to around 20 ppb, and the spread of cattails is down to two acres per day. Sugar growers—who had screamed that they would never be able to cut their phosphorus releases by one-fourth—have slashed them more than one-half. And after the sovereign Miccosukees set a powerful precedent by enacting a scientifically backed phosphorus limit of ten parts per billion—cleaner than Evian—for their slice of the Everglades, Florida eventually followed suit. The Miccosukees say that the Everglades saved their ancestors, and they're trying to return the favor.

The only problem is that it's 2007, and the sugar runoff isn't down to ten ppb yet, so it's just poisoning the Everglades a lot more slowly. And in 2003 Governor Jeb Bush and a phalanx of 46 sugar lobbyists helped push the deadline for a pristine Everglades back to 2016. Still, when it comes to water quality, the long-term trend is good, although not as good as Florida

413

officials have proclaimed. A recent report by the court offered wise advice to Pollyanna bureaucrats as well as Cassandra activists: "Chill out."

But water quality was just a piece of the problem. In October 1995, the 42 members of the business-friendly Governor's Commission produced a unanimous report, agreeing that "it is easy to see that our present course in South Florida is not sustainable." Destroying the ecosystem, the report concluded, was destroying the region's quality of life, creating lower water tables, higher flood risks, unbearable traffic, overcrowded schools and hospitals, "mind-numbing homogeneity and a distinct lack of place." South Florida was already living well beyond its means, and every new resident was demanding an additional 65,000 gallons of water per year. The region's highway mileage had quintupled in two decades, and could now circle the earth twice. Hurricane researchers warned that a repeat of the 1926 storm would cause $80 billion in damage, and warned that evacuation routes were dangerously clogged. "Time is of the essence," the report warned. "If we are to evade further catastrophe, urgent strategic action is needed."

The commission then proposed a solution: a drastic overhaul of the flood-control project, in order to capture all that fresh water that was bleeding out to the estuaries, then redistribute it to farms, cities, and the Everglades in the right amounts at the right time of year. The mission was to Get the Water Right throughout south Florida: the quality, quantity, timing, and distribution. The Army Corps began converting the commission's win-win-win vision into a technical plan, and Vice President Al Gore came to Everglades National Park to announce that the plan would include at least 100,000 acres of reservoirs on former sugar fields. Gore also endorsed a penny-a-pound sugar tax, a proposal the industry was already spending more than $25 million to defeat.

But a few hours later, while President Clinton was in the Oval Office breaking up with a then-anonymous intern named Monica Lewinsky, he excused himself to take a 22-minute phone call from Florida's most powerful sugar grower, Alfonso Fanjul, who also happened to be one of his top fundraisers. The administration stopped pushing the sugar tax, which was narrowly rejected by Florida voters. And the 4,000-page Army Corps plan only included 60,000 acres of reservoirs on former sugar fields. It was a political plan, another nobody's-ox-gets-gored plan, designed to make sure every Florida interest group could support it. It guaranteed that no resident, business, or farm would get less flood control or drinking water; in fact, it pledged to supply enough drinking water to let the region double its population, which helped ensure the support of water utilities, home builders, and business interests. Overall, the $7.8 billion plan included 180,000 acres worth of above-ground reservoirs, almost enough to blanket New York City, an unprecedented array of deep-injection "aquifer storage and recovery wells," and a complex "seepage management" plan to prevent water from escaping the Everglades underground. By increasing water storage and reducing seepage losses, this Comprehensive Everglades Restoration Plan was projected to add nearly a trillion gallons a year to the "water pie," and to create dramatic benefits throughout the ecosystem.

The goal wasn't really to "restore" the Everglades; Graham liked to say that would be like restoring the omelet you ate for breakfast to its egg. And the resulting Everglades wouldn't really be "natural;" Corps officials described their vision as a kind of "Disney Everglades," intensely managed and tightly controlled, an "Everglades on life support." But at least it would be alive. Water managers would no longer have to rely so heavily on Lake Okeechobee and the conservation areas as reservoirs;

415

they could stop blasting coffee-colored lake water into the Caloosahatchee and St. Lucie estuaries; and they wouldn't have to slurp water out of Everglades aquifers to accommodate the demands of future growth. Gore unveiled the draft plan shortly after Marjory died in 1998, calling it a tribute to her vision. "The entire south Florida ecosystem, including the Everglades, will become healthy," the Corps promised in the document. "The numbers of animals—crayfish, minnows, sunfish, frogs, alligators, herons, ibis and otters—at virtually all levels in the aquatic food chain will markedly increase."

Or maybe not. "There are unique and significant uncertainties," the Corps conceded a few thousand pages later. The plan depends on four technological gambles that account for nearly half its cost; for example, geologists believe that two new-fangled reservoirs converted from mined-out rock quarries might not hold water, and might contaminate Miami's drinking water with deadly bacteria. The co-chair of the science team for CERP joked that a better acronym would be SWAG: Scientific Wild-Ass Guess.

Everglades National Park's scientists were much less charitable. The plan, they wrote, "does not represent a restoration scenario for the southern, central and northern Everglades." They showed that the plan offered swift, sure, and lucrative benefits to south Florida's homeowners, developers, and agribusinesses, while its benefits for the Everglades were riddled with uncertainties and delayed for decades. It was supposed to expand the spatial extent of the Everglades, but it actually called for the sacrifice of more than 30,000 acres of Everglades wetlands. It did next to nothing to address endangered species or the runaway development that was whittling away the Everglades, but it was required to meet south Florida's urban water supply goals for 2050 within a decade. It sounded less like Everglades restoration than a federally subsidized water-supply project for the unborn, promoting more of the development that was destroying the Everglades.

On a deeper level, the plan abandoned Art Marshall's vision of a reconnected ecosystem. The Corps boasted that it would remove up to 240 miles of levees and canals to "reestablish the natural sheet flow through the Everglades," but the scientists noted that the plan would add more levees and canals than it would remove, and would do little to let the River of Grass flow freely again. It looked more like the Rube Goldberg–style structural engineering the Corps was famous for than a real effort to get out of Mother Nature's way. Six of the nation's best-known ecologists sent the Clinton administration a letter warning about the plan's "deep, systemic problems." Friends of the Everglades opposed the plan, and Browder churned out emails accusing the Audubon Society and other less strident conservation groups of shilling for Clinton and Gore at the expense of nature: "We are going to lose what really counts about the Everglades unless someone gets beyond cheerleading for the Administration and mounts a genuine campaign to force the federal government to meet its responsibilities to the National Parks."

Browder was already angry about Babbitt's deal with the sugar industry; he was even angrier about the Clinton administration's support for another Everglades airport, this one at Homestead Air Force base between Biscayne and Everglades National Parks. It was as if history was repeating itself, as tragedy rather than farce. Some Everglades Coalition leaders were reluctant to waste energy and political capital fighting a friendly administration (and the airport's well-connected Cuban-American developers) over a lost cause; they didn't want to hurt Gore's chances of winning Florida in 2000, endanger the larger restoration project, or fuel stereotypes of enviros as litigious people-haters who reflexively opposed economic growth. But to Browder, this was an egregious sellout of Marjory's feisty legacy. The administration was pushing an airport—and the inevitable pollution, sprawl, and noise that would follow it—on the edge of the Everglades, after an environmental review so laughable that its maps didn't even identify Biscayne Bay. Enviros weren't supposed to compromise on disasters like that. They weren't supposed to worry about relationships with friends in high places, or console themselves with the knowledge that other politicians might be worse. They were supposed to raise hell.

In the end, the compromisers won the battle over restoration. The hell-raisers persuaded the Clinton administration to add language to the plan guaranteeing an extra 79 billion gallons for the Everglades and ensuring that restoration would be the project's "primary and overarching purpose. But those new commitments infuriated Florida's economic interests and Governor Jeb Bush, who insisted that the plan could not prioritize the Everglades over his constituents. (Bush's administration had flirted with the idea of selling water rights in the Everglades to an Enron subsidiary, shortly before the company's collapse.) So, shortly after the plan arrived on Capitol Hill, the new environmental commitments disappeared. And while Friends of the Everglades still opposed it, the national environmental groups ultimately supported it with varying degrees of reluctance; the Audubon Society's lobbyist literally walked the halls of Congress arm-in-arm with Big Sugar's lobbyist to push for it. The Senate passed it with only one dissenting vote. The margin in the House was 394-14.

Clinton signed the plan into law with Governor Bush at his side on December 11, 2000—the same day the Supreme Court heard arguments in the Florida recount dispute between Clinton's vice president and Bush's brother. Even while

Florida's political swamp was dividing the nation along partisan lines, Florida's actual swamp was bringing Republicans and Democrats together. "This is a model—not just for our country, but for projects around the world," Bush said. Clinton was also delighted, although he sounded a note of caution in a chat with two Florida legislative staffers. "If we don't do something about climate change," he pointed out, "your Everglades is going to be underwater."

But the hell-raisers got their way on the airport. When Gore refused to take a stand against the project, Browder began feeding talking points to Green Party presidential candidate Ralph Nader, who started making speeches in Florida accusing Gore of selling out the Everglades for an airport. And when Gore tried to schedule an environmental speech in the Everglades, activists vowed to protest, so Gore cancelled. Even Nathaniel Reed, a compromiser who had pushed hard for the restoration plan, became a hell-raiser against the airport, warning Gore's aides that he'd pay the price if he didn't kill it before Election Day. He didn't, and he lost Florida and the election by 537 votes to George W. Bush, the candidate of mining, drilling, and logging interests. Reed estimates that the airport straddle cost Gore about 10,000 votes in Florida. "Oh, I don't think the airport was a major factor in the outcome," Gore told me years later.

Then he paused. "Well, maybe it was."

Four days before leaving office, Clinton rejected the airport. The hell-raisers had made their point. And the greenest vice president in American history, suddenly jobless, became a hell-raiser himself, launching a one-man crusade against climate change.

Today, if you want to feel optimistic about Everglades restoration, visit the Kissimmee River restoration at the ecosystem's headwaters. The Army Corps has filled in seven miles of its old C-38 Canal, recreating fourteen miles of zig-zagging river and 11,000 acres of tangled marshes. Fish, birds, and gators have returned to the floodplain, and officials from Japan, England, Brazil, Italy, and Hungary have visited to learn how to bring a river back from the dead. The secret, they have discovered, is to get out of Mother Nature's way. Everyone always talks about "fragile" ecosystems, and the south Florida ecosystem is one of the most fragile; even minuscule changes in its chemistry or topography can transform its biology. But nature isn't all that fragile. Marjory once wrote that it's as tough as an old tire. When we stop abusing it, it can come back.

On the other hand, if you want to feel pessimistic about Everglades restoration, visit the Shark Slough restoration that's supposed to rehydrate the park. It's now old enough to vote, and its $89 million price tag has ballooned to about $800 million. But it's still paralyzed by infighting and litigation over flood risks, property rights, and the possible extinction of the Cape Sable seaside sparrow. The Miccosukee lands in the conservation areas above Tamiami Trail are still much too wet, and the park lands below the Trail are much too dry, but the hulking floodgates that were supposed to move water across the Trail have never been opened. They're concrete monuments to bureaucratic sclerosis.

Everglades restoration really will be a test. It's already the national blueprint for multi-billion-dollar projects to revive the Great Lakes and Louisiana's coastal wetlands; as Governor Bush predicted, it's also a model for plans to resuscitate the Pantanal of South America and the Garden of Eden marshes that Saddam Hussein destroyed in Iraq. Success in the Everglades could usher in a global era of ecosystem restoration, and could show the world how to avoid the water wars in the 21st century, when water is going to be as precious as oil. But if Broward County and Palm Beach County can't figure out how to share water and leave enough for the bugs and bunnies, it's hard to imagine that Israel and Syria are going to be able to do it. And if we can't save the Everglades—the world's most beloved and most studied wetland, in a region with plenty of rain, plenty of money, and three million acres already in the public domain—it's hard to imagine what we can save.

So far, unfortunately, the results look a lot more like Shark Slough than the Kissimmee River. In March 2005, the Corps planner overseeing Everglades restoration warned in a memo that it was already dramatically over budget, behind schedule, and off track: "It's different from what we told Congress we would do—and it's not restoration!" Federal funding has lagged, even though the National Academies of Sciences now pegs the restoration's cost at $20 billion. And while Governor Bush kept his funding promises, he also practically took over the project, which intensified its emphasis on Florida residents and businesses over national parks and refuges. Water managers have lost faith in their plan to store water in 330 aquifer wells, and they don't seem to have a Plan B. Scientists have produced new evidence that uninterrupted flow—the missing link in the restoration plan—was as vital to the natural Everglades as water quality or quantity. And as Gore's climate crusade has gained traction, the current plan—which did not even mention the threat of rising seas once in 4,000 pages—has looked increasingly outdated. Even Reed, who once testified that the plan would "unequivocally" fix the Everglades, warned in a 2005 email that "we are witnessing the potential end of a great experiment in restoration." In May 2007, three national green groups sued the Corps, accusing the agency of neglecting and abusing "a system under assault and in jeopardy of collapse."

Many people who hear about the largest restoration project in history assume that the Everglades is already safe. The clueless United Nations even removed the Everglades from its list of endangered natural treasures. But south Florida is still nature's fool, and runaway development is still wiping out its wetlands and stressing its aquifers. The Miami-Fort Lauderdale-West Palm Beach conurbation has become America's sixth-largest metropolitan area, obliterating almost every patch of green space between the Atlantic Ocean and the Everglades perimeter levee. Everglades suburbs like Coral Springs, Miami Gardens, Miramar, Pembroke Pines, and Sunrise—all built after Marjory's book was published—have attracted 100,000 residents, and are all approaching buildout. Big Sugar is a convenient scapegoat for the problems of the Everglades, and it would be nice to wave a magic wand and achieve Marjory's dream of shutting down the industry. But the real problem in the Everglades is Big People, and industry executives are not shy about saying that if they can't grow sugar, they'd be glad to grow condos. In fact, Fanjul is already floating development plans for the edge of the Everglades Agricultural Area.

Meanwhile, southwest Florida has begun sprawling east into the Everglades, with no perimeter levee to block it. "We are permitting in SW Florida as fast as we can the same types of development and associated environmental degradation we are spending billions of dollars trying to fix on the SE coast," an EPA official wrote in a 2002 email. "Haven't we learned our lessons? Apparently not!" The EPA's top regulator in southwest Florida quit in disgust after President Bush's appointees began pushing a developer-funded study claiming that wetlands cause pollution. And the Fish and Wildlife Service has admitted the science it used to rubber-stamp thousands of homes in panther habitat was flawed; unsurprisingly, cars are now killing panthers at record rates.

The bill for a century of progress is coming due. For decades, Lake Okeechobee has been used as a reservoir and a sewer for farms, dairies, and cities; now it's suffocating in slimy gunk, and scientists are worried it could become a 730-square-mile dead zone. Meanwhile, a chilling April 2006 engineering report declared that leaks in the Hoover Dike pose "a grave and imminent danger to the people and environment of South Florida," calculating a one-in-six chance of failure in any given year, an existential roll of the dice for the 30,000 residents in the lake's shadow. That means water managers will have to flush even more of the turbid lake into the St. Lucie and Caloosahatchee estuaries, which have been clobbered by red tides so toxic that beachgoers have started wearing surgical masks. Man's impact has pervaded the ecosystem from Disney World to Key West, from the herbicide-resistant hydrilla clogging the Kissimmee chain of lakes to a 60-mile-wide cloud of "black water" that wiped out half the coral in western Florida Bay. The Everglades is under siege from species we've introduced to the ecosystem, from the Old World climbing fern that is spreading through the marsh like The Blob to the Burmese pythons that entertain tourists with their death matches against alligators. It's fair to assume that if Marjory were alive today, she'd still be raising a bit of hell.

It's become a Florida cliché to say how much we've all learned from Marjory; she's basically our state saint. But it's worth remembering how much Marjory learned along her own journey. Her instincts weren't always right—about the Tamiami Trail, or the Everglades flood-control project—but once she had all the facts, she often changed her mind. For example, she initially thought a plan to collar and track the state's remaining panthers sounded foolish and cruel, but she was ultimately persuaded that it was worth a shot, and it's helped save the cats from extinction. She was not just an educator; she was also educable. And in recent years, there have been signs that south Floridians might be educable, too. They still don't seem to understand that they live in converted wetlands; they still call animal control 18,000 times a year to get the gators out of their backyards, rarely stopping to think that they're in the gators' backyard. But they're starting to understand that ecological meltdown is bad for their own quality of life, that unrestrained sprawl in the Everglades floodplain has created gridlocked traffic, exorbitant insurance rates, and a homogenized landscape that's increasingly difficult to distinguish from the northern suburbs they fled. They're also starting to understand that ecological meltdown is bad for business. Tourists don't want to wear surgical masks at the beach, or scuba dive in barren coral reefs, or catch mercury-laden fish with disgusting lesions; they'd like to see some birds at Everglades National Park. As snowbirds move to Arizona instead, and "halfbacks" flee Florida for less spoiled paradises in the Carolinas, even the real estate industry now admits that the environment is Florida's economy.

So the hell-raisers are starting to win battles. They helped block plans to expand Miami-Dade's urban development boundary, develop a new city at the doorstep to the Keys, and build a sprawling biotech campus at the edge of the Everglades; these have all been defeated. Florida's new governor, Republican Charlie Crist, has given environmentalists key roles in his administration, and recently blocked a plan for a coal plant near the Everglades. He also pledged to find hundreds of millions of additional dollars for the Everglades ecosystem, including a new initiative to revive Lake O—which dropped to a record low the week he announced his plans. "People all over the world recognize the importance of the Everglades," Crist said. "It's amazing how quickly Mother Nature comes back just by giving her a little bit of an assist."

But environmental victories can be fleeting: The protectors

have to win again and again, while the destroyers only have to win once. And global warming is changing the rules of the game as well as the shape of the playing field; an EPA study found that sea levels around Florida are already rising two millimeters a year, and should rise at least two feet in this century. Two feet is practically an Everest in the Everglades. And if a warmer climate means stronger hurricanes, south Florida might bear the brunt.

The Everglades will indeed be a test—of our ability to live in harmony with nature, and our ability to save ourselves. It will require a delicate combination of Marjory-style hell-raising and responsible compromise. Millions of people live in south Florida, and as long as the sun shines, millions more will follow. It's a lot nicer than Buffalo or Cleveland in the winter, and for different reasons, it's a lot nicer than Havana or Port-au-Prince all year long. The challenge will be managing our growth sustainably, and adapting our lifestyles sustainably. Self-interest will help; two-hour commutes and $6-a-gallon-gas might sour us on our car-dependent culture. But Marjory was a moral leader, and she knew that the Everglades is ultimately a moral test. It will be a test of our willingness to restrain ourselves, to share the earth's resources with the other living things that moveth upon it. If we pass, we may deserve to keep the planet.

Michael Grunwald is a senior correspondent for *Time* magazine. Parts of this essay were adapted from his 2006 book, *The Swamp: The Everglades, Florida, and the Politics of Paradise.*

To keep up to date with Everglades current events refer to the official site of the Comprehensive Everglades Restoration Plan (www.evergladesplan.org) and the site of the Friends of the Everglades (www.everglades.org).

Bibliography

ALLISON, R. V., *Soil and Water Conservation Problems in the Everglades*. Soil Science Society of Florida. Proc. Vol 1.

ANDREWS, CHARLES M., *The Florida Indians in the 17th Century*. Tequesta, the Journal of the Historical Association of Southern Florida, 1943.

ANON., *A Description of the Windward Passage and Gulf of Florida*. London, 1739.

BABCOCK, WILLIAM H., *Legendary Islands of the Atlantic*. American Geographical Society, Research Series, No. 8. 1922.

BAKER, JOHN H., *Time Is Running Out In The Everglades*. National Audubon Society Pamphlet.

BAKER, MARY FRANCES, *Florida Wild Flowers*. Macmillan, 1938.

BALLINGER, KENNETH, *Miami Millions*. Miami, 1936.

BARBOUR, THOMAS, *That Vanishing Eden*. Little Brown, 1944.

BARTRAM, WILLIAM, *The Travels of William Bartram*. Facsimile Library, N. Y. 1940.

BELL, EMILY LAGOW, *My Pioneer Days in Florida, 1876-1898*. Ft. Pierce, 1928.

BICKEL, KARL A., *Mangrove Coast*. Coward-McCann, 1942.

BRINTON, DANIEL G., *Notes on the Floridian Peninsula*. Philadelphia, 1859.

——, *A Guide Book of Florida and the South*. Philadelphia, 1869.

BROOKS, A.M. (SYLVIA SUNSHINE.) *Petals Plucked from Sunny Climes*. Southern Methodist Publishing Company, 1880.

BUSHNELL, DAVID L., *Tribal Migration East of the Mississippi*. Smithsonian, No. 3237.

CALDERON, GABRIEL DIAS VARA, *A 17th Century Letter describing the Indians and Indian Missions of Florida*. Smithsonian Pub., No. 3398.

CANOVA, ANDREW P., *Life and Adventures in South Florida*. Tampa, 1904.

CARSON, RUBY LEACH, *William Dunnington Bloxham*. University of Florida, 1945.

CHURCH, A., *A Dash Through the Everglades. Ingraham's Survey.* WPA Library Service Project, 1939.

COHEN, ISIDOR, *Historical Sketches and Sidelights of Miami, Florida.* Cambridge, 1905.

COMMITTEE ON INDIAN AFFAIRS, *Eradicating Cattle Tick, Seminole Indian Reservation, Florida*. Reprint of Hearing before the Committee on Indian Affairs, U.S. Senate, 77th Congress.

CONNOR, JEANNETTE THURBER, *Translation of the Memorial of Pedro Menendez de Aviles by Gonzalo Solis de Meras*. Florida State Historical Society, 1923.

CORY, CHARLES B., *Hunting and Fishing in Florida*. Estes and Lauriat, 1896.

CURLEY, THE REV. MICHAEL J., *Church and State in the Spanish Floridas*. Catholic University of America Press, 1940.

CUSHING, FRANK H., *Exploration of Ancient Key Dwellers Remains on the Gulf Coast of Florida*. American Philosophical Society Proc. Vol. 55, No. 155, 1896.

DAVIS, C. KAY, *Soils and Water Control in the Everglades Drainage District*. University of Florida Experiment Station in Co-operation with the U.S. Dept. of Agriculture.

DAVIS, JOHN H., JR., *The Natural Features of Southern Florida*. Fla. Geol. Bull 25, 1943.

———, *The Ecology of Mangroves*. Carnegie Inst. Pub. No. 517, 1940.

DAVIS, T. FREDERICK, *Disston Land Purchase*. Florida Historical Society Quarterly, Vol. XVII, April, 1939.

———, *History of Ponce de Leon's Voyages to Florida*. Florida Historical Society Quarterly, Vol. XIV, July, 1935.

DICKINSON, JONATHAN, *God's Protecting Providence*. (Ed. by Evangeline W. and Charles M. Andrews.) Yale University Press, 1945.

DIMOCK, A. W., *Florida Enchantments*. Stokes, 1926.

DOVELL, J. E., *A Brief History of the Florida Everglades*. The Soil Science Society of Florida, Proc. Vol. 1v-A, 1942.

FLORIDA, STATE OF, *Minutes of the Proceedings of the Board of Trustees of the Internal Improvement Fund. 1855 to 1945.*

427

FONTANEDA, ESCALANTE, *Memoir*. Translated by Buckingham Smith. Historical Association of Southern Florida, Glades House, Coral Gables, Fla., 1945.

FORBES, J. G., *Sketches Historical and Topographical of the Floridas*. New York, 1821.

FREEMAN, ETHEL CUTLER, *The Seminole Woman of the Big Cypress and Her Influence in Modern Life*. America Indigent, April, 1944.

——, *Seminole Indians of Florida*. Bulletin Florida Writers Project, Florida Department of Agriculture.

——, *We Live with the Seminoles*. Natural History, Vol. 49, No. 4, April, 1942, pp. 226-236.

GATEWOOD, GEORGE W., *Ox Cart Days to Airplane Era in Southwest Florida*. Punta Gorda, Florida, 1939.

GEIGER, MAYNARD, *The Franciscan Conquest of Florida, 1573-1618*. Catholic University of America, 1937.

GIDDINGS, JOSHUA R., *The Exiles of Florida*. Columbus, Ohio, 1858.

GIFFORD, JOHN C., *The Everglades and Other Essays Relating to South Florida*. Everglades Land Sales Co., 1911.

——, *The Reclamation of the Everglades with Trees*. Miami, 1935.

——, *Some Geographical and Historical Terms Relating to Florida and Neighboring Lands*. Pamphlet.

——, *Five Plants Essential to the Indians and Early Settlers of Florida*. Tequesta, 1944.

GODARD, A. A. Dr., Henry Perrine. Manuscript.

GOGGIN, JOHN M., *The Archeology of the Glades Area, South Florida*. Manuscript.

——, *The Distribution of Pottery Wares in the Glades Archeological Area of South Florida*. New Mexico Anthropologist, Albuquerque, 1940.

——, *The Seminole Negroes of Andros Island, Bahamas*. Florida Historical Quarterly, St. Augustine, 1946.

——, *An Anthropological Reconnaissance of Andros Island, Bahamas*. American Antiquity, Vol. 5, Menasha, Wis., 1939.

——, *A Ceramic Sequence in South Florida*. New Mexico Anthropologist, Vol. 3, Albuquerque, 1939.

——, *A Pre-Historic Wooden Club from Southern Florida*. American Anthropologist, Vol. 44, Menasha, Wis., 1942.

——, *Silver Work of the Florida Seminole.* El Palacio, Vol. 47, Santa Fe, N. M., 1940.

——, *Archeological Investigation on the Upper Florida Keys.* Tequesta, 1944.

——, *A Preliminary Definition of Archeological Areas and Periods in Florida* (with map and chart). Manuscript.

GOGGIN, JOHN M. AND SOMMER, FRANK, *Excavations in Upper Matecumbe Key.* Manuscript.

GONZALEZ, THOMAS A., *The Caloosahatchee.* The Koreshan Unity Press, Estero, Fla., 1932.

GOWER, CHARLOTTE D., *The Northern and Southern Affiliations of Antillean Culture* American Anthropological Association, No. 35, 1927.

GRAY, RICHARD W., *Florida Hurricanes.* Washington, 1936.

GREENLEE, ROBERT F., *Life Cycle of the Modern Florida Seminoles.* Florida Historical Society Quarterly.

——, *Ceremonial Practices of the Modern Seminole.* Tequesta, 1942.

——, *Folk Tales of the Florida Seminole.* Journal of American Folklore, Vol. 58, No. 228. 1945.

——, *Chants of the Seminoles* (a series of recordings of songs by a medicine man).

HAKLUYT, RICHARD, *The Principal Navigations, Voyages, Traffiques and Discoveries of the English Nation.* Everyman.

HARPER, ROLAND, *Natural Resources of Southern Florida.* Florida State Geological Survey, 18th Annual Report, 1927.

HARRINGTON, MARK R., *Archeology of the Everglades Region.* American Anthropologist, 1909.

HARSHBERGER, JOHN W., *The Vegetation of South Florida.* Wagner Institute, Philadelphia, 1914.

HAY, OLIVER P., *The Pleistocene of North America.* Carnegie Institute, 1925.

HEILPRIN, ANGELO, *Explorations of the West Coast of Florida and in the Okeechobee Wilderness.* Wagner Institute, Philadelphia, 1887.

HENSHALL, JAMES A., *Camping and Cruising in Florida.* 1888.

HERSKOVITZ, MELVILLE J., *The Myth of the Negro Past.* Harper, 1941.

——, *The American Negro.* Knopf, 1928.

HIBBEN, FRANK C., *The Lost Americans.* Crowell, 1946.

HODGE, F. W., *Spanish Explorers in the Southern United States, 1528–43.* Barnes & Noble, 1907.

HOLLINGSWORTH, TRACY, *History of Dade County, Florida.* 1936.

HRDLICKA, ALES, *The Origin and Antiquity of the American Indian.* Smithsonian, 1923.

HUDSON, F. M., *Beginnings in Dade County.* Tequesta, 1943.

HURSTON, ZORA NEALE, *Their Eyes Were Watching God.* 1937.

IRVING, THEODORE, *The Conquest of Florida.* Putnam, 1851.

IVES, J. C., *Memoirs to Accompany a Military Map of Florida.* U. S. War Dept., 1856.

JORDAN, LILLIAN, *Dania, a Historical Sketch.* Florida Historical Society Quarterly, Vol. X, No. 2, October, 1931.

KENNEDY, STETSON, *Palmetto Country.* Duell, Sloan and Pearce, 1942.

KENNY, MICHAEL J., *The Romance of the Floridas.* Bruce Publishing Co., 1934.

KROEBER, A. L., *Anthropology.*

——, *Native American Population.* American Anthropologist, Vol. 36, 1934.

KURZ, HERMAN, *Florida Dunes and Scrub.* Florida Geological Bull. No. 23.

LINDQUIST, G. E. E., *The Indian In American Life.* Friendship Press.

LOWERY, WOODBURY, *The Spanish Settlements in the United States.* Putnam, 1901.

LUMMUS, J. N., *The Miracle of Miami Beach.* Miami, 1944.

MACCAULEY, CLAY, *The Seminole Indians of Florida.* Bureau of American Ethnology, 1884.

McDUFFIE, LILLIE B., *The Lures of Manatee.* Marshall and Bruce, Nashville, 1933.

McNICOLL, ROBERT E., *The Caloosa Village, Tequesta.* Tequesta, 1941.

McWILLIAMS, CAREY, *Ill Fares The Land.* Little Brown.

MOORE, CLARENCE L., *Antiquities of the Florida West Coast.* Journal Academy of Natural Sciences, Philadelphia, 1900.

MUNROE, RALPH M. AND GILPIN, VINCENT, *The Commodore's Story.* Ives Washburn, 1930.

NASH, ROY, *Survey of the Seminole Indians of Florida.* Sen. Doc. No. 314, 71st Congress, 1931.

OBER, FREDERICK (FRED BEVERLY), *Camp Life in Florida.* Forest and Stream Publishing Company, 1876.

PARKER, GARALD G. AND C. WYTHE COOKE, *Late Cenozoic Geology of Southern Florida, with a Discussion of the Ground Water.* Florida Geological Survey Bulletin, No. 27, 1944.

PERRINE, MISS, *The Pathetic and Lamentable Narrative of Miss Perrine on the Massacre and Destruction of Indian Key in August, 1840.* Lippincott, 1841.

PHILLIPS, J. MARQUETTE, *The Jesuit Mission of San Ignacio.* Translation from "La Historia de la Compania de Jesus en Nueva Espana" by P. Francis X. Alegre. Manuscript, 1941.

PRATT, THEODORE, *The Barefoot Mailman.* Duell, Sloan and Pearce.

PROCTOR, SAM, *Napoleon B. Broward, The Portrait of a Progressive Democrat.* Manuscript, University of Florida.

RANDOLPH, ISHAM, *Report of the Florida Everglades Engineering Commission.* Fla. Doc. No. 379, 1913.

REED, W. MAXWELL AND JANNETTE M. LUCAS, *Animals on the March.* Harcourt Brace, 1937.

ROBINSON, T. RALPH, *Henry Perrine, Pioneer Horticulturist of Florida.* Florida Horticultural Society reprint.

ROMANS, BERNARD, *A Concise Natural History of East and West Florida.* New York, 1776.

SAFFORD, W. E., *Natural History of Paradise Key and the Near-By Everglades of Florida.* Smithsonian Report, 1917. Pub. 2508.

SCISCO, DR. LOUIS D., *The Track of Ponce de Leon in 1513.* American Geographic Society Bull. 1913, Vol. XLV, No. 10.

SIMPSON, CHARLES TORREY, *In Lower Florida Wilds.* Macmillan, 1920.

——, *Florida Wild Life.* Macmillan, 1932.

SIMPSON, GEORGE GAYLORD, *The Extinct Land Mammals of Florida.* Florida State Geological Survey, No. 28, 1927.

SMALL, JOHN KUNKEL, *Eden to Sahara.* Science Press Printing Co., Lancaster, Pa., 1929.

——, *Explorations in the Everglades and the Florida Keys.* Journal of the N. Y. Botanical Garden, March, 1909, No. 111–April, 1914, No. 172.

——, *The Ferns of Florida.* Science Press, 1931.

——, *The Shrubs of Florida.* New York, 1913.

——, *The Coconut Palm.* Journal of the N. Y. Botanical Garden, 1929, No. 30.

SMITH, BUCKINGHAM, *Report on the Everglades.* Sen. Doc. 242, 30th Congress, 1848.

SPECK, FRANK G., *Some Outlines of Aboriginal Culture in the Southeastern States.* American Anthropologist, Vol. 9, No. 2, 1907.

SPENCER, LUCIAN A., *A History of the Florida Indians.* Manuscript.

SPOEHR, ALEXANDER, *Camp, Clan and Kin Among the Cow Creek Seminoles of Florida.* Field Museum Natural History, Vol. 33, No. 1, August, 1941.

——, *The Florida Seminole Camp—1941.* Field Museum Natural History, Vol. 33, No. 3, December, 1944.

SPRAGUE, JOHN T., *The Origin, Progress and Conclusion of the Florida War.* Appleton, 1847.

STEPHEN, L. L., *Historic and Economic Aspects of Drainage in the Florida Everglades.* The Southern Economic Journal, Vol. X, No. 3, 1944.

——, *A Little Known Sugar Bowl in Florida.* The Journal of Geography, February, 1944.

STEWART, JOHN T., *Report on Everglades Drainage Project.* U. S. Dept. of Agriculture, Soil Conservation Service, 1907.

STIRLING, GENE, *Report on the Seminoles of Florida.* Office of Indian Affairs, 1936.

STIRLING, MATHEW W., *Florida Cultural Affiliations in Relation to Adjacent Areas.* Essays in Honor of A. L. Kroeber, University of California Press, 1906.

——, *Archeological Projects.* Smithsonian Report for 1934, Pub. 3324.

STORTER, GEORGE W. WITH CAPT. J. F. JAUDON, *Footing It Across The Everglades.* Manuscript, 1921.

STRONG, W. D., *North American Indian Tradition Suggesting a Knowledge of the Mammoth.* American Anthropologist, Vol. 36, 1934.

SUGAR CORPORATION, U. S., *Sugar and the Everglades.* Clewiston, Fla.

SUTTON, D. C., *The Disston St. Cloud Sugar Plantation.* Annual Report of the State Chemist of Florida, 1919.

SWANTON, JOHN R., *Early History of the Creek Indians and Their Neighbors.* Bureau American Ethnology, Bull. 73.

———, *Social Organization and Social Usages of the Indians of the Creek Confederacy.* BAE, 42nd Annual Report, 1928.

———, *Aboriginal Culture of the South East.* BAE, 42nd Annual Report, 1928.

———, *Myths and Tales of the Southeastern Indians.* BAE, Bull. 88.

SWEITZER, M. A., *Ethnology of the Modern Mikasuki Indians of South Florida.* Essay presented to the Faculty of the Graduate School of Yale University for the Degree of Master of Arts, 1945.

TEED, CYRUS R., *Cellular Cosmogony.* Estero, Florida, 1922.

THORNTHWAITE, C. W., *The Climates of North America.* American Geological Society, 1931.

TORREY, BRADFORD, *A Florida Sketch Book.* Houghton Mifflin, 1894.

TRAPP, MRS. HARLAN, *My Pioneer Reminiscences.* Miami, 1940.

TRUE, DAVID, O., *The Freducci Map of 1514–1515.* Tequesta, 1944.

———, *Notes and Comment, Fontaneda's Memoirs, 1575.* The University of Miami and the Historical Association of Southern Florida, 1944.

VOSS, LILLIE PIERCE, *Notes on the East Coast of Florida and Hypoluxo.* Manuscript.

WALL, A. J. *The Life of Buckingham Smith.* Manuscript, the N. Y. Historical Society.

WHITEHEAD, C. E., *The Camp-fires of the Everglades or Wild Sports in the South.* London, 1891.

WILLIAMS, JOHN LEE, *The Territory of Florida.* New York, 1837.

WILLIAMSON, JAMES A., *The Voyages of the Cabots and the English Discovery of America.* London.

WILLS, DR. THOMAS E., *The Everglades of Florida.* Sen. Doc. No. 89, 62nd Congress, 1911.

WRIGHT, IRENE A., *English Voyages to the Caribbean.* Hakluyt Society, London, 1929.

NEWSPAPERS—*The Miami Herald, The Miami Metropolis* and *The Miami Daily News, The Ft. Myers News-Press, The American Eagle,* Estero, Florida, *The Belle Glade Herald, The Okeechobee News, The Collier County News.*

OTHER PUBLICATIONS—*Tequesta,* the Journal of the Historical Society of Southern Florida; the Florida Historical Society Quarterly and Proceedings of the Florida Soil Science Society.

Index

INDEX

440

INDEX

443

Index for Afterword

445

Here are some other books from Pineapple Press on related topics. For a complete catalog, visit our website at www.pineapplepress.com. Or write to Pineapple Press, P.O. Box 3889, Sarasota, Florida 34230-3889, or call (800) 746-3275.

Marjory Stoneman Douglas: Voice of the River—An Autobiography with John Rothchild by Marjory Stoneman Douglas. This is the story of an influential life told in a unique and spirited voice. Marjory Stoneman Douglas, nationally known as the first lady of conservation and the woman who "saved" the Everglades, was the founder of Friends of the Everglades, a feminist, a fighter for racial justice, and always a writer. (pb)

Exploring Wild South Florida by Susan D. Jewell. The third edition includes over 40 new natural areas and covers Broward, Collier, Miami-Dade, Hendry, Lee, Monroe, and Palm Beach counties. (pb)

Easygoing Guide to Natural Florida, Volume 1: South Florida, by Douglas Waitley. If you love nature but want to enjoy it with minimum effort, this is the book for you. To make this book, a site must be beautiful and easy to reach, it must not cost a lot of money, and it must not require an inordinate amount of exertion to enjoy. Covers south Florida sites such as the Indian River Lagoon, the St. Johns March, the Ten Thousand Islands, the Everglades, and the Keys. (pb)

Priceless Florida by Ellie Whitney, D. Bruce Means, and Anne Rudloe. An extensive guide (432 pages, 800 color photos) to the incomparable ecological riches of this unique region, presented in a way that will appeal to young and old, laypersons and scientists. Complete with maps, charts, species lists. (hb & pb)

Florida's Birds, Second Edition, by David S. Maehr and Herbert W. Kale II. Now with color throughout, this new edition includes 30 new species accounts. Sections on bird study, feeding, and habitats; threatened and endangered species; exotic species; and bird conservation. (pb)

Florida Magnificent Wilderness by James Valentine and D. Bruce Means. A visual journey through some of the most precious wild areas in the state, presenting the breathtaking beauty preserved in state lands, parks, and natural areas. Valentine has used his camera to record environmental art images of the state's remote wilderness places. Dr. D. Bruce Means has written the detailed captions and main text, "Florida's Rich Biodiversity." (hb)

Old Florida Style by Steve Kidd and Alex Menendez, Delve Productions. Saddle up on a tough little Cracker horse called a marsh tacky and explore old Florida—when cow hunters pulled the tough little Spanish cattle out of the palmettos and established this as a cattle state. This DVD showcases Florida's Cracker heritage. (DVD)

Marjory Stoneman Douglas and the Florida Everglades by Sandra Wallus Sammons. Marjory Stoneman Douglas has been called "the Grandmother of the Everglades." This biography for children ages 9–12 covers her life from her childhood up north to her inspiring time spent in south Florida. (pb)